The Discipling Church: The Church That Will Stand until Christ Comes

David W. Cloud

The Discipling Church:
The Church That Will Stand until Christ Comes
Copyright 2017 by David Cloud
This edition October, 2017
ISBN 978-1-58318-227-7

Published by Way of Life Literature
PO Box 610368, Port Huron, MI 48061
866-295-4143 (toll free) - fbns@wayoflife.org
www.wayoflife.org

Canada: Bethel Baptist Church
4212 Campbell St. N., London Ont. N6P 1A6
519-652-2619

Printed in Canada by
Bethel Baptist Print Ministry

CONTENTS

The Collapse of Independent Baptist Churches 7
A Discipling Church or a Mixed Multitude? 27
The Disappearance of Discipling Churches 59
A Discipling Church Begins with Caution about Salvation 84
A Discipling Church Guards the Door to Membership 139
A Discipling Church Has the Right Leaders 151
A Discipling Church Trains Preachers 172
A Discipling Church Has a Disciplined Environment 185
A Discipling Church Is Strong in God's Word 212
A Discipling Church Is Strong in Prayer 251
A Discipling Church Is a Reproving Church 261
A Discipling Church Maintains God's Standards for Ministers and Workers 286
A Discipling Church Is Properly Educated 302
A Discipling Church Has an Atmosphere of Charity 308
A Discipling Church Is Zealous for Biblical Separation 315
A Discipling Church Is Careful about Music 341
A Discipling Church Is a Hard Working Church 355
A Discipling Church Builds Godly Homes 361
A Discipling Church Disciples Youth 368
A Discipling Church Has a Vision for Evangelism and World Missions 419
A Discipling Church Has a First Love for Christ 424
Building a Discipling Church from the Beginning 438
Restoring the Discipling Church 445
Cultural Factors in the Weakening of Churches 452
Characteristics of a Discipling Church 480
Arguments Against a Discipling Church 481
Sample Church Covenant 485
Suggested Materials for a Discipling Church 515

The Discipling Church:
The Church That Will Stand until Christ Comes
David W. Cloud

I would beg my readers to give me a chance to present this issue properly and to answer your questions by reading the entire book. If, after reading the book, you have further questions, please feel at liberty to contact me. I live in South Asia and travel extensively, but I can be contacted by email, and I will do my best to answer any sincere question. -- *David W. Cloud*

The very best church is a deeply imperfect body of sinners saved by grace who still have the "old man" and who live in a fallen world filled with temptations. But I believe that a church that is very careful about appointing leaders and is extra careful about salvation and church membership, that is serious about discipleship and discipline, that aims to be very strong in the Word of God, etc., is a better church than one that isn't. I believe that a church that is striving to maintain a first love for Christ is far superior to a church that barely has an idea about a first love. I believe that a church that is learning from its mistakes and aiming to be ever stronger in Christ is superior to a church that is content with lukewarm as the status quo.

The Collapse of Independent Baptist Churches

Outline

A Fundamental Reason for the Collapse
Looking to the Future
The Role of Technology in the Collapse
We Don't Have to Erode
A Passionate Subject with Me
My Teaching Is Not Theory
No Boasting and No Perfection
The Church That Will Be Standing until Christ Comes

In the last twenty years, we have witnessed the capitulation of hundreds of Bible-believing churches to a contemporary philosophy of Christian life and ministry.

When I was saved in 1973, a major thing that distinguished fundamental Baptists from Southern Baptists was biblical separation, but that distinction is disappearing and there is a merging of philosophy. We live in a day of blending.

As soon as I was saved, I began to search for a biblical church. I had grown up in Southern Baptist churches but I had not seen the zealous biblical Christianity there that I now saw in Scripture. I studied the Bible intently and considered several churches, including Pentecostal and Seventh-day Adventist, finally visiting a little Independent Baptist church one Sunday morning at the invitation of the sister of a former unsaved friend.

If I remember correctly, the church was a couple of years old and was meeting in a storefront. It was founded by a family that had come out of the Southern Baptist Convention because of the liberalism, spiritual lukewarmness, and worldliness. They wanted to take the Bible seriously. They weren't afraid of being different. They wanted a church that was biblical. They were careful about salvation. A large percentage of the members were young single adults. There was a zeal for separation. There was open, plain rejection of error. For example, we distributed books by John Rice warning about liberalism in the Southern Baptist Convention and pamphlets warning about the Today's English Version (*Good News for Modern Man*) that the Southern Baptists were publishing. The little church was looked upon by the established churches in the area as fanatical, but I was convinced that this type of "fanaticism" is biblical, and I loved it!

That type of Independent Baptist church is rare today.

A large number of the fundamental Baptist churches that existed in the 1970s and 1980s have either ceased to exist, have capitulated to the contemporary philosophy, or they are well on the way to capitulation.

Consider the following testimony that describes what is happening in multitudes of Independent Baptist churches:

> "Recently, there was a large photo in the newspaper of one of the NFL football team cheerleaders dressed in her cheerleading uniform which was equivalent to a bikini. Since watching NFL football is talked about so positively from the IFB [Independent Fundamental Baptist] pulpit, the Sunday School teacher's lectern, and amongst the deacons and other men of the church, I decided to take a closer look. An internet search provided endless links--and just visiting the team's website provided many photos and videos of the cheerleaders wearing even less than the team uniform bikini, posing in sexy poses, etc. I just do not understand how something like this is promoted by the church. One can only imagine that their 'cheers' are not wholesome things to watch, but I have not seen a 'performance' to be able to evaluate that. Then there is also the advertising and other 'entertainment' that is shown, not to mention values promoted. It would seem that this 'entertainment' clearly violates separation, purity, etc., yet it is embraced by the church leadership. What am I missing here? How is this justified?
>
> "On another note, some of your recent articles have been about the decline of the IFB churches. I have just a few comments. ... it seems that pastors don't want to step on anybody's toes (and possibly lose any donors?), yet they still want to say they are IFB. So a few times a year some generalities are pronounced from the pulpit--just one or two lines--not a sermon mind you--and it sounds something like this: People ought to listen to good music (but what 'good' is,

is never defined). People ought to dress right (but what that means is never defined). People should be careful what they watch (but no examples or details are given). And so on. So it is easy to imagine each person thinking their 80s rock music, or country music, or CCM, or latest Hollywood movie, or newest TV shows are the 'good' ones, and they continue right on in their worldly behaviors, passing them to their children. But maybe this approach is considered effective because none of them are 'offended' and quit the church or reduce their donations? CCM is very, very quietly ushered in via specials, visiting evangelist singers, Christmas programs, etc. It seems that if anyone questions anything, a sermon soon follows to warn about those 'not operating in love.' I could go on, and I'm sure you have heard much more from others. It is truly a sad thing to watch the decline. Please do keep sounding the warning--maybe some will wake up before it's too late."

This church is very typical, and it will be *completely* and *unequivocally* contemporary and "non-judgmental" within a decade.

Observe that when a church first begins to go down the slippery slope of spiritual decline, the pastor usually wants to straddle the fence for some time. He wants to pretend that nothing has changed and that he still stands for things the church once stood for, but his actions and inactions speak much louder than his words.

Consider **Emmanuel Baptist Church** of Pontiac, Michigan. In the 1970s and 1980s, this was one of America's largest churches, running as high as 5,000 in attendance. It operated 80 buses and hosted the Midwestern Baptist College. The founder, Tom Malone, was one of the influential names in the Sword of the Lord circles, and the Sword still publishes several of his books, including *The Sunday School: Reaching Multitudes*. Even before Malone died in 2007, Emmanuel had shuttered its doors. The tiny remnant of Emmanuel's remaining members merged with New Beginning Baptist Church, formerly Silvercrest Baptist Church, another church once pastored by Tom Malone. New Beginning carries on as the second generation of these formerly thriving churches. It is still basically the same in character as in Malone's day (e.g., same Bible, doctrine, music, church philosophy), but it is a small work. It is pastored by Jerry Boritzki, retired Navy, a 1981 graduate of

Midwestern, a brother in Christ who is bravely trying to carry on the traditions he was taught.

Consider **Highland Park Baptist Church in Chattanooga, Tennessee**, home of Tennessee Temple where I was trained for the ministry. These institutions moved in a contemporary direction, renounced separatism, and died.

When I was a student at Temple in the mid-1970s and pastored one of the chapels, Highland Park was very conservative.

The music was sacred and glorious. I have never heard more thrilling congregational singing than I heard at Highland Park Baptist Church in those days. Dr. J.R. Faulkner was not a particularly dynamic song leader, but he was cheerful, enthusiastic, and effective, and he brought out the best from the choir, orchestra, and congregation. There was absolutely nothing contemporary about the style. Everything was built on a solid sacred foundation that sounded nothing like the world's pop music. The rejection of CCM in those days was not just lip service. The special music groups sang sacred music in a sacred manner. There was plenty of talent, but as I recall the groups did not put on "performances." The presentation was not showy or fleshly or even flashy, and this was purposeful.

One of the fundamental themes at "the old" Highland Park was the imminent return of Christ, and this is very biblical and very important. Every Sunday the choir led the congregation in singing "Behold He Comes" in harmony, and what a joy it was!

> "Behold, He comes; behold, He comes; behold, He comes, and every eye shall see Him; friend, will you be ready when Jesus comes?"

Dr. Roberson was a man of real Christian character. J.R. Faulkner, who knew Dr. Roberson as well as any man knew him, said: "He was a man of his word--great character, great integrity. He lived what he preached" (James Wigton, *Lee Roberson: Always about His Father's Business*, 2010, p. 117).

Dr. Roberson believed in dying to self, in being filled with the Spirit. He had a love for God and an unquenchable burden for souls. He was a man of prayer, a man who depended upon the Lord rather than on the arm of flesh. He lived frugally, didn't take a large salary, and refused to take his pay check until the missionary support was all paid.

There was never a hint of moral or financial scandal in Dr. Roberson's life and ministry. He was exceedingly careful about his relationship with women. There was a large glass window between his office and his secretary's office, and he refused ever to be alone with a woman other than his wife. He didn't give personal gifts to his female secretaries. He said that even if he saw his secretary walking in a driving rainstorm he would not have stopped to pick her up lest someone see it and get the wrong idea.

I am convinced that this is the reason why Tennessee Temple graduates from Dr. Roberson's era have not been known for moral scandals as the graduates of some other Independent Baptist schools have. It has happened, but it has been rare.

The daily chapels and annual Bible conferences featured some of the best preachers from across America, and there was real life-changing power in the services.

Dress standards and dating standards and such were high, and it wasn't "legalism" or "Phariseeism." It was an attempt to take God's Word seriously. The cry of "legalism" is usually a slanderous accusation made by the contemporary crowd who are lovers of the world. Even Christian rockers and emergents have standards. I don't know of one contemporary church that would allow a woman in a bikini or a man in lipstick, high heels, and a dress to sing in the praise team. No, they draw lines, too, and for them to call our lines legalism is blatant hypocrisy. It is not legalism for blood-washed, grace-saved churches to prayerfully apply the principles of God's Word (e.g. 2 Corinthians 7:1; Ephesians 5:11; Titus 2:11-12; James 4:4; 1 John 2:15-17) to issues of practical Christian living, and in my experience that's what Highland Park tried to do in those days.

It was not a matter of an emphasis on mere externals. The emphasis was on a heart for God and seeking after true godliness. The general atmosphere at the church and school was happy and spiritual.

Above all, there was a godly vision to be caught. It was a place where multitudes of lives were changed to the glory of Jesus Christ, and great masses of people heard the gospel and hundreds of Bible-believing churches were planted as a result of what was "caught" at Highland Park Baptist Church in those days. One graduate said, "During my tenure at TTU, I believe that it was truly a Biblically conservative, separated institution of higher learning, that strove to pass along godly principles for life and ministry."

Lee Roberson said:

> "In my first year at the Highland Park Baptist Church, we had one missionary. The blessings of God came down upon us, and many were saved. As we kept on preaching the Gospel at home, we were driven to a deeper concern for the rest of the world. So we began putting on missionaries with support of them through the regular offerings of the church and by special offerings on Sunday evening and Wednesday evening. We saw scores of our young people volunteer for missionary work. During my fortieth year at Highland Park [1982], we were giving support to 565 missionaries in all parts of the world. Fifty percent of the church's offerings went to home and foreign missions. Every need of the church was met, and every building was paid for. At home we were seeing the salvation of hundreds. People were happy and the blessings of God were upon us. Obey God! Don't question. Don't procrastinate! Don't quibble! Obey God! Obedience brings manifold blessings."

But by the late 1980s, Highland Park and Tennessee Temple were experiencing dramatic changes. There was a great influence from Liberty University and Word of Life, both of which had long been in the New Evangelical orbit, and it was a terrible lack of wisdom on the part of Highland Park's leaders to build bridges to these institutions.

By 1989, Tennessee Temple music groups used "soft rock" at the annual Southwide Baptist Fellowship meeting (*Calvary Contender*, Oct. 15, 1989). In 2005, Highland Park hosted a Christian rock concert in its main auditorium featuring Bebo Norman, Fernando Ortega, and Sara Groves. In April 2006, the school's College Days featured Toddiefunk and the Electric Church.

In 2008, Highland Park Baptist Church joined the Southern Baptist Convention.

In 2012, Highland Park Baptist Church ceased to exist. The name was changed to Church of the Highlands to reflect a location change as well as its new generic, contemporary flavor. Jeremy

Roberts, Highland Park's 28-year-old Southern Baptist pastor, said, "It'll be the funnest church around" ("Chattanooga's Iconic Highland Park," *Chattanooga Times Free Press*, Sept. 10, 2012).

In March 2015, Tennessee Temple announced that it was closing its doors.

In the book *The Collapse of Separatism*, we have documented the shocking collapse of Highland Park Baptist Church in greater detail, together with other churches associated with Southwide Baptist Fellowship, Baptist Bible Fellowship International, etc.

We need to ponder the reasons for these great changes. It has been said that those who do not learn from the failures of the past are doomed to repeat them. It has also been said that trying the same experiment repeatedly, expecting different results, is a mark of insanity!

God's commandment to "prove all things" (1 Th. 5:21) is a commandment to test everything continually by God's Word. The mature Christian is characterized by a never-ending process of discerning good and evil (Heb. 5:14). Testing is not something that is to be done once in a while; it must be a way of life.

Continual testing is an essential part of a biblical lifestyle and a fruitful church ministry.

I learned a lot from John R. Rice and Lee Roberson and other men of God when I was a young Christian, and I have been helped by the type of churches they founded, but God's people should follow their leaders *as their leaders follow Christ and His Word*, but not wherein they veer from God's Word or fall short of the whole counsel of God.

A Fundamental Reason for the Collapse

I have come to the conclusion that the downfall of so many Baptist churches is not the product merely of a failure in this or that area of ministry (e.g., carelessness about music). Rather the downfall is the product of a wrong philosophy of the church that has produced congregations that are too weak to stand against the hurricane force winds of end-time compromise and apostasy.

In 2011, we published *Why Most Independent Baptists Will Be Emerging within 20 Years*, and in that and subsequent editions we identified twelve reasons: (1) lukewarmness, unholiness, and worldliness, (2) biblical shallowness, (3) lack of prayer, (4) maligning warning and reproof, (5) unquestioning loyalty to man, (6) following the crowd, (7) pragmatism and big-mindedness, (8) ignorance about important issues, (9) soft separatism, (10) lack of serious discipleship, (11) carelessness about music, (12) quick prayerism.

These are important issues that must be addressed by any church that wants to be standing when Jesus comes, but there is something more foundational.

A church can have a strong Bible teaching ministry and try to maintain biblical standards for teachers and workers and be careful about its music, but if it has a mixed multitude philosophy instead of a discipling philosophy it is probably doomed to capitulate to the contemporary program.

The urgent need is to return to the New Testament pattern of a church as a discipling church.

A discipling philosophy might make the average church possibly smaller, but it will definitely make it stronger.

It is the "smaller" part of that equation that guarantees that, apart from genuine revival, many Baptist pastors will not give much attention to this exhortation, being steeped as they are in pragmatism and wanting something that "works" to build the largest church possible.

But even the "smaller" part of the equation isn't certain, because a discipling church has God's blessing and power.

> "Greg Wills notes that from 1790 to 1860, when Baptist churches maintained high rates of discipline, they also maintained high rates of growth, growing at a rate twice that of the population. But in later years, as their discipline fell, so did their growth" (*Restoring Integrity in Baptist Churches*, Kindle loc. 289).

Looking to the Future

At a recent Bible conference, I was invited to preach on "the future of Independent Baptists."

We don't have to be prophets to look to the future.

> "A prudent *man* foreseeth the evil, and hideth himself: but the simple pass on, and are punished" (Proverbs 22:3).

In this verse, which is repeated in Proverbs 27:12 by way of emphasis, we see "the prudent." Because he has God's Word and God's Spirit, the prudent can see the future and plan for it. He can see the end of present actions. He can protect himself, his family, and his church.

We also see "the simple." He doesn't observe warning signs. He is satisfied so long as there are no glaring problems *presently*. And he doesn't heed warnings given by others. He says, "Why are you criticizing good churches?" But if we wait until sin and error are full blown, it is too late to fix it.

The following communication represents the outlook of the prudent:

> "My wife and I both grew up in churches that were second generation New Evangelical. By God's grace, shortly after we were married we realized we couldn't be part of NE churches. Since then we have grown through the teaching ministries of a number of IFB churches, but have found that though they have sound doctrinal statements, practical Christian living standards are **ERODING. We greatly desire to be part of a church that is not just okay for now, but that will be there for our children in the next generation. For this reason when we visit a church we are looking not only at where it is at today, but for the direction it is moving.** Is it withstanding the onslaught of our evil culture and compromising churches or does it get along with them?"

This man understands that many churches are eroding, and he understands that erosion will ultimately result in apostasy. He wants protection for himself and his family, so he looks at a church's "direction" in order to determine its future. He looks for a church that is standing against erosion and going in the opposite direction of it. This is a mark of biblical prudence.

The Role of Technology in the Collapse

Modern technology has played a significant role in the weakening and downfall of churches.

Modern communications technology is a two-edged sword. It can be a tool for good and therefore a blessing, and it can be a tool for evil and therefore a curse. How technology is used depends on the individual's heart and wisdom.

I've been on the cutting edge of technology all my life. I've owned transistor radios, 45-rpm record players, reel-to-reel recorders, 8-track players, cassette recorder/players, portable televisions, and, since 1982, most types of personal computers and "smart devices."

And I know both sides of using these devices. Before I was saved, I used technology to serve the world, the flesh, and the devil. Since I have been saved, I have used technology in the service of God.

Radio became popular and influential in the 1920s and 1930s with vacuum tube technology. By 1930, 60% of American homes owned radios. The technology brought some good things. It broadened people's horizons and was used for the preaching of the gospel, but it also brought the world into homes in the form of such things as jazz, big band swing, professional sports, and vain entertainment, including comedians who were perpetually pushing the envelope of decency. Suddenly sleazy musicians and entertainers could enter the homes of church goers across the land and influence the minds and hearts of the family members.

Television took this phenomenon to a new level. It exploded into common usage after World War II, and by 1956 there were 37 million sets in America, a country with a population of 159 million, or one television for every four people. I was seven years old then, and that's about when my parents got our first television.

In the 1950s, the **transistor radio** (1953), **45-rpm record** (1954), and **automobile radio** (1956) made pop music portable and thus empowered the rock & roll teen culture, with its cool (arrogant), me-first attitude, generation gap, relativistic sexual mores, and distinct youth clothing fashions.

In the 1990s, I was told by a pastor that he saw a significant negative influence of Christian radio on his church members. He said, "The members that are spiritually weakest and that cause me the most spiritual problems are those who listen the most to Christian radio." This is because they were being leavened by New Evangelical principles.

But it was the **Internet** (beginning in the 1990s) and the **smartphone** (beginning especially in 2007 with the introduction of the iPhone) that have made the world and apostasy all intrusive. No church today can escape the effect of this technology, from the cities of wealthy nations to the villages of the Third World.

In the Internet/smart phone generation, church young people can access the pop culture at the touch of a finger. Church people can connect with any song writer and be influenced by his or her music, philosophy, and lifestyle. Church women can communicate with popular teachers such as Beth Moore and homeschooling gurus.

The technology of the age demands that churches take everything to a higher, stronger level if they want to be standing until Christ comes.

We Don't Have to Erode

God has given His people everything they need to stand in the midst of the fiercest apostasy. Churches don't fail because of the power of apostasy. They fail because of compromise and backsliding.

God has given us everything we need for victory.

> "According as his divine power hath given unto us all things that *pertain* unto life and godliness, through the knowledge of him that hath called us to glory and virtue" (2 Pe. 1:3).

In a major passage on spiritual warfare, Paul says that we *can* stand (Eph. 6:10-18). But standing requires putting on and using the *whole* armor of God.

In a major passage on end-time apostasy, Paul again says that we *can* stand (2 Timothy 3:1 - 4:8). The man of God can be "perfect, fully furnished unto all good works" (2 Ti. 3:17). But victory is not for the halfhearted and backslidden. Standing requires a passionate walk with Christ and attention to every resource God has given us: separation (2 Ti. 3:5), continuing in the apostolic truth (2 Ti. 3:14), supernatural salvation (2 Ti. 3:15), attention to all Scripture (2 Ti. 3:16-17), walking in the fear of God (2 Ti. 4:1), biblical preaching (2 Ti. 4:2), vigilance (2 Ti. 4:5), doing the work of an evangelist (2 Ti. 4:5), making full proof of the ministry (2 Ti. 4:5), loving Christ's appearing (2 Ti. 4:8).

A Passionate Subject with Me

To help churches stand in the next generation is my passion. It receives a large amount of my meditation, prayers, and study.

It has motivated me to produce materials such as the *One-Year Discipleship Course*, *An Unshakeable Faith*, the *Believer's Bible Dictionary*, *Keeping the Kids*, *The Mobile Phone and the Christian Home and Church*, the *Advanced Bible Studies Series* courses, and now *The Discipling Church*.

I am thankful that there was a sound church in Bartow, Florida, in 1973, where I could begin my Christian life on a good footing. It was sound in salvation, in doctrine, in teaching, in music, in discipleship, in separation, and in love.

But what about the future? What about my grandchildren? Will there be sound churches for them?

I think about my hometown. In the 1970s there were three or four pretty good churches, but now there is not one I can recommend with any enthusiasm. The one that was the strongest in the 1970s is a shell of what it was then, both in numbers and in character, and it is building bridges to the "broader church" through contemporary praise music. This church has large video screens and uses Hillsong praise music and the pastor is willfully clueless about the danger of this practice. The powerful, life-changing pulpit ministry of the 1970s and 1980s, which was characterized by biblical depth as well as clear reproof, has become soft.

My Teaching Is Not Theory

I have sought God's mind about the church for 43 years as I have served Him in the church.

This began when I was a new Christian seeking God's will about what church to join. I was led to Christ by a Pentecostal, and the day after I was saved, he went one way and I went a different way, and I have never had contact with him since. He was traveling and had no permanent address.

I began seeking a good church, believing that I could find the right church by earnest prayer and Bible study. I held to John 7:17

and 8:31-32, which are Christ's promises that the child of God can know the truth if he continues in God's Word.

I wasn't interested in following anyone's tradition, whether Catholic, Episcopal, Presbyterian, Methodist, Pentecostal, Brethren, or Baptist. I wanted to take the Bible as my sole authority.

In a few weeks, the Lord led me to an Independent Baptist church, and I have been a member of Independent Baptist churches ever since, but I am not interested in accepting Independent Baptist tradition as authoritative unless it is based solidly upon Scripture.

Independent Baptist is a multi-faceted movement, but it is also simply the description of a type of church that is Baptist in theology (e.g., not Protestant) and autonomous in polity (not part of a denominational structure or ecclesiastical union). By being Independent Baptist I do not owe allegiance to any earthly headquarters and am not obligated to follow any "crowd." Each Independent Baptist church is at liberty to mind its own business and pursue its own program before the Lord, its one Head, and to fellowship with and support only those brethren and congregations that are truly likeminded.

In other words, I can be Independent Baptist while not supporting the Independent Baptist "movement" or associating with any Independent Baptist circle.

The man who led me to Christ gave me a King James Bible. He also gave me a *Strong's Concordance* and showed me how to use it. He taught me to honor the Bible as my sole authority and gave me pointers in how to study it, and I practically wore out both volumes that first year. I probably averaged eight hours a day in Bible study, while working full time as a printer. I filled up many notebooks with my studies. My pastor was a good expository Bible teacher, and the messages were honey to my soul (Ps. 119:103). The Lord graciously gave me a Christian friend who had been studying the Bible for about a year before I was saved, and I learned much from him. I recall very clearly, for example, the time when he showed me the beauty of Psalm 119.

When I was about one year old in the Lord, I attended Tennessee Temple Bible School at Highland Park Baptist Church, which was the second largest Independent Baptist church at the time. I just wanted to study the Bible, and I had some excellent Bible teachers (as well as some mediocre ones), the most memorable for me being Bruce Lackey and John Economidis. Sitting in their classes was like "tucking into" a steak dinner. It was a spiritual feast.

But I wasn't there to accept whatever was taught and practiced. I attended Tennessee Temple with the mindset to "prove all things; hold fast that which is good" (1 Th. 5:21). There were many good things, and I thank the Lord for the help and truth I received there. But there were things that seemed to be wrong, particularly the over exaltation of man, the unquestioning loyalty given to church leaders, the shallow, salesmanship evangelism methods, and the frenzy for numbers. And there was the promotionalism: turning the church into a circus to increase the crowds. There were prizes (from candy to bicycles), cheap gimmicks, exploding cakes, evangelists parachuting into the church parking lot, swallowing goldfish, demonstrating karate techniques, challenging neighborhood men to a boxing or wrestling match. One evangelist dressed in a fire retardant suit, lit himself on fire, and called himself "the flaming evangelist"!

I have preached in probably about 550 churches, and I have always studied these churches, trying to learn from them, but also analyzing them by God's Word.

As a missionary beginning in 1979, I studied the Bible intensely to get a better understanding of the church and of New Testament missionary work. I focused on the book of Acts and the Pastoral Epistles. I wanted to leave tradition aside and "go back to the Bible."

For 37 years my wife and I have planted churches as a team like Priscilla and Aquila (Acts 18:26; 1 Co. 16:19), and throughout that experience I have sought to come to a better understanding of the nature of a New Testament church.

We continue to build churches. With our excellent co-workers, we have ongoing works in about two dozen towns and villages. We have a full-time Bible college to train preachers and Christian workers. And we are particularly focused on discipling young people. We have about 60 youth at our monthly meetings these days, and a large percentage of them are on fire for the Lord.

No Boasting and No Perfection

I don't consider myself anything special. To the contrary, I have always been amazed that God would call me and use me. I certainly have never felt worthy of such a thing. Without the Lord, I am a zero with the rim rubbed out. What I know and what I have done is 100% by God's grace, and I do not doubt that I am far from what I should be in Christ.

As far as the church, I don't believe that we have all of the answers. Far from it--but we do have *some* answers, and we are learning more each year. I am a serious student, but I have never been dependent on my own thinking and wisdom. To the contrary, for decades I have communicated widely with preachers in many parts of the world to learn everything I can from those who have godly wisdom.

We don't have any sort of perfection in our churches. We have plenty of problems, weaknesses, failures, sins. There are a lot of things that we are trying to figure out before the Lord. We have made plenty of mistakes.

The very best church is a deeply imperfect body of sinners saved by grace who still have the "old man" and who live in a fallen world filled with temptations. Within the membership of the most careful church will be found carnality, backsliding, and sin that requires discipline. Even the strongest church will be deceived by false professions and will be disappointed by people for whom it had high hopes.

Among the churches of the apostolic era, all of which were discipling churches, there were lots of sins and problems. And the individual churches were not equally sound and strong. The same is true today. Not every church that is committed to a discipling philosophy will be equally sound and strong and fruitful. There are vast differences between pastors, people, cultures, etc.

But I do believe--yea, am confident--that we have more strength and spiritual zeal in our churches because we have rejected some unprofitable and vain traditions and are more committed to a truly biblical philosophy and program. And I believe that we are getting stronger instead of weaker, which is the opposite direction of so many churches today.

I believe that a church that is very careful about appointing leaders and is extra careful about salvation and church membership, that is serious about discipleship and discipline, that aims to be *very* strong in the Word of God, etc., will be a much stronger church than one that isn't. I believe that a church that is striving to maintain a first love for Christ is far superior to a church that barely has an idea about what a first love even means. I believe that a church that is aiming to be ever stronger in Christ is superior to a church that is content with lukewarm as the status quo and is going backwards spiritually.

The Church That Will Be Standing When Christ Comes

The church that will be standing when Christ comes is simply a biblical church, but a biblical church is stronger than most churches that I have known about in my lifetime.

As we look to the future, we need to strengthen everything. We need to look at every aspect of the church anew through biblical eyes and make everything stronger.

Hebrews 10:25 supports this. "Not forsaking the assembling of ourselves together, as the manner of some *is*; but exhorting *one another*: **and so much the more, as ye see the day approaching.**"

God's Word says that as we see the day of the Lord approaching, we must be ever more faithful and watchful in the things of Christ. We can't know the day or even the year of the Lord's coming, but we can see it approaching. We see Israel back in her land and the preparations for the Third Temple. We see the globalism and the preparation for a one-world economy and government. We see the apostasy that has spread throughout "Christianity," preparing for Mystery Babylon's brief fling with the Antichrist.

We definitely see the day approaching, and as a consequence the wise are going to make sure their lamps are trimmed and filled with oil, ready to meet the Bridegroom.

It is time for Bible-believing churches to wake up and strengthen *everything*.

We particularly need to look at the fundamental philosophy of a New Testament church and make sure that we are building on a truly solid biblical foundation.

Many Independent Baptists are re-examining the church, but in many cases they are examining it by unsound principles.

The church that will be standing when Jesus comes is **not an emerging church**. Many are examining the church by contemporary emerging principles. An emerging church is a new church for a new age, but the scriptural church is an outpost of Christ's heavenly kingdom and is never fashioned according to the culture of this fallen world. The New Testament Christian is a pilgrim and a stranger in this present world. We don't need a church of the twenty-first century or the twentieth century or the nineteenth century. We need a church of *the first century*.

The emerging church offers a type of liberty that amounts to license, and for this reason it is highly attractive to people who grew up in fundamentalist churches but didn't like the "rules." It is a magnet for rebels. In *A Renegade's Guide to God*, David Foster mocks "Bible thumpers" and calls for a "renegade" type of Christianity that "resists being named, revolts at being shamed, and rebels against being tamed" (p. 8). He says, "We won't be 'told' what to do or 'commanded' how to behave'" (p. 10). We see this theme all across the Internet in testimonies of people who grew up in fundamentalist churches. They charge fundamentalists with hypocrisy and pettiness, and some of their charges are true because there has been plenty of hypocrisy and pettiness among some "fundamentalists," but the root problem was their own rebellion to authority.

I think of a testimony of a man who attended Midwestern Baptist College in the days of Tom Malone. He charges the church and school with hypocrisy (allegedly not disciplining some who should have been disciplined), pettiness (e.g., caring too much about the length of men's hair), and legalism (the "six inch rule" that kept males and females apart before marriage), but he admits that he was a rule-breaker and a fornicator or at least a wannabe fornicator.

Zach Lind, drummer for the secular rock band Jimmy Eat World, told us in an interview at the National Pastor's Conference in 2009 that he grew up in a "very conservative Baptist church" and made a profession of faith when he was young, but he only did so because he didn't want to be left out of the communion service. He secretly loved rock & roll and didn't like to hear preaching against that sort of thing, so he left church and did not return to Christianity until he discovered the emerging church. Now he has the "freedom" to be a Christian and also a drummer in a secular rock band.

Hypocrisy is always wrong, but having a zeal for obedience to God's Word is not wrong and is not "legalism." Paul cared about hair length enough to teach about it in 1 Corinthians 11. To make "hair" a complete non-issue as the emerging church does is not a biblical position. As for a "six inch rule," a good case can be made from Scripture that unmarried young men and women should not touch each other and should be exceedingly careful in this matter. A six-inch rule is not legalism; it is an attempt to take the Bible's warning about the danger of moral temptation seriously, and it is an honest and good attempt to help young people remain morally pure until marriage. A "six inch rule" is wise.

The Bible teaches extreme strictness about separation from worldly things. We are to avoid **even the appearance of evil** (1 Th. 5:22). We are to be **unspotted** by the world (Jas. 1:27). We are to have **no** fellowship with the unfruitful works of darkness (Eph. 5:11). That is not legalism. That is Bible Christianity.

There was hypocrisy and legalism and error in many of the old fundamentalist churches, and we have personally exposed that (e.g., in the book *The Hyles Effect*), but strictness of separation and "rules" and "standards" in and of themselves are not wrong. We must not "throw the baby out with the bathwater."

The church that will be standing when Jesus comes is also **not a Reformed church**. Many are examining the church by Reformed principles, but John Calvin didn't understand the New Testament church. His concept of the church came more from Augustine than from Paul. Calvin said, "If I were inclined to compile a whole volume from Augustine, I could easily show my readers, that I need no words but his" (*Institutes*, Book III, chap. 22). He said, "Augustine is so wholly with me, that if I wished to write a confession of my faith, I could do so ... out of his writings" ("A Treatise on the Eternal Predestination of God," trans. by Henry Cole, *Calvin's Calvinism*, 1987). I don't consider Calvin a safe guide to anything pertaining to the church or Bible theology.

The church that will be standing when Jesus comes is also **not a church of the Fathers**. We don't need to examine the church by the principles of the "church fathers." They didn't add one iota of truth to the New Testament Scriptures, and in fact, they were guilty of introducing corruption into the church.

The church that will be standing when Jesus comes is also ***not merely a fundamentalist church***. Some are examining the church by fundamentalist principles, but whereas we should understand the fundamentalist movement and learn from it, it isn't the standard. Fundamentalism as a movement was in error in regard to many things, such as its denominationalism (with its politics and pragmatism), inter-denominationalism, and the "in essentials unity" principle.

The church that will be standing when Jesus comes is also ***not a church of the 1940s and 1950s***. I was born in 1949 and grew up in Southern Baptist churches, which were considered very conservative in those days. But they weren't strong enough to stand. They were worldly and lukewarm at best. They were a mixed multitude of saved and unsaved, with a large portion of the membership showing no evidence of salvation. The youth were frightfully worldly. A large percentage of them dropped out when they reached adolescence and followed their hearts into the world. Emergents and New Evangelicals mock separatists as wanting to go back to the 1950s, but we need to go a lot farther back than that!

The church that will be standing when Jesus comes is also ***not a church of the Independent Baptist forefathers***. Many today are simply following "conservative" Independent Baptist tradition and thinking. But though the G.B. Vicks and the Bob Joneses and Lee Robersons and John R. Rices had a lot of truth and took a good stand on many things, they are not our authority, and it is now obvious that their principles were not far-reaching enough to stand in this terrible age.

The church that will be standing when Jesus comes is simply a biblical church, but it is stronger than most Baptist and fundamentalist churches have been in my lifetime, to my knowledge. A New Testament church is more in love with Christ, more careful about salvation and church membership, more spiritually alive, stronger in God's Word, holier, stricter about separation, and more serious about real discipleship than the majority of Baptist churches.

It is time to get stronger rather than be content with the status quo.

Yet instead of re-evaluating, tightening up, and getting stronger, most churches are loosening up, eroding, weakening, softening.

You can see the effect in the youth. How many true disciples of Christ does the average church have in its "youth department"?

You can see the effect in the families. How many men are the spiritual leaders of their homes and how many mothers are the keepers at home so they can focus on the needs of their families?

You can see the effect in the music issue. In the past 10 years, the standard position has changed from the position that contemporary music is *always* wrong to the position that contemporary music is not always wrong and can be used *selectively*.

The erosion, the collapse is everywhere, but we are convinced that we can stop the erosion by addressing the fundamental issues, beginning with going back to the biblical pattern of the church as a discipling church.

A Discipling Church or a Mixed Multitude?

Outline
A Believer is a Disciple
The Mixed Multitude Philosophy
Evidences of a Mixed Multitude
The New Testament Church Is a Discipling Church
Acts 2
Matthew 28
The Church at Antioch
Paul's Greetings to the Churches
1 Corinthians 5
The Church at Thessalonica
Pilgrim Passages
Colossians 1:28
New Testament Epistles
Revelation 3:6
Christ's Message to Ephesus

The church we see in the New Testament is a church of disciples. It is a disciplined, discipling environment. A New Testament church is not something to attend. It is a spiritual entity where disciples of Christ are trained, encouraged, and protected.

New Testament discipleship is not merely a course in Christian fundamentals; it is the essence of the true Christian life. The entire church should be geared to producing and training disciples of Jesus Christ.

A Believer Is a Disciple

A pastor friend said that at a youth camp some years ago, he asked the youth to list words that God uses to describe those who are saved. He said, "We came up with something like fifty in total, and then I pointed out to them that they had forgotten the most used word, which is 'disciple.'"

Indeed, the most common name for a New Testament believer is "disciple" or "methetes" in Greek. The term "believer" appears two times (Acts 5:14; 1 Ti. 4:12); "christian" appears three times (Acts 11:16; 26:28; 1 Pe. 4:16); "saint" appears 62 times; "brethren" appears about 135 times; but "disciple" (referring to a disciple of Christ) appears about 268 times.

Scripturally speaking, a New Testament believer and a disciple are one and the same.

Jesus Christ defined discipleship in very serious terms. Consider John 8 and John 15.

> "Then said Jesus to those Jews which believed on him, If ye continue in my word, *then* are ye my disciples indeed" (John 8:31).

In John 8:31, Christ said the "disciple indeed" is one who continues in His Word. The Lord was addressing Jews who believed on Him but not in a saving way. See John 2:23-24. They were believing in Jesus as a miracle worker, as a great prophet, as a political messiah, but they were not acknowledging their personal sinfulness and owning Him as their Lord and Saviour.

A believing in God's Word, a love for God's Word, a continuing in God's Word, a passion for God's Word is the clearest evidence of salvation and true discipleship.

> "He that is of God **heareth God's words**: ye therefore hear *them* not, because ye are not of God" (John 8:47).

> "My sheep **hear my voice**, and I know them, and they follow me" (John 10:27).

A disciple's heart burns within him at God's Word (Lu. 24:31).

Later, the crowds that had "believed" on Jesus turned away from Him (John 6:66). They turned away because they did not receive His Word (Joh. 6:64), in contrast to Christ's true disciples.

> "From that *time* many of his disciples went back, and walked no more with him. Then said Jesus unto the twelve, Will ye also go away? Then Simon Peter answered him, Lord, to whom shall we go? thou hast the words of eternal life. And we believe and are sure that thou art that Christ, the Son of the living God" (John 6:66-69).

In John 15, Christ again identified the true believer as a disciple. "Herein is my Father glorified, that ye bear much fruit; so shall ye be my disciples" (Joh. 15:8). Christ likens the believer to a branch in the vine. Christ is the vine and the believer is a branch. Fruit bearing is the evidence of the true believer. It is not possible for a branch to be attached to the vine and not share in the life of the vine. If someone seems to be a branch of Christ but does not bear fruit, he is taken away (Joh. 15:2, 6). This refers to the professor who is not a possessor (Titus 1:16). The true believer bears fruit and is pruned to bring forth more fruit (Joh. 15:2). This describes God's sanctifying and chastening work in the believer's life. This describes the true believer and the true disciple as one and the same.

Salvation and discipleship are two different things, but they are closely associated and not so sharply divided as is commonly taught today. Saving faith *produces* discipleship. Discipleship is the *evidence* of saving faith. The New Testament associates saving faith with following and obeying Christ in an intimate way.

Charles Wesley got this right in the beautiful hymn "And Can It Be," which was probably his personal testimony of salvation:

> Long my imprison'd spirit lay,
>   Fast bound in sin and nature's night:
> Thine eye diffused a quickening ray;
>   I woke; the dungeon flamed with light;
> My chains fell off, my heart was free,
>   I ROSE, WENT FORTH, AND FOLLOW'D THEE.

To follow Christ is intimately connected with salvation. Following is not salvation, but it is the sure product of salvation.

This is crystal clear in Christ's words in John 10:27: "My sheep hear my voice, and I know them, and they follow me."

This is clear in Ephesians, 2:8-10. It is common to quote verses 8-9 when sharing the gospel, but those verses cannot be divorced from verse 10. Verses 8-9 is salvation, and verse 10 is the evidence and product of salvation. The individual who has the reality of verses 8-9 will have the reality of verse 10, as well. This is true salvation as taught in the Bible.

There is no example in the New Testament of a true believer who is not also a disciple of Christ. In every case of the true believer, there is a dramatic change so that the individual becomes a follower and disciple of Christ.

The Lordship Salvation Issue

The issue of repentance and discipleship and receiving Jesus as Lord has been confused and muddied by the fathers of Quick Prayerism.

Jack Hyles included "Lordship salvation" in his book *Enemies of Soulwinning*. Here he used the bait and switch method, changing "disciple" to "100% disciple." He listed the failings of men such as Peter and concluded that Peter was not "100% a disciple." Hyles did the same thing with lordship. He said that no one makes Jesus "100% Lord" of his life.

This is a straw man. It is a deceitful way of handling the issue. I don't know anyone who has taught that the true believer makes Jesus 100% Lord or that the believer is a 100% disciple in all things.

Discipleship, as with every aspect of the Christian life, is a matter of growing. The true believer doesn't have perfection in anything, including his level of discipleship. But every true believer is a disciple *at some very real and discernible level.* And every true believer surrenders to Jesus as Lord (Ro. 10:9).

Consider Peter. When he answered Christ's call and left his nets, he was a disciple of Christ. That was evident to everyone who knew him. But he learned many things along the way and made many hard decisions. He even rebuked Jesus (Mt. 16:21-23) and momentarily denied Jesus (Mt. 26:69-75). But through it all he grew and became a stronger, more devoted disciple. He was a disciple from the beginning, but he grew in discipleship. Jesus was Peter's Lord from the beginning, but he grew in the matter of Lordship. Peter was not someone who merely prayed a sinner's prayer and never showed any further evidence of salvation, like a great many of Hyles' converts and like a lot of worldly teenagers in Independent Baptist churches.

How Much Evidence?

There is a teaching about salvation evidence that goes too far and looks too deeply.

Some don't believe in a carnal Christian, claiming that a carnal Christian is unsaved, but the Bible plainly describes carnal believers as true saints (1 Co. 3:1-4). Paul did not exhort the Corinthians to be saved; he exhorted them to put away their carnality and grow. He did conclude his second epistle to Corinth with a challenge to "examine yourselves, whether ye be in the faith" (2 Co. 13:5), but in general Paul did not question their salvation. He did not equate carnality with unregeneracy.

Some don't believe that a true Christian can backslide. But the true Christian life is not a matter of 100% anything. It is a matter of knowing Christ in a saving manner and then walking with Him and daily putting off the old man and putting on the new (Eph. 4:22-24). Romans 12:1-2 teaches that surrender is a continual thing, not a once-for-all thing.

A mark of such a ministry (those who have gone too far in identifying a true believer with full surrender) is that people tend to "get saved again" under that ministry. Many people who were counted as true believers and showed evidence of salvation come to see themselves as lost and make a new profession of faith.

I recall an American missionary in Singapore who had that type of ministry. A large percentage of people who sat under his preaching "got saved" again. If an individual had struggles with some sin or had doubts about his salvation, he was considered lost and was encouraged to seek a fuller, plainer repentance. Several short-term missionaries that I knew from Nepal visited this ministry and "got saved again." Some of the people from this ministry visited my wife when she was in the hospital in Bangkok having our third child, and they tried to make her doubt her salvation because she was physically stressed and mentally depressed.

But there is no such thing as Lordship perfectionism in this present life. The true believer confesses Christ as Lord (Ro. 10:9) and is converted and changed and becomes a follower of Christ, but his discipleship will not be 100%. Any saint who is honest before God knows that there are areas of his life that are not 100% under Christ's Lordship and there are plenty of times when his discipleship is weak.

Spirit-taught wisdom is required to understand these things and to deal with people properly about salvation and sanctification.

Believer's baptism signifies the biblical concept of discipleship. It depicts dying with Christ, being buried with Christ, and rising to new life with Christ. Paul uses baptism in this way at the very beginning of his teaching about sanctification in Romans 6-8.

> "What shall we say then? Shall we continue in sin, that grace may abound? God forbid. How shall we, that are dead to sin, live any longer therein? Know ye not, that so many of us as were baptized into Jesus Christ were baptized into his death? Therefore we are buried with him by baptism into death: that like as Christ was raised up from the dead by the glory of the Father, even so we also should walk in newness of life" (Ro. 6:1-4).

A disciple is one who has died to the old life and risen to new life. This is the true Christian.

The apostle Paul described the Christian life as being dead to the world.

> "But God forbid that I should glory, save in the cross of our Lord Jesus Christ, by whom the world is crucified unto me, and I unto the world. For in Christ Jesus neither circumcision availeth any thing, nor uncircumcision, but a new creature. And as many as walk according to this rule, peace *be* on them, and mercy, and upon the Israel of God" (Ga. 6:14-16).

This is the evidence of "a new creature." Paul emphasized that this is such a fundamental principle of Christianity that only those who walk according to this rule are the true Israel of God. This is true Christianity and true salvation and true discipleship.

At some point in recent history, it became popular to distinguish between a believer and a disciple, but the Bible makes no such distinction. Every believer described in the New Testament was a disciple, beginning with Christ's original twelve. Every one of the salvations described in the New Testament were clear conversion experiences that produced disciples of Christ (e.g., the woman at the well in John 4, the 3,000 on the day at Pentecost in Acts 2, the Ethiopian eunuch in Acts 8, Saul in Acts 9, Cornelius in Acts 10, the converts at Antioch in Acts 11, Sergius Paulus of Acts 13, Lydia and the Philippian jailer in Acts 16).

The believers we see in the New Testament Scripture were sinners saved by grace and they still had the "old man" and had to put off the old man and put on the new as a daily practice, but all of them were true disciples of Christ.

The Mixed Multitude Philosophy

But in many traditional Baptist churches today, disciples are rare, and it has become acceptable to have a mixed multitude membership filled with people who are half-hearted followers of Christ, at best.

Decades ago, Evangelist Fred Brown said that he feared that a high percentage of members of Independent Baptist churches were not born again. And Lee Roberson, pastor of Highland Park Baptist Church, said that he thought that not even 50% were saved.

There are many different types of mixed multitude churches, some much stronger than others. The percentage of the members who are true disciples of Christ as defined by Christ Himself (John 8:31; 10:27), might be 10%, 20%, 30%, 40%, 50%, even 60%. But no mixed multitude church requires that a person give evidence of being a true disciple of Christ before baptism and membership.

The mixed multitude philosophy is like fishing with a net. "Again, the kingdom of heaven is like unto a net, that was cast into the sea, and gathered of every kind" (Mt. 13:47). As net fishing is non-discriminatory, dragging in everything that is caught, so the mixed multitude church accepts pretty much anyone who professes Christ and expresses interest in membership.

The discipling church is like fishing with a single rod under strict regulations. Each catch is examined for species, sex, size, weight, and quality. Again, we're not talking about some kind of sinless perfection or 100% lordship or any such thing. We are simply talking about new life in Christ that results in New Testament discipleship. We're talking about those who hear Christ's voice and follow Him (Joh. 10:27).

R. Albert Mohler, Jr., observed: "No longer concerned with maintaining purity of confession or lifestyle, the contemporary church sees itself as a voluntary association of autonomous members, with minimal moral accountability to God, much less to each other. ... Consumed with pragmatic methods of church growth and congregational engineering, most churches leave moral matters to the domain of the individual conscience" ("Church Discipline: The Missing Mark," chapter 8 of *The Compromised Church*, edited by John H. Armstrong, 1998).

I don't remember hearing the word "disciple" growing up as a Southern Baptist, and I have rarely heard it as an Independent Baptist, except in the context of a "discipleship" course.

The mixed multitude philosophy has been modeled by the vast majority of Independent Baptist churches since at least the late 1960s.

The mixed multitude philosophy was summarized to me by a pastor with 40 years of church planting experience. He said, "A church's membership is typically composed of 10% who are with the pastor and the church's program, 10% who are opposed, and 80% who could go either way."

Even if you change the numbers to something like 40% for, 10% opposed, and 50% in the middle, this is still not a New Testament church.

Anything less than a vast majority of real disciples of Christ in a church membership is a mixed multitude.

Marks of a Mixed Multitude

Following are some of the evidences and characteristics of a mixed multitude church. The bottom line is that in a mixed multitude church, true disciples of Christ are only a small percentage of the membership.

A mixed multitude is evident in church attendance.

This has long been the situation in Southern Baptist churches. According to a 1997 study by Southern Baptist Sunday School Board, only 32.8% of the 16 million SBC church members even bother to show up on a given Sunday morning and only 12.3% participate in any further aspect of church life. "These figures suggest that nearly 90% of Southern Baptist church members appear to be little different from the 'cultural Christians' who populate mainline denominations" (*Founder's Journal*, Feb. 7, 1999).

> "Let me illustrate in rounded figures by looking at some of the churches where I have preached as a guest speaker. Each could be any Baptist church in any city. ... [One] church had 2,100 on the roll, with 725 coming on Sunday morning. Remove guests and non-member children and the figure

drops to 600 or less. Only about a third of that number came out on Sunday evening, representing less than 10% of the membership. Yet another church had 310 on the roll with only 100 who attended on Sunday morning. Only 30-35, or approximately 10%, came to the evening worship service" (Jim Elliff, president of Christian Communicators Worldwide, in an article entitled "Southern Baptists, an Unregenerate Denomination," www.ccwonline.org/sbc.html).

This has also been true in most large Independent Baptist churches. For example, in the 1970s and 1980s, Highland Park had a membership of more than 50,000, but it had about 4,000 in the Sunday morning services. The same was true of First Baptist Church of Hammond, Indiana.

In contrast, Baptist churches in the early 19th century typically had far more in attendance than in the membership.

> "The children of members were present but rarely were seen as fit subjects for baptism and church membership prior to their teenage years. Moreover, many adults would regularly attend but not seek church membership because the standards associated with membership and a regenerate life were daunting to them. A church with 100 members might well have 200 to 300 attendees" (*Restoring Integrity in Baptist Churches*, Kindle loc. 209).

We must hasten to add that church membership itself is not an evidence that a person is a disciple of Christ. Multitudes of people are faithful to church services who do not give evidence of being a disciple of Christ in their daily lives. I personally know and have met hundreds of such people.

Some people enjoy church services almost as a form of entertainment, particularly when the church has an excellent music program and good preaching, which is still true of a good number of churches.

A mixed multitude is evident in the church members' relationship with the Bible.

In a mixed multitude church, the average member does not have a passionate relationship with God's Word. He doesn't continue in the Word (Joh. 8:31). He doesn't hear Christ's voice (Joh. 10:27).

A large percentage of the members don't even have a daily Bible study habit.

If they do read the Bible, it is more like a rote ritual, something to get out of the way as quickly as possible so they can check that box. They don't have a real passion to learn it. They aren't interested in obtaining and using study tools. They don't make the effort to learn how to interpret the Bible. I think of a church member I talked to recently who told me that his daily Bible study consisted of reading a couple of verses.

In my experience, the biblical ignorance of the average church member is shocking. We put together the "Bible Knowledge Test" as a tool that pastors can use to know the condition of their flocks. This is not a test of advanced knowledge. It is a test of basic knowledge, but in my experience, the average member of the average Independent Baptist church would fail it miserably.

See http://www.wayoflife.org/free-ebooks/bible-knowledge-test.php

A mixed multitude is evident in the attitude of church members during the teaching and preaching.

In a mixed multitude church, a large percentage of the members show no sign of wanting to capture a message from God for their lives. They never write down anything. They treat the messages more like a ritual to be endured or an entertainment to be enjoyed. Many don't even look at their Bibles.

In contrast, consider the following testimony from a true disciple:

> "When I got saved at age 24, I realized that there was a lot missing from my childhood, since I grew up in a weak church. When I found a good church, the strong preaching was like honey to me. Being in a church that preached the truth was just like the Bible says; it was like honey. I just ate it up and tried to apply it."

If a church has only a few people like this, it is a mixed multitude church rather than a church of disciples.

A mixed multitude is evident in the youth.

In a mixed multitude church, only a small percentage of the youth are disciples of Christ. They don't hear Christ's voice and follow Him as Christ's true sheep (John 10:27). They make a profession of Jesus as Saviour, but they aren't earnestly seeking God's' perfect will, don't walk in sweet fellowship with Him, aren't serious Bible students, aren't making their decisions based on God's Word, and aren't diligently separating from the evil things of the world from the heart.

A mixed multitude is evident in the prayer meetings.

In a mixed multitude church, only a small percentage of the members show up for prayer meetings. I have seen this in the vast majority of churches I have preached in.

Prayer is the heart of a church, and it *shows* the heart of a church. Real disciples of Christ continue in prayer (Acts 2:42), and I don't believe that a real disciple would dream of skipping prayer meetings.

A mixed multitude is evident in the church members' passions.

In the mixed multitude church, a large percentage of the members love the things of the world as passionately as unbelievers do (e.g., music, music videos, movies, professional sports, video games, worldly literature, sensual social media, the world's clothing fashions).

What people are passionate about is witnessed by the content of and use of their cell phones.

It is witnessed by the content of their social media (e.g., Facebook, Twitter).

It is witnessed by what they spend their money on, and what they do with their free time, and what they do when they are alone.

A mixed multitude is evident in the church members' conversations.

> "O generation of vipers, how can ye, being evil, speak good things? for out of the abundance of the heart the mouth speaketh" (Mt. 12:34).

> "The heart of him that hath understanding seeketh knowledge: but the mouth of fools feedeth on foolishness" (Pr. 15:14).

In a mixed multitude church, a large number of the members don't naturally talk about Christ and the things of God. They talk about foolish things (not wise) and vain things (no eternal value) and out-and-out worldly things.

One man described his church as follows: "Most of the men stand around and talk about sports, going on cruise ships, going to Disney, etc. and when I walk up and want to talk about things of the Lord Jesus Christ, they stand there and have no idea what I'm talking about and normally walk off. I can only think of two men who will talk to me about things of the Lord."

In contrast, disciples of Christ are described by Malachi:

> "Then they that feared the LORD spake often one to another: and the LORD hearkened, and heard it, and a book of remembrance was written before him for them that feared the LORD, and that thought upon his name" (Mal. 3:16).

A mixed multitude has become the status quo. A great many pastors are content with it. Few seem to be concerned enough to re-evaluate tradition to see why the typical church is so weak and whether there is a better, more scriptural path.

But this is exactly what we must do. The flood tide of compromise and worldliness and apostasy is sweeping down upon us from every direction, enhanced by end-time technology, a sensual global pop culture, and social media, and only a thorough-going New Testament church will stand.

A New Testament Church Is a Church of Disciples

Everywhere in the New Testament we see a church membership composed of disciples. We see the true Christian described as a born again disciple. We see an emphasis on evidence of salvation. We see warnings about Christians who do not show clear evidence of salvation. We see the church as a discipling institution.

If need be, I had far rather have a membership composed of ten disciples than 500 lukewarm. Ten disciples is a powerful start to a strong church, whereas 500 lukewarm are nothing.

Again, we're not talking about any kind of perfect Christian discipleship or any kind of "100% lordship."

And we are not forgetting the issue of spiritual growth. A new Christian is a babe in Christ and must grow (1 Pe. 2:1-2), and growing is a process that continues throughout the entire life (2 Pe. 3:18).

But even a babe in Christ is a new creature who has been spiritually raised from the dead, brought out of darkness into light, and has new life in Christ, and this is a powerful transformation that can be seen.

The bottom line is what kind of church do we see in the Word of God?

Consider the following Scriptures that describe a church of disciples rather than a mixed multitude:

Matthew 28:18-20

> "And Jesus came and spake unto them, saying, All power is given unto me in heaven and in earth. Go ye therefore, and teach all nations, baptizing them in the name of the Father, and of the Son, and of the Holy Ghost: Teaching them to observe all things whatsoever I have commanded you: and, lo, I am with you alway, *even* unto the end of the world. Amen."

Here we see a New Testament church as the product of Christ's Great Commission.

First, a Matthew 28:19-20 church is a disciple-making church. Christ's command is to make disciples of all nations. The Greek word translated "teaching" is "matheteuo," a verbal form of "methetes," commonly translated "disciple."

Anything short of disciple-making is not a fulfillment of Christ's command. The Lord doesn't want professors; He wants disciples. There is not a hint in the Gospels that Christ would be satisfied with someone who merely professed Him as Saviour. To the contrary, He powerfully witnessed against such a thing (e.g., John 8:30-32).

A church composed of some disciples of Christ lumped together with a bunch of people who aren't disciples is not obedience to Christ's command.

Second, the beginning of discipleship is baptism. The mention of baptism in direct connection with making disciples is highly significant.

Scriptural baptism is a powerful, meaningful thing. It is not an empty religious ritual as it has become in so many churches. Scriptural baptism, which is baptism by immersion or "dipping," is only for those who are born again, and it is a picture of their conversion. It is a picture of being buried with Christ in His death and being raised to newness of life in His resurrection. Baptism itself does not save and is not a part of salvation, but it has rightly been called "the first step of obedience," or we could say, the first step of discipleship.

A discipling church practices scriptural baptism. It takes baptism very seriously. It is careful about who is baptized, making as sure as possible that the individuals who are baptized are qualified, meaning that they have been saved and risen to new life in Christ spiritually.

A discipling church educates baptismal candidates in the meaning of baptism and in the significance it has in identifying them as true disciples of Christ.

If a person gets baptized who has no intention of following and obeying Christ, he is lying when he comes up out of the water, because that event signifies rising to new life in Christ.

Third, it is a church that teaches all things that Christ has commanded. Matthew 28:19-20 is a description of a very serious teaching church. It is exceedingly strong in God's Word. It has the objective of teaching all of the people all of God's Word.

Fourth, a Matthew 28:19-20 church is a church that teaches the observance of all things. It is a church that isn't content that the people will have mere head knowledge of the Bible. It is a church that teaches the Bible in such a way that it gets down into every part of the believer's daily lives.

The Church at Jerusalem

A church of disciples is described in Acts 2:41-47:

> "Then they that gladly received his word were baptized: and the same day there were added *unto them* about three thousand souls. And they continued stedfastly in the apostles' doctrine and fellowship, and in breaking of bread, and in prayers. And fear came upon every soul: and many wonders and signs were done by the apostles. And all that believed

were together, and had all things common; And sold their possessions and goods, and parted them to all *men*, as every man had need. And they, continuing daily with one accord in the temple, and breaking bread from house to house, did eat their meat with gladness and singleness of heart, Praising God, and having favour with all the people. And the Lord added to the church daily such as should be saved."

This is the first church, and it is the pattern for all churches throughout the age.

Some of the characteristics of that church, such as apostolic signs and having property in common (verses 43-33), were temporary.

The permanent characteristics are found in verses 41-42 and 47.

The members were saved (Ac. 2:41). There was a clear new birth conversion experience. The *before* and *after* of their conversion was dramatic. Before Pentecost, they rejected Jesus as Christ and were fearful to confess His name, but now they gladly and publicly received Him as Lord and Saviour, and they were willing to bear before the Hebrew nation the reproach of being a follower of "Jesus of Nazareth." This is what we look for in our church work. We don't look for anything more or less than life-changing salvation.

The members were committed and faithful (Ac. 2:42). They "continued stedfastly in the apostles' doctrine and fellowship, and in breaking of bread, and in prayers." This was serious Christianity. These were real disciples *from day one of their Christian lives.* They were faithful, zealous, persistent.

The church's membership continued to grow through regeneration (Ac. 2:47). The members are described as "saved."

This is what happened to me in the summer of 1973. I had a dramatic conversion experience. My life was turned around and my feet were set on a different course.

In contrast, many churches today are mixed multitudes of saved and unsaved, hot, cold, and lukewarm, faithful and unfaithful. Pastor Bob Kirkland says,

> "Two thousand years ago when someone was baptized, publicly professing their faith in Christ, they were willing to die for the Lord. We don't have that situation today [in North America]; however, no one should be considered a member

of the Lord's local church today who is not willing to live for Him. At our church we require all members to be faithful to the services. Potential members are taught that they have the same responsibility to the church that the pastor has. If the pastor misses a service to watch some sports activity on television or to visit family, the people should find a new pastor. If a church member skips church for something like that, the church member should be instructed to get in line or find a church that allows a cheap membership. **If the church that Christ 'purchased with his own blood' is no more than an add-on in life, it is an insult to the Lord.**"

The Church at Antioch

"And some of them were men of Cyprus and Cyrene, which, when they were come to Antioch, spake unto the Grecians, preaching the Lord Jesus. And the hand of the Lord was with them: and a great number believed, and turned unto the Lord. Then tidings of these things came unto the ears of the church which was in Jerusalem: and they sent forth Barnabas, that he should go as far as Antioch. Who, when he came, and had seen the grace of God, was glad, and exhorted them all, that with purpose of heart they would cleave unto the Lord. For he was a good man, and full of the Holy Ghost and of faith: and much people was added unto the Lord. Then departed Barnabas to Tarsus, for to seek Saul: And when he had found him, he brought him unto Antioch. And it came to pass, that a whole year they assembled themselves with the church, and taught much people. And the disciples were called Christians first in Antioch" (Acts 11:20-26).

The churches that were established among the Gentiles were discipling churches in the clearest and most profound way.

Consider the church at Antioch.

It was a discipling church in that the members were truly converted.

- They "believed, and turned unto the Lord" (Acts 11:21). Here we see biblical repentance (a turning) and faith. Compare Acts 20:21.

- Their salvation is described as a supernatural work of God - "the hand of the Lord was with them." There was no human manipulation and no cheap salesmanship tactics, no empty professions. The gospel was preached and the power of God converted souls.

- Their salvation is described as being "added unto the Lord" (Acts 11:24).
- Their salvation could be *seen* by Barnabas (Acts 11:23).
- Their salvation was evident in that they were exhorted to cleave unto the Lord. It is impossible for an unsaved person to do this.

It was a discipling church in that the new work was not left to its own devices, but was overseen by the church at Jerusalem, which sent Barnabas to build up the new converts, establish them in the faith, and provide proper leadership.

And it was a discipling church in that the believers were called "disciples" (Acts 11:26).

Paul's Greetings to the Churches

Paul's greetings to the churches make it clear that a New Testament church is a church of disciples.

Note what he calls the church members:
"beloved of God, called to be saints" (Ro. 1:7)
"sanctified in Christ Jesus, called to be saints" (1 Co. 1:2)
"ye are the temple of the living God' (2 Co. 6:16)
"the saints which are at Ephesus, and to the faithful in Christ
  Jesus" (Eph. 1:1)
"the saints in Christ Jesus" (Php. 1:1)
"the saints and faithful brethren in Christ" (Col. 1:2)
"the church of the Thessalonians which is in God the Father and in
  the Lord Jesus Christ" (1 Th. 1:1)

It is obvious that Paul assumed that the members of the churches were born again.

> "The New Testament uses a number of images to describe something of the church's nature, and all of them presuppose that the church is composed of genuine believers. How could the church be 'the people of God' if the people did not, in fact, belong to God? How could the church be 'the body of Christ' if the members of that body were not, in fact, joined to Christ? How could the Holy Spirit make the church 'a holy temple' in which God dwells and is worshipped if, in fact,

God did not dwell in the individuals composing the church?" (*Restoring Integrity in Baptist Churches*, Kindle loc. 172).

1 Corinthians 5

A church of disciples is described in 1 Corinthians 5.

"Your glorying *is* not good. Know ye not that a little leaven leaveneth the whole lump? Purge out therefore the old leaven, that ye may be a new lump, as ye are unleavened. For even Christ our passover is sacrificed for us: Therefore let us keep the feast, not with old leaven, neither with the leaven of malice and wickedness; but with the unleavened *bread* of sincerity and truth" (1 Co. 5:6-8).

Paul describes the church as an entity that must be kept pure. In Paul's mind, the leaders cannot accept a permanent state of impurity. They must strive against impurity in all forms. They must purge, purge, purge.

The believers are unleavened *positionally* through the blood of Christ, but in a *practical* senses they must keep the feast of unleavened bread which followed the Passover, which is a picture of the Christian life. All leaven was to be rejected from their homes for seven days, signifying completion. The Passover pictures once-for-all redemption, and the feast of unleavened bread pictures progressive sanctification.

This is why Paul wrote to the church at Corinth to correct and reprove them for their carnality, sin, and error.

He would not accept a mixed multitude church. He had to purge out the leaven.

He would not accept a carnal church. He dealt with carnality head on, forcefully, and relentlessly. He was always gracious, but he was unbending for righteousness and truth in the churches.

He would not rest content until there was repentance and *all* of the issues were resolved to the glory of Christ.

He would not rest content with even a little leaven in the church. He warned that a *little* leaven leavens the *whole* lump.

How far this is from the mindset of the so many pastors today! They overlook sins and errors and don't believe it is their responsibility to "meddle" with the daily and private lives of the church members. I have heard pastors actually say this. Others might not say it verbally, but they say it by their actions.

Unlike Paul, while the modern pastor might not be happy with carnality in the membership, he doesn't deal with it forcefully and effectively. He countenances a carnal status quo even in the lives of those involved in ministry. Basically he accepts the mixed multitude condition of the church year after year.

And this thinking is increasing. It has taken over some of my pastor friends that were formerly stronger. It appears that they have gotten weary in the battle. They have gotten soft and have compromised. And the churches bear the evidence of the compromise in the families that have grown increasingly worldly and in the young people who have at least one foot in the world. The people know the right words to say and can conform outwardly when necessary, but they lack a true passion for Christ and His will in their daily lives. The evidence can be seen in their social media communications, which are filled with vanity if not outright worldliness, and it is seen in what the people truly love and how they spend their time and money.

The pastors know that the young people are worldly, but they don't do anything effectual about it. They don't reprove and rebuke their sins plainly, only in generalities. Even if they reprove publicly from the pulpit, they don't reprove face-to-face. They don't reprove the parents for letting their children play with the world even though they are sleeping under their roofs and eating their food. They don't exercise discipline by refusing to let worldly young people participate in ministries such as playing musical instruments, singing in the choir, and taking up the offering.

The pastors know that the older members have "settled on the lees" and live in a backslidden condition, but they don't deal with it effectually. They let the backsliders continue in ministries and thus pull down the spiritual climate of the entire congregation.

Pastors who don't deal effectually with sin and error throughout the church body are pastoring a mixed multitude and not a New Testament discipling church.

The Church at Thessalonica

A church of disciples is described in 1 Thessalonians 1:9-10.

"For they themselves shew of us what manner of entering in we had unto you, and how ye turned to God from idols to serve the living and true God; And to wait for his Son from heaven, whom he raised from the dead, *even* Jesus, which delivered us from the wrath to come."

This is a description of a true Christian and a true disciple and a true New Testament church.

The members had turned to God from idols. They had repented, and the evidence was seen in their lives. They were busy serving the living and true God.

They were looking for Christ's return.

This is a description of passionate, wholehearted Christianity. This is a church of disciples.

At the same time, there was no perfection or "100% discipleship" at Thessalonica. The church had to deal with the unruly, the feebleminded, and the weak (1 Th. 5:14).

Pilgrim Passages

A church of disciples is described in the pilgrim passages.

> "For our conversation is in heaven; from whence also we look for the Saviour, the Lord Jesus Christ" (Php. 3:20).

> "These all died in faith, not having received the promises, but having seen them afar off, and were persuaded of *them*, and embraced *them*, and confessed that they were strangers and pilgrims on the earth" (Heb. 11:13).

> "Dearly beloved, I beseech *you* as strangers and pilgrims, abstain from fleshly lusts, which war against the soul" (1 Pe. 2:11).

A New Testament church is a church of pilgrims who are citizens of another country and are journeying through a foreign land. This is how the members of New Testament churches are addressed in Scripture. It is taken for granted that this is what they are.

The true Christian is described here as one who has been persuaded of God's promises in Christ, "and EMBRACED THEM, and confessed that they were strangers and pilgrims on the earth" (Heb. 11:13). This is not a picture of nominal Christianity. It is a description of a fervent disciple of Jesus Christ who has turned his back to this world to love and serve Christ.

These are the people of whom God is not ashamed to be called their God (Heb. 11:16). They have confessed Him before an antagonistic world, and He confesses them!

The mixed multitude church might have some pilgrims but they are mixed together with a lot of people who *profess* to know Christ but who are very much at home in this present world.

Colossians 1:28

A church of disciples is described in Colossians 1:28.

> "Whom we preach, warning every man, and teaching every man in all wisdom; that we may present every man perfect in Christ Jesus."

We see that the church's goal is to present **every man** perfect in Christ Jesus; not *some* men, but every man. And the goal is to present every man **perfect**, not half-hearted and lukewarm. This is a description of a serious discipling church.

"**In Christ Jesus**" means in His will, in His pleasure. This is serious discipleship. This is not an entertainment program. This is not a seeker-sensitive program.

This describes a church in which the entire body is moving ever higher spiritually.

We see that a church *can* present God's people perfect in Christ Jesus. If this were not possible, God's Word would not teach it. Churches, even "Bible believing churches," are not all the same.

Many do not have this type of ministry, being content with a mixed multitude in which some of the members are growing and many aren't.

A Colossians 1:28 ministry requires warning.

Warning is absolutely necessary for producing disciples because we are sinners and we need warning and correction.

The New Testament is literally filled with warnings.

Note that warning is mentioned first in Colossians 1:28, even though teaching actually comes first. We don't warn someone of something until he first has been taught about that thing.

Warning is probably mentioned first because it is difficult and typically it is the first thing to be given up by churches.

Warning is against human nature; we don't naturally like to give it or receive it.

Warning is against human philosophy and psychology (e.g., "be positive so as not to injure the people's self-esteem").

Warning is against the spirit of the modern times (e.g., judge not, be tolerant). One-world globalism is driven by a "judge not" philosophy.

Warning is against the pragmatic, seeker-sensitive, church growth philosophy. If you warn, you will have a smaller church than you would otherwise have.

The ministry of warning is never intended to hurt anyone; it is intended to help the people and to present them perfect in Christ Jesus.

In our ministry we aim to warn every man. When we see a brother or sister backsliding, we warn him. We warn the old, and we warn the young.

I think of a man who had persistently missed the weekly men's discipleship meeting. I preach about being faithful and carefully teach about the reason for faithfulness and reprove those who aren't faithful, but the time came when we talked to this brother face to face. I said, "I believe the reason for your unfaithfulness is one of three things: either you are not saved, or you are lazy, or you are backslidden." I said, if it isn't one of those things, please tell me what it is. He is not a very talkative man, and he didn't reply for a while. I thought he wasn't going to answer me, but finally he said, "I am lazy." I exhorted him further that day, and he has been faithful ever since.

We are never content if a member is lukewarm and backsliding. We deal with it, and we continue to deal with it until the matter is solved.

The ministry of warning is difficult, and one of my fears for the preachers I train is that they won't exercise the ministry of warning, that they will soften the preaching and soften the personal ministry, that they will be afraid, that they will be selfish, that they will be covetous, that they will honor their friends and relatives more than God and His truth.

A Colossians 1:28 ministry requires teaching.

An effectual and extensive program of Bible teaching is necessary for true discipleship.

The church must have a plan to teach every member.

This is one reason why every member must be faithful to all services. We spend a lot of time and effort preparing messages for the services, and if God's people aren't there, there is no benefit. We tell our people, "God's business always trumps your business."

We deal with the church's teaching ministry in the chapter "The Discipling Church Is Strong in God's Word."

A Colossians 1:28 ministry requires warning and teaching **in all wisdom**. Only God can give this type of wisdom in dealing with people. Thus, Paul is saying that the teachers must lean on the Spirit of God in exercising this ministry.

The New Testament Epistles

A church of disciples is described in all of the New Testament Epistles.

Not every church we see in the New Testament is strong, but anytime we see a church that was less than what it should be, we see it as the recipient of strong and effectual correction.

Consider the church at Corinth. It was carnal, as Paul plainly stated.

It was not lukewarm, by the way. It was a church whose members gave clear evidence of a saving conversion experience (1 Co. 6:9-11). It was a church that was zealous for the things of Christ, zealous for spiritual things (1 Co. 14:12), and it was a church that abounded in "faith, utterance, knowledge, diligence, and love" (2 Co. 8:7).

But the church at Corinth was carnal and had many problems and errors, *and Paul was not content to allow the church to continue in these things.* He did not allow the church to settle down into carnality as the status quo. He dealt with the church's sins and errors head on, plainly, publicly, firmly, even sharply at times. He called the church to repentance and discipline. He didn't *suggest* discipline; he *demanded* discipline.

And the church did repent of many things. We see their repentance in 2 Co. 7:8-11, which is evidence that they were true disciples of Christ and which shows the power of godly discipline.

Paul is our example (Php. 3:17). Every pastor must imitate Paul's method of dealing with sins and errors in the churches. The pastor must not be content with carnality, lukewarmness, unfaithfulness, unrepentant sin. He must not accept it. He must ever strive for a pure body. He must remove the leaven (1 Co. 5:6-7). Carnality, backsliding, unfaithfulness, sin, and error must be dealt with, in whatever ways are necessary, and these things must never be allowed to become the status quo.

Paul did not conform to the society in which he ministered. Corinth was renowned for its sensuality, but Paul did not bend to this. He didn't say, "Well, we can't expect much more from this church, because they are Corinthians, you know." He didn't lower God's standards. He kept the bar of holiness and faithfulness as high as God demands and raised up the Corinthian saints to God's standard. In contrast, many preachers today lower the bar because of the character of their people. They let the society set the standards for the level of faithfulness and holiness.

By nature, all men are the same, but there are national and local characteristics. I've spent the major part of my life living and traveling oversea, and there are significant differences between Australians, Brits, Nepalis, Thais, Koreans, Brazilians, Russians, Nigerians, etc. And these national characteristics have the potential to affect the churches in some major ways.

The Cretians had the well deserved reputation of being "liars, evil beasts, slow bellies" (Titus 1:12). But Paul did not say to Titus, "The Cretians aren't going to be very good Christians and their churches aren't going to be very strong, because their national characteristics are just too weak. So lighten up and don't try to be too hard on them, because you won't get very far and you will probably just offend them." Instead, Paul told Titus to double down on how he dealt with the Cretian believers because they needed an even firmer hand. He said, "rebuke them sharply, that they may be sound in the faith" (Tit. 1:13).

Everywhere we look in the New Testament epistles, there is no support for, no divine authority for, accepting a mixed multitude church as the status quo.

Consider the churches addressed by James. He publicly called the members adulterers and adulteresses (Jas. 4:4). In the plainest manner he called them to repentance and holiness (Jas. 4:9-10). James was not a spiritual leader who would accept worldliness and unholiness and lack of passion for Christ as the status quo. He would not wink at it year after year. He would not keep his mouth shut in the face of it. He would never say, "I'm sorry for how the people live, but it is not my part to *force* them to serve Christ." James was not afraid to preach so hard and so fervently that he would *force* people to make a decision one way or the other!

This is our example. This is New Testament Christianity. This is a New Testament church. The leaders must not be content if the people are lukewarm and disobedient and backsliding, if they don't attend the services faithfully, if they don't love their Bibles, if they don't listen to the messages eagerly in order to capture something for their daily lives, if they are worldly, if the husbands don't love their wives and train their children, if the wives don't honor their husbands and aren't keepers of the homes, if the members join unscriptural organizations such as the Masons or the Eastern Star, if the church members adopt the ways of the world such as the world's unisex and immodest fashions and the world's music, etc.

In the culture where our church planting work is located, it is popular for men to go overseas to work. In doing so, they abandon their wives and children contrary to the teaching of God's Word, typically they don't have good Christian fellowship or even a good church to attend, and as a consequence they backslide spiritually. Further, they neglect the needy mission field of their own people. We don't ignore this type of thing. We can't force them not to go, but we definitely can teach and exhort and warn and rebuke.

Some might call this *force*, but this is exactly what we see in the New Testament churches.

I have never known a Southern Baptist pastor who is a James, and I have known *very few* Independent Baptist pastors who are Jameses.

Instead of James pastors we more typically have Eli pastors. He warned his wicked sons, but he did not control them (1 Sa. 2:21-25; 3:13 "because his sons made themselves vile, and he restrained them not"). He did not discipline them. They should have been stoned for their adultery (1 Sa. 2:22; Lev. 20:10). Instead, Eli allowed the young men to continue in the ministry. Likewise, a great many pastors do not discipline sinning members, and they allow people to continue in various ministries in the church even though they are spiritually unqualified.

If you examine even the most conservative and lively of Independent Baptist churches, with rare exceptions, you find a frightful lack of real disciples, and all too often you even find a frightful lack of concern about the matter.

A mixed multitude has become the status quo.

Revelation 3:16

The necessity of the church being a church of disciples is seen in Christ's attitude toward a lukewarm church.

> "So then because thou art lukewarm, and neither cold nor hot, I will spue thee out of my mouth" (Re. 3:16).

The church at Laodicea had become lukewarm, but Christ did not accept this and did not ignore it. He dealt with it in the plainest, sharpest manner. Christ does not accept lukewarm churches.

Christ requires "hot." He requires passion, zeal, fervor.

> "And now, Israel, what doth the LORD thy God require of thee, but to fear the LORD thy God, to walk in all his ways, and to love him, and to serve the LORD thy God with all thy heart and with all thy soul" (De. 10:12).

> "No man can serve two masters: for either he will hate the one, and love the other; or else he will hold to the one, and despise the other. Ye cannot serve God and mammon" (Mt. 6:24).

> "He that loveth father or mother more than me is not worthy of me: and he that loveth son or daughter more than me is not worthy of me" (Mt. 10:37).

> "Not slothful in business; fervent in spirit; serving the Lord" (Ro. 12:11).

> "Who gave himself for us, that he might redeem us from all iniquity, and purify unto himself a peculiar people, zealous of good works" (Tit. 2:14).

"And above all things have fervent charity among yourselves: for charity shall cover the multitude of sins" (1 Pe. 4:8).

"Nevertheless I have *somewhat* against thee, because thou hast left thy first love" (Re. 2:4).

"That religion which God requires, and will accept, does not consist in weak, dull, and lifeless wishes, raising us but a little above a state of indifference: God, in his word, greatly insists upon it, that we be good in earnest, 'fervent in spirit,' and our hearts vigorously engaged in religion. ... It is such a fervent vigorous engagement of the heart in religion, that is the fruit of a real circumcision of the heart, or true regeneration, and that has the promises of life; De. 30:6, 'And the Lord thy God will circumcise thine heart, and the heart of thy seed, to love the Lord thy God with all thy heart, and with all thy soul, and that thou mayest live'" (Jonathan Edwards, *A Treatise on Religious Affections*).

In spite of Christ's warning, the average "Bible believing" church today is lukewarm at best. Lukewarm has become acceptable. It is the status quo. In fact, a lukewarm church is considered a pretty good church. At least it isn't spiritually cold and totally dead. At least it isn't "liberal."

The average church *might* have a few members who are spiritually fervent, but the greatest number are either cold or lukewarm.

Consider the following description of a church that considers itself a separatist, Bible-believing church:

> "It is probably among the most careful Baptist churches in this area about music. The preaching has some good points but we are alarmed at the weak spiritual life of the people. Very few men will lead in prayer. There is no apparent fellowship around the things of the Lord. Before and after services people talk of work, sports, and other small talk, and even that is quick. Most arrive just in time and then head straight out the door when it's over. The pastor is a lover of sports. There is a joking toleration of gluttony in the majority of the sermons. There are three teenagers. One is a boy who seems miserably bored. He plans to go into the video game industry. The other is a quiet, sweet girl who is the only one who comes to church from her family. She wears dresses, which is the pastor's stated preference, but they are very

revealing, probably because she hasn't been taught any better, even by female teachers at the church. Most of the young wives and moms work outside the home and this is not taught against in the church."

This is a lukewarm church at very best.

If Christ does not accept lukewarm, who are we to accept lukewarm people into the membership and even allow them to participate in ministries, thus pulling down the spiritual climate of the congregation?

Christ's Message to Ephesus

A church of disciples is demanded by Christ's message to the church at Ephesus.

> "I know thy works, and thy labour, and thy patience, and how thou canst not bear them which are evil: and thou hast tried them which say they are apostles, and are not, and hast found them liars: And hast borne, and hast patience, and for my name's sake hast laboured, and hast not fainted. Nevertheless I have *somewhat* against thee, because thou hast left thy first love. Remember therefore from whence thou art fallen, and repent, and do the first works; or else I will come unto thee quickly, and will remove thy candlestick out of his place, except thou repent" (Re. 2:2-5).

A true New Testament church is a church of the first love for Jesus Christ.

We look at the church's first love relationship with Christ more extensively in the chapter "A Discipling Church Is a Church of the First Love."

Here we make the point that a church of the first love cannot possibly be a mixed multitude church.

A New Testament church is not merely a church that is sound in doctrine. Sound doctrine and the right Bible is essential, but it is not enough. Truth alone is not enough. The church at Ephesus had more truth and more *zeal* for truth than the *vast* majority of Independent Baptist churches or fundamentalist churches or Bible-believing churches.

We see that the church at Ephesus **had a first love previously**. This describes a church of true disciples who are passionate in their relationship with Jesus Christ. This was no mixed multitude.

First love Christianity is no nominal, half-hearted Christianity. It is born again, converted, turned upside down, inside out Christianity so that you love the things you once hated and you hate the things you once loved. Having a first love is talking about a passionate relationship with Jesus Christ, knowing Him personally as Paul did (2 Ti. 1:12), seeking to please Him because He loves me and I love Him, considering His Word sweeter than honey and more valuable than gold (Psa. 119:103, 127). Love. Passion. Zeal. Enthusiasm. On fire. This is a first love for Christ.

We see first love Christianity in all of the cases of conversion that are described in the New Testament. The woman at the well had it when she left her water pot and ran back to her village to tell the people about Jesus. Zacchaeus had it when he pledged to pay back anything he had stolen. Joseph of Arimathaea had it when he devoted his own new tomb for Jesus' burial. The 3,000 on the day of Pentecost had it when they publicly professed Christ before a wicked nation and continued stedfastly in the apostles doctrine and fellowship, and in breaking of bread, and in prayers. Paul had it when he immediately began to preach the Christ he previously persecuted. The Ethiopian eunuch had it when he urgently sought baptism and went on his way rejoicing. Lydia had it when she urged Paul and Silas to lodge at her house. The Philippian jailer had it when he washed Paul and Silas' wounds.

A great many members of Bible-believing churches have never had a first love passion for Jesus Christ because they have never been born again.

A great many churches have only a relatively few members who have actually experienced a first love. How can such a mixed multitude be called a New Testament church? If Ephesus, which actually had a first love but had left it, did not please Christ, how much more does the typical church today not please Him which has never had a first love?

First love Christianity is real Christianity and a first love church is a real New Testament church.

We see that the church at Ephesus **had left its first love**. Christ uses strong language to describe what had happened. They had "fallen." It was a serious matter.

Christ did not overlook this backslidden condition. He requires first love from His churches. He warned that He would remove their candlestick out of its place. The candlestick signifies a true church of Christ (Re. 1:20). The candlestick church is the church that Christ walks in the midst of (Re. 1:13; 2:1). The removal of the candlestick would mean that Christ no longer owns that church as a true church. This doesn't mean the church ceases to exist. Often such a church will continue for a long time going through the motions after Christ has removed the candlestick.

This is a very serious matter. It tells us that there is more to a sound church before God than doctrinal correctness. We say, "That is a good church." But is it really? Does it abide in a first love passion for Christ?

Christ calls the church to repentance. "Remember therefore from whence thou art fallen, and repent, and do the first works..." (Re. 2:5).

We don't know how long the church had before this judgment would fall. But the warning is clear: if it did not repent, it would no longer be owned by Christ as one of His churches.

The church we see in the New Testament is a discipling church rather than a mixed multitude!

Are There any Discipling Churches among Independent Baptists?

I have had the privilege of preaching in some Independent Baptist churches that are true discipling churches. They are very careful about salvation and church membership. They have a strong ministry of God's Word, and their people are learning to be effectual Bible students. They are building godly families, discipling the youth, and training preachers.

I wrote to two pastors of such churches and asked them about their congregations, and they replied as follows:

> "As far as I can see all of our men are spiritual leaders of their homes and the thirteen men that have children still at home

are discipling them with 'family Bible time,' etc. All the wives are keepers at home. Only two of our married women work outside the home and both are in feminine jobs (nursing and house-cleaning) and testify that they are very careful to not allow their outside work to hinder all responsibilities to the home. One no longer has children at home and the other doesn't have children yet and is committed to quitting her job as soon as she does. Our Jr./Sr. High group numbers 11 and all seem to be true disciples. I teach them every Sunday morning at 10 and I lead all camps, activities, etc. They are active singing, serving, giving, etc."

"I would say that we have 5-7 men that are striving to be spiritual leaders and about that many that are passive. It's probably 50/50. If by keepers at home you mean that they do not work outside the home, besides my wife and our deacons's wives, we have four other ladies that do not work. Some that do work, work part time. Overall, again, it's probably 50/50 of ladies working outside the home. I think that several would prefer not to, but because of past financial decisions and/or husbands losing their jobs, they must. Only a couple would prefer to work over being at home. If by young people you mean teenagers, then we have currently around 10-12 that are faithful. Of those ten, I would say that 8 of 10 would be serious about following Christ."

A discipling church will have new Christians who are learning and progressing.

In a discipling church, not every father will yet be the spiritual leader of his home nor every mother the keeper at home that God wants her to be. It takes time to build these kinds of Christian lives and homes even when you start with true disciples, and how long this takes and how far they will progress depends to some degree on the background of the converts.

Some of our fathers and mothers were saved later in life out of darkest Hinduism and have a very poor education, if that. They love the Lord, and they are faithful and doing their best in most cases, but their spiritual progress has been very slow, and teaching them to train, discipline, and oversee their children has been an uphill battle.

In this situation we have put our focus on training the young people and preparing them for marriage so they can start out their marriages with a knowledge of God's will. We are doing what we can for the older crowd, but more of our attention is on training the youth. And this includes preparing a school program to educate the children of our families so they can start learning God's Word and ways in childhood and not be sent to public school to be steeped in Hinduism and Humanism.

The Disappearance of Discipling Churches

Outline
Apostasy Destroyed the Discipling Church
Bible-believing Churches Held to New Testament Discipline
Protestants Kept Rome's Church Doctrine
Old Baptist Churches Were Discipling Churches
Apostasy in the Convention Baptist Churches
Independent Baptist Churches

In this chapter we aim to give a brief history of the New Testament discipling church from the first century until today.

New Testament churches were churches of disciples and churches of discipline. We saw this in the previous chapter.

Apostasy Destroyed the Discipling Church

In the centuries after the apostles, large numbers churches were corrupted. A regenerate church membership was destroyed by infant baptism and a sacramental gospel. People became Christians by rituals. The church members and the pastors were not born again. They had a form of godliness but denied the power thereof (2 Ti. 3:5), as Paul had prophesied.

By Augustine's day (AD 353-430), churches that rejected infant baptism were persecuted.

The Roman Catholic Church gradually took control of most churches across Europe.

The moral climate of these churches was terrible. When Martin Luther visited Rome in 1511, he expected to find a holy place, but that was not his experience. Instead of a city of prayers and alms, of contr...ite hearts and holy lives, Rome was full of "mocking hypocrisy,. defiant skepticism, jeering impiety, and shameless revelry." He commented, "If there be a hell, Rome is built over it."

This history can be found in *A History of the Churches from a Baptist Perspective*, available from Way of Life Literature.

Bible-believing Churches Held to New Testament Discipline

During that era, Bible-believing churches continued to exist and to hold fast to a regenerate church membership and New Testament discipline, but they were terribly persecuted.

Consider the Waldenses of northern Italy and southern France. Following are statements from their church covenants:

> "By this ordinance [water baptism] we are received into the holy congregation of God's people, previously professing and declaring our faith and **change of life**."

> "We contend, that **all those in whom the fear of God dwells, will thereby be led to please him, and to abound in the good works [of the gospel] which God hath before ordained** that we should walk in them—which are love, joy, peace, patience, kindness, goodness, gentleness, sobriety, and the other good works enforced in the Holy Scriptures."

> "We hold that the **ministers of the church ought to be unblameable** both in life and doctrine; and if found otherwise, that they ought to be deposed from their office, and others substituted in their stead."

The following are testimonies about the Waldenses from the mouths of their Roman Catholic persecutors. These quotes are from the chapter "The Waldenses" from *A History of the Churches from a Baptist Perspective*, available from Way of Life Literature.

- "In morals and life they are good."
- "They avoid vices."
- "They avoid lying and cheating in business."
- "Even when they work, they either learn or teach."
- "Their women are very modest, avoiding backbiting, foolish jesting, and levity of speech, especially abstaining from lies or swearing."
- "They fulfill their promises promptly."
- "They withdraw company from those who talk lasciviously or blasphemously."
- "They avoid dancing and taverns."
- "They memorize large portions of Scripture. Many of them can repeat by heart the whole text of the New Testament and great part of the Old."

Diverse groups of Christians continued to hold to a regenerate church membership and New Testament church principles, to various degrees, throughout the Dark Ages of Rome's rule over Europe.

Protestants Kept Rome's Church Doctrine

The Protestant Reformation did not produce New Testament discipling churches.

When the Protestants came out of the Roman Catholic Church in the 16th and 17th centuries, they brought many errors with them.

One of these was infant baptism, and another was state churchism. They formed territorial "churches," such as the Church of England, and every person was required to be baptized as an infant and became a member of the "church."

Consider the Lutheran doctrine of baptism: "Being by nature sinners, infants as well as adults, need to be baptized. Every child that is baptized is begotten anew of water and of the Spirit, is placed in covenant relation with God, and is made a child of God and an heir of his heavenly kingdom" (*The New Analytical Bible and Dictionary of the Bible*, Chicago: John A. Dickson Publishing Co., 1973)

By this means, the Protestant churches were mixed multitudes. Whereas many of the first generation Protestants were born again by personal faith in Jesus Christ, subsequent generations quickly deteriorated because the people (including the pastors) trusted their infant baptism and confirmation and church membership and outward conformity to morality.

John and Charles Wesley, founders of the Methodists, are examples of this. They grew up in the Church of England; their father was a pastor; but it was a long time before they knew Christ personally. They trusted their good works until they were born again at about age 30. Before that, when John Wesley was asked by a Moravian preacher the reason for his hope of salvation, he replied, "Because I have used my best endeavours to serve God."

(See the chapter "The Protestant Reformation" in *A History of the Churches from a Baptist Perspective*, available from Way of Life Literature, www.wayoflife.org.)

By the 1700s, a large percentage of Protestant churches in America were characterized by "having a form of godliness but denying the power thereof."

> "The difference between the church and the world was vanishing away. Church discipline was neglected, and the growing laxness of morals was invading the churches. ... The young were abandoning themselves to frivolity, and to amusements of dangerous tendency, and party spirit was producing its natural fruit of evil among the old. ...
>
> "A very lamentable ignorance of the main essentials of true practical religion and the doctrines nextly relating thereunto, very generally prevailed. The nature and necessity of the new birth was but little known or thought of. The necessity of a conviction of sin and misery, by the Holy Spirit opening and applying the Law to the conscience, in order to a saving closure with Christ, was hardly known at all to the most. ...
>
> "The necessity of being first in Christ by a vital union, and in a justified state, before our religious services can be well pleasing and acceptable to God, was very little understood or thought of. But the common notion seemed to be, that if people were aiming to be in the way of duty as well as they could, as they imagined, there was no reason to be much afraid. ...
>
> "In public companies, especially at weddings, a vain and frothy lightness was apparent in the deportment of many professors; and in some places very extravagant follies, as horse-running, fiddling and dancing, pretty much obtained on those occasions.
>
> "Thus religion lay as it were dying, and ready to expire its last breath of life in this part of the visible church..." (Joseph Tracey, *The Great Awakening: A History of the Revival of Religion in the Time of Edwards and Whitefield*, 1842).

Old Baptist Churches Were Discipling Churches

Beginning in the 16th century, Baptist churches multiplied greatly, and they were discipling churches.

They renounced infant baptism, requiring a regenerate church membership and exercising strict discipline.

Baptist churches practiced church discipline for centuries. In the book *Corrective Church Discipline: with a Development of the Principles upon Which It Is Based* (1860), Patrick Hughes Mell, former president of the Southern Baptist Convention, stated,

"The views which are presented in the following pages are such as have been held by the Baptist churches from time immemorial. The Author attempts to do no more than to exhibit the sentiments of our Fathers, and to defend them by showing that they are sustained by the Scriptures."

From the 16th to the 19th centuries, most Baptist churches were doctrinally sound and separated. They were careful about receiving members, requiring evidence of salvation.

Following are some of the materials published in the 18th and 19th centuries on church discipline:
- *A Short Treatise on Church Discipline*, Philadelphia Association, 1743
- *A Summary of Church Discipline*, The Baptist Association, Charleston, South Carolina, 1774
- *A Short Treatise of Church Discipline*, Sansom Street Baptist Church, Philadelphia, Pennsylvania, 1818
- William Crowell, *The Church Member's Handbook*, 1858
- John Dagg, *A Treatise on Church Order*, 1859
- Edward Hiscox, *The Baptist Directory*, 1859
- Patrick Hughes Mell, *Corrective Church Discipline*, 1860
- James Pendleton, *Church Manual*, 1867
- Williams Rutherford, *Church Members' Guide for Baptist Churches*, 1885
- William Everts, *Baptist Layman's Book*, 1887
- Edward Hiscox, *The Standard Manual for Baptist Churches*, 1890

The churches had strict covenants that the members were required to agree to and obey, and they practiced discipline of sin and error.

Following is part of the Somerset Confession of 1656:
THAT it is the duty of every man and woman, that have repented from dead works, and have faith towards God, to be baptized (Acts 2:38; 8:12, 37, 38), that is, dipped or buried under the water (Ro. 6:3, 4; Col. 2:12), in the name of our Lord Jesus (Acts 8:16), or in the name of the Father, Son, and Holy Spirit (Mt. 28:19), therein to signify and represent a washing away of sin (Acts 22:16), and their death, burial, and resurrection with

Christ (Ro. 6:5; Col. 2:12), and being thus planted in the visible church or body of Christ (1 Co. 12:3), who are a company of men and women separated out of the world by the preaching of the gospel (Acts 2:41; 2 Co. 6:17), do walk together in communion in all the commandments of Jesus (Acts 2:42), wherein God is glorified and their souls comforted (2 Th. 1:11, 12:2 Co. 1:4).

THAT we believe some of those commandments further to be as followeth.

CONSTANCY in prayer (Col. 2:23, 24)

BREAKING of bread (1 Co. 11:23, 24)

GIVING of thanks (Eph. 5:20)

WATCHING over one another (Heb. 12:15)

CARING one for another (1 Co. 12:25) by visiting one another, especially in sickness and temptations (Mt. 25:36)

EXHORTING one another (Heb. 3:13)

DISCOVERING to each other, and bearing one another's burdens (Ga. 6:2)

LOVING one another (Heb. 13:1)

REPROVING when need is one another (Mt. 18:15)

SUBMITTING one to another in the Lord (1 Pe. 5:5)

ADMINISTERING one to another according to the gift received, whether it be in spirituals, or temporals (1 Pe. 4:10)

THE offender to seek reconciliation, as well as the offended (Mt. 5:23, 24)

LOVE our enemies and persecutors, and pray for them (Mt. 5:23, 24)

EVERY one to work if he be able, and none to be idle (2 Th. 3:10, 11, 12)

THE women in the church to learn in silence, and in all subjection (1 Ti. 2:11; 1 Co. 14:37)

PRIVATE admonition to a brother offending another; and if not prevailing, to take one or two more; if he hear not them, then to tell it to the church; and if he hear not them, to be accounted as an heathen and publican (Mt. 18:15.)

PUBLICK rebuke to publick offenders (1 Ti. 5:20.)

THE brethren in ministring forth their gifts, ought to do it decently and in order, one by one, that all may learn and all may be comforted (I Co. 14:31, 40)

A SPECIAL care to assemble together, that their duty to God, and the church may not be neglected (Heb. 10:24, 25.).

AND all things in the church, done in the name and power of the head, the Lord Christ Jesus (Col. 3:7)

THAT in admitting of members into the church of Christ, it is the duty of the church, and ministers whom it concerns, in faithfulness to God, that they be careful they receive none but such as do make forth evident demonstration of the new birth, and the work of faith with power (John 3:3; Mt. 3:8, 9; Acts 8:37; Eze. 44:6, 7, Acts 2:38; 2 Co. 9:14; Ps. 26:4, 5; 101:7)

Following is a standard Baptist church covenant which was written by John Newton Brown and published in J.M. Pendleton's *Baptist Church Manual* of 1853:

Having been led, as we believe by the Spirit of God, to receive the Lord Jesus Christ as our Savior and, on profession of our faith, having been baptized in the name of the Father, and of the Son and of the Holy Spirit, we do now, in the presence of God and this assembly, most solemnly and joyfully enter into covenant with one another as one body in Christ.

We engage, therefore, by the aid of the Holy Spirit, to walk together in Christian love; to strive for the advancement of this church, in knowledge, holiness and comfort; to promote its prosperity and spirituality; to sustain its worship, ordinances, discipline, and doctrines; to contribute cheerfully and regularly to the support of the ministry, the expenses of the church, the relief of the poor, and the spread of the Gospel through all nations.

We also engage to maintain family and secret devotions; to religiously educate our children; to seek the salvation of our kindred and acquaintances; to walk circumspectly in the world; to be just in our dealings, faithful in our engagements, and exemplary in our deportment; to avoid all tattling, backbiting and excessive anger; to abstain from the sale of, and use of intoxicating drinks as a beverage; and to be zealous in our efforts to advance the kingdom of our Savior.

We further engage to watch over one another in brotherly love; to remember one another in prayer; to aid one another in sickness and distress, to cultivate Christian sympathy in feeling and Christian courtesy in speech; to be slow to take offense, but always ready for reconciliation and mindful of the rules of our Savior, to secure it without delay.

> We moreover engage that when we remove from this place, we will, as soon as possible, unite with some other church where we can carry out the spirit of this covenant and the principles of God's word.

This covenant called for private and family devotions, which would include the study of God's Word. It called for the religious education of children by the parents, intercessory prayer, strict separation from the world, and aggressive evangelism.

The Baptist churches practiced discipline "because **they could not in good conscience call themselves Christians while ignoring a clear command of Christ**" (Gregory Wills, *Democratic Religion: Freedom, Authority, and Church Discipline in the Baptist South*).

The Baptists in Georgia in the 19th century "**placed discipline at the center of church life**" (Wills).

"To an antebellum Baptist [referring to the time before the American Civil War of 1861-65], **a church without discipline would hardly have counted as a church.** ... Baptists ,,, required their members to submit to the church's authority. Nineteenth-century Southern Baptists exercised church discipline on a remarkable scale. ... By the time of the Civil War Southern Baptists had excommunicated more than forty thousand members in Georgia alone. Baptist churches in the southern states brought to trial between 3 and 4 percent of their membership every year. They excommunicated about half of those brought to trial, excluding between 1 and 2 percent of their membership annually" (Wills).

Jesse Mercer of the Georgia Association of Baptist Churches, in a circular letter entitled "Church Discipline" dated 1806, wrote,

> "We would awaken you to, and exhort you to be promptly active in the execution of discipline--**discipline, without which there can be no union, order, peace or fellowship in the church; no, nor church itself--discipline**, which, in its right use, is the church's ecclesiastical life--bond of union and peace--spring of order and fellowship--and great source of harmony and love."

The *Summary of Church Discipline,* published by the Baptist Association of Charleston, South Carolina, 1813, said that when churches do not require a regenerate membership, "**they make the church of Christ a harlot.**"

In 1860, David Benedict wrote on church discipline, saying, "**The free circulation of the blood ... is not more necessary to the health of the body, than a good discipline to the prosperity of a Christian church**," and, "that churches, like armies and families, may be said to be well disciplined, not when punishments are often inflicted, but when, by due care and faithfulness, they are seldom required" (*Fifty Years Among the Baptists*, chapter 29).

J.L. Dagg, *Manual of Church Order*, 1857, wrote, "It has been remarked, that **when discipline leaves a church, Christ goes with it**" (p. 274).

This is borne out in Christ's messages to the seven churches in Revelation 2-3. He warned that if a church loses its first love, it will lose its candlestick (Re. 2:4-5), and Christ was standing *outside of* the lukewarm church of Laodicea (Re. 3:20).

In that day, the churches disciplined for drunkenness, **absence from services, resisting the authority of the church**, interpersonal hostility, slander, anger, quarreling, cursing, swearing, profanity, falsehood, adultery, fornication, fighting, abuse, theft, debt evasion, **neglecting family, neglecting duty**, dancing, horse-racing, and gambling (Wills, *Democratic Religion: Freedom, Authority, and Church Discipline in the Baptist South*).

Churches held regular **Days of Discipline** "when the congregation would gather to heal breaches of fellowship, admonish wayward members, rebuke the obstinate, and, if necessary, excommunicate those who resisted discipline."

In these meetings, the brethren would sometimes accuse themselves of unchristian behavior and ask for discipline.

> "Brother Lovall accused himself of drinking too much spiritous liquor and of getting into a great rage of anger at the same time," or "brother Dread Wilder came forward and observed that he had lately gotten very angry, for which ordered that he be reproved by the Moderator which was done" (Wills).

Many of the churches read the church roll during the Lord's Supper, and absentees were dealt with as offenders.

The Broadmead Church of England "had all the members' names engrossed in parchment, that they might be called over always at breaking bread, to see who did omit their duty" (J.J. Goadby, *Discipline in Early British Churches*).

The churches exercised discipline for neglect of the assembly.

"The general Baptists of the 16th and 17th centuries so respected the nature and importance of assemblies for public worship that the wilful neglect of them was considered as disorderly conduct, which called for the censure of the church. A constant inspection was exercised over the attendance of the members: persons were appointed to take down the names of the absentees, and report them to the elders; and nothing but reasons of obvious importance were admitted as a sufficient apology for their non-attendance. When the societies grew numerous, the members were ranged into districts, according, to the proximity of their habitations: and proper persons appointed to superintend each district. If any member did not appear in his place, on the Lord's-day, he was certain of a visit, in the course of the week, from one of the inspectors of the district, to call him to account for his absence. These regulations were rendered effectual, by being acted upon with steadiness, impartiality, and decision; and, for nearly a century, contributed much to the order and prosperity of the general baptist churches. In 1655, an 'Order' was made, by the general consent of the congregation at Fenstanton, that 'if any member of this congregation shall absent himself from the assembly of the same congregation, upon the first day of the week, without manifesting a sufficient cause, he shall be looked upon as an offender, and proceeded with accordingly. At the same meeting, it was devised, that, if any member should, at any time, have any extraordinary occasion to hinder him from the assembly, he would certify the congregation of the same before hand, for the prevention of jealousy.' And, in 1658, the same society, after considering the case of a wife who had been kept back, by the threatenings of her husband, concluded 'that, unless a person was restrained by force, it was no excuse for absenting himself from the assemblies of the congregation.' Resolutions of a similar purport are frequent in the records of these churches: and numbers of cases prove that they were constantly enforced" (Adam Taylor, *The History of the English General Baptists*, London: 1818, Vol. I).

A Baptist church in East Tennessee disciplined members who failed to attend services for 60 days "without legal excuse." This church disciplined a member who "comes to Sunday School and leaves before preaching" ("Brief Survey of Historical Background to Church Discipline," pastorhistorian.com).

"The oversight of the members was minute and persistent. Their general conduct, their domestic life, their business, their connections in civil society, their recreations, and even their dress, were all deemed legitimate subjects for the strictest supervision" (J.J. Goadby, *Discipline in Early Baptist Churches*, 1871).

Consider examples of discipline from J.M. Cramp's *Baptist History*:

A "Sister Watkins" was disciplined by Broadmead Baptist Church for not paying her debts, not keeping her promises, and not working. "Tidings came to the ears of the church that she walked disorderly and scandalously in the borrowing of money, up and down, of many persons--of some ten shillings, of some twenty shillings, of some more, some less, as she could get them to lend-- and took no care to pay it again, promising people and not performing, spending much if not most of her time going up and down; and so did not work, or but little, to endeavor honestly to live and eat her own bread. And thus, she walking disorderly and scandalously in borrowing, contrary to the rule (2 Thessalonians 3:6, 10, 12)."

After being admonished several times and not repenting, she was withdrawn from the church fellowship, the ruling elder, "Brother Terrill, declared to her, before the church, how that for her so sinning against the Lord, she rendered herself among the wicked ones, as Psalm 37:21, and, therefore, the church, in faithfulness to the Lord and to her soul, must withdraw from her, seeing she had by several of the members been admonished once and again, and by several together witnessing against her evil in so doing; yet she had lately done the like, so that there was a necessity upon them to do their duty. And also acquainted her that if the Lord should hereafter give her repentance of the evil that she should reform to the satisfaction of the congregation, they should be willing to receive her into full communion again. And then the sentence, by the said ruling elder, was passed upon her, viz.: That in the name of our Lord Jesus Christ, and by the authority he had given to the Church, we did declare, that Sister Watkins, for her sin of disorderly walking, borrowing and not paying, making promises and not performing, and not diligently working, was withdrawn from, and no longer to have full communion with this church, nor to be partaker with them in the holy mysteries of the Lord's Supper, nor privileges of the Lord's house [that is, 'if she doth come to the meeting, not to be suffered to stay when any business of the church is transacted']; and the Lord have mercy upon her soul" (*Broadmead Records*, pp. 211, 413, cited from J.M. Cramp, *Baptist History*).

John Blows, a preacher, absented himself from a day of fasting and prayer at Fenstanton Church in order to attend a "great football play, he being one of the principle appointers thereof." After being confronted about the matter, he confessed that he had done wrong and "promised to abstain from the like for time to come." Nevertheless, as he had "dishonored the Lord," "grieved the people of God," and "given occasion to the adversary to speak reproachfully," it was resolved that "he should not be suffered to preach until further fruits meet for repentance did appear" (Fenstanton *Baptist Church Records*, pp. 126, 244, cited from Cramp, *Baptist History*).

The church at Warboys withdrew from Mary Poulter, "for forsaking the assembling with the church and neglecting holy duties, and walking disorderly in pride and vanity" (Cramp).

John Christmas was disciplined "for not loving Ann his wife as he ought, and for speaking hateful and despising words against her, giving her occasion to depart from him by his unkindness." Happily, "John Christmas, afterward sending for Ann his wife again and promising amendment, after her coming again to him, desired to be a partaker with the church, in holy duties, was joined in fellowship again" (Cramp).

Mary Drage was disciplined "for sundry times dissembling with the church, and out of covetousness speaking things very untrue, at length it being plainly proved against her in her hearing, and she having little to say for herself, was withdrawn from" (Cramp).

Thomas Bass was disciplined "for telling of lies and swearing" (Cramp).

Ellen Burges was disciplined "for lying and slandering of her relations, and counting them and her mother witches, which we have no ground to believe..." (Cramp).

In 1817, a "Brother Lancaster" was brought before Powelton Baptist Church of Georgia and disciplined for allowing the young people to dance to fiddling music at his daughter's wedding (Wills). The disciplinary proceeding was overseen by the church's pastor, James Mercer, who later was president of the Georgia Baptist Convention.

The Broadmead Baptist Church did not admit a Mrs. Bevis into the communion "by reason of her selling strong drink" (Goadby, *Discipline in Early British Baptist Churches*).

As we have seen, in all cases of discipline the door was open for repentance and restoration.

Another example of this is "Brother Osman" who was disciplined for leaving his farming work during harvest and spending the day wasting his money in an alehouse." A few months later, he "did, in the presence of the congregation, publicly declare his fall, acknowledge his sin, and manifest great trouble for the same. The church gladly embraced him again, believing that God had given him repentance to the acknowledgment of the truth; he was admitted to his membership."

Baptist churches in America restored about one-third of those who were excommunicated (Wills, *Democratic Religion: Freedom, Authority, and Church Discipline in the Baptist South*).

Those who expressed repentance were not always received back into membership immediately but were often put on probation. They were required to attend the worship services regularly and "to persevere in righteous behavior" for three to twelve months. "They then appeared before the church, confessed their sin, vindicated the church's action and authority, and pledged to lead a moral life" (Wills).

Strict biblical discipline has been the characteristic of Bible-believing churches throughout the church age except in times of backsliding and apostasy.

The Split of American Baptists

The Baptists of America split in 1845 over the issue of slavery, forming the Northern Baptist Convention and the Southern Baptist Convention.

There were Baptist churches that remained independent, but they were few and far between.

Baptist churches of the north and south were similar in character until toward the end of the 19th century, as we have seen. The typical Baptist church was a discipling church.

Apostasy in Convention Baptist Churches

By the end of the 19th century, the Baptist churches in America were very weak and had stopped practicing strict discipline.

Confidence in the Bible was weakened by theological liberalism and Darwinian evolution.

The Northern Baptists became liberal in theology at the beginning of the 20th century. (They were known as the Northern Baptist Convention until 1950, when the name was changed to American Baptist Convention.) For example, in 1918, Harry Emerson Fosdick, pastor of the influential Riverside Church in New York City, published *The Manhood of the Master*, denying that Jesus Christ is God. In 1926, the Northern Baptist Convention voted by a margin of three to one *not* to evict Riverside Church from the convention.

Liberalism entered the Southern Baptist Convention in the first half of the 20th century.

By 1902, J.W. Bailey of North Carolina wrote in the *Biblical Recorder* that there were a multitude of "theologies" in the Southern Baptist Convention. He said, "Theologies change every day. ... [Baptists do not stand for] formulated dogmas."

For theological and cultural reasons, the churches became increasingly weak and rejected New Testament discipline.

Even as early as 1874, William Whitsitt, a professor at Southern Baptist Theological Seminary, said, "[I]t is now very difficult to exclude a person for drunkenness or any other ordinary crime" (*Restoring Integrity in Baptist Churches*, Kindle loc. 2138).

In 1878, J.C. Hiden, pastor of First Baptist Church, Greenville, South Carolina, wrote a series of articles in the *Baptist Courier* "lamenting the recent trend of lax discipline."

By 1921, Z.T. Cody, editor of South Carolina's *Baptist Courier*, wrote,

> "Our churches have practically no discipline. As to worldliness and minor offences, many of our churches do nothing. But what is far worse, our churches often allow the most serious moral transgressions to go unnoticed. Even at times, to save a disturbance in the church, they will grant a minister a letter who, as they know, has grossly violated, not only the proprieties of life, but the moral law of God. ... What we dread today more than aught else is a disturbance in the 'peace' of a church. ... We do not know what is the remedy for this lapsed condition."

A pastorate that was probably largely unregenerate turned from the Bible as sole authority (in practice if not profession) and looked to the world of science for help. The churches stopped depending on spiritual weapons and turned to carnal weapons such as programs and an efficient organization. For example, instead of depending on prayer to prepare for special meetings, they depended on advertising.

There was an emphasis on "efficiency" and "pragmatism" (using whatever works to produce a desired goal).

> "Efficiency consisted not in purity or obedience, but in system, organization, and rationality in all areas of church activity. ... progressive church leaders held that the church in the modern age needed a polity based not on ancient authority but on science, rationality, and system. They looked to social scientists and efficiency experts such as Frederick Winslow Taylor, who in this era developed management into a science for producing efficient organizations" (*Restoring Integrity in Baptist Churches*, Kindle loc. 2167-2174).

In the 1920s, the Southern Baptist Theological Seminary appointed Gaines Dobbins as a "professor of church efficiency." His 1923 book *The Efficient Church* had a wide influence. He claimed that Christ's ministry in the Gospels was "the perfection of efficiency" and Paul was the "world's greatest efficiency expert in religion."

The churches began leaning to the spirit and wisdom of the times instead of God's Spirit and God's Word. Instead of separating from the world and its fallen thinking, they learned from the world.

They bowed to the American spirit of individualism and consumerism. They stopped requiring evidence of salvation and practicing discipline so as not to offend potential members. The churches appeased the people's idolatrous, me-centered desire to shop for a church that met their felt needs. They lowered the spiritual standards, became entertainment-oriented, borrowed from the world to make Christian music more appealing to the unsaved and carnal, softened the preaching, created "youth ministries" that encouraged the generation gap and were merely Christianized versions of the world's pop culture.

By the last half of the 20th century, this spiritual appeasement produced the seeker-sensitive movement. A regenerate church membership and discipline only gets in the way of the seeker-sensitive philosophy and will never produce a megachurch today.

The churches bowed to the influence of the "new morality" and allowed church members to live worldly lives. Such things as dating, pre-marital sex, drinking, jazz, rock, divorce, unisex fashions flooded the weak churches.

They bowed to the philosophy of non-judgmentalism and non-dogmatism that permeated society.

The concept of the church as pilgrims and strangers in a foreign country was replaced by Americanism and flag waving.

The Social Gospel produced an emphasis away from evangelism and church planting. Building God's kingdom on earth through social-justice projects, honest business practices, and maintaining good social order began to replace "saving brands from the burning."

In 1910, William Poteat, president of Wake Forest College, told the annual Southern Baptist Convention that Baptists were in the best position to save civilization.

In 1920, Richard Edmonds wrote, "Upon the Baptists of the South may rest the salvation of America and of the world from chaos and from sinking back into the darkness of the middle ages" (*The South, America and the World*).

This was the condition of the church I grew up in. I remember one of my non-church friends saying to me, "Why should I come to your church? You folk are no different than we are."

There was no looking for evidence of salvation. Any profession of faith was accepted and the individual's salvation was never doubted thereafter. As a result, every generation brought a larger percentage of unregenerate people into the membership.

There was no caution about receiving members. The old church covenant from the 1800s hung on the wall, but it was an historic relic, a museum piece. Its principles were not taught or enforced.

There were no serious biblical standards for workers.

There was no serious discipleship, separation, or discipline. I heard the Bible preached and taught, but I was not given a biblical worldview and there was no emphasis on true discipleship.

The churches adapted to the pop culture. They entertained pagan fables such as Santa Claus and the Easter Bunny. Like the proverbial frog in the pot, they followed Hollywood's descent into ever-deeper moral filth. They didn't have a testing mindset. They weren't thorough-going Bible people. They weren't true disciples of Jesus Christ. They weren't pilgrims and strangers in a foreign world. Almost no one in the SBC in those days saw Walt Disney or Ed Sullivan as enemies of the truth. The fact that Disneyland had no church on Main Street didn't register as a warning that Disney was promoting an atheistic worldview and was drawing the hearts and minds of youngsters away from the God of the Bible like a Pied Piper. The fact that *The Disney Hour* and *The Ed Sullivan Show* were weakening Sunday evening church attendance with their enticing wares was not a matter of deep concern by the preachers.

The vast majority of Southern Baptist preachers were as soft as their hero Billy Graham. The preaching lost its rebuking, discipling power.

This is the type of Baptist church that was on nearly "every street corner" in the American South, which was why it was called "the Bible belt." Southern Baptist churches were one of the most prominent influences in southern society, but because of their spiritual weakness, church was a thing of little significance and social impact. At some point in childhood, most people went through the motion of "receiving Christ" and then continued to live their lives as they pleased with little to no serious reference to Scripture.

The rock & roll pop culture conquered these churches quickly in the 1950s. At first there were a few voices lifted against rock music and its "live as you please" philosophy, but the resistance faded quickly. By the 1960s, Southern Baptist church kids partied as much as non-church kids. Church kids loved the same music and held the same philosophy of life.

Independent Baptist Churches

The Independent Baptist movement exploded in the middle of the 20th century. Many came out of the Baptist conventions to separate from liberalism. Others were new churches founded as independent Baptists. Bible Colleges were established to train pastors and missionaries.

Thousands of fundamental Baptist churches were planted worldwide during the last half of the twentieth century.

The heyday was the 1970s and 1980s.

By the 21st century, a new generation of fundamental Baptists was collapsing in spiritual character and capitulating to compromise in the same way that the Southern Baptists and other New Evangelicals did in the 20th century.

A dramatic change is taking place. The scenario that existed when I was saved in the early 1970s and joined an Independent Baptist church is radically different from the one that exists today.

A large number of fundamental Baptist churches have not kept their spiritual character much beyond the first generation.

Consider two groups of Independent Baptists as an example of what has happened:

Baptist Bible Fellowship International (BBFI) was the first group of fundamental Baptists to reject biblical separatism and to go in a contemporary direction.

The BBFI was founded in 1950 by pastors who left the World Baptist Fellowship as a result of a dispute with J. Frank Norris. Prominent among the roughly 100 founding pastors and missionaries were G.B. Vick and Noel Smith. They located their headquarters in Springfield, Missouri, and founded the Baptist Bible College there.

The BBFI grew quickly and became very influential among Independent Baptists. In the 1970s, enrollment at Baptist Bible College peaked at 2,481. The number of affiliated BBFI pastors and missionaries probably peaked in the late 1990s when 3,326 pastors were listed in the Fellowship Directory and 880 BBFI missionaries were working on 111 mission fields.

In the late 1970s, Jerry Falwell, who graduated from Baptist Bible College in 1956 and was associated with the BBFI throughout his career, took an ecumenical stance with the founding of the Moral Majority political organization in 1979. Half of the state chairmen of the organization were members of the BBFI (Daniel Williams, *God's Own Party: The Making of the Christian Right*, p. 177). In that capacity these Baptist pastors joined hands with practically every denomination and cult in direct contradiction to 2 Corinthians 6:14-18. By February 1986, Falwell told *Christianity Today* that Catholics made up the Moral Majority's largest constituency (30%). In his autobiography, *Strength for the Journey*, Falwell referred to the "Catholic brothers and sisters in the Moral Majority" (p. 371). Falwell endorsed Chuck Colson's 1992 book, *The Body*, which urged evangelicals to join forces with Roman Catholics and charismatics. Colson said, "... the body of Christ, in all its diversity, is created with Baptist feet, charismatic hands, and Catholic ears--all with their eyes on Jesus" (*World*, Nov. 14, 1992).

In spite of this incredible compromise and error, Falwell remained in good standing with the BBFI and continued to speak at their meetings. Very, very few BBFI preachers publicly decried Falwell and his heretical thinking and practice.

Even in the late 1980s, the music was moving rapidly in a contemporary direction through the specials. I recall attending BBFI meetings in those days and being disgusted with the special music accompanied by pre-recorded background tapes that featured a Nashville sound. Most of the preachers didn't seem to have a clue about the difference between sacred music and worldly music. As long as the people liked it and it got the preacher's toe tapping, it was fine. I stopped attending those meetings because of the music, the biblical shallowness of the preaching, and the religious politicking.

In the 1990s, some prominent BBFI leaders supported the ecumenical Promise Keepers even though PK promoted unity between Protestants and Catholics. Roman Catholics were featured as speakers at PK conferences and were appointed as leaders within the organization. In 1996, Billy Hamm, pastor of the Mountain States Baptist Temple, Denver, Colorado, spoke at a Promise Keepers seminar and wrote a report justifying his involvement. Hamm had served five terms as treasurer of the Baptist Bible Fellowship, and in the late 1970s he had taught at BBFI-connected Pacific Coast Baptist Bible College. Again, there were hardly any voices lifted publicly against Hamm's blatant disobedience of Scriptures such as Romans 16:17 and 2 Timothy 3:5.

The direction of the BBFI was clear by 2002 when Bethlehem Baptist Church in Fairfax, Virginia, was chosen to host the fellowship's annual conference. The music was led by a contemporary "worship team" composed of four young women. Around that time Bethlehem Baptist had dropped the "King James Only" clause from the by-laws, and the New Living Translation and other corrupt versions began to be used from the pulpit. The pastor sent out a letter to members saying, "With regard to dress and modesty issues, we enforce NO RULE on our folks. ... apparel issues are really of no concern to us." (This type of statement is always a lie, because these churches don't allow women to teach Sunday School in bikinis or men to sing specials in lipstick, dresses, and high heels.) The church's Skate Night, which was sponsored by raunchy secular skateboarding companies, featured "throbbing Christian rock." The church's youth pastor in 2002 had an earring and in the church's newsletter sported a T-shirt promoting the rock band P.O.D.

Following is a testimony of someone who attended the 2002 conference:

"All of us from our church got up and walked out. It was sickening to see the cutesie young women in their tight pants and high boots, sitting with legs crossed on high stools, leading the worship music. I was stunned. A far cry from what I had known when I attended back in the Viet Nam days when my husband was serving in the Air Force."

Since then, Bethlehem Baptist Church has changed its name to Expectation, a very cool emerging-type name.

In 2003, BBFI in the Philippines invited the country's Roman Catholic president to speak at an evangelism conference.

There are still some "conservative" BBFI churches (though they are usually not outspoken about reproving the compromise of the mother organization, which in itself is compromise and sin), but as a movement it is well on its way to the emerging church.

Southwide Baptist Fellowship was founded in 1955 by Lee Roberson, pastor of Highland Park Baptist Church, Chattanooga, Tennessee, and was formerly one of the largest Independent Baptist church networks.

But by the mid-2000s, Southwide was rocking out and clearly renouncing separatism.

Many of the speakers who preached at the Southwide annual conference in October 2003 were from churches with rock & roll worship services. Bo Moore, Moderator of Southwide that year, was the pastor of Heritage Baptist Church of Kentwood, Michigan, which advertised itself as "a progressive Independent Baptist church" with a "High Impact" Sunday evening service consisting of "praise and worship choruses led by our worship leader, praise team and band." Johnny Hunt, another Southwide speaker in 2003, is senior pastor of First Baptist Church, Woodstock, Georgia, a rocking Southern Baptist congregation that decidedly rejects "separatism." A man wrote to me in 2003 to say, "I visited there [Hunt's church] and got up and left because of the wild, party-like atmosphere in their 'worship' service."

The 51st Southwide Baptist Fellowship, October 22-25, 2006, at Trinity Baptist Church in Jacksonville, Florida, featured Jerry Falwell. The music was led by Mike Speck, whose choral book *Everlasting Praise* features many songs that are on the CCLI list of top 25 contemporary "praise and worship" songs in America, including "Shout to the Lord" by the ecumenical charismatic rocker Darlene Zschech. We have already seen how that Falwell had promoted unity with Rome since the 1980s.

By 2007, the number of Southern Baptist speakers at Southwide equaled the number of Independent Baptists, and two contemporary rock musicians provided music, including one who had appeared on the Crystal Cathedral television program with Robert Schuller (Don Boys, "Rise and Fall of Southwide," CSTNews.com, May 16, 2007).

In 2012, Highland Park Baptist Church, Southwide's founding church, ceased to exist, and in 2015 Highland Park's Tennessee Temple University closed its doors. It had been the largest fundamental Baptist school in the 1970s.

In 2016, the choir of Marcus Pointe Baptist Church, which hosted the Southwide meeting in 2009, sang backup for homosexual Barry Manilow on his *One Last Time Tour*.

The more conservative churches of Southwide have pulled away and coalesced around Crown Baptist College, but they haven't renounced the things that resulted in the downfall of most of the churches. They didn't re-examine anything, because they don't believe in saying anything critical about former leaders, even when it is the truth.

We could continue the description of the collapse at great length. Large numbers of schools and churches that were fairly sound in the 1970s are gone today, either entirely defunct or spiritually compromised and well down the contemporary path.

In *The Collapse of Separatism*, we document the changes at GARBC, Northland Baptist College, Bob Jones University, Central Baptist Seminary, Trinity Baptist Church and College, Calvary Baptist Seminary of Pennsylvania, Cedarville University, Southside Baptist Church of Greenville, South Carolina, Temple Baptist Church of Detroit, Michigan, New Testament Baptist Church of Ft. Lauderdale, Florida, Akron Baptist Temple of Akron, Ohio, and Landmark Baptist Church, Cincinnati, Ohio.

The list could be multiplied endlessly. The change, the downgrade, the erosion, is evident everywhere.

I see it in preachers that I have known since the 1970s and 1980s, a large number of whom have gone in a different direction. Their children are carrying the changes to an even greater degree.

I see it everywhere I travel.

All of my preacher friends tell me that a great many of their friends are changing and moving in a weaker, contemporary direction. The following communication is typical of hundreds I have received:

"Your stand and articles on the Burlington fiasco have echoed what was in my heart. Once again it's been an issue that has revealed how some MINISTRY FRIENDS ARE CHANGING WITH THE TIMES AND SO LACKING IN DISCERNMENT. Very sad. I thank God for those who are standing for and walking in truth."

We see the effect of the changes in the lives of young people. Many Independent Baptist churches don't have even one on-fire young person who is a true disciple of Jesus Christ, who has a first love for Christ, who is passionately seeking God's will, who is an effectual Bible student, who is separating from the world zealously and is extremely cautious about music and social media, etc., and who *loves* holiness and modesty *from the heart*.

While there are many reasons for this collapse, I am convinced that a fundamental element is the rejection of the biblical pattern of a discipling church for the mixed multitude philosophy.

The churches that came out of the Southern Baptist Convention rejected liberalism and improved on the Southern Baptist program in many ways, such as preaching separation and supporting missionaries directly, but they did not reject the mixed multitude philosophy of the church.

Few of the churches in the Independent Baptist movement were ever dedicated to a thorough-going New Testament church principle. The goal was not to build discipling churches; the goal was to build the biggest church possible with the highest number of "salvation decisions."

Such things as being *very* careful about evangelism, exercising great caution in receiving members, *requiring* the faithfulness we see in Acts 2:42, and exercising strict biblical discipline would actually get in the way of this program.

Highland Park Baptist Church of Chattanooga, Tennessee, was one of the chief models of what multitudes of Independent Baptist churches aimed for.

It was the second largest church in America in the late 1960s and early 1970s (Elmer Towns, *America's Ten Largest Sunday Schools*, 1969). But this statistic was measured by Sunday School attendance, which was the product of a fleet of 15 large buses and hyper promotionalism gimmicks. The Sunday School numbers also included the attendance figures of Highland Park's chapels (42 in 1969) which were scattered all across that part of the country, as far as 70 miles from Chattanooga.

Highland Park had many excellent characteristics, as we described in the chapter "The Collapse." Many people were saved. Hundreds of churches were planted by the graduates of Tennessee Temple Bible College.

But Highland Park was a mixed multitude.

There was an aggressive evangelistic program, but it followed the Jack Hyles "Roman's Road" formula which emphasized a quick, simple presentation of the most basic points of the gospel followed by a push for the individual to pray the "sinner's prayer." This was followed by giving the individual "assurance of salvation."

We will look at this in the chapter "A Discipling Church Begins with Caution about Salvation."

When people came forward at the invitation, they would be dealt with right during the invitation and expected to pray the sinner's prayer. It was impossible to deal with them properly in this context, and the pressure to make a quick profession was intense. From the pulpit, Dr. Roberson would then ask the individuals the following questions: (1) Do you believe that Jesus died on the cross to save sinners? (2) Are you trusting Jesus as your personal Saviour? (3) Do you want to follow the Lord in baptism and live for him? Those who replied in the affirmative (and I never saw someone respond otherwise) were baptized immediately and became church members.

The church reported 50,000 members, but a large percentage were nowhere to be found. Most had prayed a sinner's prayer, been baptized, then disappeared. In that sense, the church hadn't changed since it was in the Southern Baptist Convention. When Dr. Roberson came to Highland Park in 1942, the membership was 1,000 but there were only about 300 members in the Sunday morning service and much fewer in other services. At least two-thirds of the members were inactive. That percentage probably held true over the lifetime of Dr. Roberson's pastorate.

Only five things were expected of church members: (1) faithful attendance of services, (2) read the Bible, (3) pray, (4) witness to someone every day, (5) tithe.

There was no church discipline except in a few prominent cases, such as when Dr. Roberson's associate pastor, Cliff Robinson, committed adultery with Dr. Roberson's secretary. And even that case was more like a "slap on the hand," and Robinson was soon restored to a traveling ministry. It would be impossible to exercise discipline in a church in which most of the members are nowhere to be found.

This is the mixed multitude program, and I am convinced it is at the heart of the collapse we are witnessing.

A Discipling Church Begins with Caution about Salvation

Outline
Biblical Salvation Has Evidence
A conversion experience that changes the life
Personal knowledge of the Lord
Believing the gospel
Continuing in the gospel
Love of God's Word
Love of righteousness
Led by the Spirit
Looking for Christ's return
Divine chastisement
Southern Baptist Churches a Mixed Multitude
Independent Baptists Prior to the 1970s
Independent Baptists after the 1970s
Dealing with Children

Salvation is the fundamental of fundamentals. Disciples can be made only of born again saints. A "nominal" Christian who has "prayed the prayer" but is not born again cannot be discipled.

Salvation is the thing that is often missing in young people who grow up in Christian homes and churches. They go through the motions of professing Christ. They know how to give the right answers and to act right when necessary, but the reality of the kind of supernatural salvation that we see in Scripture is foreign to their daily lives.

Consider the following testimony which is typical of hundreds we have received through the years:

> "Having taught in my church's Christian school, I truly believe that out of an enrollment of 40-50 kids, most likely more than 95% were lost. It breaks my heart to see so many young people have a head knowledge of Christ, but they have never truly believed from the heart. What concerns me even

more than that is that many parents and even church leaders seem to not want to acknowledge the reality of the situation. We comfort ourselves with the fact that our kids memorize Bible verses and come to church, when in reality most of them come because Mom or Dad make them, and then during the services most of them are sleeping, laughing and talking to their friends, or checking their cell phones. Most youth groups in Independent Baptist Churches are an absolute joke. My wife and I spent 20 months on deputation visiting Independent Baptist Churches, and we could not believe some of the things we were seeing from the youth groups. It is high time that Independent Baptist churches face the issue of our unconverted youth, because if we don't our churches are headed for disaster."

I know this by experience. I grew up in a Baptist church and professed Christ at about age 10 or 11, but I wasn't saved. I had no inner motive and compulsion to do right. I had zero personal love for the Bible. I broke my parents' rules, snuck around, lied, pursued every worldly thing, and found a way to do what I wanted to do. As soon as I could, I left home and "followed my heart," eventually to a Hindu/New Age faith.

Biblical Salvation Has Evidence

The church that wants to build a solid biblical foundation must look for biblical evidence as described in Scripture. We are warned about those who "profess that they know God; but in works they deny *him*, being abominable, and disobedient, and unto every good work reprobate" (Titus 1:16).

Consider nine biblical evidences of salvation:

A born again conversion experience that changes the life.

> "Therefore if any man *be* in Christ, *he is* a new creature: old things are passed away; behold, all things are become new" (2 Co. 5:17).

Jesus described salvation as being born again (John 3:3) and being converted (Mt. 18:3). Paul said the saved person is a new creature in Christ (2 Co. 5:17). Salvation is a spiritual resurrection; it is life from the dead (Eph. 2:1; Col. 2:12). It is Christ living in me (Ga. 2:20).

The Spirit ministers *to* the unsaved in various ways, but the Spirit does not indwell the unsaved.

It is not possible to experience the salvation described in the Bible without some clear evidence of it appearing in the individual's life.

Every salvation recorded in the New Testament involves a life-changing, born again, spiritual resurrection, conversion experience (e.g., the woman at the well, Zacchaeus, the Jews on the day of Pentecost, the Ethiopian eunuch, Lydia, the Philippian jailer).

The Great Awakenings in America focused on salvation with evidence. The churches had grown lukewarm and nominal. In a great many cases, even the preachers were not born again. The members were trusting in baptism and church attendance and good works.

> "[T]he most important practical idea which then received increased prominence and power ... was the idea of the 'new birth' ... [**This is**] **the doctrine, that in order to be saved, a man must undergo a change in his principles of moral action, which will be either accompanied or succeeded by exercises of which he is conscious, and can give an account; so that those who have been thus changed, may ordinarily be distinguished from those who have not; from which it follows that all who exhibit no evidence of such a change, ought to be considered and treated as unregenerate, and on the road to perdition, and therefore not admitted to the communion of the churches.** ... The history of the 'Great Awakening' is the history of this idea, making its way through some communities where it had fallen into comparative neglect, and through others where it was nearly or quite unknown; overturning theories and habits and forms of organization inconsistent with it, where it could prevail, and repelled by them, where it could not..." (Joseph Tracy, *The Great Awakening*).

An interesting example of a biblical conversion from that era is that of Noah Webster, author of *The Blue-Back Speller* and the *American Dictionary of the English Language.*

His conversion occurred during the Second Great Awakening, which began in Kentucky and soon spread to all parts of the young nation. In 1807, the revival came to Webster's church, First

Congregational Church of New Haven, Connecticut, pastored by Moses Stuart.

Webster made a public profession of faith in April 1808, together with his two oldest daughters.

It was a life-changing conversion experience. Following is a description by Alan Snyder, Webster's biographer:

> "**Webster's conversion was the intellectual and moral watershed of his life**. As such, it provided him with a spiritual and intellectual framework which extended into every sphere of life, including perceptions of and judgments about man, morality, government, education, and the very purpose of being. ...
>
> "Internal conversion results in a profound alteration of an individual's conception of the nature of God, man, sin, and brings a transformation in both thought and action. ... conversion is a return to God, a restoration of the relationship God originally had intended to have with man, through a turning away from sin (i.e., rebellion against God's commands) and a turning to the mercies of a forgiving Father. ...
>
> "Having once read it [Webster's testimony], one can have no doubt that Webster's conversion was authentic and **produced a basic reorganization of his entire life. In Webster's world, God moved from the periphery to the center, providing him a new purpose and focus**" (Snyder, *Defining Noah Webster: Mind and Morals in the Early Republic*, pp. 221, 222).

Consider some details of Webster's life prior to his conversion:
- He was an active church member.
- From age 20 he had resolved "to pursue a course of virtue through life, and to perform all moral and social duties with scrupulous exactness."
- He believed in God and was thankful to God. "... for some years past, I have rarely cast my eyes to heaven or plucked the fruit of my garden without feeling emotions of gratitude and adoration."
- He believed that Christ died for man's sins.
- He doubted some doctrines of the Bible, believing that religion should conform to man's reason and if something wasn't

"reasonable," it could be rejected. His ultimate authority, then, was his own mind.

- He believed that one should not be passionate about religion. When the Second Great Awakening first came to his town, he was opposed. "I felt some opposition to these meetings, being apprehensive that they would by affecting the passions too strongly, introduce an enthusiasm or fanaticism which might be considered as real religion."

Following is Webster's own fascinating account of his spiritual conversion, written in response to a letter from his brother-in-law, Judge Thomas Dawes of Boston, who had written to Noah to oppose the revival:

> "My wife [Rebecca], however, was friendly to these meetings and she was joined by my two eldest daughters [Emily and Frances] who were among the first subjects of serious impressions. I did not forbid but rather discouraged their attendance on conferences. Finding their feelings rather wounded by this opposition, and believing that I could not conscientiously unite with them in a profession of the Calvinistic faith, I made some attempts to persuade them to join me in attending the Episcopal service and ordinances. To this they were opposed. At some times I almost determined to separate from my family, leaving them with the Congregational Society and joining myself to the Episcopal. ...
>
> "During this time, my mind continued to be more and more agitated, and in a manner wholly unusual and to me unaccountable. I had indeed short composure, but at all times of the day and in the midst of other occupations, I was suddenly seized with impressions, which called my mind irresistibly to religious concerns and to the awakening. These impressions induced a degree of remorse for my conduct, not of that distressing kind which often attends convictions, but something which appeared to be reproof.
>
> "These impressions I attempted to remove by reasoning with myself, and endeavoring to quiet my mind, by a persuasion, that my opposition to my family, and the awakening was not a real opposition to a rational religion, but to enthusiasm or false religion. I continued some weeks in this situation, utterly unable to quiet my own mind, and without resorting to the only source of peace and consolation. The impressions

grew ever stronger till at length I could not pursue my studies without frequent interruptions. My mind was suddenly arrested, without any previous circumstance of the time to draw it to this subject and as it were fastened to the awakening and upon my own conduct. I closed my books, yielded to the influence, which could not be resisted or mistaken and was led by a spontaneous impulse to repentance, prayer and entire submission and surrender of myself to my maker and redeemer. My submission appeared to be cheerful and was soon followed by that peace of mind which the world can neither give nor take away. ...

"I now began to understand and relish many parts of the scriptures, which before appeared mysterious and unintelligible, or repugnant to my natural pride. ... **In short my view of the scriptures, of religion, of the whole Christian scheme of salvation, and of God's moral government, are very much changed, and my heart yields with delight and confidence to the divine will.** ...

"**I am taught now the utter insufficiency of our own powers to effect a change of the heart and am persuaded that a reliance on our own talents or powers, is a fatal error, springing from natural pride and opposition to God, by which multitudes of men, especially of the more intelligent and moral part of society, are deluded into ruin.** I now look, my dear friend, with regret on the largest portion of the ordinary life of man, spent 'without hope, and without God in the world.' I am particularly affected by a sense of my ingratitude to that Being who made me, and without whose constant agency, I cannot draw a breath, who has showered upon me a profusion of temporal blessings and provided a Savior for my immortal soul. To have so long neglected the duties of piety to that Being on whom I am entirely dependent, to love whom supremely is the first duty, as well as the highest happiness of rational souls, proves a degree of baseness in my heart on which I cannot reflect without the deepest contrition and remorse. And I cannot think without trembling on what my condition would have been had God withdrawn the blessed influences of his Spirit, the moment I manifested opposition to it, as he justly might have done, and given me over to hardness of heart and blindness of mind. I now see in full evidence, the enormous crime, the greatest, man can commit against his God, of resisting the influence of his holy Spirit. Every sting of conscience must be considered as a direct call from God to obey his commands; how much more then ought man to yield to those pungent and powerful convictions of sin which are unequivocally sent to chastize his disobedience and compel him to return to his Heavenly Father."

This type of dramatic, worldview-changing, life-changing conversion experience is the first evidence of salvation.

Personal knowledge of the Lord

"And this is life eternal, that they might know thee the only true God, and Jesus Christ, whom thou hast sent" (John 17:3).

"For the which cause I also suffer these things: nevertheless I am not ashamed: for I know whom I have believed, and am persuaded that he is able to keep that which I have committed unto him against that day" (2 Ti. 1:12).

The essence of salvation is a personal relationship with and walk with God in Jesus Christ. Salvation is not a reformation or a new religion. It is to know the Lord personally, to walk and talk with Him as Lord and Saviour, Father and Friend. It is to cry, "Abba, Father" (Ro. 8:15; Ga. 4:6). Heartfelt prayer to a God who is personally known is an evidence of salvation. Salvation is to love God (De. 30:6; 1 Joh. 4:19). The apostle Paul said, "I know whom I have believed ..." (1 Ti. 1:12).

When people express doubts about their salvation, I ask them if they *know* the Lord and when and how it was that they came to *know* Him.

Many young church people are like Samuel who knew *about* the Lord but did not *know* the Lord (1 Sa. 3:7).

Jesus warned about those who profess Him as Lord, but to them He will say, "I never *knew* you" (Mt. 7:21-23). See also Mt. 25:12, "Verily I say unto you, I know you not."

Believing the gospel

"For I am not ashamed of the gospel of Christ: for it is the power of God unto salvation to every one that believeth; to the Jew first, and also to the Greek" (Ro. 1:16).

"Moreover, brethren, I declare unto you the gospel which I preached unto you, which also ye have received, and wherein ye stand; By which also ye are saved, if ye keep in memory what I preached unto you, unless ye have believed in vain. For I delivered unto you first of all that which I also received, how that Christ died for our sins according to the scriptures; And that he was buried, and that he rose again the third day according to the scriptures" (1 Co. 15:1-4).

Salvation is believing and receiving the gospel of Jesus Christ.

Salvation is not "receiving Jesus into my heart." That concept is never found in the Bible. Christ does come into the life of the person who is saved, but he must first be cleansed by Christ's blood through believing the gospel.

Salvation is not surrendering my life to God. Surrendering to God's authority is the essence of repentance, but repentance alone is not salvation. God does not accept my life until I have been cleansed by the blood of Christ, and that happens through believing the gospel.

You don't have to be a theologian to be saved, but you must know the gospel. There is a certain doctrine that must be believed from the heart (Ro. 6:17), and that is the doctrine of the gospel.

A great many Christians we meet don't know the gospel. A church-going taxi driver in South Africa is typical. He told me that the gospel is "obeying Jesus."

Consider some lessons about the gospel from 1 Corinthians 15:1-4:

Believing the gospel means that I know who "Christ" is.

- I can't believe that Christ died for my sins in a saving way unless I know who He is. I must understand that *Christ* means *Messiah, Christ* being Greek and *Messiah* being Hebrew. Jesus is the fulfillment of Old Testament prophecy. He is the Son of God and the Son of David. The prophets said that Messiah would come to earth the first time to be cut off or die for man's sins (Da. 9:25-26) and He would come again to rule on the throne of David and to establish the kingdom of God on earth (Isaiah 9:6-7). These prophecies are fulfilled in Jesus. He is the Christ.

- Believing the gospel requires that I not believe in a false christ. A false christ, such as the Roman Catholic host-christ, does not save.

Believing the gospel means that I admit I am the sinner that the Bible says I am ("Christ died for our sin").

- To be saved, the individual must see himself as a wicked sinner before God who is deserving of eternal condemnation. I must understand and acknowledge that I am not good (Ro. 3:12). There is no righteousness that I have that is acceptable to God (Isa. 64:6). In contrast, we think of a man in California who prayed a sinner's prayer but still believed his good works would get him to heaven. It is obvious that he was not saved.

- It is the Holy Spirit who shows me my sin and impresses this to my heart so that I am convicted and found guilty before God (John 16:8). The soul winner must look to the Holy Spirit to do this supernatural work, and must look for evidence of this work in the sinner's life.

Believing the gospel means that I believe that Jesus died for my sins.

- I deserve eternal judgment, and that judgment fell upon Christ. Salvation is an exchange (2 Co. 5:21).

- The Bible emphasizes that Christ's atonement was sacrificial, vicarious. This is repeated 12 times in Isaiah 53 (vv. 4, 5, 6, 8, 10, 11, 12). See also Ro. 4:25; 5:6; 1 Co. 5:7; 15:3; 2 Co. 5:21; Ga. 1:4; 3:13; Eph. 1:7; 5:2; Col. 1:14; 1 Ti. 2:6; Tit. 2:14; Heb. 9:12, 26; 10:12; 1 Pe. 2:24-25; 3:18; 1 Joh. 2:2; 4:10; Re. 5:9.

- This means I must believe that Christ was the virgin born, sinless Son of God, for only the sinless Son of God could die in the place of sinners. In contrast, we think of a Southern Baptist seminary student who told us that believing in the virgin birth is not necessary for salvation.

- Believing the gospel means that I will not trust in anything other than Christ's atonement for salvation. If I am still trusting in baptism or sacraments or the church or my good works, I am not believing the gospel and am not saved. I think of John and Charles Wesley, who were so zealous for Christianity that they formed a "holy club" at Oxford University, were mockingly called "Methodists" for their methodical habits of prayer and fasting and

Bible reading, were ordained as Anglican priests, and hazarded the dangerous voyage across the Atlantic Ocean to America in order to preach to the natives. But the Wesleys were trusting in their good works rather than the grace found in the gospel of Christ. They knew *about* the Lord, but they didn't know Him personally. When a Moravian preacher asked John if he had a hope to be saved, he replied, "I do." But when the preacher asked him the reason of his hope, he said, "Because I have used my best endeavours to serve God."

Believing the gospel means that I believe that Christ died for my sins according to the Scripture.

- This refers to the amazing prophecies that described His death in great detail. These were written down hundreds of years before Jesus was born. Following are just a few of these prophecies from Psalm 22: *The Scripture prophesied that Jesus would die by crucifixion* (Ps. 22:14-16; Joh. 19:16-18). This is a perfect description of death by crucifixion, and when the prophet David wrote it 1,000 years before Christ came, crucifixion was not yet practiced! It began to be practiced in the days of the Roman Empire not long before Jesus was born. To punish murderers and robbers, the Roman government would nail their hands and feet to a wooden cross and leave them there to die. *The Scripture prophesied that the soldiers would gamble for Jesus' robe at the foot of the cross* (Psalm 22:18). The cruel soldiers did this while Jesus was suffering (Mt. 27:35). *The Scripture prophesied the very words that Jesus spoke from the cross* (Ps. 22:1; Mt. 27:46). *The Scripture prophesied that Jesus would thirst* (Ps. 22:15; Joh. 19:28). *The Scripture prophesied that the people would mock Jesus* (Ps. 22:6-8; Mt. 27:39, 41-43). *The Scripture prophesied that the people would sit and stare at Jesus* (Ps. 22:17; Mt. 27:36).

Believing the gospel means that I believe that Christ was buried.

- His burial proved that He really died. He did not merely faint or merely appear to die as some have claimed. The reason the soldiers did not break Jesus' legs is because He was already dead (Joh. 19:31-34).

- His burial fulfilled prophecy. It was *"according to the Scriptures."* The Bible prophesied that Jesus would be buried in the tomb of a rich man (Isaiah 53:9). This prophecy, written about 710 years before Jesus was born, was fulfilled when Jesus was taken down off the cross by a wealthy disciple and buried in that disciple's own tomb (Mt. 27:57-60).

Believing the gospel means that I believe that Jesus rose from the dead the third day according to the Scripture.

- To be saved, I must believe that Jesus Christ is alive, having proven that He is the Son of God, and that He is ready to receive me when I call upon Him.

- The evidence of the resurrection is the eyewitnesses and the changed lives, such as Saul who was converted after meeting the risen Christ.

- His resurrection was according to the Scripture in that it was prophesied in Psalm 16:10. This was written about 1,000 years before Jesus came. His resurrection proved that He is the Son of God (Ro. 1:4). Jesus prophesied that He would rise again the third day (Mt. 16:21), and if he had not done so it would have proven that he was a deluded man or a false prophet and not the Son of God that He claimed to be.

Continuing in the gospel

> "Moreover, brethren, I declare unto you the gospel which I preached unto you, which also ye have received, and wherein ye stand; By which also ye are saved, if ye keep in memory what I preached unto you, unless ye have believed in vain" (1 Co. 15:1-2).

> "And you, that were sometime alienated and enemies in *your* mind by wicked works, yet now hath he reconciled In the body of his flesh through death, to present you holy and unblameable and unreproveable in his sight: If ye continue in the faith grounded and settled, and *be* not moved away from the hope of the gospel, which ye have heard, *and* which was preached to every creature which is under heaven; whereof I Paul am made a minister" (Col. 1:21-23).

Salvation is evident by continuing in the gospel. Those who profess the gospel and then renounce it are not saved and never were saved.

Paul had doubt about the salvation of the churches in Galatia because they had left the gospel of grace (Ga. 1:6-8; 4:20).

I have seen many examples of this through the years.

This is one of the many reasons why I know that I did not get saved when I professed Christ as a boy. Not only did I abandon church, but I abandoned the gospel and turned to a Hindu/New Age faith that there are many paths to God. This is a complete rejection of the gospel and of Jesus Christ as only Lord and Saviour.

A born again child of God will not become an atheist. I think of a man I knew when I was a young Christian in the 1970s. He and his wife helped disciple me, and I spent a lot of time in their home. After I went off to Bible School I heard that they had quit church and divorced, so on a visit back to my home town I looked him up. He told me, "David, I don't even believe in God anymore."

I think of a pastor's son who had a testimony of salvation and was looked up to by the other church youth, but he rejected the Bible and became an atheist.

Adoniram Judson, the famous missionary to Burma, grew up in a strong Christian home and made a profession of faith in Christ, but he became associated with worldly friends in college and became a Deist, believing that God is not involved with the creation and has no plan of salvation. This proved that he had never been saved.

I think of Hindus who have attended our services and Bible studies in Nepal and professed to "believe in Jesus" but who turned back to Hinduism and idolatry.

Rejecting the gospel proves that the individual is not saved and never has been saved.

Love of God's Word

> "He that is of God heareth God's words: ye therefore hear *them* not, because ye are not of God" (John 8:47).

A person's attitude toward the Bible is one of the clearest evidences of his spiritual condition. It is impossible that an individual could be saved if he doesn't love God's Word. Jesus said, "My sheep hear my voice, and I know them, and they follow me" (Joh. 10:27). Words could not be plainer.

A saved person will be interested in the Bible, will want to study the Bible, will respond to the Bible's teaching.

After I made a profession of faith at about age 11, I had zero interest in the Bible. I had a Bible, but I never read it. I wasn't interested in preaching and teaching. Everything pertaining to the Bible was boring. I was at church because my parents took me, not because I had an interest in spiritual things. That is not the condition of a saved person.

But as soon as I repented and trusted Christ as my Lord and Saviour at age 23, I *loved* the Bible and everything about the Bible.

A born again child of God can backslide and become disobedient and his spiritual life might grow dim, but there will still be something of a love of the Bible in his heart, and he will not forget the Master's voice (John 10:27). Peter backslid terribly but He was restored by the Master's words (John 21:6-19).

Love of righteousness

> "And hereby we do know that we know him, if we keep his commandments. He that saith, I know him, and keepeth not his commandments, is a liar, and the truth is not in him" (1 John 2:3-4).

It is impossible for a born again child of God to continue in his old rebellious attitude toward God's commandments. He still has "the old man" and can still sin, but there is going to be a great change in his attitude toward righteousness and unrighteousness.

Consider the testimony of David Sorenson, a pastor's son. He made a profession of faith at age five in an evangelistic meeting. He was coached to tell others that he was saved, and he did that for 15 years. But he says, "I had no interest in the things of God. I only went to church because my dad was the pastor, and I had to go. I could not have cared less about the Bible." At age 20 he was saved in Bible College and his life changed because he began to love the things he used to hate and to hate the things he used to love.

One thing that will always change is the individual's attitude toward authority. If a child is saved, there will be a change in his attitude toward the authority of his parents and teachers and church leaders.

Led by the Spirit

> "But ye are not in the flesh, but in the Spirit, if so be that the Spirit of God dwell in you. Now if any man have not the

Spirit of Christ, he is none of his. And if Christ *be* in you, the body *is* dead because of sin; but the Spirit *is* life because of righteousness. But if the Spirit of him that raised up Jesus from the dead dwell in you, he that raised up Christ from the dead shall also quicken your mortal bodies by his Spirit that dwelleth in you. Therefore, brethren, we are debtors, not to the flesh, to live after the flesh. For if ye live after the flesh, ye shall die: but if ye through the Spirit do mortify the deeds of the body, ye shall live. For as many as are led by the Spirit of God, they are the sons of God. For ye have not received the spirit of bondage again to fear; but ye have received the Spirit of adoption, whereby we cry, Abba, Father. The Spirit itself beareth witness with our spirit, that we are the children of God" (Ro. 8:9-16).

The true believer has the indwelling Spirit, communes with the Spirit, and is led by the Spirit.

The believer can grieve the Spirit by sin (Eph. 4:20), but the believer has an entirely new orientation in life. He is oriented toward the Spirit of God as opposed to prior to conversion when he was oriented toward the flesh.

Looking for Christ's return

"For since the beginning of the world *men* have not heard, nor perceived by the ear, neither hath the eye seen, O God, beside thee, *what* he hath prepared **for him that waiteth for him**" (Isa. 64:4).

"And not only *they*, but ourselves also, which have the firstfruits of the Spirit, even we ourselves groan within ourselves, **waiting for the adoption,** *to wit,* the redemption of our body" (Ro. 8:23).

"Henceforth there is laid up for me a crown of righteousness, which the Lord, the righteous judge, shall give me at that day: and not to me only, but unto **all them also that love his appearing**" (2 Ti. 4:8).

"So Christ was once offered to bear the sins of many; and **unto them that look for him** shall he appear the second time without sin unto salvation" (Heb. 9:28).

These passages make it clear that the saved are those who are anticipating Christ's coming.

Divine chastisement

> "For whom the Lord loveth he chasteneth, and scourgeth every son whom he receiveth. If ye endure chastening, God dealeth with you as with sons; for what son is he whom the father chasteneth not? But if ye be without chastisement, whereof all are partakers, then are ye bastards, and not sons" (Heb. 12:6-8).

A child of God can and does sin, but there is an indwelling, loving Disciplinarian who chastens him. There is even a sin unto death (1 Joh. 5:16-17).

The saved person will have a sensitivity to sin and a conviction about sin. I think of a young teen who got saved and afterwards became concerned about sins she had committed when she was younger and had "gotten away with." Before salvation, if her parents were not watching, she would do things behind their backs. For example, she took her father's socks and stuffed them down a hole in the back hallway. The disappearance of the socks was an unsolved mystery in the home, but after she got saved she came weeping to her mother and confessed that sin, though no one had ever caught her. That is an evidence that something real was happening in her life. She stopped being "sneaky." She starting being trustworthy to obey even if no one was watching. Those are simple but profound evidences of a spiritually-converted life in a child.

Jerry was my best buddy growing up. We went through school together, graduated together, went to Vietnam in the Army about the same time, and came back to America and became drug-using "hippies" together. I came to Christ at age 23, but Jerry never did. He mocked my faith in Christ and refused to listen to me when I tried to talk to him from the Bible. Eventually he got involved in "Native America" spirituality, which is demonism. He died a few years ago at about age 62, and I visited his mother. His mother and father were faithful church goers, and the mom had been a Baptist Sunday School teacher. She told me that she had hope of Jerry's salvation because he went to church when he was a boy, but there was zero evidence that he was ever saved.

What about Christian growth?

When we talk about evidence of salvation, we are not ignoring the issue of spiritual growth. A new Christian is a babe in Christ and must grow (1 Peter 2:1-2), and growing is a process that continues throughout the entire life (2 Pe. 3:18). There is the process of adding to one's faith (2 Peter 1:5-8). There is a process of laying off the old man and putting on the new man (Eph. 4:22-24). There is an ongoing surrendering to Christ, separating from the world, and being transformed by God's Word (Ro. 12:1-2).

But even a babe in Christ is a new creature who has been spiritually raised from the dead, brought out of darkness into light, and has new life in Christ, and this is a supernatural transformation that can be seen.

What about carnality?

The born again child of God can be carnal. We see this in 1 Corinthians 3:1-3. The carnal Christian is a born again saint who has fleshly elements in his life.

But the carnal Christian is not a person who merely professes Christ with the mouth and does not show evidence in his life.

The Corinthian believers were passionate Christians. They gave clear evidence of salvation (1 Co. 6:9-11). They were zealous for spiritual things (1 Co. 14:12). They abounded in "faith, utterance, knowledge, diligence, and love" (2 Co. 8:7).

That is not the description of a nominal Christian who is not zealous for the things of Christ, but rather loves the world while merely professing Christ.

What about backsliding?

The born again child of God *can* backslide. This is evident in Christ's messages to the seven churches of Asia. For example, Ephesus had backslidden from its first love and was exhorted to repent (Re. 2:4-5). The potential for backsliding is evident in 2 Peter 1, where Peter exhorts the believer to grow by adding to his faith virtue, knowledge, temperance, patience, godliness, brotherly kindness, and charity. This exhortation is accompanied by the warning that the believer who doesn't do this "is blind, and cannot see afar off, and hath forgotten that he was purged from his old sins" (2 Pe. 1:9). That is backsliding.

The Christian life is not a direct upward progression. It is not continual revival. There are spiritual ups and downs, and we must be careful not to look at a true believer who might be on a spiritual low and misjudge him as unsaved.

At the same time, there will still be evidence of spiritual life at the lowest ebb of a true believer's experience.

What about Lot?

First of all, Lot was not a New Testament believer, and he should not be used as an example of a New Testament believer.

At the same time, Lot cannot be used as an example of a believer who shows no sign of spiritual life. Peter says Lot was "just," which only comes by faith in God's promise in Christ. And he gave evidence that he was just. Lot was a carnal believer who made unwise decisions that resulted in sorrow and destruction, but he was "vexed with the filthy conversation of the wicked" (2 Pe. 2:7). And unlike his wife and married children, Lot obeyed the angel and fled Sodom.

Lot is not an example of someone who prays a sinner's prayer but shows no sign of new life in Christ, and Lot is not an example of a worldly teenager that professes Christ but secretly loves the filthy conversation of the wicked.

Beware of looking for perfection

We look for a change, but we don't look for any kind of perfection, because there is no such thing. The "old man" remains after salvation and must be dealt with. The Christian life is a progression of putting off the old man and putting on the new, and it involves a lot of real "struggle" with the flesh. The believer's level of surrender is never absolute in any area of his life. There is the potential for carnality and backsliding.

When "testing" others, the child of God must not forget how imperfect *he* is! We are simply looking for a regenerated heart and a changed direction in life.

I have known of a few churches that require a "lordship" conversion, meaning that in practice they look for the individual to make "Jesus completely Lord." If there are areas of holdout in that individual's life and if there is still a struggle with sin, doubting, carnality, they tend to believe that the individual is unsaved. The mark of such churches is that an inordinate number of people "get saved" when no one around them doubted their salvation previously. I think of a missionary in Singapore whose ministry was characterized by this type of thing. Most of the Christians who visited his church began to doubt their salvation and eventually "got saved." A group of missionaries we knew visited his work, and they all "got saved."

This type of thing can be devastating. It causes the individual to look at himself too much rather than keeping his eyes on Christ. In fact, this missionary's own son took over that church and later got out of the ministry when he doubted his salvation and "got saved."

What about emotional experiences?

We don't look for any certain type of emotional experience. Emotional reactions differ from person to person. Some will feel elated; some will feel nothing.

What about a certain type of conversion experience?

We don't look for one kind of experience. Some conversions are more dramatic than others. In some the change is quicker and more dynamic. I had a very dramatic conversion experience. Literally I hated the Bible one minute and loved it the next. I was a New Ager in my heart one minute and a staunch Bible believer the next. Not everyone has exactly that type of experience. No one is saved without a life-changing conversion experience, but the details and timing are not always the same.

What about a pattern of conversion experience?

We don't look for a certain pattern of experience. In the Great Awakenings there was often an attempt to trace a certain pattern of experience (e.g., conviction of sin, feelings of guilt, a sense of helplessness and hopelessness, settled peace and joy). Jonathan Edwards explained that this is an error. "It is to be feared that some have gone too far towards directing the Spirit of the Lord, and marking out his footsteps for him, and limiting him to certain steps and methods. Experience plainly shows, that God's Spirit is unsearchable and untraceable, in some of the best of Christians, in the method of his operations, in their conversion. Nor does the Spirit of God proceed discernibly in the steps of a particular established scheme, one half so often as is imagined" (A Treatise on Religious Affections).

Man's part is not to try to trace the steps of conversion. Man's part is to observe the effect of the conversion. "As to the steps which the Spirit of God took to bring that effect to pass, we may leave that to him."

What about an exact time and place?

We don't require knowledge of an exact time in every case.

The new birth does happen at a certain time, and usually the time and place will be clear in the individual's mind, as we have noted.

> "Paul knew the time of his conversion (Acts 26:13). Men are frequently at a loss whether their conversion were true or not; but surely men that are converted must take some notice of the time when God made a change in them: conversion is a great change, from darkness to light, from death to life, from the borders of despair to a spirit of faith in Christ. As for the outward conversion, there is sometimes little difference men might carry very well before; but as to the frame of men's hearts, there is a very great difference. ... Conversion is the greatest change that men undergo in this world, surely it falls under observation. The Prodigal knew well enough the time of his return to his Father's House. The children of Israel knew the time of their passing over Jordan" (Solomon Stoddard, *Defects of Preachers Reproved*, 1723).

But in some cases, particularly when the individual was younger when it occurred, he might not be able to pinpoint it.

If a person does not know the exact time of his conversion, that does not mean he or she is not converted. The most important thing is whether the individual knows Christ as personal Lord and Saviour and has a changed life to back it up.

With children growing up in Christian homes and churches, it is not uncommon for them to make two professions of faith, one when they are young and another when they are older. Usually this means that they weren't saved earlier, but not always.

What about repentance?

Repentance is real and necessary but it is not complicated.

Repentance is absolutely necessary for salvation. Christ's Great Commission requires preaching "repentance and the remission of sins" (Luke 24:47). Paul preached repentance to the citizens of Athens (Acts 17:30). Peter described salvation as coming to repentance (2 Pe. 3:9).

Paul taught that salvation consists of repentance toward God and faith toward our Lord Jesus Christ, not only one or the other (Acts 20:21).

Repentance was the missing element in my life as a boy who professed Christ as Saviour, and this is what is missing in the lives and hearts of many church members. I "believed in Jesus," but so do the devils (Jas. 2:19). In fact, the devils tremble, which is far more than the average church member today does!

But repentance is not complicated.

Repentance is to surrender to God's authority. It is to acknowledge that I have wickedly sinned against God's holy law and have not honored Him as God by loving Him with all my being, and it is *to be ready to* live in a different way. Repentance is a change of direction *in the heart*. It is *not* a change of life (as some have falsely claimed that we teach); it is a change of mind that *results in* a change of life.

Repentance is turning *to* God *from* one's false ways, like the idolaters at Thessalonica (1 Th. 1:9). It means to turn around and go another way. It is something that happens in the heart and has consequences in the life.

Repentance is the prodigal son *turning his face toward the father* and *away from* the pig pen and saying, "I have sinned against heaven and before thee" (Lu. 15:18). He had a dramatic change of mind and attitude toward God and this was evidenced in his change of attitude toward his father and life in general.

Those who argue that our doctrine of repentance is complicated or difficult are those who have made repentance into NOTHING! We explain this later in this chapter.

Salvation is not difficult and it is not for the future

Recently I heard of some young women who are in "limbo" about salvation. They made professions of faith when they were younger and believed they were saved and gave some evidence thereof, but they have begun to doubt that, believing that their salvation was based only on "a mental assent" to the gospel.

I replied to this situation as follows:

I don't understand why the girls don't just go to Christ and settle the matter. Being in a limbo land of not knowing you are saved is a very dangerous place where the devil could work overtime.

The Bible presents salvation as something that the sinner can receive right now:

> It is receiving a gift that is offered (Eph. 2:8-9).
> It is coming to Christ for salvation rest (Mt. 11:28).
> It is drinking the living water (John 4).
> It is believing on Christ with all the heart (John 3:16; Acts 8:37; 16:30-31).
> It is calling on Christ (Romans 10).
> It is believing the gospel (1 Corinthians 15:1-4).
> It is gladly receiving the gospel (Acts 2:41).
> It is repenting toward God and exercising faith toward our Lord Jesus Christ (Acts 20:21).
> It is fleeing for refuge and taking hold of Christ (Heb. 6:18).
> It is receiving salvation today (2 Co. 6:2).

Salvation can be rejected as in the case of the rich young ruler. It can be falsified by believing on a false christ or a false gospel (John 2:23-25; Mt. 7:21-23). But salvation is never described as something that is difficult or complicated, that I can see. That would defeat the purpose of it as a free gift.

Salvation is described as a transaction between the sinner and the living Christ, a transaction that changes the life, but the transaction itself is simply coming to Christ as a needy, repentant sinner and receiving Him as Lord and Saviour.

The Bible never presents salvation as something that should be put off until later. God's Word gives no promise of tomorrow. "(For he saith, I have heard thee in a time accepted, and in the day of salvation have I succoured thee: behold, now *is* the accepted time; behold, now *is* the day of salvation.)" (2 Co. 6:2).

If someone is having doubts, he should settle it right then and there. He should simply come to Christ as a needy sinner who wants to be saved. He should take Christ at His word:

> "Come unto me, all *ye* that labour and are heavy laden, and I will give you rest. Take my yoke upon you, and learn of me; for I am meek and lowly in heart: and ye shall find rest unto your souls. For my yoke *is* easy, and my burden is light" (Mt. 11:28-30).

He should say, "Lord, I have been laboring and am heavy laden. I want to be saved, but I have doubts about my salvation. I am now coming to you for the free salvation that you offer and that you purchased on the cross for needy sinners. I am that needy sinner, and I want to receive you as my Lord and Saviour."

If you do that sincerely, you can trust Christ's promise that He will receive you and give you the gift of salvation rest.

Once you have come to Christ for salvation rest, you should obey Him and take His yoke and begin learning about Him and from Him and learning how to serve Him in your daily life.

Salvation is no more complicated than this.

The necessity of spiritual discernment

Keen spiritual discernment is required when dealing with souls about salvation. This is the discernment that is essential for pastors and teachers and evangelists.

We're not talking about perfect discernment, for there is no perfection in the Christian life and ministry, but we're talking about good spiritual discernment that comes by knowing and walking with God.

Discerning salvation in others requires that one has experienced salvation himself.

> "Now, will anyone pretend, that persons who have been through this process themselves, cannot, by examination, form a reasonable judgment whether others have been through it or not? What teacher, what school committee man, cannot ascertain whether a boy has seen for himself and understands the nature and reason of the rule for working

simple addition, or whether he has only learned it by rote? Cannot pretenders in any branch of science be detected? ... If discrimination is possible in such cases as these, it must also, on the same principle, be possible for those who are qualified, to judge whether a man has made those discoveries of religious truth ... which are essential to Christian experience" (Joseph Tracy, *The Great Awakening).*

God has promised wisdom to those who seek it (Pr. 3:5-6; James 1:5).

The necessity of patience

We would also note that patience is very important in this matter. The tare looks like wheat until the fruit appears (Mt. 13:25-26). It is better to err on the side of caution, because to pronounce someone saved and to baptize them is very harmful to the individual as well as to the church if they are brought into membership.

The importance of unanimity

Unanimity is a helpful protection in discerning salvation. Before we baptize an individual, he or she must appear before the church leaders and their wives and give account of his salvation. If something isn't clear, the leaders ask appropriate questions. We look for unanimity in these decisions, believing it is better to err on the side of caution. In the last session we interviewed four and baptized three. In the session before that, we interviewed 15 individuals and baptized 13. There were doubts about three of the individuals, and we kindly asked them to wait until things were more clear in their minds and lives and so we can have more time to teach them and work with them.

Southern Baptist Churches

Carelessness in the matter of salvation has long been the status quo in Southern Baptist churches.

According to a 1997 study by Southern Baptist Sunday School Board, only 32.8% of the 16 million SBC church members even bother to show up on a given Sunday morning and only 12.3% participate in any further aspect of church life. "These figures suggest that nearly 90% of Southern Baptist church members appear to be little different from the 'cultural Christians' who populate mainline denominations" (*Founder's Journal*, Feb. 7, 1999).

Jim Elliff, president of Christian Communicators Worldwide, in an article entitled "Southern Baptists, an Unregenerate Denomination," says,

> "Let me illustrate in rounded figures by looking at some of the churches where I have preached as a guest speaker. Each could be any Baptist church in any city. ... [One] church had 2,100 on the roll, with 725 coming on Sunday morning. Remove guests and non-member children and the figure drops to 600 or less. Only about a third of that number came out on Sunday evening, representing less than 10% of the membership. Yet another church had 310 on the roll with only 100 who attended on Sunday morning. Only 30-35, or approximately 10%, came to the evening worship service" (www.ccwonline.org/sbc.html).

This was true in the Southern Baptist church in which I grew up. They didn't look for any evidence of repentance. I don't recall even one genuine Christian among the youth. They never questioned an individual's salvation. No one was ever taken off the membership roll.

Most Independent Baptists are little better. They are so eager for members that they aren't careful. In fact, careful is the last thing they want to be! As a result, the average Independent Baptist church is a mixed multitude of saved and unsaved, disciples and lukewarm.

Independent Baptists Prior to the 1970s

Prior to the 1970s, Independent Baptist churches were spiritually stronger, and one reason was that they were more careful about salvation.

Consider some prominent examples:

J. Frank Norris, 1930s and 1940s - Norris stated plainly that repentance is "turning to God with unfeigned contrition, confession, and supplication for mercy" and that the "proper evidence" of the new birth "appears in the holy fruits of repentance and faith and newness of life." He warned about those who instructed people to make mere "decisions" for Christ and invited sinners merely to come forward for prayer. Of this kind of preaching, he said it "did not have enough gospel in it to save an ant" (J. Frank Norris, *What Do Fundamental Baptists Believe*, an address delivered at the annual meeting of the American Baptist Association at First Baptist Church, Fort Worth, Texas, 1935). In the 1940s, Norris preached an entire week on the subject of hell without giving an invitation. Only after a full week of such preaching did he give an invitation, and more than a hundred and fifty were saved. He believed in plowing the ground of sinner's hearts with the law of God to prepare the soul for genuine conviction, repentance, and saving faith.

John R. Rice, 1940 - "To repent literally means **to have a change of mind or spirit toward God and toward sin. It means to turn from your sins**, earnestly, with all your heart, and trust in Jesus Christ to save you. You can see, then, how the man who believes in Christ repents and the man who repents believes in Christ. The jailer repented when he turned from sin to believe in the Lord Jesus Christ" (*What Must I Do to Be Saved?* 1940).

Baptist Bible Fellowship International, 1950 - "We believe that Repentance and Faith are solemn obligations, and also inseparable graces, wrought in our souls by the quickening Spirit of God; thereby, being deeply convicted of our guilt, danger and helplessness, and of the way of salvation by Christ, **we turn to God with unfeigned contrition**, confession and supplication for mercy at the same time heartily receiving the Lord Jesus Christ and openly confessing Him as our only and all-sufficient Saviour" (Baptist Bible Fellowship, Articles of Faith, 1950).

Harold Sightler, 1963 - "Recognizing his guilt, there is **a turning from sin**. There is a turning to God. The actual word 'repentance' means a turning completely around: a change of course; a change of mind. ... **To think of repentance that does not cause the sinner to turn gladly from his sins is impossible**. ... I know that we have a shallow religious movement in our times that will allow men to profess faith in Christ and at the same time continue to live in the world. Such a shallow religious faith is not real. These are mere professors and have no part with God in salvation" (*Chastening and Repentance*, 1963).

B.R. Lakin, 1964 - "Repentance toward God--that's **turning away from all your sin** and everything you know to be wrong, and **turning right about face**, then trusting Jesus Christ as your complete Redeemer" (*Prepare to Meet Thy God*, 1964).

Lester Roloff, 1965 - "Repentance is a godly sorrow for sin. Repentance is a forsaking of sin. **Real repentance is putting your trust in Jesus Christ so you will not live like that anymore.** Repentance is permanent. It is a lifelong and an eternity-long experience. You will never love the devil again once you repent. **You will never flirt with the devil as the habit of your life again once you get saved.** You will never be happy living in sin; it will never satisfy; and the husks of the world will never fill your longing and hungering in your soul. **Repentance is something a lot bigger than a lot of people think. It is absolutely essential if you go to heaven**" (*Repent or Perish*, 1965).

Highland Park Baptist Church c. 1965 - "Here are some things the sinner must do to be saved. He must want to be saved (Isa. 1:18-19). He must be willing for God to save him (Rev 22:18). He must acknowledge himself a sinner (Ps. 51:3; Lu. 15:17). **He must repent - turn his back on sin and turn to God** (Acts 20:21; Lu. 13:2). He must believe on Christ and His finished work of Redemption (Act 16:31; Joh. 1:12; Ro. 10:10; Joh. 3:16)" (*Handbook for Our Members*, Highland Park Baptist Church, Chattanooga, Tennessee, c. 1965, p. 32).

Oliver B. Greene, 1960s - He preached 25 radio messages in a row on *the wrath of God*. He said, "True repentance is sorrow for sin committed against a holy God and **not only sorrow for sin, but turning from sin, forsaking sin and turning to God**. Sin nailed the Savior to the cross and certainly that fact alone is sufficient reason why **all who have genuinely repented hate sin and forsake sinful ways**" (*Commentary of Acts of the Apostles*, Acts 2:37-38).

Leon Maurer, 1970 - "**A rotely memorized prayer or some repeated statement without true repentance and faith never saves anyone.** He must be very serious about it and really mean it. ... Consider a case where the person being dealt with is going to repeat a prayer after the soul winner as he calls on the Lord to save his soul. Here is a pattern which can be followed merely as an example: 'Lord, I realize I am a sinner. I am lost in my sin. **I turn**

from my sin. I repent of my sin. Right here and now I do trust the Lord Jesus Christ as my personal Saviour...' (*Soul Winning: The Challenge of the Hour*, The Sword of the Lord, 1970).

When these men talked of turning from sin, everyone in those days knew what they meant. They weren't talking about reformation or a works salvation. They were talking about something that occurred in the heart. They were talking about a radical change of mind that put them on a different path.

Independent Baptists after the 1970s

Soul winning changed dramatically in the late 1960s and early 1970s.

There was a frenzy for bigness, and this was the motivation for a change in soul winning doctrine and methodology.

The *Sword of the Lord* promoted the "biggest" and "the fastest growing" concept. This is the way that preachers were often introduced at Highland Park in the 1970s and 1980s.

A new evangelistic program was introduced and spread rapidly. I experienced this program at Highland Park Baptist Church in Chattanooga, Tennessee, as a student at Tennessee Temple from 1974-1977.

Jack Hyles was by far the most influential teacher of the new soul winning and church planting methods. In 1962, The Sword of the Lord published Hyles' *Let's Go Soul Winning* and *Let's Build an Evangelistic Church*.

Second in influence, beginning in the late 1970s, was Curtis Hutson, who became the editor of The Sword of the Lord upon the death of John R. Rice in 1980. Hutson's book *Winning Souls and Getting Them Down the Aisle* (Sword of the Lord, 1978) was very influential. Hutson's mentor was Jack Hyles.

Jack Hyles taught that every church problem could be solved by his soul winning program:

> "Soul winning is the basic secret of every other problem in the church. For example, here a church is having cold services. There is no warmth. There. The Lord does not meet with them. Now how do you overcome it? Get to winning souls. If somebody walks down the aisle every Sunday and professes their faith in Christ, that will warm the service up a great deal.

Here is a church having trouble with its business. It doesn't have enough folks who know business. It is having trouble handling its legal affairs. It doesn't have enough wisdom. The Bible says, "He that winneth souls is wise.' So God gives extra wisdom to those who win souls" (Hyles, *Let's Build an Evangelistic Church*, p. 34).

I call this program "Quick Prayerism," and following are its characteristics:

1. The emphasis of soul winning changed from an emphasis on repentance to an emphasis on "going to heaven when you die."

This was the heart and soul of Jack Hyles' soul winning program.

> "It may be done thusly. 'Now, Mr. Doe, let me ask you a question: Do you know that if you died this minute you would go to Heaven?'
>
> "'No, I don't believe I do.'
>
> "'Let me ask you this: Would you like to know? Don't you think it would be fine if you could know that if you died you would go to Heaven?'
>
> "'Yes.'
>
> "Well, let me ask you this: If I could take the Bible and explain to you how you could know beyond any shadow of a doubt, that you could know right now, and you could see it and you could understand it, would you believe it? Would you do what the Bible says?'
>
> "Do you see what I'm trying to say? It is good to get him committed that he will do it; then you have gone a long way toward getting him saved before you ever present the plan. So these three questions: (1) 'Do you know that if you died today you would go to Heaven?' (2) 'Would you like to know?' (3) 'If I could show you how you could know, would you do it?'" (Hyles, *Let's Go Soul Winning*).

The most atrocious example of this we have seen is *My John 3:16 Book: Lola Mazola's Happyland Adventure*. The cover depicts a gleeful child on a roller coaster holding a Bible. Children are taught that heaven is an exciting place, sort of like an eternal Disneyland, and they can go there "when they die" by saying a sinner's prayer.

It includes a "commemorative certificate" that is signed and dated to proclaim the child's eternal security. The cover says, "Best-selling author Robert J. Morgan has told this story to children for years and personally witnessed hundreds of them in turn express faith in Jesus."

Not once in the book of Acts do we find a preacher saying, "Do you want to go to heaven when you die? If so, you need to do this..." There is not a hint of that type of thing in Scripture.

Preachers in the New Testament promised eternal life through Jesus Christ, but they never used the "do you want to go to heaven" approach in evangelism. The emphasis is on knowing and serving Christ in this present life. The emphasis is on discipleship in the here and now rather than obtaining a ticket to heaven. It is on doing works *meet for repentance* (Acts 26:20). It is on being ordained to walk in good works (Eph. 2:10). It is on living soberly, righteously, and godly in this present world (Titus 2:12).

2. The "sinner's prayer" became the focus of soul winning.

The emphasis and aim was to get the individual to pray a sinner's prayer.

An example of a sinner's prayer is the following from the gospel tract *God's Simple Plan of Salvation*:

> "Dear Jesus, I know I am a sinner; I know I deserve hell for my sins. I believe You died for me, and I am trusting You to save me from hell and give me the gift of eternal life. Thank you Jesus for saving me. Amen."

The sinner's prayer can be traced to about the middle of the 20th century. The American Tract Society was founded in 1825 during the Second Great Awakening, but it was not until 1955 that it published its first tract containing a sinner's prayer.

Billy Graham popularized the sinner's prayer in his gospel tracts, beginning in the 1950s with *Steps to Peace with God*. The sinner's prayer was also popularized by Bill Bright and Campus Crusade for Christ.

It was Jack Hyles who popularized sinner's prayer soul winning among Independent Baptists. This was the emphasis of his soul winning books and annual Pastor's Schools. He said, "You must try to get them to pray."

At a recent Bible conference, some men challenged me, saying, "What about the sinner's prayer? Do you believe in using the sinner's prayer?"

My reply is simple: "Show me the sinner's prayer in the New Testament."

Jesus Christ never led an individual in a sinner's prayer, and Paul never led anyone in a sinner's prayer.

In our evangelism course *Sowing and Reaping*, we urge people to do their own studies of the following passages to learn how to deal with people in a biblical way:
- Nicodemus - John 3:1-16
- The Woman at the Well - John 4:1-43
- The Rich Young Ruler - Mark 10:17-27
- Zacchaeus - Luke 19:1-10
- The Ethiopian Eunuch - Acts 8:26-39
- Lydia - Acts 16:14-15
- The Philippian Jailer - Acts 16:23-40
- The Athenians - Acts 17:14-34

Instead of focusing on a sinner's prayer, biblical evangelism has the following characteristics:

Biblical evangelism presents the gospel (Mark 16:15-16; Ro. 1:16). The job the Lord has given His people as ambassadors of Christ is to preach the gospel to every person on earth. The gospel is defined in a nutshell in 1 Corinthians 15:1-4. This is the message that must be proclaimed and explained. A sinner does not have to become a theologian to be saved, but he does have to understand and receive the gospel. To understand the gospel, the individual must come to understand the character of God as a holy judge. He must understand that he is a sinner according to the Bible's definition, meaning that he is not good and has *no* righteousness that is acceptable to God. He must understand who Jesus Christ is and the significance of Christ's death as an atoning sacrifice. He must understand that Christ rose from the dead. He must understand what it means that Christ died and rose "*according to the Scriptures.*" We have dealt with what it means to believe the gospel earlier in this chapter.

The soul winner's job is to explain the gospel. How long this takes depends on the listener's religious background, receptivity, and other factors.

Biblical evangelism is *bringing sinners to wholehearted faith in Jesus Christ* (Acts 8:36-37). Salvation is not a prayer; it is a personal relationship with God in Christ. "And this is life eternal, that they might know thee the only true God, and Jesus Christ, whom thou hast sent" (John 17:3).

Biblical evangelism urges sinners to *call on Jesus Christ as Lord and Saviour* (Romans 10:9-13).

> "That if thou shalt confess with thy mouth the Lord Jesus, and shalt believe in thine heart that God hath raised him from the dead, thou shalt be saved. For with the heart man believeth unto righteousness; and with the mouth confession is made unto salvation. For the scripture saith, Whosoever believeth on him shall not be ashamed. For there is no difference between the Jew and the Greek: for the same Lord over all is rich unto all that call upon him. For whosoever shall call upon the name of the Lord shall be saved."

Here salvation is described as confessing the Lord Jesus with the mouth, believing from the heart that God has raised Him from the dead, and calling on Him.

The word "Lord" is mentioned three times in this key passage. To say that a person can receive Christ as Saviour and not as Lord has no biblical support. Jesus *is* Lord, and every soul will bow to Him as Lord, either in salvation or in judgment.

To believe on Christ savingly after the fashion of this passage (to confess Him, to believe unto righteousness, to call upon Him) requires that the individual understand and believe the gospel that Paul preached in Romans 1-3. Romans 1-3 gives the content of the gospel: man's totally lost and condemned condition before a holy God and his inability to save himself by good works and law keeping (Ro. 1:18 - 3:20) and Christ's work of atonement for man's behalf on the cross (Ro. 3:21-29).

To call on the Lord in the sense of Romans 10:13 is not a "sinner's prayer" in the way that sinner's prayer evangelism has been taught. It is simply a personal receiving of Jesus Christ.

A sinner's prayer might be helpful to some people who don't know what to say to the Lord in calling on Him for salvation. My wife was helped by a sinner's prayer when she got saved as a teenager. But a sinner's prayer is not the goal of evangelism. To get the sinner to receive the living Christ is the goal. If a sinner's prayer is used at all, it must be used very carefully and wisely at the right time and with the right person.

And if a sinner's prayer is used, it must be a good sinner's prayer that helps the individual express biblical repentance and faith. Many of the sinner's prayers that we have seen totally neglect repentance.

3. The biblical concept of plowing the soil of man's heart with the law to prepare it for Holy Spirit conviction and salvation was discarded for a quick salesmanship program.

When we refer to plowing the soil, we refer to sowing the seed of the gospel, carefully explaining it, using the law to show the sinner his plight, praying over it, and patiently waiting for the fruit that comes only by God's Spirit.

The law of Moses was given to show man his fallen condition and to lead him to the Saviour (Ga. 3:24-25).

In Romans 1-3, we see Paul's use of the law in this manner. He spends nearly two full chapters exposing man's fallen condition and God's righteous judgment upon all men before he mentions anything about the grace of God in Christ's atonement.

This is the true "Romans Road"! It is careful to get the sinner totally and thoroughly lost before it tries to get him saved.

The "old" Baptists believed in plowing the soil with the law to cause the sinner to see himself as exceedingly sinful and undone. We have seen how that J. Frank Norris preached a full week on hell before giving a salvation invitation and Harold Sighter preached 25 messages in a row on the wrath of God.

But this careful, patient preparation is done away with in the "Quick Prayerism" program.

Jack Hyles taught dozens of psychological tricks. Consider how he used prayer to manipulate individuals:

> "There are several ways to do this, but you must try to get them to pray. If he is really ready, say, 'Could I pray for you, and while I pray, would you pray and ask God to save you today?' Maybe he is not quite that ready. Maybe you don't know. You could say, 'Could I pray that you will get saved?' Maybe you don't think he will let you pray for him to get saved. Then you say, Could I have a word of prayer with you before I go?'

"Anyway, to get your head bowed is good. If you are talking to him, he might interrupt, but if you are talking to the Lord, he won't. You can preach him a little sermon in the prayer. If you can't win a fellow to Christ, and if he won't let you present the plan to him, the best way to tell him how to be saved is to tell the Lord and let the sinner hear you.

"I go into a home and say, 'Sir, would you like to know how to be saved?'

"'No, don't have time for it. The wife's sick and I'm busy.'

"Could I have a prayer for your wife before we go, that she will get well?"

"With his wife lying there sick, a man would be a fool not to let the preacher pray for her. He says, 'Well, O.K.'

"I pray, 'Dear Lord, bless this wife and make her well, and help this man to know that Romans 3:10 says, 'As it is written, There is none righteous, no, not one.' And if people die in their sins, according to Romans 6:23 'the wages of sin is death.' O dear Lord, show him that Romans 5:8 is true when it says that 'God commendeth his love toward us, in that, while we were yet sinners...'

"Pray him the plan. He won't interrupt you. You can get by with a lot of things talking to the Lord that you wouldn't talking to him. ...

"I stop abruptly in my prayer. I pray a simple prayer. Never pray a big prayer. You must pray a prayer so simple that he won't mind his prayer following yours.

"But you can pray this, 'Dear Lord, here is a fellow who needs to get converted. I pray You will help him get saved. May he receive Christ. You love him, dear Lord...' 'Now fellow, will you pray?' You pray like that, and he can pray his little prayer in a minute.

"I always stop in the middle of my prayer. I say, 'Dear Lord, lead this man to be saved. You led me here and I pray that he will be saved today. May his wife have a Christian husband and the little children a Christian daddy. May this be the day of his salvation.' Now while our heads are bowed in prayer, 'Mr. Doe, would you be willing today to ask God to forgive you and tell Him you want to get saved?'

"See, you stop in the middle of your prayer and lead him to pray. Let me say this: Fifty per cent of the time when you get this far the lost person is going to pray" (Hyles, *Let's Go Soul Winning*).

That is cheap psychological manipulation. It is tricky. It is dishonesty. If you tell a man that you want to pray for him, but your goal actually is to preach to him and get him to pray a sinner's prayer, that is deception. We see no hint of this in the Gospels or Acts.

Consider the following example of this methodology. Carl Hatch was called "the world's greatest soul winner" by *Sword of the Lord* editor Curtis Hutson and by Jack Hyles:

> *The Carl Hatch Squeeze*
>
> I don't ask anybody if they want to be saved. If you want a positive answer you must ask a positive question. If you want a no answer ask a no question. If you want a yes answer ask a yes question. **Soul winning is positive. And in soul winning you use a lot of psychology.**
>
> For instance, if you are lost and I say, "Mr. Smith, let me ask you a question. You don't want to go to hell, do you?"
>
> He will answer, No.
>
> I say, "Wonderful, you want to go to heaven, don't you?" He will say, Yes. I will reply, "Sure you do. Sure you do. Sure you do. I thank God for a man that doesn't want to go to hell."
>
> **Did you get that? I am reinforcing the fact that he wants to go to heaven. I'm keeping everything positive.**
>
> I don't say, "Can I show this to you?" or "Do you mind if I read the Bible to you?" That's negative and you will probably get a negative answer. I just say, "I'm so glad you don't want to go to hell and I will just take a minute here to show you some verses. I don't have long and I know you don't, either. There's three things that you need to know. First, Jesus died for you. Isn't that wonderful? Two, Jesus loves you. Isn't that wonderful? Three, Jesus wants you to go to heaven. Isn't that wonderful? And I'm so glad that you want to."
>
> **See, I am being positive.**

He may say he has a lot of questions, but unsaved people don't have questions. **Don't get on unsaved people's questions. Tell them that you will answer their questions later**, but first you want to read a few verses of Scripture. Unsaved people don't have questions. If you get them saved, that answers all of them.

Let me tell you how to deal with someone who has a dumb spirit who bucks getting saved. You share the gospel and get them to the point of praying the sinner's prayer, but they stop. How do you get that type of person saved? Now, this will work in most cases. If he is a man, put your hand on his shoulder and say, "Mr. Jones, I want to have prayer for you. I'm thrilled you want to go to heaven. God has been good to you. Bow your head with me. Then I pray, "Lord, I'm so thankful for this man that doesn't want to burn in hell. I'm so thrilled he wants to go to heaven and not take his kids to hell. I thank you for this man. And I pray you will help him to see that need."

While our heads are still bowed, I say, "Mr. Jones, if you want heaven as your home and Christ as your Saviour, pray this prayer. Lord Jesus." And **if he doesn't repeat that and tries not to pray, I squeeze his shoulder**. I use this technique. If I am dealing with the president of the bank, I take his hand and when it comes time for him to pray, I squeeze his hand. We've titled that the Carl Hatch squeeze. **It works**. If I am dealing with a woman, I ask her to put her hand on the Bible, and when it comes time to pray I just tap her hand gently. **It works; it works!** (This is from a Carl Hatch soul winning seminar at Texas Baptist University. Hatch was called the world's greatest soul winner by *Sword of the Lord* editor Curtis Hutson and by Jack Hyles.)

    This is a damnable practice that has turned biblical evangelism into cheap salesmanship. Hatch didn't take the time to deal carefully and clearly with any part of the gospel. Who is God? Who is Jesus Christ? What is sin? What does it mean that Christ died for my sins? What does it mean that He died according to the Scriptures? What does it mean that He rose from the dead?

    And Carl Hatch didn't even hint at repentance. He was simply offering people a ticket to heaven.

4. The presentation of the gospel is brief and quick.

Jack Hyles' soul winning books encouraged evangelists to try to lead a complete stranger in a sinner's prayer after just a few minutes. Many times he described leading people in a sinner's prayer in 10 or 15 minutes.

One afternoon I went soul winning with a pastor who was trained in this method. He is a man of God, but he has unthinkingly adopted the methodology he was taught. At each door he would go through Hyles' plan. He would ask the individual if he or she would like to go to heaven when he died and if he would listen while he told him how to do that. None of them even let us into the house, as I remember, and they really showed zero interest in Jesus Christ. But when they didn't actually close the door, the pastor would quickly go through the most basic points of the "Romans Road" (e.g., you are a sinner, the wages of sin is death, the gift of God in Christ is eternal life). After that presentation, which took only a few minutes, he said, "Do you have any questions?" None did. And then he said, "Would you like to pray now to receive Christ as your Saviour?" None of the people were interested enough even to let us into their houses and they had no questions, but he was ready to lead them in a sinner's prayer in such a circumstance. That is Quick Prayerism. And these were mostly university students who were steeped in evolution and humanism. Later I asked the pastor why he didn't even hint at repentance in his presentation, and he said that he hadn't thought about it.

Following is the full content of Jack Hyles' Romans' Road:

> I always use the following: "Now, Mr. Doe, there are only four things you must know to be saved. First, you must know that you are a sinner. For example, Romans 3:10 says, 'As it is written, There is none righteous, no, not one.' Let me illustrate. If there is none righteous, that means I'm not righteous, doesn't it? (Notice, I didn't get him unrighteous first; I got me unrighteous. Never put the sinner below you. You always let him know that but for the grace of God you would be in the fix he is in. You get yourself lost first.) So if there is none righteous, I'm not righteous. If there is none righteous, then Mr. Doe, you are not righteous. Also, it says, 'For all have sinned, and come short of the glory of God.'

Now if all have sinned, that means I've sinned-- right? That means your wife has sinned, and that means you have sinned."

If he still acts like he is not a sinner, you just list a few sins and you will catch him. A lot of times I say this: "You do realize that you are a sinner? For example, the Bible mentions some sins such as evil thinking, bad literature, ugly disposition, etc." Somewhere along that line there will be something that he does. Show him that he is a sinner.

Second, show him the price on sin. Romans 5:12: "Wherefore, as by one man sin entered into the world, and death by sin..." What kind of death? All death, both spiritual and physical death, the sum total of death. "... and so death passed upon all men, for that all have sinned." And Romans 6:23, "For the wages of sin is death..." So there is a price on sin. What is that price? Death. What kind of death? That includes the second death of Revelation 20:14, and that second death is the Lake of Fire. So ultimately a person who is a sinner must pay for it by going to Hell. That is the basic price on sin.

Third, the next thing we must do is show that Jesus paid the price. So I say this: "Mr. Doe, God looked down from Heaven and saw that you were a sinner. He saw that you were in debt. He saw that you and I deserved to go to Hell. He wanted to save us and made a plan to do it. He came to the world Himself. His name was Jesus. He was God in a human body. For thirty-three years He lived here in this world. He did not commit one single sin. This is important. Mr. Doe, suppose that Jesus Christ had sinned one time only. The price on sin being death or Hell, where would Jesus have had to go when He died? The answer is Hell, but He did not sin. He did not commit one sin, but He went to the cross, and on the cross He suffered spiritual death when He said, 'My God, my God, why hast thou forsaken me?' He suffered the same thing that a lost person will have to suffer in Hell. I'll go farther than that. I believe that He suffered as much in that moment on Calvary as the sum total eternal suffering of all the lost people who will ever go to Hell to stay forever. Actually He was paying our price for our sins. He was becoming our substitute."

Fourth, "If we will receive that price as our hope for Heaven and receive Him as our Saviour from sin, He will make us His children and take us to Heaven when we die" (Hyles *Let's Go Soul Winning*).

This is not even the complete gospel, because Hyles says nothing about Christ's resurrection. Compare 1 Corinthians 15:3-4.

But even if it included the resurrection, it is an extremely shallow presentation of the gospel. It might be enough for someone who has grown up in a Bible-believing church in the Bible Belt of America and has been taught the principles of the Bible all his life. But it isn't enough for an individual who has never heard the gospel. It isn't enough for an atheistic Humanist, a Hindu, a Buddhist, or a Muslim. It's too shallow, too basic, too quick.

Consider the fact that man is a sinner. No one can be saved if he does not believe and acknowledge that he is a sinner, and that he is *such a sinner* that he absolutely *deserves* eternal hell.

When asked if they believe they are a sinner, many people will answer in the affirmative simply because they know that they are not perfect, but at the same time, they do not believe that they are so wicked as to deserve God's wrath. Most people will admit that they aren't perfect, but they also think of themselves as basically good or at least that their good can outweigh the bad. They know they have done wrong, but they don't think of themselves as deserving of hell. In their minds, they redefine "sin" to be a lack of perfection or a lack self-esteem or (if Catholics) they divide sin into "categories" of mortal and venial, or some such thing.

They do not believe that they are sinners from conception (Psalm 51:5) and that even their very righteousness is as filthy rags before a holy God (Isaiah 64:6).

An example of *not* plowing the ground sufficiently was told to me by a pastor friend who had the following experience at Lancaster Baptist Church in Lancaster, California:

> "We went out with their staff on Saturday morning for soul winning. We were immediately partnered up with some of the veterans. The first door we went to, we spoke to a friendly Catholic guy and to my surprise, the guy got 'saved' before my very eyes as ------- took him from a few scripture passages to the sinner's prayer so smoothly that I was caught off guard. I caught myself and while ------- was recording this man's contact details and writing it down, I asked the man whether

(1) he believed that he was a good person and (2) that it is possible to go to heaven by being a good person. This man who had just got 'saved' told me 'YES.' I looked around and the other two men beside me said nothing and did nothing. We went to a few more places and eventually reached a home with a Roman Catholic young lady who came to the door. She said she was a professing Christian. Even though she said that all churches were the same ------- gave her assurance of salvation by quoting 1 John 5:13."

It is unconscionable to deal with people in such a shallow way. The "Catholic guy" acknowledged that he is a "sinner," but he didn't mean by that that he was deserving of hell. He didn't mean what the Bible means. He still thought of himself as basically a good person deserving of heaven because of his "good deeds"! Obviously he wasn't ready to get saved and should *not* have been led in a sinner's prayer. It was all too hasty and shallow.

One time I was on visitation with a man in Oklahoma City when a woman invited us into her house. Her teenage children were in the living room, so we accepted the invitation and my partner began to talk to her. Though it was soon evident that her language was Portuguese and her English was *very* rudimentary, he proceeded to give her the Romans Road and lead her in a sinner's prayer. I suggested that we should try to obtain a Portuguese Bible and find someone who speaks her language.

Jack Hyles told of a man in Texas who supposedly led a hitchhiker to Christ even though the man was deaf and dumb and couldn't read.

> "He picked up a hitchhiker and tried to witness to him. The hitchhiker shook his head. He then talked real loud, but the hitchhiker pointed to his ears and shook his head. So this new convert started writing the Gospel out and the hitchhiker pointed down and shook his head. He couldn't read, he couldn't hear, he couldn't talk. So this soul winner, who went to the third grade and couldn't even spell Jesus, stopped the car and got out, took his Bible, pointed to the Bible, pointed to his heart, pointed to Heaven, made a motion to open your heart and let Him come in, got on his knees and began to pray. The deaf and dumb fellow got on his knees and mumbled a bit, got up with a smile of Heaven on his face,

pointed to the Bible, pointed to Heaven and pointed to his heart" (*Let's Build an Evangelistic Church*).

This isn't biblical evangelism; it is blind mysticism.

This evangelistic methodology is so brief and quick that it is expected to produce salvation during the few minutes of a gospel invitation in a church service or an evangelistic meeting. Earlier we mentioned the practice of the old Highland Park Baptist Church in Chattanooga, Tennessee. Every Sunday morning people would come forward for "salvation," be dealt with in the front of the auditorium, be led in a sinner's prayer, and then be baptized after answering a few simple questions in the affirmative. ---

I have always thought that this program is unscriptural and even ridiculous. At the very least, seekers should be taken to another room and dealt with carefully, for as long as it takes, and there should be no pressure whatsoever.

5. Quick Prayerism immediately pronounces people saved and gives them assurance just because they have prayed a sinner's prayer, with zero evidence to back it up.

This is what Hyles taught:

> "Then you say, 'Dear Lord, thank You that this man has trusted Jesus. And if the Bible is true and he has been sincere, he is Your child. Help him to see it now. In Jesus' name. Amen.'

> "God bless you, brother. 'Let me ask you this question now: According to this Book, where would you go if you died right now?'

> "'To Heaven.'

> "Do you believe this Book? When you get to the judgment seat, are you willing to trust your eternity on what this Book says?

> "'Yes, sir.'

> "That means you are God's child. Now, suppose somebody asks you tomorrow, 'Mr. Doe, Are you a Christian?'--what are you going to tell them?

> "'I'll tell them yes.'

"If somebody says, 'When did you become a Christian?'-- what are you going to tell them?

"'Yesterday'" (*Let's Go Soul Winning*).

We believe in eternal security and we believe in assurance of salvation, but the assurance must come from the Lord, as He is the only who knows the hearts. See Romans 8:16; Galatians 4:6; 1 John 5:10. The Lord knows those that are His. The believer's part is to demonstrate his salvation by departing from iniquity (2 Ti. 2:19).

6. Quick Prayerism does not look for evidence and the vast majority of professions are empty.

Quick Prayerism produces a large number of professions, but a large percentage are empty.

I was discussing the doctrine of repentance with a missionary some years ago in England. He had told me that many people were being saved through their soul winning outreach, but when I asked about the church services, he said that they had a small number of people in the services and admitted that most of the people being "saved" were not interested enough even to attend the services. I challenged him about the claim that the people were actually being saved. I asked, "How can you say they are saved when there is no evidence of it in their lives?" He became agitated and strongly countered that I had no right to judge the salvation of people who were making professions through his ministry. He said, "You cannot know who is saved." This man had recently attended Hyles Pastor's School, and he said the featured topic that year was repentance!

The idea that you cannot tell if someone is saved is heresy. It is possible, of course, for a person to show false signs of salvation and to deceive people, as Judas did. And we are not saying that a genuinely saved person will suddenly be sinlessly perfect or that every true believer is equally zealous to serve Christ or that a saved personal makes "Jesus Lord of his entire life." But the Bible is clear that if someone is genuinely saved, there will definitely be evidence in his or her life. I don't know of one example of conversion in the New Testament that did not result in a dramatically changed life. Do you?

For several weeks in 1977, my wife and I followed up on a Phoster Club soul-winning program in a fundamental Baptist church. Though the Phoster Club ladies reported many salvations and had a stack of cards representing "decisions for Christ," we did not find even one person who demonstrated biblical evidence. In fact, most of the people we tried to follow up on didn't even invite us into the house for a talk.

Churches reported thousands of souls saved annually, though these numbers were not reflected in the active membership. Jack Hyles claimed that his church saw more people saved on May 3, 1998, than were saved and baptized on the day of Pentecost. He estimated that around 15,000 people were saved and 5,112 were baptized on that one day. But the Wednesday night crowd, which is the truest indication of the real church, was not more than several hundred, and that included the Hyles-Anderson students.

First Baptist Church's Spanish department reported 35,000 professions from 1977-1987, but the average attendance was never more than 1,400 (www.firesofevangelism.org/Origin.html).

Longview Baptist Temple in Longview, Texas, claims that more than one million people were won to Christ in 25 years, which is an average of 40,000 a year (www.lbtministries.com/Pastor/Meet_Our_Pastor.htm). Yet on an average mid-week service, which is the truest reflection of an American church's active membership, you will find only a few hundred people in attendance. Literally hundreds of thousands of these souls that have been "won" are nowhere to be found.

When we were given the "decision" cards to follow up a county fair ministry in Oklahoma in the late 1990s, of the hundreds of professions that were recorded we could not find *even one* person who gave any evidence of salvation or was even interested in attending church.

A pastor friend followed up on the more than 100 "salvation decisions" that were made at a county fair ministry in Kentucky in 2011, and he *did not find one soul* who was even interested enough in Christ to attend church.

Quick Prayerism with its empty statistics is not something that is practiced only by Independent Baptists.

In the 1990s, the Assemblies of God had an evangelistic outreach called "Decade of Harvest," and out of 3.5 million professions, only five out of 100 actually joined a church, and much fewer than that proved to be true disciples of Christ.

The same is true for the Southern Baptist Convention. SBC Evangelist Jim Elliff says, "Our largest pizza supper may bring in a hundred new 'converts,' but we will likely get only a few of those on the roll. [And even the vast majority of these will not become faithful church members.] In other words, if you compare all who we *say* have become Christians through our evangelistic efforts, to those who actually *show signs* of being regenerate, we should be red-faced" ("Southern Baptists, An Unregenerate Denomination," ccwtoday.org).

7. Repentance was redefined to justify this program.

There was a change in the doctrine of repentance. We have seen that former Independent Baptist preachers taught a clear doctrine of repentance as a turning, a surrender, a change of mind that results in a change of life, but this changed. (More examples can be found in the book *Repentance and Soul Winning*, available from Way of Life Literature.)

Instead of repentance and faith as two different things, as Paul taught (Acts 20:21), repentance and faith become one thing. Repentance became faith.

Instead of turning to God from sin and false religion, repentance became *turning from unbelief to belief*.

Instead of repentance as something that always produces evidence (Acts 26:20), repentance became something that *might not be seen*.

Consider some examples:

Curtis Hutson - "The problem and confusion is not preaching repentance but attaching the wrong definition to the word. For instance, to say that repentance means to turn from sin, or to say that repentance is a change of mind that leads to a change of action, is to give a wrong definition to the word" (*Repentance: What Does the Bible Teach?* Sword of the Lord, 1986, p. 16).

Jack Hyles - "So, yes, there is a repentance from unbelief in order to believe. ... With your will you believe and rely upon Christ to save you. In order to believe, you have to repent of unbelief. That which makes a man lost must be corrected" (*Enemies of*

Soulwinning, 1993). Hyles taught that repentance *does not* mean "to turn from sin."

Bob Gray - "10,446 professions of faith in 1995. ... Repentance is not a doctrine. The word 'repent' is not even found in the book of John. It is obviously assumed by God that 'repentance' is a part of 'believing.' ... Repentance is not turning from your sins. ... Repentance is to change one's mind from unbelief to belief in Christ" ("A Message from the Pastor," *The Soulwinner*, January 1996, Longview Baptist Temple, Longview, Texas).

Fred Afman of Tennessee Temple - "The many false conditions of salvation [include] water baptism and repentance" ("The Way of Salvation," Sunday School class, Highland Park Baptist Church, Chattanooga, Tennessee, May 1996; quoted from Chris McNeilly, *The Great Omission*, pp. 25, 26).

Tolbert Moore - "If someone says: repent for sins and you are not saved, what do they mean by that? ... repentance in the true sense of the word really means to turn from being an unbeliever and to become a believer" ("Repentance and Lordship Salvation," *The Gospel Preacher*, September 1996).

In the 1980s, The Sword of the Lord stopped publishing Leon Maurer's *Soul Winning: The Challenge of the Hour* and John Rice's *Here Are More Questions,* in which Rice said that repentance is to turn from sin. Further, *The Sword Hymnal* was purged of many references to repentance.

8. The doctrine of eternal security was corrupted.

The biblical doctrine of eternal security is never divorced from a life-changing salvation experience.

Consider the following passages carefully: John 10:27-30; 1 Co. 15:1-2; Col. 1:21-23; 2 Ti. 2:19; Heb. 6:8-11; 10:38-39; 1 John 3:1-3.

But in the 1970s, eternal security was divorced from a change of life and the evidence of an obedient walk. The typical soul winning program aimed to lead someone in a sinner's prayer and then give him "assurance of salvation" immediately, even if there was no evidence that the person was even sincere in the prayer, even if the person would not so much as invite the soul winner into his house.

Once my wife was taken on "soul winning visitation" by a supposed expert who led a man in a sinner's prayer. While the expert was writing down the man's information, the man told my wife, "I don't really believe that stuff." Yet he was given "assurance" and reported as a convert.

As we have noted, granting assurance of salvation is the work of the Spirit of God (Ro. 8:16; Ga. 4:6; 1 Joh. 5:10). We can show the individual where assurance can be found, which is in God's Word, but we can't give the assurance. The Lord knows those that are His, and the believer's part is to demonstrate his salvation by departing from iniquity (2 Ti. 2:19).

9. There was a focus on "child evangelism."

A huge emphasis was placed on winning little children to Christ and baptizing them. The Vacation Bible School program was geared toward this. It was at a VBS that I made a profession of Christ and was baptized when I was 10-11 years old.

In the Southern Baptist Convention, there was a 96% growth rate from 1970 to 2010 *in baptisms of pre-schoolers*. Consider the statistics for 2013: A full 60% of SBC churches baptized *zero* youth between ages of 12-17 and 80% baptized zero or just one young adult ages 18-29. But there was an explosion in the baptisms of "five and under" (*Annual Church Profile*, 2013).

That is Baptist infant baptism!

A child can believe on Jesus Christ savingly, but it is doubtful that a pre-schooler can do this.

We know that there were no small children baptized on the day of Pentecost, because all of the 3,000 that were baptized "continued stedfastly in the apostles' doctrine and fellowship, and in breaking of bread, and in prayers" (Acts 2:42). That is not the description of a five-year-old child.

I grew up under this type of ministry and philosophy, and the fruit was wretched. It played a major role in building mixed multitude churches. The vast majority of the children that got "saved" at a young age either fell away to the world in adolescence or stayed in the church as nominal, lukewarm, worldly Christians.

Church planters actually tried to build churches on child evangelism, driven by bus ministries and gimmicks, which is not what we see in Acts 13-14, and this is a passage of Scripture specifically given as the preeminent example of missionary church planting for the entire church age.

An early Independent Baptist missionary to Thailand in the 1980s, a Hyles-Anderson graduate, reported impressive numbers of salvations and attendees to his services, but the majority turned out to be children that he was enticing with gimmicks.

Shallow, unscriptural soul winning and neglect of repentance have produced incredibly weak churches. It has produced churches that are mixed multitudes instead of churches of disciples.

If professing Christians are rebels against God's Word and refuse to obey the preaching, refuse to be faithful, refuse to separate from the world, are insubordinate to pastoral authority, it is probably because they aren't saved. As we have seen, the Bible is very clear on this point. See, for example, John 8:47; 10:27; Titus 1:16; 1 John 2:3-4.

Most churches are far too careless about salvation. They pronounce people, including children, saved on a mere profession with no regard for biblical evidence.

Long ago I rejected this tradition. My sole authority for faith and practice is the Bible, and in the Bible we see an emphasis on genuine spiritual conversion with evidence. One of my early books was *Does Salvation Make a Difference?* For 40 years I have warned about the carelessness I have witnessed both in Southern Baptist and Independent Baptist churches. We want to follow the Bible, not anybody's church tradition; the biblical example is Acts 2:41-42. This is a description of a church of true disciples.

Dealing with Children

The church must be very careful when dealing with children and youth; they can be saved (Mt. 19:14), but they are easily manipulated. Every child growing up in a Bible-believing church "believes in Jesus," but so do the devils (Jas. 2:19). Salvation is not a mere belief in Jesus; it is a supernatural conversion experience that sets an individual on an entirely different course in life.

Following are some suggestions for dealing with children about salvation:

Fill their minds with God's Word (2 Ti. 3:15; Heb. 4:12; Ps. 19:7; 119:130).

Of one of his daughters, Pastor Kerry Allen says, "I began a program of memorizing salvation Scriptures with her, and rewarding her for her efforts. In less than one month, with numbers of these same Scriptures at work in her heart, she fell under deep conviction of sin. ... Don't wait until they are teens, you will have lost them by then! ... start memorizing with them as soon as they are able to speak, surely not later than three to four years old. ... begin reading the verses to your child as soon as they are born. They will hear each verse dozens of times before you even begin memorizing, and that is a great way to begin the process from the very earliest days. Sow the Seed of the Word of God faithfully and consistently every day, and wondrous things will occur!" (Allen, *How Can I Except Some Man Guide Me?*).

Pastor Allen has published 150 salvation verses that can be used for a Scripture memorization program for children and has posted it on the web for free download. See the following forwarding link: www.wayoflife.org/memory-cards.pdf

It is important to try to make the Bible as understandable and as interesting as possible for the children. They are children, not adults.

Candidly, I do not understand the thinking of some churches that despise children's ministries. Such ministries can be operated in a wrong way, but I believe it is very important to get the Bible down to a child's level, and the teaching in the adult ministries is not geared to that.

We deal more with filling the home with God's Word later.

Teach them the gospel.

The gospel is the power of God unto salvation (Ro. 1:16). The gospel is described in a nutshell in 1 Co. 15:1-4. It must be explained (Acts 8:30-31). Many people grow up in Bible-believing homes and churches and cannot give a clear definition of the gospel.

Missionary Jeremy Johnson says of his children ages one to eight, "We talk with them about salvation when different topics come up. At the dinner table, in casual conversation, etc. We do not push them, but when the conversation arises, we talk about it: Where a person goes when he dies, why people don't go to heaven, what is sin, what did Jesus do for us, does everyone go to heaven, can I get saved by praying a prayer, etc. When they have false ideas or beliefs about salvation or where they would go, we do not overlook it or ignore it, we speak against it and correct it. We continually try to bring them to an understanding of the truth, yet not pushing them to a decision."

Practical teaching on the gospel can be found in the first few lessons of the One Year Discipleship Course.

Deal with repentance (Lu. 17:3; Acts 17:30; 20:21).

Though I made a profession of faith at age 10-11, the missing element in my life was repentance toward God, and this is what is missing in the lives and hearts of many young people. I "believed in Jesus," but so do the devils (Jas. 2:19). In fact, the devils tremble, which is far more than the average "Christian" young person does! I knew about Jesus and believed in Him, but I did not surrender to God's authority. That is the essence of repentance. The sinner has rebelled against God and broken His law, and he must repent of this. Repentance is not a change of life; it is a surrender to God and change of direction in the heart.

Repentance is not a complicated thing. It simply means to come to Jesus, but when you turn to Jesus you have your back to the old life. It is like a man and marriage. He receives one woman as his spouse, and he has his back to all other women. Jesus taught that it is impossible to have two masters (Mt. 6:24).

Two great biblical examples of repentance are the Prodigal Son (Lu. 15:17-19) and the idolaters at Thessalonica (1 Th. 1:9).

We deal with how to teach repentance in the evangelistic course Sowing and Reaping, which is available from Way of Life Literature.

Don't pressure them.

The parent/teacher must be careful not to pressure the children. Children are so easily manipulated, and pressure can happen even when the adult thinks he is avoiding it. One grandfather told me how he keeps a record of his grandchildren's professions of faith in Christ in a notebook, and he shows it to the other grandchildren and asks, "When will I be able to add you name to my book?" This could be a great pressure in a child's mind, because he or she wants to please granddad and wants to go to heaven.

Invitations given in Sunday Schools and youth meetings can put undue pressure on children. I responded to an invitation at a Vacation Bible School because other kids were responding. Unwise, manipulative invitations have caused a world of harm and confusion. At the very least, children should be asked to stay behind so they show that they are serious. One missionary says, "In dealing with children in an invitation, we often ask them to stay behind if they want to talk to someone. Children will easily raise a hand for many reasons. But a child who is willing to stay behind or make some kind of an effort to speak to someone is much more serious."

It is better for parents and teachers to leave this important matter in the Lord's capable hands as they pray earnestly for Him to perform the work of salvation in the children's hearts. The Lord can and will reveal himself to each child as He did to Samuel (1 Sa. 3).

Discipline them.

> "Withhold not correction from the child: for if thou beatest him with the rod, he shall not die. Thou shalt beat him with the rod, and shalt deliver his soul from hell" (Proverbs 23:13-14).

God's Word ties the proper discipline of a child directly together with the salvation of his or her soul. One reason for this is that proper discipline teaches the child a proper fear and respect of authority, which in turn leads to the fear of God. Pastor Allen asks, "If children don't respect parent's authority, who stand as God ordained police in the home, how will they ever respect the God whom the parents represent?" Also proper discipline teaches the child about law and sin and punishment, which are fundamental principles of the gospel. Further, the parent's love and mercy in the midst of discipline instructs the child about God's love for sinners.

In this light, we can see more clearly why the Bible says that the parent who "spares the rod" and lets the child get away with disobedience and rebellion hates the child (Pr. 13:24).

Pray, pray, pray (Jas. 5:16).

Nothing is more important in the evangelism of our children and grandchildren than effectual prayer. My maternal grandmother was a prayer warrior, and her prayers were doubtless instrumental in my conversion. She taught me three "secrets" of answered prayer:

Persistence (Lu. 18:1).

Fasting (Mt. 17:21). There is a study on fasting in our *One Year Discipleship Course*.

Prayer partners. Paul taught the importance of this by his frequent, earnest requests for prayer (Ro. 15:30; Eph. 6:19; Col. 4:3; 1 Th. 5:25; 2 Th. 3:1). Your first prayer partner should be your husband or wife; pray together for each of your children from the time before they are born; don't keep problems to yourself; that is often an act of pride, because we don't want others to know of our imperfections; ask Christian friends to pray for you; be faithful to prayer meeting and ask the church to pray for your situation.

Look for the convicting, drawing work of the Holy Spirit (Joh. 12:32; 16:7-11).

Salvation is a supernatural work of God. There is no salvation apart from a convicting, enlightening, drawing work of God. The sinner must respond to the Spirit's wooing, but there is no salvation apart from the wooing. The soul winner's job is to look for the Spirit's work and help the sinner understand it and respond properly to it.

If the child shows a persistent desire to be saved (not a mere passing interest), explain how he can be saved and let him call on the Lord in his own way. Missionary Jeremy Johnson describes his dealing with his oldest son: "Our oldest boy had a lot of questions about salvation just after he turned five. When we were back to the States on a furlough, he claimed to make a decision for salvation after a church service, but there was no real change in his life. He quickly changed his mind about having made that decision and actually verbalized his refusal to be saved because he did not want to get baptized. (He was not confusing it as part of salvation, but he did know that if he got saved the next step in obeying Christ is to identify in baptism. Since he knew that obeying in one would lead to the other, he refused and would verbalize it in passing conversations.) Almost a year later, shortly after turning six, he put up his hand during a Sunday morning invitation. I did not call him out, planning to talk with him later. He came to me after the service and wanted to talk, and I said we would talk at home. It was a busy Sunday with a meal and fellowship time after the service, a busy afternoon, an evening service, and then I had to transport people home. When I arrived home late that evening, my wife said our oldest son wanted to talk with me. I went to his room, and he was waiting to talk to me about salvation. He was anxious about wanting to be saved, his rebellion against baptism was gone, and he wanted it settled. I told him that if he understood and wanted to be saved, salvation was between him and God and not me and he needed to talk to God. Without hesitation, in the middle of our conversation, he dropped his head and began to pray, asking God to forgive him, to save him, and to help him do right. After he prayed, we talked a little more. I actually tried to shake his belief with some questions. Are you saved now? Why are you saved? What if I don't think you are? The purpose was to see if he understood that salvation was not a decision of words (prayer) but a decision of heart. I explained that only he and God know whether he is saved, because God looks at his heart."

Pastor Kerry Allen says of his fourth daughter after she memorized verses about salvation, "She approached me in tears, and after further questioning, she stated she was afraid of dying without Christ, and going to Hell. She then readily trusted the Lord Jesus Christ as her Saviour, and shows good evidence of it now" (Allen, *How Can I Except Some Man Guide Me?*). Note that she approached him. She showed evidence of conviction.

If a child does profess saving faith in Christ, encourage him or her to seek the Lord and His will (2 Ti. 2:19).

Receiving Christ as Lord and Saviour is not the end of salvation, it is the beginning! (We don't mean to say that salvation is a process; we are simply saying that salvation is a new life, not a mere ritual.) Salvation is a life of walking with and serving Jesus Christ. If a child gets saved, it is time for that child to grow and seek God's will.

Look for scriptural evidence of salvation in the child's life
(Titus 1:16)

We have dealt with evidence of salvation earlier in this chapter.

When looking for evidence, we aren't looking for any kind of sinless perfection. The "old man" is still present in the Christian life. We are simply looking for a new life in Christ evidenced by a new direction.

Let God confirm to the children that they are saved (Ro. 8:15-16; Ga. 4:6).

Don't tell them they are saved. Don't give them a "spiritual birth certificate" like some churches do.

Don't remind them of when they professed Christ when they were little. One grandfather told me how that he writes down the date of his grandchildren's professions of faith and reminds them of it each year. He says, "Each year, I phone them on their salvation date to ask them if they know what important date this is, and then I ask them about their progress in their walk with the Lord since the last year." It is wonderful for a parent/grandparent to inquire about a child's walk with the Lord and to encourage the child in his spiritual life, but it is dangerous for a parent or grandparent to tell a child he is saved or "remind" him that he is saved. That is the Lord's work. Missionary Jeremy Johnson says: "I do not claim to know for certain that either of my older sons are saved. I believe that Scripture clearly teaches that children can be saved and that God wants them to be. We have seen changes in their lives, a desire and concern for others to be saved, and a brokenness over sin. We do not ever tell them they are saved. When asking them about salvation, we do not point to a time or place. We look for what they remember. Both of them, although they cannot remember the exact day (month/day/year), will immediately go to the circumstances and events happening on that day, reminding us of when and where they made that choice. We do not go over this often trying to get them to memorize it. Children are not saved because of their parents' memory or their parents' leading; they are saved when they make a choice in their hearts, and if they do they will remember it on their own. If they ever come to me with doubts, I will try to prayerfully help them examine why, but I will not tell them I know they are saved. Only God knows their hearts."

If the child later expresses doubt about salvation, encourage him to settle it.

A great many young people who grow up in Christian homes make two professions of faith in Christ, one when they are young and another when they reach maturity.

Don't baptize a young child.

There is no example of the baptism of a young child in Scripture.

How old should a child be before he is baptized? He should be old enough to do what we see in Acts 2:41-42, which is to receive the gospel gladly and "to continue steadfastly in the apostles' doctrine and fellowship, and in breaking of bread, and in prayers."

The Jewish custom is to receive a boy into the full privileges of the synagogue at age 13. This is called bar mitzvah, which means "son of the covenant." At this point, the boy can read the Scriptures publicly.

In my estimation, this would be the very youngest age for baptism, but even that is probably too young.

As for the timing of baptism, the main thing to look for is the sure fruit of salvation. If a teenager demonstrates a changed life, if he has a love for God's Word and doesn't have to be prodded to read and study the Bible, if he has a godly attitude toward authority, if he loves to talk about spiritual things, if he is making wise decisions of his own accord, then he is old enough to be baptized, because he is showing the fruit of true salvation.

If a teenager shows the evidence found in Acts 2:42 and loves Bible doctrine and spiritual fellowship and breaking of bread and prayers, then we have a sound biblical basis for baptizing him.

Children should not be discouraged from believing in Christ savingly, but they aren't old enough to be baptized and to function as church members. If they do repent and trust Christ savingly, it doesn't hurt them to wait until they are old enough to fit the description of Acts 2:41-42, since baptism doesn't save them.

> "At a time when he is too young to choose his clothes for himself, at a time when he is too young to choose a life's

vocation, at a time when he is too young to serve on a church committee, at a time when he is really too young to vote intelligently on business matters in the church, at a time when he is not considered legally responsible by any agency in the community, there has been a tendency to feel that he is sufficiently responsible to make a life-binding, permanent-type decision concerning his relationship to Christ and his church. If we are unwilling to feel that the child is capable of making lesser decisions, how can we justify our confidence in the efficacy of this greater decision at this age?" (Kenneth Chafin, "Evangelism and the Child," Review and Expositor 60, no. 2, 1963).

"The question is not whether a five-year-old or a ten-year-old can savingly confess Christ. The question is one of the congregation's ability to discern. The large number of nominal Christians and rebaptisms in Southern Baptist churches seems to answer the question clearly in the negative. We are not meant to be able to fully distinguish a child's love and trust in God, from their love and trust in adults, especially their own parents. That grows up over time, as the distinct outlines of the young adult's life comes into place as he or she feels the pull of the world, the flesh, and the Devil and yet follows Christ. Baptists around the world know this; Baptists here in America used to know this. We can again" (Restoring Integrity in Baptist Churches, Kindle loc. 643).

"So, what is the proper response when your eight-year-old daughter [says she has trusted Jesus as Saviour?] Well, the last thing you want to do is throw cold water on her. Remember, she is very sincere in what she believes. She believes in Jesus and she believes the Gospel. If she expresses faith in Christ this is something in which you should encourage her. Say something like, 'That's wonderful, sweetheart! I'm so thankful that you are growing in your understanding of who Jesus is and what He did for us. I pray for you every day that God will draw you to Him. I want us to continue to learn and grow together.' Encourage her in her desire to learn more about the Gospel. ... God made children to be especially teachable and malleable for a reason. This is the season of their lives in which you will have the most influence over what they will believe as they mature. It is your sacred duty as a parent to teach them the Scriptures and encourage them to continue to grow in their knowledge of Jesus Christ and His Gospel. ... However, wait on her baptism. Tell her, 'Sweetheart, baptism is a very, very serious commitment, and when we look at the Scriptures, the only people who were baptized were adults. Your Mom and I love you very much, and we want what is best for you. We want to follow the Scriptures to the very best of our ability. We are going to wait on your baptism until you are older, just like those who were baptized in the Bible. And when you are older, your baptism will be much more meaningful to you than it would be right now" (Justin Peters, Do Not Hinder Them, pp. 104, 105).

In this chapter we have seen that building a New Testament discipling church requires great caution about salvation. We need to understand the evidence of salvation and look for it by God's wisdom.

We have seen that Southern Baptists became careless about salvation in the early 20th century.

Prior to the 1970s, Independent Baptists were more careful about salvation and believed in life-changing repentance.

But through the influence of Jack Hyles and The Sword of the Lord, repentance was redefined and evangelism was cheapened into a shallow salesmanship routine. It appears that the motive was to justify the program of "big-ism."

The result of this change in method and message of evangelism was to create very weak, mixed multitude churches, and this is a major reason why these churches have not stood the test of time. In our experience, most of them have either died or are in the process of dying or are on the road to a worldly contemporary philosophy.

A Discipling Church Guards the Door to Membership

Outline
Regenerate Membership is an Ancient Baptist Principle
Spurgeon's Care in Receiving Members
Our Standards for Church Membership
Caution and Patience

This chapter is connected intimately with the previous chapter, "A Discipling Church Begins with Caution about Salvation."

A regenerate church membership is an ancient Baptist principle based on clear biblical teaching, and it was practiced by most Baptist churches in America until the beginning of the 20th century.

The Somerset Confession of 1656 stated,

> "In admitting of members into the church of Christ, it is the duty of the church, and ministers whom it concerns, in faithfulness to God, **that they be careful they receive none but such as do make forth evident demonstration of the new birth**, and the work of faith with power."

The Charleston *Summary of Church Discipline* of 1774 said,

> "The temple of the Lord is not to be built with dead but living materials, 1 Pe. 2:5. None have a right to church membership but such as Christ will own as his sincere followers at the last decisive day, whatever pretensions they may make to an interest in his favor, Mt. 7:22, 23. ... **None are fit materials of a gospel church, without having first experienced an entire change of nature, Mt. 18:3.** ... By nature we are dead in trespasses and sins, and **Christ does not place such dead materials in his spiritual building.** It is certain the Ephesian church was not composed of such materials, Eph. 2:1. ... The members of the church at Colosse are denominated not only saints, but faithful brethren in Christ, Col. 1:2, or true believers in him. None but such have a right to ordinances, Acts 8:37. Without faith none discern the Lord's body in the

Supper, and consequently must eat and drink unworthily, 1 Co. 11:29. ... Their lives and conversations ought to be such as becometh the gospel of Christ, Php. 1:27; that is holy, just, and upright, Psalm 15:1, 2; **if their practice contradicts their profession they are not to be admitted to church membership.** ... Persons making application are to be admitted into the communion of a church by the common suffrage of its members; being first satisfied that they have the qualifications laid down in the preceding section; **for which purpose candidates must come under examination before the church; and if it should happen that they do not give satisfaction, they should be set aside until a more satisfactory profession is made** 1 Ti. 6:12."

In 1859, Edward Hiscox wrote,

> "**Church members are supposed to be regenerate persons** bearing the image and cherishing the spirit of Christ, in whom the peace of God rules, and who walk and work in the unity of the Spirit, and the bond of peace'" (*The Standard Manual for Baptist Churches*).

In 1867, J.M. Pendleton's influential *Church Manual Designed for the Use of Baptist Churches* emphasized a regenerate church membership:

> "**Let it never be forgotten that the only suitable materials of which to construct a church of Christ, so far as spiritual qualifications are concerned, are regenerate, penitent, believing persons. To make use of other materials is to subvert the fundamental principles of church organization.** It is to destroy the kingdom of Christ; for how can there be a kingdom without such subjects as the King requires? ... **Great care should be exercised in receiving members.** ... There is much danger of this, especially in times of religious excitement. Pastors should positively assure themselves that those who are received for baptism have felt themselves to be guilty, ruined, helpless sinners, justly condemned by God's holy law; and under a sense of their lost condition have trusted in Christ for salvation" (Pendleton, *Church Manual*, 1867).

In 1874, William Williams wrote,

> "**The members of the apostolic churches were all converted persons, or supposed to be converted**. In the various epistles they are addressed as 'saints,' 'faithful brethren,' 'the sons of God,' sanctified in Christ Jesus. The many exhortations to a godly life and a holy conversation presume that they are 'new creatures in Christ Jesus' ... **This--a converted church membership, a membership composed only of persons who are believed to have exercised personal repentance and faith--is, of all others, the most important peculiarity that characterized the apostolic organization of the church**" Williams, *Apostolic Church Polity*, 1874).

At the Baptist World Conference in 1905, J.D. Freeman said,

> "**The principle of regenerate Church membership more than anything else, marks our distinctiveness in the world today**. ... both logic and experience teach its importance as a safeguard to the Church from intrusion of unregenerate life" ("Baptists and a Regenerate Church Membership," *Review and Expositor*, Spring 1963).

As we saw in the chapter "The Disappearance of Discipling Churches," the New Testament principle of a regenerate membership was destroyed in ancient times by the practice of infant baptism and the sacramental gospel (faith in Christ plus sacraments and good works). In the early centuries of the church age, churches became filled with unregenerate members who were brought in by infant baptism. This practice became a fundamental element of the Roman Catholic Church, and most Protestants brought this error with them when they departed from Rome.

For example, the Church of England baptized infants with the following prayer by the officiating minister:

> "We yield thee hearty thanks, most merciful Father, that it hath pleased thee to regenerate this infant with thy Holy Spirit, to receive him for thine own child by adoption, and to incorporate him into thy holy church."

So long as the baptized person attended church and did not live a scandalous life, he was accepted as a true Christian.

When a baptized person died, so long as he had not been excommunicated or committed suicide, the minister said at the funeral:

"Forasmuch as it hath pleased Almighty God, of his great mercy, to take unto himself the soul of our dear brother here departed, therefore we commit his body to the ground; earth to earth, ashes to ashes, dust to dust; in sure and certain hope of the resurrection to eternal life, through Jesus Christ."

This practice destroyed the power of the church because it filled it with unregenerate people, from the Sunday School to the Pulpit.

Regenerate church membership is being corrupted in Baptist churches today, not by infant baptism and a sacramental gospel, but by shallow evangelism and hastiness and carelessness in receiving members. This is usually done in the pragmatic rush to have a bigger church regardless of its spiritual health.

Today, the unregenerate church member doesn't trust his infant baptism and confirmation; he trusts his "sinner's prayer."

As we saw in "A Discipling Church Begins with Caution about Salvation," the Southern Baptist Convention has been called "an unregenerate denomination" because in a typical SBC congregation only 30% of the members attend Sunday morning services and only 12% "participate in any further aspect of church life."

The same has been true of a large number of Independent Baptist churches of the past 50 years.

If we love God's Word, we will want a church of disciples, not a mixed multitude. We will, therefore, be very careful about receiving members, as this is the most fundamental thing in building a spiritual church.

In his book on church discipline, James Crumpton divided discipline into constructive church discipline, corrective church discipline, and punitive church discipline, and he said that constructive church discipline begins with care in receiving members.

> "**A very important measure in constructive church discipline is that of exercising care in receiving members into the church. The devil could tuck his horns behind his ears, walk down the aisle of the average church, ask for membership, and be received without one dissenting vote.** ... To bring the person seeking membership in one of the local churches of our Lord Jesus Christ face to face with what church membership really means is for his good, the

good of the church, and the glory of the Saviour. Many churches receive members, never telling them that they have a covenant. With too many of our day, church membership has degenerated into a trivial ceremony that has absolutely no place of value or lasting interest in their lives. Folk by the hundreds and thousands join the church yet never support it with their testimony, time, money, talents, presence, influence, labor, or prayers. Therefore, the purpose of constructive church discipline is to so change this sad state of affairs that being a church member will really have a vital meaning" (James Crumpton, *New Testament Church Discipline*).

Charles Spurgeon's Care in Receiving Members

Charles H. Spurgeon began pastoring the Metropolitan Tabernacle of London, England, in 1854 at age 20, and was the senior pastor until his death in 1892. His superlative preaching drew massive crowds, and the church grew from "a handful" to a membership of over 5,300.

The church was very cautious in receiving members. Following is an account from *Wonders of Grace: Original testimonies of converts during Spurgeon's early years*, compiled by Hannah Wyncoll, copyright 2016 by Wakeman Trust:

> "On a weeknight evening each week church elders would see enquirers at the Tabernacle. For each one they would write an account of their spiritual journey. Often the discernment they exercised can be seen in the advice given, and in further visits over weeks or months until they were sure that the enquirer was truly saved. The core of the testimony would need to show that the person was relying only on the blood of Christ for salvation. They would also be asked if they understood the need for the imputed righteousness of Christ. They would talk about the doctrines of grace and whether they would-be member was looking only to Christ rather than their own merit. If the applicant was not quite clear on some things, the elders might give further questions to be answered, Bible passages to be read and prayed over, or as one elder put it, he 'prescribed her some pills of precious promise with a little draught of sympathetic experience to wash them down.' They might be given the *Baptist Confession of Faith* to study, or be

directed to attend one of the Bible classes to help them further. ...

"*The Sword and the Trowel of 1865* says that elders look for four things: Tenderness of conscience, attachment to the means of grace, desire to come out of the world, and deep interest in the unconverted.

"If satisfied, an interviewing elder would give a card, with the number matching the report, for the enquirer to see C.H. Spurgeon...

"Spurgeon would spend several hours every Tuesday afternoon seeing many such people, taking a brief interval to compare notes with his elders. He would then appoint an elder or deacon to visit to ensure the applicant was living a consistent, godly life at home. Attendance at as many meetings as possible on Sundays and during the week was seen as a sign of true Christian life. Many were in service and had very little free time away from their work, but their new Christian instinct should be seen--to assembly together whenever possible. ...

"[A] theme which shines out distinctly in the vast majority of records is the forsaking of worldliness at conversion. All is changed for the convert. Worldly pleasures are given up and the life devoted to Christ and his people from that time on. Pursuits such as the penny theater, public houses, music parties, the use of popular songs, and gambling are spoken of repeatedly as holing no pleasure for the new believer. The markedly different life of believers is often mentioned as instrumental in bringing others to enquire into Christian things. The change was not limited to church attendance, but extended to all areas of life."

Our Standards for Church Membership

Acts 2 gives us the preeminent biblical example for church membership.

"Then they that gladly received his word were baptized: and the same day there were added *unto them* about three thousand souls. And they continued stedfastly in the apostles' doctrine and fellowship, and in breaking of bread, and in prayers" (Acts 2:41-42).

We don't believe that this biblical pattern can be ignored or weakened. People with a shaky testimony of salvation and who are not faithful after the fashion of the members at the church of Jerusalem are not qualified to be church members.

Following are the things we look for in receiving members into our church:

1. A clear testimony of salvation and a changed life to back it up, whether joining by profession and baptism or from another church.

Those who joined the church at Jerusalem on the day of Pentecost had gladly received the gospel. There was no manipulation or coercion. Their salvation was clear and was evidenced by the fact that they publicly confessed Jesus as the Christ before an antagonistic Jewish nation and by the fact that they continued in the things of Christ.

In seeking to maintain a regenerate church membership, we are following the Bible and we are following in the footsteps of sound Bible-believing churches through the church age. Consider the ancient Waldensians:

> "We believe that in the ordinance of baptism the water is the visible and external sign, which represents to us that which, by virtue of God's invisible operation, is within us--namely, the renovation of our minds, and the mortification of our members through [the faith of] Jesus Christ. And by this ordinance we are received into the holy congregation of God's people, previously professing and DECLARING OUR FAITH AND CHANGE OF LIFE" (Third Waldensian Confession of Faith, AD 1544).

We, too, look for the evidence of a changed life. We look for a life-changing conversion experience, as we have discussed in the chapter "A Discipling Church Begins with Caution about Salvation."

We don't look for any kind of sinless perfection or "100% lordship" or anything like that. We simply look for salvation, believing that salvation is a miraculous, life-changing thing.

We want to see the reality of the following Scriptures in the lives of those we baptize and receive into membership:

> "Therefore if any man *be* in Christ, *he is* a new creature: old things are passed away; behold, all things are become new" (2 Co. 5:17).
>
> "Nevertheless the foundation of God standeth sure, having this seal, The Lord knoweth them that are his. And, Let every one that nameth the name of Christ depart from iniquity" (2 Ti. 2:19).
>
> "And hereby we do know that we know him, if we keep his commandments. He that saith, I know him, and keepeth not his commandments, is a liar, and the truth is not in him" (1 John 2:3-4).

We simply look for the type of salvation that we see in every case in the New Testament, whether it be the woman at the well, Zacchaeus, Cornelius, the Ethiopian Eunuch, the Philippian jailer, or Lydia.

We would gladly and readily accept into our membership *any* individual described in the New Testament as a saved person. As soon as we see this type of salvation, we proceed to baptize the individual.

We don't want to receive an empty profession, because Scripture warns about that in the plainest manner:

> "They profess that they know God; but in works they deny *him*, being abominable, and disobedient, and unto every good work reprobate" (Titus 1:16).

We do not allow a person to join our church if he is still living in gross sin, such as fornication, adultery, homosexuality, drunkenness, drug abuse, theft, extortion, and idolatry.

It would be confusion to bring an individual into membership who is committing the type of sin that should be the subject of discipline.

> "But now I have written unto you not to keep company, if any man that is called a brother be a fornicator, or covetous, or an idolater, or a railer, or a drunkard, or an extortioner; with such an one no not to eat" (1 Co. 5:11).

Last year a man wanted to join our church by baptism, but he owns a liquor store and he refused to promise that he would find a way to give it up. We did not baptize him, and subsequently he has demonstrated that he probably is not yet saved.

2. Scriptural baptism (Acts 2:41)

Scriptural baptism is baptism by immersion as a public testimony of one's saving faith in Jesus Christ.

If a person was baptized before he was saved, that is not scriptural baptism.

If a person was baptized by sprinkling or pouring, that is not scriptural baptism, because it is not a picture of the death, burial, and resurrection of Christ (Ro. 6:3-4).

If a person was baptized by a church with an unsound gospel or otherwise identifies itself as an unscriptural church, that is not scriptural baptism. For example, we do not receive baptisms performed by Pentecostal or charismatic churches or other churches that do not believe in eternal security. Not believing in eternal security is to pervert the gospel of the grace of Christ.

3. Faithfulness ("continued steadfastly" Acts 2:42)

We don't receive an individual into the church's membership until he or she has *demonstrated* faithfulness to the services and to the general "program" of the church.

One man wanted to join our church from another church, a weaker church, because he wanted his children to serve the Lord and he had seen good fruit in our young people. But he didn't want to attend all of the services at our four-day missions conferences. These are held during the largest Hindu festival of the year, and each year he had made a lot of money selling various things from his shop at that time. He sought advice from a preacher who is a close friend of our church, and the preacher said, "If you don't want to be faithful, you need to stay at the weaker church." He determined to obey God's Word (Heb. 10:25); we received him into the membership; and he has been perfectly faithful ever since.

4. Agreement in doctrine and practice (1 Co. 1:10)

We require that the individual read our covenant, including read every Scripture that is referenced, and acknowledge agreement with it 100%.

Our church covenant is very extensive. See the chapter "A Sample Church Covenant."

We have had people attend faithfully for a long time without joining, because they don't agree with everything we hold in our church covenant. Usually it is something having to do with separation.

Non-members are welcome to attend and benefit from our church's ministry, as long as they don't cause trouble, and we do our best to minister to them as we do to our own members, but they cannot partake in the Lord's Supper, participate in church business, or hold any type of ministry.

We are planning to require the members to read the covenant again once a year as individuals and families, to discuss the covenant and write down questions, and we will have a business meeting to answer the questions. The church will use this occasion to make any desired adjustments to the covenant. Unlike the Bible, our church covenant is not infallible and not "settled in heaven."

5. Submission to authority (Heb. 13:17)

God requires submission to authority, and so should the church.

We don't want to receive rebels into our church family, whether they are young or old. If we detect stubbornness toward authority, we hold off on receiving that individual as a member.

Caution and Patience

We are careful and patient when it comes to baptism and church membership.

Before an individual is baptized and joins our church, he must be known to us, meaning we don't baptize and receive strangers. We want to know the testimony and life of the individual.

When we believe that a person we have been working with is saved, we invite him to go through a short baptismal class that deals with salvation and the purpose of baptism.

After that, the individual appears before the church leaders and their wives to give his testimony and to answer any questions we might have. Remember, these are people we already know.

If we don't have 100% agreement among the leaders, we don't baptize the person or receive him into membership. We kindly ask him to wait until the next baptism so that things will be clear in everyone's mind. It is harmful to the individual and the church to baptize someone who isn't saved.

Most recently, for example, we interviewed four and baptized three. Prior to that, we interviewed 15 and baptized 13.

This practice is in accordance with old Baptist churches, as witnessed by David Benedict who traveled nearly 7,000 miles on horseback in the early 19th century to write a history of the churches of his day.

Benedict's history frequently mentions the caution with which the churches received members. They had a custom called "hearing the experience" which preceded baptism. The following, for example, is a description of a revival that took place in 1807 in Argyle, Nova Scotia:

> "Twenty-four have TOLD THEIR EXPERIENCES, who are not yet baptized, and a number of others are under hopeful impressions. The work is still going on in this place, and spreading rapidly in different parts of the province" (Benedict, *A General History of the Baptist Denomination*, vol. I, chapter 8, 1813).

Observe how that these churches received members. They required a plain testimony of salvation of those who would be baptized. They required that the professors "tell their experiences" before the church. It is obvious that they were looking for more than mere lip service. And they did not confuse "hopeful impressions" with genuine salvation. They knew that a person can be very interested in Christ and can be convicted of his sin without being genuinely saved. We see many examples of this in the Gospels, and we have witnessed this type of thing hundreds of times in our own ministry.

After appearing before the church leaders and being accepted for baptism and church membership, the individual is recommended to the church by the leaders. He then gives his testimony to the entire congregation, and afterwards he is baptized and received as a member. We have our baptisms on the same day as the Lord's Supper so new members can take the Lord's Supper as soon as they are baptized.

A large number of Baptist churches are not this careful and would even disagree with our policy, but I can see that our caution in receiving members has made our congregation much stronger spiritually.

Ninety-five percent of our people are totally faithful, including faithful to the prayer meetings. The *vast* majority of our young people who are church members are actively seeking God's will for their lives and separating from the world from the heart.

A Discipling Church Has the Right Leaders

Outline

Right in His Calling
Right in His Testimony
Right in His Family Life
Right in His Walk with Christ and His Devotional Life
Right in His Study Life
Right in His Preaching
Right in the Exercise of Authority
A Biblicist as Opposed to a Pragmatist

A church will never rise higher than its leaders. Pastors set the agenda and spiritual temperature of the church.

The late Lee Roberson said, "Everything rises and falls on leadership."

The importance of the right leadership is seen in the fact that there are two entire chapters of Scripture on this subject, plus portions of others (1 Timothy 3; Titus 1).

Many godly people have written to me about the lack of vision in their churches and serious failings in their churches, but there is little to nothing they can do if the pastors aren't qualified, don't care, are ill informed, and aren't interested in change. They complain of such things as lack of serious Bible training, preaching with little substance, lack of discipline, weak standards for workers, partiality toward family members, worldly youth leaders, prayerlessness, carelessness about music, and shallow evangelism.

We teach people how to be good church members and how to submit to pastoral authority in a scriptural way (e.g., *Keys to Fruitful Church Membership* and *The Pastor's Authority and the Church Member's Responsibility,* both of which are available as free eBooks from www.wayoflife.org), but this is a difficult matter when the pastors aren't biblically strong.

Consider some ways that the pastor must be right in his life and ministry:

Right in His Calling

I suspect that many Baptist pastors aren't called of God, or at the least they haven't been properly prepared for the ministry.

This is no light matter. God's Word warns, "My brethren, be not many masters, knowing that we shall receive the greater condemnation" (James 3:1). Greater responsibility means greater judgment. A church leader must answer to God, not only for his own life and family, but for his entire congregation or sphere of ministry, whatever that might involve. Even the unbelievers in the community observe church leaders' lives closely and judge Christ and the Bible by these men.

We find a number of tests of calling in Scripture. These can help a man determine if God is calling him to be a pastor, and these can enable churches to examine men before ordination.

1. The test of desire (1 Timothy 3:1)

This speaks of a strong, compelling desire; a passion; a zeal. This verse could also be translated "if a man *reach out to grasp* the office of a bishop" (John Economidis).

Paul speaks of such compulsion in 1 Co. 9:16 when he says, "... for necessity is laid upon me; yea, woe is unto me, if I preach not the gospel!"

Those in Israel who did the work of building the Tabernacle were men "whose hearts stirred them up, to come unto the work to do it" (Ex. 36:2). Likewise, men who lead the churches must be men whose hearts have been divinely stirred for this great task. There must be a divine call. This desire must be more than a mere interest; it must be a passion, a powerful, divine summons to the ministry. It has been said, and rightly so, that if a man can refrain easily from preaching and from church leadership, he should refrain, because God's call to such ministry is attended by a powerful, unmistakable summons. A man might say no to God's call, as Jonah temporarily did, but he will not mistake the call or lightly ignore it!

Charles Spurgeon, in addressing the men in his Pastor's College, warned, "If any student in this room could be content to be a newspaper editor, or a grocer, or a farmer, or a doctor, or a lawyer, or a senator, or a king, in the name of heaven and earth let him go his way ... If on the other hand, you can say that for all the wealth of both the Indies you could not and dare not espouse any other calling so as to be put aside from preaching the gospel of Jesus Christ, then, depend upon it, if other things be equally satisfactory, you have the signs of this apostleship."

This is the type of calling I experienced after I was saved in the summer of 1973. I was consumed with the desire to study the Bible and to pursue God's will. That's all I wanted to do. Immediately I started witnessing to my old friends. Within the first year I started printing my testimony and little booklets containing the spiritual truths I was learning. I was working as a printer at the Florida Citrus Commission in Lakeland, Florida, and I did my work well and had a good testimony on the job, but I wasn't satisfied. I was consumed with the desire to study the Bible and teach and pursue God's calling, and the Lord soon gave me the freedom to do that.

Consider Psalm 37:4 - "Delight thyself also in the LORD; and he shall give thee the desires of thine heart."

We see that God's guidance is for those who delight in Him. The verse does not say that whatever an individual desires he will have. Desire itself is not evidence of God's leading and calling, because there are many wrong desires in a man's heart. The promise is for those who delight in the Lord, those who love the Lord walk with Him in sweet fellowship and love His Word and are pursuing His holy will.

To those who love Him, God imparts the right desires. He imparts His will into that individual's life in the form of right desires, then He fulfills those desires.

To delight in the Lord is a passionate thing. It is not a casual, half-hearted thing. Lukewarm is not delight. Delight is first love passion (Re. 2).

Delight in the Lord is fed by God's Word. Through Scripture the mind is renewed (Ro. 12:1-2) so that we find the mind of Christ (1 Co. 2:15-16). We see this in Psalm 1. Delight in the Lord is the man who separates from evil and error because he meditates in God's Word day and night.

2. The test of life (1 Timothy 3; Titus 1)

Desire is important, but this, in itself, is not enough. The individual's life must also meet the requirements of the calling.

Some people who desire to be pastors, deacons, or missionaries are deceived about God's call. They feel strongly that God is calling them to that work, but it is obvious that He is not, because God would not give detailed standards for elders and deacons, then ignore His own standards and call unqualified people.

Consider some examples of how the test of life restricts the calling:

If a woman, for example, feels God is calling her to be a pastor or deacon, she is wrong, because the Bible says plainly that this is a man's work.

If a man has a poor reputation in his community, or is given to wine, or has an angry, combative spirit, or loves money, or does not have faithful children and a good home life, or has more than one wife, etc.,--he can be certain that God does not want him in the pastorate.

In 1980, I was invited to teach a group of pastors in Nepal in an all-day Bible conference, and I chose the book of Titus as my text. After we had gone through the standards for pastors in chapter one, I was informed that one of the men had three wives. He maintained three different families on three different properties that he owned and he visited them on a sort of circuit. I told the national pastors that this man could not be a pastor because of his marital status. He spoke up and said that he knew that God had called him to pastor because he had a vision. The entire group of men chose to ignore the clear teaching of the Bible in favor of the man's alleged "vision"!

We would note here that the call to preach is not necessarily the same as the call to pastor. A man can preach in many ways without being a pastor: in the highways and byways, in the jails and nursing homes, on the street corners and from house to house, in a bus ministry, etc. Men who are not qualified to be a pastor or deacon can still preach the Word of God in many ways if they are faithful to Jesus Christ.

3. The test of ability (Titus 1:9-11)

When God calls, He equips. He will not call someone to do something without giving that person the ability to do it. When the Lord wanted the tabernacle built in the time of Moses, He prepared men for this work.

"See, I have called by name Bezaleel the son of Uri, the son of Hur, of the tribe of Judah. And I have filled him with the spirit of God, in wisdom, and in understanding, and in knowledge, and in all manner of workmanship" (Exodus 31:2-3).

We see here the main aspects of God's call for special service. First, it was an individual call. God called Bezaleel, the son of Uri, the son of Hur. Second, it was a call to a particular work. Third, the call was accompanied by the ability to perform that work.

It is true that God loves to use the weak things of this world for His service. In this way Jesus Christ receives the glory. God often calls men to preach who seem unlikely candidates by man's natural standards. He will not, though, call a man to be a pastor who cannot do the work of a pastor.

No man without such ability is qualified to be a pastor, even if he has a strong desire and a good Christian life and testimony. Such a man should heed Romans 12:3 - "For I say, through the grace given unto me, to every man that is among you, not to think of himself more highly than he ought to think; but to think soberly, according as God hath dealt to every man the measure of faith."

Consider some of the things the pastor must be able to do:

The pastor must be able to feed and shepherd the Lord's sheep (1 Peter 5:1-2). He must be apt to teach God's Word (1 Ti. 3:2). He must be able to preach God's Word effectively (2 Ti. 4:2). He must be able to teach all the counsel of God (Acts 20:27). The man called to be a pastor must, therefore, be able to read and study well enough to do this work. The qualified pastor is a studious man, a man who "labours in the word of God and doctrine" (1 Ti. 5:17). He must be a serious student of God's Word (2 Ti. 2:15). He must have the spiritual discernment to understand people and to deal with them in a wise way.

The pastor must be able to make disciples by teaching the believers "to observe all things" (Mt. 28:20). This involves more than teaching facts. It involves teaching how to walk with Christ, how to live the Christian life, how to do the work of the ministry.

The pastor must be able to take oversight of the church. He must have the ability to lead and oversee and supervise all areas of church life and ministry (Acts 20:28; 1 Peter 5:2; Hebrews 13:17). The qualified pastor is a leader, a manager, an overseer, a supervisor. He must have leading ability and planning ability. He should be a man of ideas. He has to lead the church in accomplishing everything Christ has commanded. He has to take God's commands and apply them to his cultural setting and figure out the best way to do God's work in that particular situation. He isn't a man who blindly follows tradition. That is not a leader. Yet many pastors don't ever rethink things. They don't analyze the services and programs to see if things could be done better.

The pastor must be able to protect Christians from error (Titus 1:9-13; Acts 20:28-30). This includes rebuking when necessary (Titus 1:13). It requires the exercise of discipline (Titus 3:9-11). It requires the courage to confront sin and error. It requires spiritual discernment to know true believers from false (Titus 1:16). The qualified pastor is the opposite of the simple man who "believeth every word" (Pr. 14:15). The pastor must have keen doctrinal and spiritual discernment and a shepherd's heart for protecting and watching over the sheep. He must be informed about any danger that his church faces, such as New Evangelicalism, charismaticism, ecumenism, contemplative prayer, and contemporary music, and he must be able to protect the church from such things.

The pastor must be able to train Christian workers (2 Ti. 2:2). A qualified pastor is a serious educator.

The man who lacks the ability to do the work of a pastor is not qualified to be a pastor, even if he has a good Christian life and testimony and even if he has the ability to do *some* of the work of a pastor.

There are many good Christian men who can even preach and teach, but they don't have the full gifting to be pastors. They might not be strong enough to exercise discipline as they should. They might not have the spiritual wisdom to deal with people effectually in a pastoral way. They might not be good leaders.

4. The test of recognition (Acts 13:1-3)

When God called Paul and Barnabas to a particular missionary work, their church recognized that call. This is an important test. The normal Bible pattern is for an individual's call to be recognized by the church that knows him best. The same was true when Timothy was called to accompany Paul on his journeys (Acts 16:1-3).

There will be occasions when a church is controlled by unsaved or carnal men and that church's judgment might be wrong.

Consider this statement by Charles Spurgeon to the preachers in his Bible college:

> "Considerable weight is to be given to the judgment of men and women who live near to God, and in most instances their verdict will not be a mistaken one. *Yet this appeal is not final nor infallible, and is only to be estimated in proportion to the intelligence and piety of those consulted.* I remember well how that a godly Christian woman tried to dissuade me from preaching, but her opinion was outweighed by the judgment of persons of wider experience ... I have noted that you students, as a body, in your judgment of one another, are seldom if ever wrong. There has hardly ever been a case when the general opinion of the entire college concerning a brother has been wrong. Meeting as you do in class, in prayer, in conversation, and in various religious engagements, you gauge each other. And a wise man will be slow to set aside the verdict of the house" (C.H. Spurgeon, *Lectures to My Students*).

As Spurgeon noted, there are exceptions to this rule. When a church is controlled by unsaved or carnal men, the church's judgment will be wrong. There have been instances when God called a man or woman to a certain work, but the church refused to recognize the call or support the ministry. In fact, there are examples of this in the Bible.

- Jesus was rejected by His own people (Joh. 1:11).
- Paul was rejected by the Galatians and by some in the Corinthian church (Ga. 4:15-17; 1 Co. 9:1; 2 Co. 6:11-12; 3:1).
- John and other men of God were rejected by the proud Diotrephes (3 Joh. 9-10).

5. The test of proving (1 Timothy 3:10; 2 Corinthians 8:22)

The Scriptures show that churches must be careful in ordination. Men must demonstrate their zeal and faithfulness *before* ordination, not *by* ordination.

This is true for every position of service in the church. The believer should show by his godly manner of life that he is qualified for a special place of service, regardless of how "lowly."

A man will show by his life and zeal whether he is called. The man who is called of God will serve the Lord in that capacity, or at least prepare for serving, without pay and without having a "position."

The Scriptures warn about hasty ordinations (1 Ti. 5:22). Timothy was warned to be cautious about ordaining men to positions of leadership. The context of 1 Timothy 5:17-25 concerns leaders in the church. By laying on of hands, those performing the ordination are testifying publicly that they believe God has called the person being ordained. Ordination is a recognition of a divine call. Those performing the ordination are identifying themselves with the one being ordained. If the church makes a mistake because of hastiness and failure to prove the person by God's standards, they become partaker of the sins of the man wrongly ordained.

6. The test of fruit

The Bible emphasizes the importance of fruit (Psalm 1:1-3).

Note that the fruit is personal and individual ("his fruit"). Fruit is different for different people. We have different gifts and callings, but there will be fruit.

If you are called to a certain ministry, you should have some fruit, some success, some evidence. The blessing of God should be evident in some tangible way. "... make full proof of thy ministry" (2 Ti. 4:5).

There are pastors who are never successful in the ministry. In fact, there are pastors who only kill churches. They always have an excuse for their failures, and the excuse might sound reasonable, but there should be some evident blessing and fruit if a man is called of God.

Many men simply don't have the ability to do the work of the pastorate. They are good Christian men. They have a good testimony and a good family, and they love Christ and love the Word of God, but they simply don't have the gifting and wisdom and ability and discernment to lead a church.

One fruit of a pastor should be more pastors. Many pastors never reproduce themselves, never raise up and train more preachers, never start any new churches. After 20 years, there are no more preachers in the church than when his ministry started.

We don't see this type of thing in Scripture. The great missionary church that is put before us in Scripture is Antioch. Paul and Barnabas worked for two years to establish the foundation of that church, and by the time God called them to go out as foreign missionaries, there were many other preachers in the church (Acts 13:1).

Fruit is an important test in all areas of ministry. There are missionaries who never start sound, self-governing, self-supporting, self-propagating churches. There are Sunday School teachers who do not grow their classes either spiritually or numerically. There are song leaders who do not raise the standard and blessing of the church's song service.

A God-called pastor will show evidences of his calling in all of the aforementioned ways: by the test of desire, the test of life, the test of ability, the test of recognition, the test of proving, and the test of fruit.

A man who does not have the biblical evidence of God's calling should be content with doing something other than pastoring. There are many ways to preach without being a pastor. The "call to preach" is not necessarily the call to the pastorate. A man can preach and teach in a Bible College, a jail, a home Bible study, on the streets, etc., without being a pastor.

Churches must be very careful in ordaining men. They must measure men by God's standards, not by human standards. By ordaining the wrong men, they are doing both those men and the churches a disservice, and this business will doubtless be addressed at the judgment seat of Christ.

Right in His Testimony

The pastor must be right in his spiritual and moral testimony.

This is the emphasis of 1 Timothy 3 and Titus 1. The pastor must be blameless and of good behaviour in his testimony. If he is a man of poor character, this will hinder the power of his preaching and teaching. It will hurt the reputation of the church. It will harm the families and especially the youth.

One pastor wrote,

> "In a past church, many young people were hurt due to the fall of the pastor into sin and rebellion. They idolized the

pastor as mentor and friend. We are not to look to the man, but many young people have no defense against this, especially in a Christian school situation. At least four of the girls became pregnant soon after the incident. Two are in church today with their children. Three never married; the one that did is now divorced. One has had three children out of wedlock. Some of the boys became alcoholic and rebellious; some have returned to the Lord and overcome."

Bad pastoral character has been rampant in some circles of Independent Baptist churches (adultery, homosexuality, lying, theft, worldliness), as we have documented in *The Hyles Effect*, which is available as a free eBook from www.wayoflife.org.

Consider some biblical examples of the wrong kind of pastors:

- The lording pastor (Diotrephes, 3 John 9-11) - He is proud rather than humble and Christlike. He treats the church as his private possession rather than the flock of Christ. He is controlling and manipulative after the fashion of a cult leader. He forbids the people to hear preachers that he doesn't like, regardless of whether or not they are sound. He prats against sound preachers, not with gracious words of biblical warning but with malicious words of personal attack.

- The soft pastor (Jer. 23:22) - He doesn't turn the people from evil. He doesn't reprove and rebuke sin and error. He allows the people to live as they please and remain in good standing.

- The devouring pastor (Jer. 23:1)

- The careless, neglecting pastor (Jer. 23:2)

- The profane pastor (Jer. 23:11) - He loves the profane things of the world that are characterized by the lusts of the flesh, the lusts of the eyes, and the pride of life (1 John 2:16).

- The adulterous, lying pastor (Jer. 23:14)

- The light pastor (Jer. 23:32) - His ministry is light and shallow. He isn't serious enough in his preaching and ministry. He is spiritually shallow. He doesn't rebuke sin and error effectively.

Right in His Family Life

The pastor must be right in his family life. This is emphasized in Scripture (1 Ti. 3:4-5; Titus 1:6), and the reason is given.

"For if a man know not how to rule his own house, how shall he take care of the church of God?" (1 Ti. 3:5).

A weakness in a pastor's family life is often reflected throughout the church in weak marriage relationships, weak homes, and rebellious young people.

A pastor who does not have strength in this area cannot effectually help the families be what they should be. He will tend to neglect necessary teaching on the subject. If his own children are rebellious, they will greatly affect the spiritual climate of the congregation.

Right in His Devotional Life

"I commend you to God, and to the word of his grace, which is able to build you up" (Acts 20:32).

"... his delight is in the law of the LORD; and in his law doth he meditate day and night" (Ps. 1:2).

"O how love I thy law! it is my meditation all the day" (Ps. 119:97).

A man's devotional life is his walk with Christ. If the preacher lacks an intimate walk with Christ and is slack in his personal devotional life, in his private time in God's Word, in his private prayers, in meditating on God's Word day and night, he will be lacking in spiritual wisdom and power and passion.

"Many of the pastors I counsel are in serious trouble because of weakness in their devotional life. ... You cannot do the work of the ministry in your own power and be sloppy in your devotional life. Many times the pastors I counsel with have not been reading their Bibles except to get a message" (Terry Coomer, "How to Have a Daily Time with God," For Love of the Family Ministries).

"The need of the hour is for young preachers to get their noses out of contemporary theology books and get their minds into the Word on an in-depth basis, 365 days a year, year in and year out. The Bible must be more than just a source of proof text for preaching. As one saturates his mind with the Word of God, it will begin to soak down into his heart and modify his theology, his behavior, his dedication, his morals, his convictions, and his philosophy of life.

Incidentally, when one so saturates his mind with the Word of God, separation from the world and from apostasy will flow naturally. It is the view of this author the reason many young preachers are weak on separation at whatever level is because they are weak in their absorption of the Word of God. ... The devil is all too happy to see young preachers spending more time in contemporary theology books than in the Book of Books. It is no wonder there are so many defections and failures in the ministry. Furthermore, the devil will happily see to it that a preacher is super busy. ... Some are too busy to spend significant time in the Word. Such are on a collision course with trouble; whether theologically, philosophically, or morally" (David Sorenson, *Broad Is the Way: Fundamentalists Merging into the Evangelical Mainstream*).

The pastor who is weak in his own devotional life will be weak in leading the church in spiritual matters. Things such as intimacy with the Lord, Spirit filling, love of the brethren, and prayer will not be emphasized in his preaching and ministry. And he will lack in the spiritual wisdom necessary to protect the church.

Right in His Study Life

A qualified preacher is a serious student. Following are the biblical characteristics of a preacher who is right in his study life:

- He has been taught (Titus 1:9).
- He is strong enough in God's Word to protect the flock (Titus 1:9-16).
- He is nourished up in good doctrine (1 Ti. 4:6).
- He gives attendance to reading and to doctrine (1 Ti. 4:13).
- He labors in the Word and doctrine (1 Ti. 5:17).
- He is apt to teach; capable of training others (1 Ti. 3:2; 2 Ti. 2:2, 24).
- He labors to rightly divide God's Word (2 Ti. 2:15).
- He preaches God's Word with doctrine (2 Ti. 4:2).

A pastor friend who has been in the ministry for many decades wrote the following to me in 2014:

"I asked a missionary what books he had read lately that were a blessing, and he replied that all he reads is a magazine on running. I fear that Independent Baptists may be the *illiterati* of the 20th and 21st centuries. And the present addiction to iPhones and social media only makes it worse. John Nordman, who worked with Hyles years ago at Hyles Anderson, led the Bible college in Brisbane for some years until the pastor's son did a Schaap on some kids there and the wheels fell off. He sent me their college prospectus one year hoping to get some of our kids, and I wrote him back and asked him why there was not a course on theology. I later found out that Hyles Anderson never allowed theology to be taught because Jack Hyles thought it would turn their students into Calvinists. Some years ago I started asking preachers questions when we sat around talking or when we drove down the road. Questions on what doctrine was especially precious to them at that moment, or what book of the Bible they love the most this week, or what good book they are reading, or which one has helped them grow the most, or what authors are the most challenging to them spiritually, or what they think about this or that verse (and I pick the hardest ones to ask about). If they are driving, I take my Bible and read to them some passage I am meditating on and ask them to explain it to me. Most of them are out of their depth within ten seconds. Some stare at me with open mouth and shake their head. The Presbyterian pastors I know are the most adept at discussing solid Bible doctrine. Most of the Independent Baptist pastors have never read anything deeper than John Rice or Curtis Hutson. We had a missionary here this weekend who tells great stories, but doesn't know ANY solid Bible doctrine."

This preacher said further:

"There is abysmal ignorance concerning the doctrine of Christ, concerning the doctrines of justification, sanctification, and glorification. One of our major problems is that expository preaching is not politically correct in fundamental churches. For a pastor to preach through a book of the Bible is a rare thing. Most of the men I know don't do that because it doesn't draw big crowds and they like fireworks in the pulpit or fairy tales."

A large percentage of the Independent Baptist preaching I have personally heard over the past 43 years has been Pablum (baby food) with no serious exegesis of Scripture and little spiritual depth and content. In my experience, most preachers are not serious students.

The church must be a Bible institute, and the pastors are the head masters, training the church in everything that is necessary to build it up and protect it.

I do not mean that the pastors do all of the preaching and teaching; they must train up preachers and teachers to enlarge the ministry. Pastors should be teachers of teachers.

The preacher must be the example. He can't teach the people to be Bible students unless he shows the way. He can't teach them to put God first in their daily schedule (Mt. 6:33) unless he leads the way.

The preacher must have good study habits. It is impossible to be an effectual student unless you have a daily study schedule and stick to it jealously as much as is humanly possible.

The preacher should have a time and a place for his devotions and study and should get rid of all potential distractions, especially the phone, texting, messaging, and Internet. Turn those things off! I start my daily study time with devotional Bible reading, and I don't use the computer for that because it is too easy to get distracted with other things.

The distraction can be anything. I make sure to close my laptop so I am not distracted by the photos that rotate through my screensaver. One pastor told me that he removed all of the colorful dust jackets from the books in his library because they caught his eye and distracted him.

The preacher should have the habit of writing things down and doing them later. This way, when a distracting thought comes, urging him to do this or that thing, instead of getting sidetracked he jots it down for later and goes on with his study.

The battle against distraction is an ongoing one. This is not a battle that is won once and forgotten. I often find myself slipping in this and allowing myself to be distracted when I should be studying God's Word.

A pastor must teach his people the importance of his study time and exhort them to respect that time and help him guard it. He should explain that there are certain times when he is unavailable except for real emergencies. If they want a godly pastor who has a rich personal devotional life and if they wanted an educated pastor and a rich preaching/teaching ministry, they will understand and respect this.

One preacher said, "I carve out a time away from everything in order to avoid distractions. I notify my wife, and others so that I can get into my study mode. I gather the necessary materials ahead of time. My desk has most, if not all of the resources that I will need or consult. I will have water and peanuts on the desk also so that I don't need to waste time getting up and breaking my concentration. My cell phone is on airplane mode, a no disturbance sign on the door."

I know of a pastor who does some of his study in a back corner of a public library.

There are occasions, of course, when a pastor must interrupt his study schedule, but it should be for a true emergency only. If the preacher allows himself to be at the beck and call of people during his study time, he will get into the bad habit of being hit and miss. The preacher must honor God by honoring God's Word and giving it the right priority in his daily life. In case of emergency, the pastor can make some arrangement for being contacted during his study time. Perhaps the people can call his wife, secretary, or a deacon and inform them of the problem, and they can decide whether or not to inform the pastor at that time or to wait until later.

It is impossible for a pastor who is weak as a Bible student to feed the church properly unless he works especially hard at it. Recently a pastor told me, "Brother Cloud, I am not naturally a good student, but I know that this is a necessary part of the ministry, and I work hard at it." Actually this man puts large numbers of Independent Baptist preachers to shame by his studiousness. Not only is he a diligent student of the Bible, but he is a student of all things necessary for the ministry. He keeps informed about current events and dangers facing his people so he can protect them.

Right in His Preaching

"I charge *thee* therefore before God, and the Lord Jesus Christ, who shall judge the quick and the dead at his appearing and his kingdom; Preach the word; be instant in season, out of season; reprove, rebuke, exhort with all longsuffering and doctrine. For the time will come when they will not endure sound doctrine; but after their own lusts shall they heap to themselves teachers, having itching ears; And they shall turn away *their* ears from the truth, and shall be turned unto fables" (2 Timothy 4:1-4).

In this passage we see the major characteristics of a sound preaching and teaching ministry. Few things are more needed in Bible-believing churches today. A sound preaching/teaching ministry is a major part of producing disciples of Jesus Christ and disciplining the church. It is a major part of building godly homes and raising up youth who know and serve Christ.

In the chapter "A Discipling Church Is Strong in God's Word" we describe the elements of a sound preaching/teaching ministry.

Right in His Exercise of Authority

Pastors have real authority in the church (Heb. 13:17), but Scripture strongly emphasizes that it is a different kind of authority than that exercised by worldly lords.

> "The elders which are among you I exhort, who am also an elder, and a witness of the sufferings of Christ, and also a partaker of the glory that shall be revealed: Feed the flock of God which is among you, taking the oversight thereof, not by constraint, but willingly; not for filthy lucre, but of a ready mind; Neither as being lords over God's heritage, but being ensamples to the flock" (1 Peter 5:1-3).

> "But Jesus called them to him, and saith unto them, Ye know that they which are accounted to rule over the Gentiles exercise lordship over them; and their great ones exercise authority upon them. But so shall it not be among you: but whosoever will be great among you, shall be your minister: And whosoever of you will be the chiefest, shall be servant of all. For even the Son of man came not to be ministered unto, but to minister, and to give his life a ransom for many" (Mark 10:42-45).

Note some of the differences between lordship and pastoring:

Scriptural pastors love the flock and lead by compassion (1 Th. 2:7-8), but lords typically despise compassion. While a pastor has the authority to demand (Titus 2:15), and he *must* demand that the people obey God, it is a different kind of demanding than that of a worldly lord. There is a time to reprove and rebuke, and even to rebuke sharply, but the rebuking must be in the context of teaching, exhorting, challenging, entreating, and beseeching. There is warning, but it must be with tears in the sense of coming from a caring heart (Acts 20:31).

Scriptural pastors lead by example, but lords merely make demands with little or no concern that they must exemplify what they demand (1 Pe. 5:3).

Scriptural pastors know that the flock is not their own, but lords feel that they own the people and thus can control them according to their own desires (1 Pe. 5:2, 3 "flock of God" "God's heritage").

Scriptural pastors care more about the welfare of the saints than their own profit, but lords rule for personal gain and typically are not afraid to abuse the people (1 Pe. 5:2).

Scriptural pastors are humble and do not consider themselves greater than the flock, but lords exalt themselves high above the people. Pastors are over the flock (Heb. 13:17), but they are also among the flock (1 Pe. 5:2). They are to be clothed with humility (1 Pe. 5:5).

Scriptural pastors aim to build up the people and free them to do God's will, but lords want to control the people and hold them down (Eph. 4:11-12; 2 Co. 10:8). The Greek word translated "destruction" in 2 Corinthians 10:8 is elsewhere translated "pulling down" (2 Co. 10:4).

For an extensive study on this subject see *The Pastor's Authority and the Church Membership's Responsibility*, available as a print edition as well as a free eBook edition from www.wayoflife.org.

A Biblicist as Opposed to a Pragmatist

The church that will be standing until Christ returns is a church that is led by pastors who are Christ-centered biblicists.

A biblicist is a man who has one Master and one final authority, and that authority is the Bible rightly translated from the right text and rightly divided by sound principles of interpretation.

He is a man who isn't following a crowd, isn't following tradition, isn't exalting a man or an institution to the place of unquestioning loyalty.

The biblicist is a man who tests everything by the Bible like the Bereans (Acts 17:11) and seeks the mind of Christ in all things. He proves all things by God's Word, not just some things (1 Th. 5:21). He is a man who preaches the whole counsel of God in season or out of season (2 Ti. 4:2).

The greatest frustration I have is that so few preachers will study for themselves and make their own decisions. I would that they were all like my preacher friend in Kentucky. He tells his buddies in the "Sword crowd" and "Chappell crowd," "We have many pulling us to the left, why can't we have one man pulling us to the right?" This man has made the effort to read my teaching and warnings for himself.

A biblicist is not a pragmatist. A large percentage of Independent Baptist preachers are pragmatists. Pragmatism is a philosophy and methodology that focuses on the practicality of a decision.

Consider some dictionary definitions of "pragmatism":

> "a reasonable and logical way of doing things or of thinking about problems that is based on dealing with specific situations instead of on ideas and theories" (Merriam-Webster).

> "the quality of dealing with a problem in a sensible way that suits the conditions that really exist, rather than following fixed theories, ideas, or rules" (Cambridge Dictionary).

A preacher friend commented about church pragmatism along this line:

> "It is to do something on a practical level without diligently considering the theological implication. It is when the practice *overtakes* the theological principle. It is to do whatever it takes to get a good result even if it violates biblical principles or undermines divine power."

The pragmatic preacher makes decisions about the church and ministry based on what "works" to produce a desired goal as opposed to making decisions based *strictly* on Bible truth, though he will give lip service to the latter.

The pragmatic preacher will not be faithful to the whole counsel of God because he has other objectives that are more pressing.

The goal might be getting big numbers and building a big church.

The goal might be not to offend prominent people in his church or even not to offend the women in his church.

The goal might be not to offend some prominent preacher or his own circle of preacher friends. A brother wrote to me about a pastor he had talked to regarding the danger of being a soft separatist and not drawing the lines against West Coast Baptist College (in particular) and its influence. This pastor told him that "he didn't agree with the music at West Coast and wouldn't attend their pastors' conference as a result, but he saw some good fruit come from the school." Yet when this preacher has Bible conferences, he invites speakers who are strong supporters of West Coast. The man who talked to the pastor to express his concern made this observation: "I can see that the implications to this pastor, of taking a Biblical stand, are great. To take a stand against West Coast/Lancaster would send waves through the network of Pastors/Churches in our area and bring isolation." The pragmatist cannot bear isolation.

The goal of the pragmatic preacher might be to keep his preaching engagements open. For example, a Bible conference speaker or evangelist who is a pragmatist will weigh his preaching and the stance he takes by whether or not it would close doors. He learns how to preach in generalities so as to "keep his options open." He can even become an expert in sounding strong when in reality he is very soft. Recently an evangelist published his stand on separation, but though he made some good biblical points, the position was so vague and shallow (being based on only one Scripture passage as opposed to the whole counsel of God and not being practically applied in a clear manner) that it was almost useless. It appears that his objective was to be thought of as a separatist while not really separating in a practical sense.

The goal of the pragmatist might be to get students for a school or to get subscriptions for a paper or orders for his books.

The pragmatic preacher might give lip service to separatism and to being faithful to the whole counsel of God, and he might talk strongly for it in private, but his practice speaks louder than his words.

A few years ago I met the editor of a prominent Independent Baptist publication for a lunch that was arranged by a pastor friend. As soon as we met at the restaurant, this editor asked me to keep the discussion "off the record." He then proceeded to agree with me about many issues, including my concerns about Quick Prayerism. I was greatly puzzled, because his publication has long promoted the men most responsible for teaching these practices and has never warned of them, to my knowledge.

The apostle Paul was not a pragmatist. He had only one objective, and that was to be faithful to Christ his Master. He called himself a "doulos" or bondservant. He had been purchased by Christ from the slave market of sin and did not own himself. His objective was to be faithful to God's truth. Period. He had no other objective. He would not have dreamed of having another objective. The non-pragmatist Paul testified,

> "For I have not shunned to declare unto you all the counsel of God" (Acts 20:27).

He didn't weigh his message by practical considerations, as to whether it would offend someone he wanted to impress or close doors of ministry or reduce the size of his crowd.

Paul even solemnly commissioned Timothy to keep the New Testament commandments "without spot," which refers to "small" things (1 Timothy 6:13-14).

Every preacher is commanded to preach the Word, all of the Word, in season and out of season, no matter what happens, no matter how popular or unpopular it is, no matter who is offended, no matter what doors it closes.

> "Preach the word; be instant in season, out of season; reprove, rebuke, exhort with all longsuffering and doctrine" (2 Timothy 4:2).

The churches desperately need courageous, faithful preachers, not pragmatic politicians.

May each preacher pray, "Lord God, help me not be a pragmatist or a politician. Help me be faithful to you and to your holy Word. While multitudes have been willing to rot in prison cells, to be torn asunder, and to be burned, woe unto me if I am not willing to bear whatever offense or cost comes for being faithful to the truth in a compromising hour."

We preachers need to aim to be better, and we need to encourage the next generation of preachers to be better.

> "My brethren, be not many masters, knowing that we shall receive the greater condemnation" (James 3:1).

A Discipling Church Trains Preachers

Outline
Paul's Example of Training Preachers
Faithful Men
Ministry Teams
Praying for Laborers
A Training College
Training Methods and Materials
Teaching Children/Discipling Youth
Building up the Families

The training of preachers should be a major emphasis of every church, because they are so necessary for God's work.

This is one of the greatest needs in every nation. We cannot have good churches without good preachers and teachers. While we must give training for all of the saints, we must have special training for preachers and this must be a special focus.

Prominent men of the First Great Awakening saw the training of God-called, biblically qualified preachers as one of the pre-eminent needs of that hour.

Consider the following plea from Gilbert Tennent in his 1740 sermon "The Danger of an Unconverted Ministry." He warned that a large number of preachers were unconverted. In the boldest language he called them swarms of locusts and crowds of Pharisees "that have as covetously as cruelly, crept into the Ministry, in this adulterous Generation!"

The situation is similar today. Large numbers of preachers even in "Bible-believing churches" aren't what they should be to lead, build up, and protect the Lord's flocks in this day.

> "And indeed, my Brethren, we should join our Endeavours to our Prayers. The most likely Method to stock the Church with a faithful Ministry, in the present Situation of Things, the public Academies being so much corrupted and abused generally, is, To encourage private Schools, or Seminaries of Learning, which are under the Care of skilful and experienced

Christians; in which those only should be admitted, who upon strict Examination, have in the Judgment of a reasonable Charity, the plain Evidences of experimental Religion. Pious and experienced Youths, who have a good natural Capacity, and great Desires after the Ministerial Work, from good Motives, might be sought for, and found up and down in the Country, and put to Private Schools of the Prophets; especially in such Places, where the Public ones are not. This Method, in my Opinion, has a noble Tendency, to build up the Church of God."

In referring to the "public Academies," Tennent was referring particularly to Harvard and Yale, which had deteriorated in spiritual character.

Tennent called for private schools of the prophets to train men for the ministry. That is exactly the need today. But these schools must reject every tradition that has weakened and corrupted the churches, including shallow evangelism techniques, hastiness in receiving members, weak discipleship that doesn't rise above spiritual infancy, a shallow ministry of God's Word that doesn't produce strong Bible students, an entertainment-oriented youth ministry, and weak discipline.

We need schools of the prophets that will prepare church leaders who can build true discipling churches.

Paul's Example of Training Preachers

This was one of the things that Paul emphasized. Paul trained many preachers, who in turn trained others. In this way he multiplied his ministry in a wonderful way.

He taught this in 2 Timothy 2:2.

> "And the things that thou hast heard of me among many witnesses, the same commit thou to faithful men, who shall be able to teach others also."

We see Paul's emphasis on high standards for leaders in 1 Timothy 3 and Titus 1.

We see Paul's own training of the preachers at Ephesus in Acts 20:26-27 and of the preachers in Crete in Titus. We see his training of Timothy in the epistles of 1 and 2 Timothy.

Faithful Men

Consider some lessons from 2 Timothy 2:1-2:

1. The strength for God's work comes from God (2 Ti. 2:1). We cannot do any spiritual work in our own power and wisdom. We must constantly cast ourselves upon God and call out to God and trust God. The strength comes by understanding God's grace in Christ. The more you know of God's grace, the more effectively you can serve Him.

Our weekly men's discipleship meetings focus on helping the men to understand God's marvelous character and the riches they have in Christ. We teach them to see Christ everywhere in Scripture and everywhere in their daily lives.

2. A church must train preachers for the sake of the future. Paul's preacher's training program looks to the future. It is training men who train other men, generation after generation. Well-trained men of good Christian character and sound doctrine will keep the churches on the right track.

3. The training requires teaching the Bible. Paul taught God's Word, not his own opinions and traditions.

4. The training requires faithful men. Faithfulness is a major requirement for any position of ministry in the church. Compare 1 Co. 4:2; Mt. 25:21; Lu. 16:10; 19:17.

Scriptural examples of faithful saints are Lydia (Acts 16:15), Timothy (1 Co. 4:17), Epaphras (Col. 1:7), Tychicus (Col. 4:7), Onesimus (Col. 4:9), and Silvanus or Silas (1 Pe. 5:12).

Faithfulness is our requirement for students we receive into our Bible college. Unfaithful people are welcome to attend our church services and sit under the preaching and teaching, and our prayer is that they will receive the Word of God and become faithful disciples of Christ. But I am not going to pour myself into training unfaithful men and women in special training programs like a Bible college, because they don't have the spiritual character to receive the training and to teach others.

Consider the characteristics of a faithful man:

Faithful means **dependable, diligent, having a good testimony** (e.g., the brother chosen to carry the offering, 2 Co. 8:18, 22). Contrast Proverbs 10:26 and 29:15. If you say you will do something, do it. Have a heart to do what you are asked to do without grudging (2 Co. 9:7; 1 Pe. 4:9). If you accept a job, do it with all your heart; do it right; try to do it better and better. If you can't be available, inform someone in leadership and try to find a replacement. A faithful man is responsible and dependable.

A faithful man is **a teachable man**. He is not a know-it-all (Pr. 26:16). He is not content to learn just a little, just enough to get by. He wants to continue learning more and more. He isn't a person that considers himself an expert when he is no such thing.

A faithful man is a man who **serves the Lord from the heart** (Eph. 6:6-7). A faithful man serves the Lord from his innermost being, not to please or impress man and not only when someone is watching.

A faithful man **keeps the teaching** (2 Ti. 2:2). The teaching is committed to him as a solemn obligation, and he is responsible before God to keep it. A faithful man doesn't <u>change it</u> (e.g., Seventh-day Adventists change the definition of grace to grace plus works). A faithful man doesn't <u>add to it</u> (e.g., heretics in early centuries adding infant baptism, etc; SDA adding Ellen White prophecies; charismatics adding gibberish tongues, falling down, worldly dancing, women preachers). A faithful man doesn't <u>take away from it</u> (e.g., failing to reprove and rebuke; avoiding preaching on unpopular subjects). Many men have a bad habit of changing things because they think they know better, even when they don't.

A faithful man is **faithful in little things** (Lu. 16:10; 19:17). An individual's character is seen in how he handles "small" responsibilities. This is how the saints are proven (1 Ti. 3:10). They are not proven by being given large responsibilities and ministries, but by being given small ones and proving themselves in the small ones.

Even unbelievers can do great things when they follow the principles of faithfulness. We see this in the Apollo program that landed 12 men on the moon between 1969 and 1972. All of the hundreds of thousands of scientists, engineers, and technicians who worked on that massive project were faithful. Everything had to be exact. Every object, large or small, had to be designed, engineered, fashioned, and installed in the most exacting manner. One small error could doom the Apollo missions.

A faithful man **teaches others** (2 Ti. 2:2). He doesn't hide what he learns. Every believer is to become a teacher at some level (Heb. 5:12-14). The child of God should be eager to learn and then he should teach this to others. The faithful man is ready to teach. He looks for opportunities. He accepts invitations.

Faithfulness **must begin when you are a new Christian** (Acts 2:42). It means learning to honor the Lord by doing His pleasure rather than your own pleasure. We see this in Isaiah 58:13-14. The sabbath and the temple were for Israel, but we have the house of the Lord which is the church (1 Ti. 3:15). The principle of honoring the Lord is the same. The believer honors God by not doing his business when he should be doing God's business. We teach our people that when the church assembles, that is time for God's business, and it is therefore time for you to forget your own business. The believer honors God by delighting in His holy business, which means serving Him from the heart.

A faithful man **continues in the teaching even when he is no longer under his teacher's authority**. I have seen many men veer away from sound teaching and practice when they got away from their teachers. Consider the fearful example of Ahaziah (2 Ch. 24:1-2, 15-22).

Every church leader should seek to continually raise up faithful men. This is not man's natural way. In his natural self, man tends to be jealous of his position and authority. He wants other men to be his servants, not his equals. But the Word of God shows a different example (Mt. 20:25-28).

Consider Barnabas, who knew that he needed help and did not hesitate to invite Paul to join him in the ministry, knowing that Paul had a greater calling (Acts 11:21-26). Soon Paul exceeded Barnabas, but humble, godly Barnabas was not concerned about such things.

The Advantage of Ministry Teams

The early churches were established and led by teams of ministry-gifted men, and we have practiced this from the beginning of our church planting work.

(The Baptist practice of pastors and associate pastors is a leadership/ministry team.)

This is something I pray much for and it is something I would urge young preachers to pray for as a priority. Pray for help. Pray that God would raise up a ministry team. Since we see this in Scripture, we can pray in confidence that it is God's will.

When we started our first church in the early 1980s, I prayed for this. I said, "Lord, I am not able to do this by myself. My wife is a great help, but we can't do this alone. We need a ministry team like we see in the Bible." The Lord answered that earnest prayer and brought two other men alongside, one from India and one from Switzerland, and we worked in harmony for several years in founding that church. The three of us together were much stronger and more effectual than any one of us would have been alone. I was the senior leader, but we functioned as a team. We made plans together and made decisions together. Together we trained "national" men who rose up to leadership positions.

We see this in the church at Jerusalem (Acts 15:6).

We see this in the church at Antioch, which is set before us as the preeminent missionary church.

- Paul and Barnabas worked together to establish this congregation (Acts 11:22-26).

- Soon there were many other preachers at Antioch (Acts 13:1).

- Then Paul and Barnabas were sent out as a missionary team to plant churches across the Roman Empire (Acts 13-14).

- When they had laid the foundation for a new church, they ordained a team of pastor/elders to rule it (Acts 14:23).

Consider some of the advantages to ministry teams:

More gifts (Eph. 4:11; Ro. 12:6-8). When men minister as teams, many different gifts are available. We see this in our church planting ministry. Presently, four of us are functioning as a leadership team. There is an American, a Korean, and two Nepalis. We are different ages. We have different spiritual gifts, personalities, training, and backgrounds, and these differences are an advantage in the ministry.

For example, we have monthly youth meetings, and each month a different leader plans and leads the meeting. As a result, each meeting is different and the youth benefit from the difference.

More eyes. When you have a multiplicity of ministers, you have more eyes to see spiritual danger and error (Acts 20:28-31). You have more eyes to discern hypocrites, deceivers, and false teachers.

More mouths (1 Pe. 4:10-11). When there is a multiplicity of ministers, there is greater variety in preaching and teaching. This is a great benefit to the people.

In our church planting ministry, not only do the leaders share preaching and teaching duties, but we also give many opportunities for younger preachers in training to minister God's Word. The churches benefit greatly from the multiplicity of voices. Currently we have 13 preachers in addition to the four leaders.

More hearts. When there is a multiplicity of ministers, there are more hearts. Different men have different grace. Christ has all grace, but we only have grace in part (John 1:16). When men minister together as a team, their differences in personalities and approaches and gifts make the work stronger. Some are encouragers like Barnabas, while others are reprovers like James. I think of a preacher friend who says he can't preach as hard as me in the matter of reproof and rebuke, but he supports my reproof and believes it is a blessing. Ministry teams make it possible for all types of men to minister together in harmony.

More hands. When there is a multiplicity of ministers, there are more hands to work.

Because we have many ministers in our team, we can have more ministries, more Bible studies, more house fellowships, more children's ministries, more personal visits, etc.

More feet. When there is a multiplicity of ministers, there are more feet to carry the gospel to more people.

Our ministry teams make dozens of outreaches each month to carry the gospel to various parts of our city and to many other towns and villages.

More equality. When there is a multiplicity of ministers, there is more potential for equality in the church. God does not show preference, and we are taught to follow God (1 Ti. 5:21), but the temptation to show preference is very strong in fallen sinners. We have relatives and friends. We have favorites. Multiple leaders can help one another not to show preference.

When it comes to team leadership, in a practical sense we believe there will always be a senior leader or a head pastor. I believe we see James in this role in Acts 15:13-22. After the others had their say about the issue at hand, James summarized the matter and made a practical suggestion about how they should proceed. The other leaders and the church members agreed, and the matter was settled.

Whether complete unanimity is required in every decision is something that each church must decide before the Lord.

Praying for Laborers

We can't train faithful men until God raises them up. We can train a faithful man, but only God can create a faithful heart.

The Lord has specifically instructed us to pray for this.

> "Therefore said he unto them, The harvest truly *is* great, but the labourers *are* few: pray ye therefore the Lord of the harvest, that he would send forth labourers into his harvest" (Luke 10:2).

In our main services every week, we have one of our young men lead the congregation in prayer for God to raise up laborers for His harvest. We pray this prayer believing that God would not instruct us to do it unless He was ready to answer.

We began this practice many years ago, and the Lord has answered these prayers in a marvelous way, and we are busy training those He gives us. The first ones the Lord called were the very young men who were appointed to lead in this prayer.

The need for earnest prayer for the Lord for laborers was mentioned by Gilbert Tennent in his 1740 sermon "The Danger of an Unconverted Ministry" -

> "And more especially, my Brethren, we should pray to the LORD of the Harvest, to send forth faithful Labourers into his Harvest; seeing that the Harvest truly is plenteous, but the Labourers are few. And O Sirs! how humble, believing, and importunate should we be in this Petition! O! let us follow the LORD, Day and Night, with Cries, Tears, Pleadings and Groanings upon this Account! For GOD knows there is great Necessity of it. O! thou Fountain of Mercy, and Father of Pity, pour forth upon thy poor Children a Spirit of Prayer, for

the Obtaining this important Mercy! Help, help, O Eternal GOD and Father, for Christ's sake!"

A Training College

We operate a full-time Bible college for the purpose of training preachers. It is a difficult ministry, but it has been one of the most important and fruitful things we have ever done.

We only accept students from our own church and a couple of seriously likeminded churches. The requirement is that the individual be a true disciple of Christ who is earnestly seeking God's will. The individual must have a good testimony in the home, at school, at work, and in the church. We are not looking for quantity, but for spiritual quality.

The discipline is serious. One of the major goals of the Bible college is to teach discipline. We teach honesty, punctuality, dependability, and hard work. We teach about the importance of correction and how to receive correction in a godly manner. The disciplinary atmosphere is strict, but also kind and gracious. We want our students to learn discipline so they can lead the churches in discipline, so they can discipline their own children, and to prepare them for Christ's kingdom.

The Bible training is serious. We tell our new students, "You are going to work harder in the next three years than you have ever worked. If you aren't ready to work like that, you are in the wrong place."

The classroom work is serious. We have 12 hours of teaching per week plus a chapel.

We teach discipline in the classrooms by means such as the following:

- The students must be on time (and this is in a culture that does not value punctuality).

- If the student has a responsibility, he must be fully prepared. For example, if an individual is leading singing in chapel, he must have everything ready beforehand, including choosing a keyboard player.

- We require the students' best effort. If they make low grades, I ask them if they have done their best, and if so, that is acceptable, but nothing less than their best is acceptable. They are training for the service of the King of kings.

- We challenge them to aim for excellence, not mediocrity.
- Tests are timed and when the teacher says, "Time's up," they must stop writing immediately.
- We give unannounced tests.
- We aim for understanding. We teach them to ask questions any time they don't understand something. We don't want to train parrots who merely repeat things back for a test.
- We train the students not to study just for a test but to learn the material well for the future. The classroom study is just a beginning. They must go over the notes and read every Scripture and make sure that they understand everything that is taught.

And the classroom teaching is just part of the overall training of serving in the church.

The students preach regularly. We have many preaching opportunities that are geared to giving young preachers opportunities to exercise and grow, as well as to edify our people. For example, we have two messages in our main weekend services, a 20 minute gospel message geared to the visitors and a longer message geared to believers. The young preachers are assigned the gospel messages. On Wednesday evening, we usually have two 15 minute messages to give the young men further opportunities. The young men also preach at mid-week prayer services in other parts of the city. They preach in the village ministries. Sometimes they also preach at the school chapel.

The song leaders and preachers are critiqued by the leaders and by their fellow students, with the aim of constantly improving. This also helps the student learn how to receive correction in a right spirit.

The preachers in training attend and participate in our weekly church leaders meetings. They hear the things that we discuss, except some matters of a private nature, and they are encouraged to ask questions and share their thoughts, though they don't make the final decisions.

Training Methods and Materials

The training must be thorough and extensive.

We publish a Bible training curriculum currently consisting of 32 courses that churches can use to educate and disciple preachers (and the congregation as a whole) and that preachers can use for self-study.

Acts
Baptist Music Wars
Bible History and Geography
Bible Times & Ancient Kingdoms
The Bible Version Issue
Defense of the Faith
The Discipling Church
The Effectual Bible Student
First Corinthians
The Four Gospels
Genesis
Give Attendance to Doctrine
Hebrews
A History of the Churches from a Baptist Perspective
Holiness: Pitfalls, Struggles, Victory
How to Study the Bible
James
Job
Keeping the Kids
Mobile Phone and the Christian Home and Church (Youth Discipleship)
Music for Good or Evil (9 video presentations)
The New Testament Church
Pastoral Epistles
The Pastor's Authority and the Church Member's Responsibility
Proverbs
Psalms
Revelation
Romans
Sowing and Reaping: A Course in Evangelism
An Unshakeable Faith: A Christian Apologetics Course
Understanding Bible Prophecy

These courses contain about 9,000 pages of material plus 150 PowerPoint presentations with roughly 15,000 slides.

The following new courses are scheduled for publication in 2017:

-The Bible's Teaching on Marriage

- Daniel
- God the Trinity
- Isaiah
- New Testament Prayer
- Preaching God's Word
- World History

The courses can be used in every type of forum and situation, including preaching, Sunday School, home Bible studies, private study, husbands and wives studying together, Bible Institutes, and home schooling.

We train our preachers to preach expositorily, to deal with the context, to define words, to preach with substance, to apply the Scripture to daily life, to be real students.

Training Children/Discipling Youth

A major way that we train faithful men is to train children and disciple the youth.

These are our potential faithful men of the future. The children and youth are the future of the church, together with those we win to Christ from outside and bring into the membership.

Our goal is not to lose one young person to the world. We don't always succeed, but this is our goal and this is our focus and passion. We do everything possible to win every child to Christ and present him as a true disciple of Christ. We have had the blessing of seeing a large percentage of our young people grow up to serve Christ.

We deal with this extensively in the chapter of this book "A Discipling Church Disciples Youth" and even more extensively in the course *The Mobile Phone and the Christian Home and Church*.

Building the Families

To prepare children and youth to be disciples of Christ and faithful men in the Lord's harvest requires building spiritual families. God's will for each family with children is that it raise a godly seed for His glory (Malachi 2:15).

The home and the church are both ordained of God, and these two institutions should work together for the glory of Jesus Christ.

The church should build the home, and the home should build the church.

This must be a major and continual focus. It must permeate every aspect of the church's ministry. The leaders must have a clear plan about how to build strong families.

We deal with this in the chapter in this book "A Discipling Church Builds Godly Homes."

The book *Keeping the Kids* also goes into all aspects of this important work even more extensively. It deals with such things as the husband wife relationship, fathers as the spiritual leaders of the home, mothers as keepers of the home, child discipline, protecting the home from the influence of the world, leading children to Christ, family devotions, and prayer and fasting. It also deals with the kind of churches that are necessary to build spiritual families.

A Discipling Church Has a Disciplined Environment

Outline
Preparing Spiritual Athletes and Soldiers
Preparing the Saints for Christ's Kingdom
Many Facets of a Disciplined Church
Discipline Is an Exercise of Godly Wisdom and Love
The Exercise of Discipline
A Disciplined Environment and the Lord's Supper
Abuse of a Disciplined Environment

The church we see in the New Testament is a disciplined church.

It is an institution with a solemn eternal purpose with a disciplined environment toward the fulfillment of that purpose.

The church is the divinely-ordained institution to train and discipline God's people for His business on this present earth, which is the Great Commission (Mt. 28:18-20). The saints are to be taught to observe all things Christ has commanded, which is a big task requiring a lot of very serious training and discipline.

A disciplined environment is necessary for every good thing in life: for effective education, for mastering skills, for achieving excellence in all things.

A disciplined environment is the only type of environment that produces true disciples of Jesus Christ. A church with a weak disciplinary environment will tend to produce soft, lukewarm, worldly Christians.

Neglect of discipline is one of the roots of the lack of spiritual power and zeal in Bible-believing churches today.

Preparing Spiritual Athletes and Soldiers

The Christian life is described in terms of discipleship and discipline. These things are intimately associated. The New

Testament church is a church of disciples that are being discipled in an atmosphere of compassionate, godly discipline.

The Christian life is described in athletic terms.

> "Know ye not that they which run in a race run all, but one receiveth the prize? So run, that ye may obtain. And every man that striveth for the mastery is temperate in all things. Now they *do it* to obtain a corruptible crown; but we an incorruptible. I therefore so run, not as uncertainly; so fight I, not as one that beateth the air: But I keep under my body, and bring *it* into subjection: lest that by any means, when I have preached to others, I myself should be a castaway" (1 Co. 9:24-27).

The keen athlete focuses his entire attention and energy on the objective of winning. He is careful about diet. He gets the best instruction and submits to it. He trains relentlessly. He avoids anything that would hinder his progress, regardless of how harmless and innocent that thing would be in another context.

This is the picture of a New Testament discipling church. The objective is to fulfill God's calling and hear, "Well, done, thou good and faithful servant." Toward this end there is single-minded focus, submission to authority, training, exercise, temperance, and separation.

The Christian life is also described in military terms.

> "Thou therefore endure hardness, as a good soldier of Jesus Christ" (2 Ti. 2:3).

> "Finally, my brethren, be strong in the Lord, and in the power of his might. Put on the whole armour of God, that ye may be able to stand against the wiles of the devil. For we wrestle not against flesh and blood, but against principalities, against powers, against the rulers of the darkness of this world, against spiritual wickedness in high *places*. Wherefore take unto you the whole armour of God, that ye may be able to withstand in the evil day, and having done all, to stand. Stand therefore, having your loins girt about with truth, and having on the breastplate of righteousness; And your feet shod with the preparation of the gospel of peace; Above all, taking the shield of faith, wherewith ye shall be able to quench all the fiery darts of the wicked. And take the helmet of salvation, and the sword of the Spirit, which is the word of God:

Praying always with all prayer and supplication in the Spirit, and watching thereunto with all perseverance and supplication for all saints" (Eph. 6:10-18).

A New Testament church is a training institute for the Lord's soldiers. It's the headquarters for global spiritual warfare. It's a boot camp. It's an advanced training school. It's an officer's training college. It's an armory. It's a supply depot. It's a communications network.

Preparing the Saints for Christ's Kingdom

The church prepares the saints for entrance into the coming kingdom. The church is an outpost of Christ's kingdom. The members are citizens of a heavenly country and pilgrims in this present world (Php. 3:20; Heb. 11:13; 1 Pe. 2:11). The believer enters Christ's kingdom spiritually when he is born again ("hath translated us into the kingdom of his dear Son," Col. 1:13). What he does in the church and in the service of Christ in this present life affects his future in the literal kingdom of Christ.

> "Wherefore the rather, brethren, give diligence to make your calling and election sure: for if ye do these things, ye shall never fall: For so an entrance shall be ministered unto you abundantly into the everlasting kingdom of our Lord and Saviour Jesus Christ" (2 Peter 1:10-11).

Peter tells us that by pursuing spiritual growth diligently as described in 2 Peter 1:5-7, the child of God gains an abundant entrance into Christ's kingdom. This refers to rewards and positions in Christ's kingdom. The entrance into Christ's kingdom is a gift of God's grace; the abundant entrance is a matter of pleasing the Lord who has saved me.

> "Charge them that are rich in this world, that they be not highminded, nor trust in uncertain riches, but in the living God, who giveth us richly all things to enjoy; That they do good, that they be rich in good works, ready to distribute, willing to communicate; Laying up in store for themselves a good foundation against the time to come, that they may lay hold on eternal life" (1 Timothy 6:17-19).

Again we see that the believer's works in this present life affect the future. By giving and otherwise serving Christ, the believer lays hold on eternal life, not in the sense of gaining eternal life but in the sense of gaining rewards in the eternal state.

> "And he that overcometh, and keepeth my works unto the end, to him will I give power over the nations: And he shall rule them with a rod of iron; as the vessels of a potter shall they be broken to shivers: even as I received of my Father" (Revelation 2:26-27).

> "To him that overcometh will I grant to sit with me in my throne, even as I also overcame, and am set down with my Father in his throne" (Revelation 3:21).

The overcomer of Revelation 2-3 is the true saint that continues to serve Christ throughout his life (Re. 2:26). He is promised a position of authority with Christ in His kingdom.

The church is tasked with preparing overcomers.

Many Facets of a Disciplined Church

The New Testament epistles describe a multi-faceted disciplinary environment. New Testament discipline is *everything* that is necessary to produce disciples of Christ.

- Maintaining high standards for leaders and workers (1 Ti. 3; Titus 1)
- Requiring faithfulness (1 Co. 4:2). If God requires faithfulness of His stewards, how can the church require less?
- Continuing steadfastly in fundamental disciplines (Acts 2:42)
- Teaching the observance of all things (Mt. 28:19-20)
- Reproof and even *sharp* rebuke when necessary (2 Ti. 4:2; Titus 1:13; 2:15). We deal with this in the chapter "A Discipling Church Is a Reproving Church."
- Obedience to authority (Heb. 13:17)
- Good order (1 Co. 14:40)
- Striving toward the *perfection* of the saints (Eph. 4:12-13; Col. 1:28)
- The "one another" ministry of the body edifying itself by admonition and exhortation (e.g., Ro. 15:14; Eph. 4:16; Col. 3:16; Heb. 10:25)
- Strict separation from the sins of the flesh ("cleanse ourselves from all filthiness," 2 Co. 7:1)

- Strict separation from the world ("have no fellowship with the unfruitful works of darkness," Eph. 5:11; Jas. 4:4; 1 Joh. 2:15-17)
- Strict separation from error and compromise (Ro. 16:17; 2 Th. 3:6; 2 John 10-11)
- Discipline of sin (Mt. 18:15-18; Acts 5:1-11; 1 Co. 5:6; 1 Ti. 5:19-22)
- Rejection of heretics (Titus 3:9-11)

The goal of the all-encompassing New Testament church discipline is for the members to make spiritual progress so that there will be no need for exclusion or excommunication.

> "... churches, like armies and families, may be said to be well disciplined, not when punishments are often inflicted, but when, by due care and faithfulness, they are seldom required" (David Benedict, *Fifty Years Among the Baptists*, 1860, chapter 29).

James Crumpton called this discipling, disciplined environment "constructive church discipline."

> "The fundamental meaning of the word *discipline* is 'to disciple.' Discipline is a very vital part in leading believers into a life of discipleship. ... God never intended that His church should be a nursery, convalescent ward, rest home, delicatessen, 'powder room,' or house of entertainment. He purposed that it should be an armory where His soldiers are trained and disciplined for the battle. The Christian life is a constant warfare. Too many are POW, AWOL, or on furlough in the Lord's army. To believe the New Testament is to believe in the saved being disciplined and trained for the Lord's service" (Crumpton, *New Testament Discipline*).

J.M. Pendleton called the discipling, disciplined environment "formative church discipline."

> "It is clear from these Scriptures (Eph. 2:21, 22; 4:12, 13; 2 Pe. 1:5-7; 3:18) that Christians should ever be in a state of progressive spiritual improvement. They must not retrograde, nor remain stationary, but be constantly advancing in the divine life. The 'perfecting of the saints' is an object of vast importance. ... **Formative church discipline** contemplates the vigorous growth of the 'babe in Christ' till it is developed into 'a perfect man.' Bringing the baptized disciples into local church organizations has this purpose in view. They are to be

taught 'to observe all things whatsoever Christ has commanded.' By such observance alone can a church edify itself in love, building up its members on their most holy faith. By such observance is promoted the symmetry of Christian character, and in it are included all the activities of the Christian life. *Formative discipline*, in its sanctifying influences, ought to reach every church-member. The old, with their gray hairs, should exhibit its beneficial power in the ripeness of the fruits of the Spirit. The middle-aged, in the perfection of physical strength, should also show that it makes them 'strong in the Lord and in the power of his might.' And the young, in the morning of life, should yield to its plastic touches, that they may become useful laborers in the vineyard of the Lord. All have been redeemed with the precious blood of Christ and 'should live, not to themselves, but to him who died and rose again'" (Pendleton, *Church Manual Designed for the Use of Baptist Churches*, 1867).

A disciplined environment can produce continual revival. The spiritual revival we see in the New Testament epistles is a revival *lifestyle*, not a revival *meeting*.

A disciplined environment can keep the Lord's people walking in the truth and living in the Spirit. In contrast, a revival *meeting* can get people stirred up, but the effect will fade away if the church doesn't have the proper disciplined environment in place to keep the spiritual life advancing.

Discipline Is an Exercise of Godly Wisdom and Love

Discipline is terribly misunderstood in today's society, but sound biblical discipline is an exercise of godly wisdom and love. The God of the Bible is a God of discipline.

"... as many as I love, I rebuke and chasten" (Re. 3:19).

"He that spareth his rod hateth his son: but he that loveth him chasteneth him betimes" (Pr. 13:24).

"... reproofs of instruction are the way of life" (Pr. 6:23).

"For whom the Lord loveth he chasteneth, and scourgeth every son whom he receiveth" (Heb. 12:6).

"For this is the love of God, that we keep his commandments: and his commandments are not grievous" (1 John 5:3).

James Crumpton observed,

> "There is not much true love--God's kind of love--known and practiced today. There is a lot of sentimental selfishness that is passed off as love. I might illustrate what I am talking about by referring to the pastors who 'cut corners' and compromise when it comes to preaching the whole counsel of God (and that would include church discipline). They claim to love their people and cannot press for these points that reprove and rebuke. But the truth is that they so love themselves they fear the criticism which Satan would foster against them, if they were true to the teachings of our Lord, if they really loved their people, they would teach them and lead them to practice what our Lord taught. Certainly, He loves the people and knows what is best and a necessity for all. It is never right to do wrong to make an opportunity to do right, and love--real love--true love--always constrains us to do right" (*New Testament Church Discipline*).

The Exercise of Discipline

(For examples of discipline in old Baptist churches see the chapter "The Disappearance of Discipling Churches.")

Bible discipline is training and chastening with the goal of conforming the church and its individual members to the will of God. It involves teaching, encouragement, correction and reproof, exclusion when required, and restoration. Church discipline involves everything necessary to keep a church pure before God (1 Co. 5:7-8). Church discipline encompasses everything discussed in this book, and more.

Discipline is a matter of love—love for God, love for holiness, love for the truth, love for Christ's testimony in the church, love for the brethren, and love for the unsaved who are observing the church's testimony.

The Goals of Church Discipline

1. To protect the purity of the church, to keep it from being permeated with sin and false doctrine (1 Co. 5:6-8). The passover depicts salvation through faith in Christ's blood, and the feast of unleavened bread depicts sanctification. See Lev. 23:4-8. The putting away of all leaven depicts putting sin out of the Christian

life and church. The believers have died and risen with Christ that they should no longer serve sin (Ro. 6:6). We are to cleanse ourselves from all filthiness of the flesh and spirit, perfecting holiness (2 Co. 7:1). Christ gave himself for us to redeem us from all iniquity (Titus 2:14). Being saved, we are to live unto righteousness (1 Pe. 2:24).

Both of these passages are written in the context of church discipline. In fact, the very epistles themselves (1 Corinthians and Galatians) are examples of the process of church discipline. The apostle was writing to correct sin and error; he was teaching, pleading, rebuking, warning. All of these things are involved in church discipline. Sin and false teaching are called "leaven," because if moral and doctrinal impurities are not corrected and removed from the assembly, they will permeate the body and destroy the church. Unrepentant sin and false teaching cannot be ignored in the vain hope that the problem will somehow disappear on its own. It must be dealt with in a biblical fashion.

Note that a little leaven leavens the whole lump. The church must be strict about dealing with sin and error. Unrepentant sin and false teaching cannot be ignored in the vain hope that the problem will somehow disappear on its own. It must be dealt with in a biblical way, or it will spread and destroy the church. We see the right example in the apostle Paul. He did not ignore *any* of the problems at Corinth. He taught, preached, exhorted, pleaded, warned, rebuked, and called for exclusion of unrepentant sinners. All of these things are involved in church discipline.

2. To maintain a good testimony before the unbelieving community (1 Co. 5:1; Php. 2:14-15; 1 Pe. 2:9-12).

3. To please and glorify the Lord (1 Co. 5:4). In Titus 2:14 we learn that a pure church pleases the Lord because this was His purpose in our redemption. In 1 Peter 2:9, 11-12 we see that a pure church is a praise and glory to the Lord.

4. To restore erring church members (1 Co. 5:5; 2 Co. 2:6-8). As we exercise church discipline, we must ever keep in mind that our goal is not to harm people, but to help them. Even when a member must be expelled from the assembly, the ultimate goal is to see that one restored.

5. To restrain sin (De. 13:11; 17:12-13; 19:18-20; Acts 5:1-11; 1 Tim. 5:20). "It would be ideal if men could be encouraged to live

godly lives without any warning of judgment upon ungodliness. But to suppose they will do so is idealistic and contrary to all observation, as well as to Scripture. God warns of impending judgment and says, 'It is a fearful thing to fall into the hands of the living God' (Heb. 10:31). 'Because there is wrath, beware...' (Job 36:18). If sin goes unjudged in a church, we are thereby inviting others to become self-indulgent. It will not do to plead 'love' as a basis for neglect. ... God does not put love and punishment in opposition to each other. He says, 'For whom the Lord loveth he chasteneth...' (Heb. 12:5-11). The church has a solemn responsibility to restrain sin by proper discipline. If we do not exercise the judgment, the Lord will (1 Co. 11:31-32)" (Paul R. Jackson, *The Doctrine and Administration of the Church*).

6. To keep the church ready for Christ's return (Tit. 2:11-15). We are warned that those who do not remain pure and ready for Christ's appearing will be ashamed when He comes (1 Jn. 2:28).

The Right Attitude of Discipline

God's people must be careful to maintain the proper attitude when dealing with sinning Christians and not to give place to the devil.

1. The attitude of humility (Ga. 6:1)

2. The attitude of impartiality (De. 1:17; 1 Ti. 5:21). "Also, discipline should be strictly impartial. The fact that a wrongdoer is related to us by ties of nature, for instance should in no wise influence our decision in the matter. Respect of persons must not be shown" (William MacDonald).

3. The attitude of compassion (2 Co. 7:12). Discipline must be exercised with much spiritual care and tenderness. Anything less than compassion is not Christlike. We think of how Christ dealt with Peter when he denied him. Christ reproved Peter with a look (Lu. 22:61). Peter repented in bitter tears (Mt. 26:74-75), and Christ restored him with a solemn, public exhortation (John 21:15-17).

4. The attitude of mourning (2 Co. 2:4). "Nothing can be more solemn or affecting than the act of putting away a person from the Lord's table. It is the last sad and unavoidable act of the whole assembly, and it should be performed with broken hearts and weeping eyes. Alas how often it is otherwise! How often does this

most solemn and holy duty take the form of a mere official announcement that such a person is out of fellowship. Need we wonder that discipline, so carried out, fails to tell with power upon the erring one, or upon the church" (C.H. Mackintosh).

5. The attitude of firmness of purpose (1 Co. 5:3-5, 13)

The Patience and Wisdom for Discipline

Church discipline requires patience and much godly wisdom. Each situation is different. There are general biblical principles, as we will see, but the application of these principles requires the Lord's wisdom. He alone knows the hearts. The church and all of its members belong to the Lord. The under-shepherds must constantly seek wisdom from the Great Shepherd. If they are ready to receive, He is ready to give, and each situation will have the necessary wisdom and power and blessing.

> "Discipline calls for discernment. Paul writes, 'Now we exhort you, brethren, warn them that are unruly, comfort the feebleminded, support the weak, be patient toward all *men*' (1 Th. 5:14). We should not encourage the unruly, but admonish him. We should not admonish the fainthearted or weak, but encourage and help them. Sometimes, a newer believer is in sin due to ignorance of God's Word. He is weak. But, if he continues defiantly in the sin after you show him what the Word says, he then becomes unruly. I find the analogy of child rearing helpful here. If my three-year-old was acting like a three-year-old, I tried to help him learn how to behave in a more mature manner. But I didn't discipline him for being three. But when your three-year-old is defiant, you must deal with his rebellion. If a believer is overcome by a sin, but is repentant and wants help, you help him. But if he says, 'I have a right to do as I please,' he is defiant and needs discipline" (Steven Cole, "Dealing with Sinning Christians," Aug. 13, 2006, Bible.org).

The Authority for Discipline

See 1 Corinthians 5:4 and Matthew 18:18-19. Dismissing someone from the church is not an easy matter. There are often doubts and fears. Will it hurt the church? Has everything possible been done to correct the problem in other ways? Do we have the right attitude? How will the erring one(s) react? How will his or her friends or relatives react? Will some protest and sympathize with the offender?

I know of a church that had to discipline a member for marrying a deceitful, crooked man; and the offending party's mother and sister sided with her and all of them left the church. This is not uncommon. The power of God is needed in exercising church discipline, and the Bible promises that His power and blessing will be available when His people are earnestly trying to walk in obedience to Him.

Discipline of Interpersonal Problems

The discipline of problems between church members is dealt with very clearly in Matthew 5 and 18.

> "Therefore if thou bring thy gift to the altar, and there rememberest that thy brother hath ought against thee; Leave there thy gift before the altar, and go thy way; first be reconciled to thy brother, and then come and offer thy gift" (Mt. 5:23-24).

> "Moreover if thy brother shall trespass against thee, go and tell him his fault between thee and him alone: if he shall hear thee, thou hast gained thy brother. But if he will not hear *thee, then* take with thee one or two more, that in the mouth of two or three witnesses every word may be established. And if he shall neglect to hear them, tell *it* unto the church: but if he neglect to hear the church, let him be unto thee as an heathen man and a publican. Verily I say unto you, Whatsoever ye shall bind on earth shall be bound in heaven: and whatsoever ye shall loose on earth shall be loosed in heaven" (Mt. 18:15-18).

"There are two commands of Christ, which, if faithfully obeyed, would in almost every instance prevent personal offences from assuming such form and magnitude as to require church action" (J.M. Pendleton, *Church Manual Designed for the Use of Baptist Churches*, 1867).

Note that God is very concerned about interpersonal relationships. Maintaining right relationships lies at the heart of loving my neighbor as myself, which is the second great commandment (Mt. 22:36-40). This is so important to God that He instructs His people to put it before worship (Mt. 5:23-24).

The objective is to clear up problems and achieve reconciliation and spiritual harmony - "first be reconciled to thy brother" (Mt. 5:24), "if he shall hear thee, thou hast gained thy brother" (Mt. 18:15). "If this is not his purpose, he violated the spirit of Christ's law though he may obey it in the letter" (Pendleton).

Following are the practical steps in dealing with interpersonal problems in the church:

First, *the matter should be discussed privately between the two church members* ("go and tell him his fault between thee and him alone," Mt. 18:15).

- The Scripture puts the responsibility of reconciliation equally upon both parties. In Matthew 5, the case is when a brother realizes that another brother has something against him, whether legitimate or not. In Matthew 18, the case is when a brother has trespassed against me. "The offended brother is not to wait till the offender goes to him and seeks reconciliation" (Pendleton).

- The individual who takes the initiative should go personally to the other person rather than writing a note or sending a text or talking on the phone. A face-to-face interview is what is needed. An exception to this would be if there is concern for personal safety or if meeting privately with the individual would put one into a compromising situation, such as meeting with a member of the opposite sex.

- The individual who takes the initiative should go not only to confront the other person but also to listen. Oftentimes the problem lies in misunderstanding and lack of information or wrong information. "Your objective is not to 'set him straight' or to 'get things off your chest' by letting him know how wrong he is. Your aim is to get him to listen so as to win him back to the Lord. The Greek word translated 'show him his fault' is a legal term that means to convince in a court of law. The best way of convincing someone of his sin is to take him to Scripture. Your opinion really doesn't matter. God's Word is the authority" (Steven Cole, "Dealing with Sinning Christians," Aug. 13, 2006, Bible.org).

Second, *if this doesn't solve the problem, the injured brother should take two or three others* (Mt. 18:16). "The brethren selected by the aggrieved brother to go with him should be very judicious and eminently spiritual. Sound judgment and ardent piety will be needed" (Pendleton).

Third, *if that doesn't solve the problem, the matter should be brought before the church* (Mt. 18:17). Even here, there is opportunity for reconciliation, and the goal continues to be reconciliation.

Fourth, *if the trespasser refuses to hear the church, he is to be disciplined* (Mt. 18:17).

What does it mean "let him be unto thee as an heathen man and a publican"?

It doesn't mean never to speak with him or to forbid him to attend church. This is not how we deal with publicans.

- It means that the church member that is under discipline is not allowed to serve in a church ministry or to participate in church business and ordinances (such as taking the Lord's Supper). The heathen or unsaved are not allowed to do these things.

- It means that the offender is not to be allowed to participate in the close fellowship that is normal between church members. This is for the purpose of making the offender ashamed. "And if any man obey not our word by this epistle, note that man, and have no company with him, that he may be ashamed" (2 Th. 3:14).

> "If individual members act contrary to this rule, and carry on freely toward an offender, as if nothing had taken place, it will render the censure of the church of none effect. Those persons also who behave in this manner will be considered by the party as his friends, and others who stand aloof as his enemies, or at least as being unreasonably severe; which will work confusion, and render void the best and most wholesome discipline. We must act in concert, or we may as well do nothing. Members who violate this rule are partakers of other men's sins, and deserve the rebukes of the church for counteracting its measures" (Andrew Fuller, *Works*, vol. III, pp. 334-335).

The seriousness of church business is seen here (Mt. 18:18). Men often take the church and its business lightly, but God doesn't.

> "If any man defile the temple of God, him shall God destroy; for the temple of God is holy, which *temple* ye are" (1 Co. 3:17)

"Not forsaking the assembling of ourselves together, as the manner of some *is*; but exhorting *one another*: and so much the more, as ye see the day approaching" (Heb. 10:25).

"Obey them that have the rule over you, and submit yourselves: for they watch for your souls, as they that must give account, that they may do it with joy, and not with grief: for that *is* unprofitable for you" (Heb. 13:17).

The "binding" does not pertain to a person's eternal destiny but to his earthly life.

Discipline of Backsliding and Halfheartedness

What should be done if a member is exhibiting backsliding and halfheartedness, such as missing services, not reading his Bible, a father not being the spiritual leader of his home, a mother not being a keeper at home.

These things must not be overlooked. Backsliding pulls down the spiritual climate of the entire church, ruins the spiritual climate of the homes, can greatly harm the children, and sometimes leads even to shipwreck. The saint who is not going forward spiritually is going backward.

The means of correcting these things is manifold, such as the following:

- Backsliding and halfheartedness is corrected through the preaching and teaching ministry. Backsliders are dealt with through teaching, exhortation, reproof, and rebuke.

- Backsliding and halfheartedness is corrected through personal, private ministry. When we see one of our members backsliding, we spend more time with them on a personal basis to try to correct the problem and to heal that situation. We pray more for him.

- Backsliders are corrected by not being allowed to have a ministry in the church.

- If the person stops attending church for two months, we put him on a non-active membership list, and if he is inactive for another three months, he is removed from membership. During this time we try to restore him. Our authority for this is the standard of the first church in which the members were characterized by steadfast continuance in the things of Christ (Acts 2:42).

Discipline for unfaithfulness was common in old Baptist churches.

The Broadmead Church in England "had all the members' names engrossed in parchment, that they might be called over always at breaking bread, to see who did omit their duty" (J.J. Goadby, *Discipline in Early British Churches*).

The Fenstanton Church exercised discipline for neglect of the assembly. The church made an order "that if any members of the congregation shall absent themselves from the assembly of the same congregation upon the first day of the week, without manifesting a sufficient cause, they shall be looked upon as offenders and be proceeded against accordingly," and "it was desired that if any member should at any time have any extraordinary occasion to hinder them from the assembly, that they would certify the congregation of the same beforehand, for the prevention of jealousies, &c." (J.M. Cramp, *Baptist History*).

A Baptist church in East Tennessee disciplined members who failed to attend services for 60 days "without legal excuse." This church disciplined a member who "comes to Sunday School and leaves before preaching" ("Brief Survey of Historical Background to Church Discipline," pastorhistorian.com).

Discipline of Disorderly Conduct

2 Thessalonians 3:6-15 calls for separation from a church member that seems to fall short of excluding. One difference is that the 2 Thessalonians 3 offender is not turned over to the devil as in 1 Corinthians 5.

The context of 2 Thessalonians 3 is a church member who is engaged in disorderly conduct such as refusing to work and being a busybody in the affairs of others (1 Th. 3:6-15).

We believe this principle applies to other cases of refusing to obey the Word of God that fall short of 1 Corinthians 5 discipline. It would seem preposterous to think that churches are to discipline members who refuse to work while ignoring other things, such as the following:

- A wife who refuses to submit to her husband's authority in the home (Eph. 5:22)

- A husband who refuses to love and care for his family (Eph. 5:25 - 6:4; 1 Ti. 5:8)

- A father who neglects his duties (1 Ti. 5:8)
- A young person who is rebellious against his parents (Eph. 6:1-4)
- An individual who is a reproach to Christ because of his actions in the workplace (Eph. 6:5-8)
- A young widow who is idle and a busybody (1 Ti. 5:11-14)
- Those who refuse to practice Bible separation (Ro. 16:17-18; 2 Co. 6:14-17; 1 Ti. 6:3-5; 2 Ti. 2:16-21; 3:5; 2 Joh. 9-11). An example of this would be participation in ecumenical organizations and ventures.

The old Baptists called this type of discipline "suspension." It entails removing the individual from the fellowship and not allowing him to partake of the Lord's Supper or participate in church ministry or business until he repents.

> "Suspension is to be administered in case of crimes which do not amount so high as to deserve excommunication" (*Summary of Church Discipline*, Charleston Association, 1774).

> "Suspension, considered as a church censure, is that act of a church whereby an offending member, being found guilty is set aside from office, from the Lord's table, and from the liberty of judging or voting in any case. ... [T]he suspended member is not to be accounted as an enemy, but admonished as a brother, 2 Th. 3:15, and upon a credible profession of repentance the censure is to be taken off and the delinquent restored to all privileges of the church" (Ibid.).

Discipline of Public and Grave Offenses

Excommunication is required for certain types of sins, particularly those of a public and grave nature. This is dealt with in 1 Corinthians 5.

> "But now I have written unto you not to keep company, if any man that is called a brother be a fornicator, or covetous, or an idolater, or a railer, or a drunkard, or an extortioner; with such an one no not to eat" (1 Co. 5:11).

The nature of the sin that calls for this type of church discipline is as follows:

It is public sin (1 Co. 5:1 -- "it is commonly reported").

It is grave sin (1 Co. 5:11). The moral evils referred to in this passage are listed under six categories: immorality, covetousness, idolatry, railing, drunkenness, and extortion. All of these evils are definite causes for church discipline, because the church which allows its members to partake in such things without exercising discipline becomes a reproach to the name of Christ (2 Sa. 12:14).

Fornication. This is a broad term for sexual impurity. It refers to fornication outside of marriage (1 Co. 7:2) and to adultery within marriage (Mat. 5:32). It is likened to "concupiscence" in 1 Th. 4:3-5, which refers more particularly to the lusting aspect of sexual impurity. A believer would be a fornicator, therefore, who engages in such things as homosexuality, incest, rape, bestiality, and the use of pornography.

Covetousness. This means "to desire inordinately; to desire that which it is unlawful to obtain or possess; excessively eager to obtain and possess" (Webster). A church member who is covetous and therefore who should be disciplined for this sin will be characterized by the following:

(1) Covetousness is to be greedy. Covetousness is to desire that which is not my own or that which is forbidden (Ex. 20:17; Deut. 5:21; Josh. 7:21).

(2) Covetousness is to obtain things by oppressing others; by cheating, stealing, borrowing and not paying back (Prov. 28:16; Mic. 2:2). Corrupt government officials and legal officials cheat because they are covetous. This is the way of the world, but it must not be the way of God's people.

(3) Covetousness is to love and pursue money instead of being content with the basic needs of life and pursuing the will of God (1 Ti. 6:6-11). It is to make money and possessions the focus of one's life (Lk. 12:15-21). The man who puts his business before God is a covetous man.

Idolatry. This refers to worshipping idols or to putting some material possession or pleasure in the place of God and to bestow upon it the love and devotion that belongs to God alone. The first law is to love God with all the heart, soul, and strength (De. 6:5).

Railing. This means to heap abuse upon another, to revile. The same Greek word (*loidoros*) is translated "reviler" in 1 Co. 6:10. It refers to speaking hatefully, calling people ugly names by way of attack. Christ hates this and will not allow it in His kingdom (Mat.

5:21-26). We had to expel a Bible college student one time because he was guilty of this. He called his fellow students "fools" and "dogs" and proudly told one humble student that his character was "a stench in God's nostrils." "A reproachful man; a man of coarse, harsh, and bitter words; a man whose characteristic it was to abuse others; to vilify their character, and wound their feelings" (Barnes).

Drunkenness. To be intoxicated with foreign substances, either by alcohol or drugs. We believe that this sin also involves selling liquor, because he contributes to and is a party to drunkenness (Hab. 2:15).

Extortion. This is the act of taking things from others by means of force or abuse of authority. It refers to cheating, blackmailing, kidnapping, requiring bribes, unjust or unauthorized taxation, fees, penalties (e.g., the publicans). See Ps. 109:11; Eze. 22:12. Those who work in the government, police, or courts in corrupt nations are particularly tempted by this sin.

It is sin that would destroy the church if ignored (1 Co. 5:6). There will always be sin of one sort or another in a church that is populated by sinners, but there are some sins that have the ability to destroy the church if left alone, and these must be disciplined by exclusion.

It is important that the church leaders investigate the matter thoroughly and not act on partial facts and hearsay. The leaders can appoint mature deacons or other mature church members to help conduct the investigation.

When the church is satisfied that it has all of the relevant facts, it can take one of several actions.

First, it can find the accused innocent and dismiss the charges. This happened about half the time in Baptist churches in America in the 19th century. If it was found that a member had brought an accusation against another without sufficient cause, "the church generally charged the accuser with slander or hostility" (*Restoring Integrity in Baptist Churches*, Kindle loc. 2126).

Second, it can rebuke the offender, receive his confession of repentance, and forgive him without further action.

Third, it can give the individual time to reflect on his sin and the church time to pray for him.

Fourth, it can put the offender under discipline according to 1 Corinthians 5:4, 5, 13. This is called exclusion or excommunication.

> "If the offender continues obstinate and appears to be incorrigible, the church is under a necessity of proceeding to the execution of the great censure against him. ... [B]y the authority of the Lord Jesus Christ, and in the name and behalf of that church, [the minister] cuts off and secludes the offender by name from union and communion with the church; he having broke his covenant with them, they also excluded him from the privileges of a member, as unworthy; yet praying the Lord Jesus Christ, who is the Good Shepherd, to restore him by giving him unfeigned repentance that he may again be received into the sheepfold" (*Summary of Church Discipline*, Charleston Association, 1774).

The old Baptists would sometimes exclude even if the individual expressed repentance.

> "Exclusion always ensued if there was no repentance. But repentance did not always save. For grave sins that brought particular dishonor to the Saviour or that involved habitual deceit or fraud, churches usually excluded even if the accused repented. About 50 percent of those whom the church brought before its discipline experienced exclusion" (*Restoring Integrity in Baptist Churches*, Kindle loc. 2121).

Exclusion

Exclusion means the following:

1. It means that the individual is turned over to Satan (1 Co. 5:5). This refers to turning the unrepentant offender over to Satan's domain, the world, and over to Satan's power for chastisement. Compare Lu. 22:31-32; 13:16.

2. It means that the individual is put out of the church membership (1 Co 5:13).

3. It means that the members should not have close fellowship with the individual so that he will be ashamed and brought to repentance (1 Co. 5:11; 2 Th. 3:14). The eating in this verse probably refers both to eating socially and to eating the Lord's Supper (1 Co. 11:26, 29). "[A]ll contact is not forbidden, but we

aren't to relate on a normal, buddy-buddy level that ignores the person's sin. Any contact must communicate, 'We love you and we want you back in the fellowship of the church, but we can't condone what you're doing and we can't accept you back until you genuinely repent'" (Cole, "Dealing with Sinning Christians," Aug. 13, 2006, Bible.org).

4. The members should pray much for the individual that he will repent and they should take any opportunity to exhort him to do this.

Restoration

When the excluded individual seeks restoration, the church tries to determine whether his or her repentance is sincere. They look for ready, hearty, and full admission of guilt. They look for admission of and naming of the specific sins they have committed, as opposed to merely saying, "I'm sorry," or, "I'm sorry for what I did." If the individual is still blaming others and otherwise making excuse for his sin, this is not true repentance and should not be accepted. See 2 Corinthians 7:11 for a description of true repentance.

> "For behold this selfsame thing, that ye sorrowed after a godly sort, what carefulness it wrought in you, yea, *what* clearing of yourselves, yea, *what* indignation, yea, *what* fear, yea, *what* vehement desire, yea, *what* zeal, yea, *what* revenge! In all *things* ye have approved yourselves to be clear in this matter."

See also David's repentance in Psalm 51:3-6.

Those who show genuine repentance should be forgiven and restored (2 Co. 2:7).

Sometimes it is wise to put the individual on probation. During probation the individual is required to show repentance for a determined period of time. Old Baptist churches expected a longer period of probation for "sins that were especially grave or involved deceit."

In Baptist churches in America in the 19th century, 30-40% of those excluded sought and gained restoration (*Restoring Integrity in Baptist Churches*, Kindle loc. 2126).

Forgiveness and restoration to church membership does not mean there are no abiding consequences to sin and that things can necessarily return to the way they were before the sin. If a pastor commits adultery, for example, we believe that he should never again hold the office of a pastor. If a girl runs off with a boy and commits fornication, she can never regain her virginity. A church member who has been disciplined for theft should probably not be placed into the position of church treasurer. There are many consequences to sin in this present life. We think of David. Though he repented deeply of his sin as recorded in Psalm 51 and was forgiven, he suffered consequences for the rest of his life.

Discipline of False Teachers

The apostle Paul warned the leaders at the church in Ephesus that false teaching would come from without and from within (Ac. 20:20-21). This is even more applicable in these closing days of the church age, days of great apostasy and of serious compromise even among those who claim to be Bible-believers. We must be constantly alert to this danger and deal with every false doctrine that reveals itself within the assembly (Ep. 4:11-14).

The discipline of heretics (those who have chosen to cleave to a false teaching) is described in Titus 3.

> "But avoid foolish questions, and genealogies, and contentions, and strivings about the law; for they are unprofitable and vain. A man that is an heretick after the first and second admonition reject; Knowing that he that is such is subverted, and sinneth, being condemned of himself" (Titus 3:9-11).

The terms "heretic" and "heresy" refer to the willful choice of false doctrine, a willful alignment with error.

A heretic is not a person who is merely ignorant of sound doctrine. If the heresy is a matter of ignorance on the part of a true believer, the individual will respond to the truth and turn from it.

I know a pastor who was saved out of a hippie lifestyle and went to Bible college only a few months after he was saved. Soon after arriving he saw a book in the bookstore entitled "Is Jesus God?" and in his mind he said, "Of course, Jesus isn't God!" But this great heresy was only an ignorance problem, and as soon as this brother was taught about Christ's deity he readily accepted it.

The heretic is to be admonished two times (Titus 3:10). An effort is to be made to reclaim the heretic from his error. It is possible that he is not truly a heretic but that he is only holding a heresy out of ignorance.

But the heretic is to be admonished only two times (Titus 3:10). We are not instructed to get involved in endless efforts to win heretics to the truth. When it is obvious that a person is set in his false ways, he must be rejected and put out of the assembly.

The heretic *condemns himself* by his self-willed commitment to error (Titus 3:11). There is something wrong in the heretic's heart. "Subverted" is from the Greek word "ekstrepho," which means "to be twisted or turned inside out." Something has perverted the person's heart so that he is not willing to hear the truth. "Such a one is subverted or perverted--a metaphor from a building so ruined as to render it difficult if not impossible to repair and raise it up again. Real heretics have seldom been recovered to the true faith: not so much defect of judgment, as perverseness of the will, being in the case, through pride, or ambition, or self-willedness, or covetousness, or such like corruption, which therefore must be taken heed of" (Matthew Henry).

Discipline of Church Leaders (1 Ti. 5:19-22)

> "Against an elder receive not an accusation, but before two or three witnesses. Them that sin rebuke before all, that others also may fear. I charge *thee* before God, and the Lord Jesus Christ, and the elect angels, that thou observe these things without preferring one before another, doing nothing by partiality. Lay hands suddenly on no man, neither be partaker of other men's sins: keep thyself pure."

Pastor/elders are members of the church body, and they are subject to discipline just as other members. In addition to the things we have stated above about discipline, which would apply to any church member, including a pastor, there are some important lessons in 1 Timothy 5:19-22 about the discipline of church leaders in particular:

1. It is essential that the church be very cautious about selecting and ordaining pastors (1 Ti. 5:22). This is a fundamental issue of keeping the church pure. Haste and carelessness in ordaining leaders will result in great injury to the work of God. If the congregation is careful to ordain only God-called, scripturally qualified men who have proven themselves, it will rarely need to go

through the heartache of disciplining an erring pastor. And the right leaders are necessary to create the discipling atmosphere that builds up the church spiritually.

2. Accusations must not be received against a pastor unless they can be substantiated by two or three witnesses (1 Ti. 5:19). This principle was a part of the law of Moses (De. 19:15). See also Mt. 18:16 and 2 Co. 13:1.

3. Pastors that sin in such a manner that requires discipline should be rebuked publicly (1 Ti. 5:20). This action would be occasioned by the type of sins listed in 1 Co. 5:11.

4. God's people are solemnly charged not to show partiality in these things (1 Ti. 5:21). Because of fallen human nature, it is a great and constant temptation to show partiality in judgment.

Inactive Membership

If an individual ceases to attend our services faithfully, the church leaders or appointed church workers meet with that individual to try to restore him.

If he continues to absent himself for two months, he is put on the inactive membership roll and cannot participate in the Lord's Supper, ministries, and church business.

For another three months, the church leaders continue to try to restore the individual. If that is unsuccessful, he or she is removed from the membership altogether.

According to the standard of Acts 2:42, an individual who is unfaithful is not qualified to be a New Testament church member.

A Disciplined Environment and the Lord's Supper

The proper exercise of the Lord's Supper is an important part of a disciplined church.

It is one of the major elements mentioned in Acts 2:42. "And they continued stedfastly in the apostles' doctrine and fellowship, and in breaking of bread, and in prayers."

Paul issued a strong warning to the church of Corinth about abusing the Lord's Supper (1 Co. 11:20-22).

> "When ye come together therefore into one place, *this* is not to eat the Lord's supper. For in eating every one taketh before *other* his own supper: and one is hungry, and another is

drunken. What? have ye not houses to eat and to drink in? or despise ye the church of God, and shame them that have not? What shall I say to you? shall I praise you in this? I praise *you* not."

The Lord's Supper, rightly conducted, maintains discipline in the following ways:

- It is an occasion of remembering Christ and His atonement (1 Co. 11:24-25).

- It is an occasion of reaffirming Christ's lordship over the believer's lives. The word "Lord" is used eight times in 1 Co. 11:20-32.

- It is an occasion of being reminded of Christ's imminent return (1 Co. 11:26).

- It is an occasion of solemn examination in fear of God's chastisement (1 Co. 11:27-32). We always begin the Lord's Supper with a time of quiet personal confession.

The Lord's Supper is part of the church's disciplinary system.

> "But now I have written unto you not to keep company, if any man that is called a brother be a fornicator, or covetous, or an idolater, or a railer, or a drunkard, or an extortioner; **with such an one no not to eat**" (1 Co. 5:11).

The fact that the Lord's Supper is an aspect of the church's discipline is why the church must control who partakes of it. The church member who is under discipline cannot partake.

We practice the Lord's Supper in a separate service when only members in good standing are in attendance so that visitors are not confused and embarrassed.

I am always shocked by the practice of open communion. Some time ago I visited a church on a Sunday morning and after the sermon they had the Lord's Supper. Visitors were invited to partake, even though they were not a part of the church body and were not therefore under the church's discipline, and some of them were complete strangers. I quietly slipped out of the auditorium.

I believe that the church can invite select visitors to participate if they and their home churches are well known and if the host church is confident that these visitors are in good standing. This is called "close communion," and it is what we practice. We don't routinely invite visitors from other churches, but we do invite short-term missionaries and visiting preachers who are gathering with us and ministering with us on a temporary basis.

Abuse of a Disciplined Environment

The right exercise of authority and discipline depends largely on the character of the leaders.

A Diotrophes will abuse his authority over the church (3 John 9-11).

Diotrophes loved to have the preeminence (3 John 9). Pride was the root problem. I have seen this ruin many churches. Humility enables the pastor to recognize that the church is not his and the members are not his. They belong exclusively to the Lord. They are His purchased possession, and the pastor is appointed to watch the flock for the Lord and by His laws and under His direction. Any preacher can become a Diotrophes if he is not careful, because the old nature is selfish, proud, controlling, and does not like "criticism."

Diotrophes refused to receive John (3 John 9). He did not submit to the authority of the Lord's apostles and the New Testament faith.

Diotrophes forbade men and things that God had not forbidden. He was a law unto himself. The pastor's authority is God's Word, not his own thinking. This is the sin of being "self-willed" (Titus 1:7). The preacher does not have the authority to reject sound men who follow the Bible.

Diotrophes prated against men of God with malicious words (3 John 10). He wasn't speaking the truth in love. He wasn't protecting the flock from compromise and error. Rather, he was slandering men of God in order to poison the minds of the people against them for his own selfish purposes.

John was speaking against Diotrophes, and Diotrophes was speaking against John. But John was speaking the truth in love, and Diotrophes was speaking lies in hatred. John was serving God, but Diotrophes was serving himself.

A Diotrophes spirit often arises when someone challenges a church or denomination or ecclesiastical organization with God's Word and points out genuine error.

- This happened during the First Great Awakening. The "old lights" who supported the status quo of the unregeneracy in the Protestant churches slandered the "new lights" who were warning of it. The latter were forbidden to preach and were locked out of congregations. George Whitefield was called Satan and a deceiver.

- This happened when I challenged the Nepal Christian Fellowship in the early 1980s with their disobedience to the Scripture, such as their acceptance of polygamous pastors and their distribution of perverted Bible translations such as the Nepali equivalent of the Today's English Version. They held an ecclesiastical trial, condemned me for "dividing the body of Christ in Nepal," and demanded that I stop all of my work and leave the country.

- Some big-name Baptist pastors have protected their empires by slandering men who have tried to warn of their errors. They have said that such men should not meddle in "the affairs of a local church," but when a man has a public ministry that influences many churches, his preaching is no longer merely the business of his local church.

Diotrophes' work was an evil work, and John solemnly warned that "he that doeth evil hath not seen God" (3 John 11). There are many preachers who haven't seen God. In the 18th century, Gilbert Tennent warned of this in his sermon "The Danger of an Unconverted Ministry."

Another example of abuse of discipline was a Shepherding Movement within Pentecostalism in the 1990s. The shepherding movement taught that each believer must be directly shepherded by an appointed leader, and this leader had complete authority over the individual, even to the extent of determining what employment he could take and who he or she could marry.

It is one thing for a spiritual leader to give biblical counsel to the Lord's people; it is quite another thing when a spiritual leader takes control of the believer's life, thus taking the Lord's rightful place.

In this chapter we have seen many aspects of church discipline.

The church that will be standing when Christ comes is the church that takes biblical discipline seriously and refuses to neglect any aspect of it.

New Testament Church Discipline by James Crumpton is available as a free eBook at www.wayoflife.org.

There is a lengthy study on church discipline in the *Way of Life Encyclopedia of the Bible and Christianity*.

A Discipling Church Is Strong in God's Word

Outline
This Begins with the Preachers
This Requires Desire on the Part of the People
This Requires the Right Type of Preaching
This Requires a Plan to Teach the Whole Word of God
The Benefit of Multiple Preachers
This Requires Training the People to be Effectual Bible Students
Public Bible Reading
Bible Memorization
Challenging the People
Re-evaluating Services and Programs
One-on-one Discipleship
Men's Discipleship Meetings
Women's Discipleship Meetings
Youth Ministry
Bookstore
Bible Conferences
Bible College

Churches that aren't serious Bible education institutions are building on sand, and they won't stand for long in today's spiritual climate.

One of the reasons why so many Independent Baptist churches have collapsed over the past 20 years is their biblical shallowness. The preaching is shallow. The teaching ministries are shallow. And most of the members aren't serious Bible students.

The Bible must be the church's chief Book. Every church should *be* a Bible Institute, not just *have* a Bible Institute.

Acts 2:42 mentions doctrine as the first activity of a sound church.

1 Timothy 3:15 says the church is the pillar and ground of the truth. Truth is the *preeminent* business of a sound church, and God's Word is truth (John 17:17).

Colossians 3:16 describes the church that is strong in God's Word. "Let the word of Christ dwell in you richly in all wisdom..."

Note that the Word of God is to *dwell richly*. The congregation's knowledge of God's Word must not be shallow and superficial. It must be deep and rich and solid.

And we see that the knowledge of God's Word is in *all wisdom*. This refers to spiritual wisdom and practical application. This is not a church that only reads and memorizes Scripture. It is a church that has spiritual understanding. It's a church that lives the Scripture.

Begins with the Preachers

Note what the Bible says about the studiousness of a qualified preacher:

- He labors to rightly divide God's Word (2 Ti. 2:15).
- He is apt to teach; *capable* of training others (1 Ti. 3:2; 2 Ti. 2:2, 24).
- He is nourished up in good doctrine (1 Ti. 4:6).
- He gives attendance to reading and to doctrine (1 Ti. 4:13).
- He labors in the Word and doctrine (1 Ti. 5:17).
- He preaches God's Word with doctrine (2 Ti. 4:2).
- He has been taught (Titus 1:9).
- He is strong enough in God's Word to protect the flock (Titus 1:9-16).

But many preachers are not serious Bible students. As a consequence, their preaching is shallow and repetitious. Many preachers are not like the scribe of the kingdom of heaven described by Jesus who "bringeth forth out of his treasure things new and old" (Mt. 13:52). The preacher who is not a serious student rarely has anything new to enrich his preaching and teaching. He studies only enough to get messages. The preaching doesn't come from the *overflow* of a serious study habit.

Some preachers even despise commentaries.

When I was a young Christian, I determined to read and study the Bible alone and to forgo consulting any commentaries or study books. I did this religiously for some time, perhaps a couple of weeks, but the Lord made it plain to me that I need help from other men and that He is not going to give me everything by direct enlightenment. It is not that the Bible is insufficient; it is that I am only one weak man and can't possibly know and understand everything without help. When I rejected the use of commentaries, I was left with my own meager resources, and though I have some gifts in understanding and teaching the Bible, I am still only a very puny man with very limited ideas when left to my own.

Any man who is honest before God will acknowledge that a great deal of his knowledge and understanding is gleaned from other men. God has ordained this. That is why we start life as a child and are dependent upon parents and tutors, and even as we grow older, we remain very dependent upon the help of others.

God has given ministry-gifted men to the churches, and He uses them to edify the saints (Ephesians 4:11-14; 2 Ti. 2:2). If I were shut up on a remote island with only the Bible, I am sure the Lord would give me everything I needed for that situation directly through His Word, but that is not His normal way of operation.

I am thankful that some of the excellent teaching of past and present generations has been captured in print so I can possess it and consult it whenever I please. Such material is worth its weight in gold.

But I have found that the most difficult place to sell serious Bible study books and associated materials is at the average Independent Baptist preachers' meeting. There are exceptions, but this has generally been my experience through the years.

A pastor friend who has been in the ministry for many decades wrote the following to me in 2014:

> "I asked a missionary what books he had read lately that were a blessing, and he replied that all he reads is a magazine on running. I fear that Independent Baptists may be the *illiterati* of the 20th and 21st centuries. And the present addiction to iPhones and social media only makes it worse. John Nordman, who worked with Hyles years ago at Hyles Anderson, led the Bible college in Brisbane for some years until the pastor's son did a Schaap on some kids there and the

wheels fell off. He sent me their college prospectus one year hoping to get some of our kids, and I wrote him back and asked him why there was not a course on theology. I later found out that Hyles Anderson never allowed theology to be taught because Jack Hyles thought it would turn their students into Calvinists. Some years ago I started asking preachers questions when we sat around talking or when we drove down the road. Questions on what doctrine was especially precious to them at that moment, or what book of the Bible they love the most this week, or what good book they are reading, or which one has helped them grow the most, or what authors are the most challenging to them spiritually, or what they think about this or that verse (and I pick the hardest ones to ask about). If they are driving, I take my Bible and read to them some passage I am meditating on and ask them to explain them to me. Most of them are out of their depth within ten seconds. Some stare at me with open mouth and shake their head. The Presbyterian pastors I know are the most adept at discussing solid Bible doctrine. Most of the Independent Baptist pastors have never read anything deeper than John Rice or Curtis Hutson. We had a missionary here this weekend who tells great stories, but doesn't know ANY solid Bible doctrine."

This preacher said further:

"There is abysmal ignorance concerning the doctrine of Christ, concerning the doctrines of justification, sanctification, and glorification. One of our major problems is that expository preaching is not politically correct in fundamental churches. For a pastor to preach through a book of the Bible is a rare thing. Most of the men I know don't do that because it doesn't draw big crowds and they like fireworks in the pulpit or fairy tales."

Another man commented:

"I agree about the importance of the study of Bible prophecy. Unfortunately, fundamental Baptist preachers seem very reluctant to delve into prophecy. I think it might be because most preachers have not studied much beyond the first three chapters of Revelation. I don't think I have ever heard a really solid message from an IFB preacher from the mountain of Old Testament prophecies with momentous future fulfillment."

A large percentage of the Independent Baptist preaching I have heard personally over the past four decades has been motivational Pablum (baby food) with no serious exegesis of Scripture and little spiritual depth and content.

It has been said, "The man who *doesn't* read is no better off than the man who *cannot* read," and, "Five years from now you will be the same person except for the people you meet and the books you read."

Wise men of God through the centuries have valued the written and printed page.

The apostle Paul was a student to the end of his life. Even when in prison awaiting his death, he said to Timothy, "The cloke that I left at Troas with Carpus, when thou comest, bring with thee, and the books, but especially the parchments." (2 Timothy 4:13).

Bring the books said the stalwart old warrior! Bring the books said the man whom we are told to imitate. "Wherefore I beseech you, be ye followers of me" (1 Co. 4:16). "Brethren, be followers together of me, and mark them which walk so as ye have us for an ensample" (Philippians 3:17).

John Wesley exhorted a preacher friend as follows:

> "What has exceedingly hurt you in time past, nay, and I fear to this day, is want of reading. I scarce ever knew a preacher read so little. And perhaps by neglecting it you have lost the taste for it. Hence your talent in preaching does not increase. It is just the same as it was seven years ago. It is lively, but not deep: there is little variety; there is no compass of thought. Reading only can supply this, with meditation and daily prayer. You wrong yourself greatly by omitting this. You can never be a deep preacher without it any more than a thorough Christian. O begin! Fix some part of every day for private exercises. You may acquire the taste which you have not; what is tedious at first will afterwards be pleasant. Whether you like it or no; read and pray daily. It is for your life; there is no other way; else you will be a trifler all your days, and a petty, superficial prayer" (John Wesley to John Trembeth, August 1760).

The revivalist preacher George Whitefield read Matthew Henry's complete commentary set through four times during his lifetime. And this is a man who preached an estimated 18,000 sermons, an average of ten a week, and traveled massive distances on terrible roads and no roads, by horseback, buggy, etc.

Charles Spurgeon, who has been called the Prince of Preachers, advised the preachers in his Bible College, "Sell your shirt and buy books."

Spurgeon did not have a lot of patience with preachers who despise commentaries. He addressed the following statement to his Bible School students:

> "Of course, you are not such wiseacres as to think or say that you can expound Scripture without assistance from the works of divines and learned men who have laboured before you in the field of exposition. If you are of that opinion, pray remain so, for you are not worth the trouble of conversion, and like a little coterie who think with you, would resent the attempt as an insult to your infallibility. It seems odd, that certain men who talk so much of what the Holy Spirit reveals to themselves, should think so little of what he has revealed to others. My chat this afternoon is not for these great originals, but for you who are content to learn of holy men, taught of God, and mighty in the Scriptures. It has been the fashion of late years to speak against the use of commentaries. If there were any fear that the expositions of Matthew Henry, Gill, Scott, and others, would be exalted into Christian Targums, we would join the chorus of objectors, but the existence or approach of such a danger we do not suspect. The temptations of our times lie rather in empty pretensions to novelty of sentiment, than in a slavish following of accepted guides. A respectable acquaintance with the opinions of the giants of the past, might have saved many an erratic thinker from wild interpretations and outrageous inferences. Usually, we have found the despisers of commentaries to be men who have no sort of acquaintance with them; in their case, it is the opposite of familiarity which has bred contempt" (Spurgeon, *Two Lectures Addressed to the Students of the Pastor's College, Metropolitan Tabernacle*, http://www.book-academy.co.uk/lectures/index.html).

Spurgeon advised his Bible students to read the entire multi-volume Matthew Henry commentary set in the twelve months after they graduated from Pastor's College. How do you measure up to that standard, preacher friend?

Spurgeon observed that a good commentary will provide new lines of thought to the student. Of Matthew Henry, Spurgeon said,

> "You will find him to be glittering with metaphors, rich in analogies, overflowing with illustrations, superabundant in reflections. ... You will acquire a vast store of sermons if you read with your note-book close at hand; and as for thoughts, they will swarm around you like twittering swallows around an old gable towards the close of autumn."

It is obvious that many men of God of former times were more studious than the average preacher today, and wiser about the value of good books.

Nearly every day for forty-three years, I have had the privilege of accessing a wealth of commentary and Bible study material and delighting as new thoughts swarm around me like twittering swallows!

To have discipling churches we must have studious preachers.

Requires Desire on the Part of the People

If there were a true passion for learning God's Word on the part of more church members, stronger preachers would be raised up and called.

A baby that does not desire milk is physically sick, and a professing Christian that does not desire the Word of God is spiritually sick.

> "As newborn babes, desire the sincere milk of the word, that
> ye may grow thereby" (1 Peter 2:2).

We have often been amazed at the lack of passion for Bible study in the membership of Baptist churches. So few have an effectual daily Bible study habit. So few are interested in serious Bible training. Even if the church has Bible Institute classes, it is typical that few care enough to participate.

I am convinced that the equivalent of a Bible Institute education is the *beginning* of an effectual, fruitful Christian life and ministry. I am not talking about preachers. I am talking about every Christian.

Every child of God has a God-given ministry that requires serious Bible education. Every child of God is an ambassador for

Christ (2 Co. 5:20). Every child of God is a king and priest (Re. 1:6). Every child of God is to be a teacher (Heb. 5:12-14). Every Christian father is the spiritual leader of his home; he is to nurture his wife (Eph. 5:25-26) and train up his children (Eph. 6:4). Every Christian mother is to love her children, which involves educating them in God's Word and discipling them (Titus 2:3-5).

Yet what a frightfully small percentage of those who profess to be God's people are passionate enough to pursue serious Bible training, even though it is readily available.

This comes back to being very careful about baptism and receiving members. There is no biblical authority for receiving lukewarm, half-hearted people into the church's membership. Let such people attend the services if they please, but let them also understand that they are not qualified to be a member of one of Christ's congregations. They don't continue in doctrine (Acts 2:42).

Requires the Right Kind of Preaching Ministry

> "I charge *thee* therefore before God, and the Lord Jesus Christ, who shall judge the quick and the dead at his appearing and his kingdom; Preach the word; be instant in season, out of season; reprove, rebuke, exhort with all longsuffering and doctrine. For the time will come when they will not endure sound doctrine; but after their own lusts shall they heap to themselves teachers, having itching ears; And they shall turn away *their* ears from the truth, and shall be turned unto fables" (2 Timothy 4:1-4).

In this passage we see the major characteristics of a sound preaching and teaching ministry.

Few things are more needed in Bible-believing churches today. A sound preaching/teaching ministry is a major part of producing disciples of Jesus Christ and disciplining the church. It is a major part of building godly homes and raising up youth who know and serve Christ.

A really strong, effectual preaching ministry can often build a decent church even when some other things might be lacking. I have seen this many times. I don't mean to refer to preaching merely as shouting and storytelling and reproving. I don't mean to refer merely to a "good pulpiteer." I mean preaching that is solidly biblical, with biblical depth, preaching by a man who enriches his messages with a lot of study, both of the Bible and of life in general, but also preaching with zeal, enthusiasm, real exhortation, reproof, and rebuke.

I think of Pastor J.B. Buffington and Calvary Baptist Church of Lakeland, Florida, in its heyday in the 1970s and 1980s. Buffington was a powerful preacher. He was enthusiastic. He was forceful. He reproved and rebuked. But his messages were rich and had a lot of depth. He preached with doctrine. There was nothing soft or shallow or frivolous. There was almost no joking around. And his preaching was interesting; he could hold the attention of an audience for long periods of time. The church practiced what I called "Quick Prayerism," and was not careful about salvation and church membership and was therefore very much a mixed multitude, because Pastor Buffington graduated from Tennessee Temple and followed the Lee Roberson model of church philosophy, and that made the ministry weaker than it could have been, but the strong preaching in itself had tremendously good fruit. That preaching built many good Christian lives and homes. It separated many from the world. Many young people surrendered to Christ in those days and attended Bible college and entered full-time ministry.

How we need good preaching!

2 Timothy 4:1-2 instructs us that there are many necessary elements to an effectual preaching ministry.

Biblical preaching is CONSCIOUS OF GOD'S SOLEMN CHARGE. The preacher must be conscious of the fact that he will give account to God (2 Ti. 4:1). The call to preach is a solemn obligation that is laid upon him. Paul impressed Timothy in the most imposing manner possible of the seriousness of his calling. This is the main thing that will keep a preacher straight in his ministry and that will give him the courage to preach the hard things of the Scriptures as well as the "positive" things, to preach the things the people like to hear and the things they don't like to hear.

Biblical preaching is CONSCIOUS OF DIVINE AUTHORITY. The preacher is the spokesman of Jesus Christ. He must not preach his own message; He must preach God's message. He is not proclaiming his own judgments; he is proclaiming the judgments of God, and as he does this he has God's authority. He is to preach as the "oracles of God" (1 Pe. 4:11). In Romans 3:2, Paul calls the Scripture "the oracles of God." The preacher must make sure that he is God's man with God's message, then he must preach with "all authority" (Titus 2:15). The preacher is not to make *suggestions* or to share *opinions*; he is not to preach with apology and hesitation and uncertainty. If a man is not convinced of his call to preach and if he is not convinced of the divine authority of his message, he should not preach. "My brethren, be not many masters, knowing that we shall receive the greater condemnation" (James 3:1). The preacher must not fear the face of man, or God will confound him (Jer. 1:17; Eze. 2:6-8).

2 Timothy 4 plainly implies that a preacher can know the truth for certain and can therefore preach with conviction and authority. Timothy was instructed to study so that he could rightly divide the Word of God (2 Ti. 2:15). He would not have been so instructed if it were not possible to know for sure how to interpret the Scriptures properly. Christ promised that a man *can* know the truth if he continues in God's Word (Joh. 8:31-32). It is a promise. John said that the believer has the Holy Spirit as his teacher and that he can know all things (1 John 2:20, 27).

Speaking with authority means the preacher must teach the people to respect God's Word and God's messenger. See Neh. 8:2-8. They must be taught to sit quietly and listen carefully, and try to capture a message for their lives. They must be taught to turn off their cell phones, to not talk with their friends, to keep the children quiet, etc.

Biblical preaching is *TO PREACH THE WORD OF GOD*. The preacher is not to preach his opinions or extra-biblical traditions or extra-biblical prophecies; he is to preach the Bible. That Book and that Book alone is the God-called preacher's Textbook.

Biblical preaching is *TO PREACH ALL OF GOD'S WORD* (2 Ti. 4:2). Timothy was instructed to "preach the word." Paul did not designate which part of it, because he was referring to the whole Bible. The preacher has no authority to pick and choose what he will preach and what he will not preach. Billy Graham once said that he was only responsible to preach the gospel, but that is not true. Every preacher is responsible to "preach the word," and those who narrow their message for the sake of a broader fellowship and a wider ministry will give account to God.

Biblical preaching is "INSTANT" (2 Ti. 4:2). The preaching must be active, aggressive, confrontational, stalwart, unyielding. The Greek word "epistemi" is elsewhere translated "assault" (Acts 17:5), "come unto" (Acts 12:7), "stand by" (Acts 22:20). It means "stand up to it" (*Robertson's Word Pictures*). It is used for the Jewish leaders' confrontation with Jesus ("came upon him," Lu. 20:1) and the arrest of the disciples ("came upon them," Acts 4:1; 6:12).

Likewise, the preacher confronts the people with God's Word. He supports God's Word before his hearers. He must exercise enthusiasm, energy.

> "Men are apt to be drowsy in hearing the Word, and the liveliness of the preacher is a means to stir up the attention of the hearers, and beget suitable affection in them" (Solomon Stoddard, "The Defects of Preachers Reproved," 1723).

Biblical preaching is to preach "IN SEASON AND OUT OF SEASON" (2 Ti. 4:2).

This refers to preaching when the preaching is popular as well as when it is unpopular.

It refers to preaching when people have gathered for the express purpose of hearing the Word of God and preaching when people are not so gathered. Paul preached in church meetings and he also preached in the marketplaces.

It refers to preaching when the preaching is legal and preaching when it is illegal, when it is safe and when it is dangerous, in times of peace and in times of persecution. We see this example in the ministry of the apostles (Acts 4:19; 5:29). Paul preached when he was free, and he preached when he was bound.

It refers to preaching to every sort of men, to the poor, who are often more responsive to God's Word, but also to the rich, who commonly do not receive God's Word as readily. The Bible commands us to preach the gospel to *every* creature (Mr. 16:15), to do good to *all* men (Ga. 6:10), and to sow our seed on *all* waters (Ec. 11:1, 6).

It refers to preaching when there is obvious fruit and preaching when nothing appears to be happening. It was admonitions such as these that kept Adoniram Judson preaching for six years before he saw his first Burmese convert and ten years before he had 18 converts.

It refers to preaching in times of encouragement and preaching in times of discouragement. "It is easy for the preacher to let the attitude of the congregation control him and to allow himself to become discouraged, but he must strengthen himself in the Lord and lift the congregation up" (Bruce Lackey).

Biblical preaching is *TO REPROVE* (2 Ti. 4:2). This is from the Greek word "elegcho," which means "to confute, admonish." It is elsewhere translated "convict" (Joh. 8:9), "convince" (Joh. 8:46), "tell a fault" (Mt. 18:15). It means to show people their false ways and to convince them of the right way of God's Word. This is a difficult task, because human nature does not like to be told that it is wrong. The natural response to reproof is to become offended and to justify oneself and to lash out at the reprover. Giving reproof implies a responsibility on the part of the preacher to make judgments based on God's Word about the condition of the people to whom he is preaching. Today the popular cry is "judge not," but those words in Matthew 7:1 are taken out of context and made to mean that it is not God's will to judge sin and doctrine, but in Matthew 7:1-5 Christ was warning against hypocritical judgment. He was not saying that the believer cannot judge anything. Elsewhere we are told that the believer *is* to judge sin and doctrine. In 2 Ti. 4:2, the preacher is commanded to judge things that are wrong and to reprove and rebuke them. In so doing, he is not exercising his own judgment; he is exercising God's judgment.

Reproof involves proving. It means "to bring to proof" (*Robertson's Word Pictures*). The preacher must know the Word of God well enough and be so well informed about the people to whom he is preaching that he can prove to them that what he is saying is true. He disproves error and proves the truth. It involves apologetics. It requires knowledge of whatever error the people might be tempted to follow. It requires a lot of study and preparation.

Biblical preaching is *TO REBUKE*. This is from the Greek word "epitimao," which means "to tax upon, to censure, to forbid." It is also translated "charge" (Lu. 9:21). It means to tell people that they are wrong; to rebuke them for being in the wrong; to charge them before God that they are wrong and that they are obligated to turn from their error. It is to call people to repentance from sin and error.

This requires plain speaking so that the people know exactly what you are rebuking.

Rebuking is a difficult ministry, but every preacher is obligated to do it and will give account to God if he shuns it.

Rebuke of sin and error requires courage that can only come from God. The fear of God must outweigh the fear of man. The love of God and man must outweigh the love of self.

This is a ministry that is contrary to the prevailing philosophy of the hour.

Rebuke is contrary to humanistic psychology, which seeks to build self-esteem and avoids anything degrading of self-esteem. The very popular Robert Schuller said that Christianity "must cease to be a negative religion and must become positive" (*Self-Esteem: The New Reformation*, p. 104). He said that it is damaging to call people sinners. He said, "I have no right to ever preach a sermon or write an article that would offend the self-respect and violate the self-dignity of a listener or reader."

Rebuke is contrary to New Evangelicalism, which avoids the negatives and focuses on the positive. It avoids "dealing with personalities." Typically, it deals with sin and error only in generalities.

Rebuke is contrary to the relativistic, judge-not philosophy of modern secular society.

Rebuke is contrary to feminism. It is amazing how dramatically feminist thinking has permeated society and even influenced Bible-believing churches. This has resulted in a softening effect even on the military. A masculine approach is not wanted. Strong discipline is not understood or appreciated, not even in a military boot camp. Typically, the female way is not the way of rebuke and chastening but the way of finding more gentle ways of discipline.

Why rebuke, she thinks, when you can deal with things in a softer way? But rebuke is what God's Word calls for.

The feminization effect has resulted in a softening of the preaching and the militant stance of the church. God is a "man of war," but very few preachers are. Christ took on the Pharisees and Sadducees, and Paul took on every heretic that raised his head, but such zeal is foreign to most so-called preachers. Martin Luther took on Rome and called the pope the antichrist and called the pope's bull "all impiety, blasphemy, ignorance, impudence, hypocrisy, lying." Charles Spurgeon took on the Baptist Union and railed against "mild and gentle men, of soft manners and squeamish words" in the pulpit, calling for ""the fiery Knox" who will "ding our pulpits into blads" [smash them with forceful preaching]. Gilbert Tennent took on the Presbyterians of his day, lifting his voice in 1740 in the midst of a synod (a regional governing body) to warn that many preachers were unregenerate and calling them "rotten-hearted hypocrites, and utter strangers to the saving knowledge of God and of their own hearts" (Joseph Tracy, *The Great Awakening*, 1842).

This type of boldness is entirely unknown among convention Baptists, and it is exceedingly rare among fundamental Baptists. The protest has long gone out of most Protestants, and the "fundamentalism" has largely gone out of fundamentalists.

But whether people like it or not, the preacher's job is to preach the Word of God without compromise and without narrowing down and softening the message. Compromising, soft-peddling preachers are responsible for the downgrade in the level of holiness in the churches. It was the same in Jeremiah's day.

> "Therefore thus saith the LORD of hosts concerning the prophets; Behold, I will feed them with wormwood, and make them drink the water of gall: for **from the prophets of Jerusalem is profaneness gone forth into all the land.** ... I have not sent these prophets, yet they ran: I have not spoken to them, yet they prophesied. But **if they had stood in my counsel, and had caused my people to hear my words, then they should have turned them from their evil way, and from the evil of their doings**" (Jer. 23:15, 21-22).

Observe that it was because of the compromise of the prophets that profaneness had gone forth into all the land. God held the preachers responsible. They were the well-spring of profaneness. Jeremiah says that the true prophet will turn the people from their evil ways. That is still the mark of a God-called preacher.

Consider the preaching of the ancient prophet Enoch,

> "And Enoch also, the seventh from Adam, prophesied of these, saying, Behold, the Lord cometh with ten thousands of his saints, to execute judgment upon all, and to convince all that are ungodly among them of all their ungodly deeds which they have ungodly committed, and of all their hard speeches which ungodly sinners have spoken against him" (Jude 1:14-15).

Observe that Enoch was preaching about conditions that will exist in the world before Jesus returns. He is preaching about our day! And that is exactly the kind of preaching we need. We don't need soft, ear-tickling teaching; we need the "reproofs of instruction" that will turn us away from evil and keep us hedged into the narrow way of the truth (Proverbs 6:23).

To be effective, rebuke has to be plain and forthright. All of the preachers in the Bible were plain spoken. Paul said, "... we use great plainness of speech" (2 Co. 3:12). Bible preachers condemned sin plainly; they rebuked error unhesitatingly. Consider Jesus' message to the Pharisees in Matthew 23:13-33. Consider Paul's description of false teachers; in 1 and 2 Timothy alone he named the names of false teachers and compromisers 10 times (1 Ti. 1:20; 2 Ti. 1:15; 2:17; 3:8; 4:10, 14). Consider Peter's description of false teachers (2 Peter 2). Consider James's rebuke of worldliness (Jas. 4:4).

The leaders of the First Great Awakening in America in the early 18th century complained that most of the preaching was soft and did not awaken the sinners to their plight. In contrast, the revivalists preached with great plainness and reproof. Consider the following excerpt from Gilbert Tennent's "Solemn Warning," 1735:

> Awake, Awake Sinners, stand up and look where you are hastning, least you drink of the Hand of the Lord, the Dregs of the Cup of his Fury; the Cup of trembling, and wring them out, Isai. 51.17.
>
> Awake ye Drunkards, and weep and howl, Joel 1.5. For what can ye expect (so continuing) but to drink of that Cup of

Trembling I but now mention'd. Awake ye profane Swearers, and remember ye will not get a drop of Water to cool your cursing cursed Tongues in Hell, when they and you shall flame in the broad burning Lake, Luke 16.24. God has said he will not hold you Guiltless, that take his Name in vain, Exod 20.7.

Awake ye unclean Adulterers, and Whoremongers, and remember that without a speedy Repentance, your dismal abode shall be ever with unclean Devils, the Soul of a God shall be avenged upon you, Jer. 5.8, 29.

Awake ye Sabbath-Breakers, and reform; or God will break you upon the Wheels of his Vengeance, and torture you eternally upon the Rack of his Justice, Neham. 13.16, 17, 18. And let all other sorts of profane Sinners be entreated to awake out of Sleep and consider their Danger.

Awake ye covetous griping Nabals, and read what the Apostle James says to you, Chap 5. 1 to 6. Go to now, ye rich Men, weep and howl for the Miseries that shall come upon you. The Rust of your Gold and Silver shall be a Witness against you. Ye have lived in Pleasure upon Earth, and been wanton, you have nourished your Hearts as in a Day of Slaughter. Here we may Note by the Way, that those who live like Beasts here, and will not be induc'd by any Perswasive to repent, reform and act like Men, shall howl like Beasts hereafter, without being heard or pitied, 1 Co. 16.13. Pr. 1.26.

Awake ye secure Moralists, and lifeless, sapless Formalists, who are Strangers to the Power of experimental Religion: Remember your shadowy Appearances, can't deceive the Rein trying God, Ga. 6.7. Nor your dry Leaves of husky spiritless Duties, secure your guilty Souls, from an astonishing overwhelming Inundation of his high and terrible Displeasure, Mt. 5.20.

Awake every of you that are yet in a Christless unconvinced State! Are you not asham'd to sleep all the Day in Sloth, while some are trembling, troubled and distress'd about their Souls, who are not greater Sinners than your selves? Nay, perhaps not near so great; what sleep? while others are crying Night and Day with Tears, and heavy Groans to God, for pardoning Mercy, who have no more precious Souls than you. Sleep! While others are labouring hard and taking Heaven by

Storm! What sleep! While some are travelling fast to the heavenly Jerusalem, and rejoicing in the Way with Joy unspeakable and glorious. What will ye draw the Curtains of a carnal Security, and false Hope about you, and sleep to Death and Hell, even when the meridian Sun of the Gospel shines full in your Face, and Life and Immortality is brought to Light, and God, and Christ, his Ministers, Word, Providences, and your own Consciences, are ringing a loud Alarm, a Peal of Thunder in your Ears to awake you: That you may consider your Ways, and turn your Feet to God's Testimonies. Will you sleep with Fire in your Bosoms? (the unpardon'd Guilt of Sin) with the Curse of God upon your Souls, the Heavens frowning upon you, and shut against you, the burden'd Earth travelling under you, and Hell yawning wide to devour and consume you I Mayn't I say to you as Moses to Israel, De. 29.4. Yet the Lord hath not given you a Heart to perceive, and Eyes to see, and Ears to hear, unto this Day. O! Is it not to be fear'd that God in Justice has left you to a Spirit of Slumber? Because you shut your Eyes against the Light, John 3. That you should sleep and never awake. Jer. 51.57. And I will make drunk her Princes, and her wise Men, and her Rulers, and her mighty Men; and they shall sleep a perpetual Sleep, and not awake, saith the King, whose Name is the Lord of Hosts. Pr. 6. 9. How long wilt thou sleep, O Sluggard? when wilt thou arise out of thy Sleep?

The preaching must warn about judgment and damnation. Consider another example of the First Great Awakening:

> "... if sinners don't hear often of judgment and damnation few will be converted. Many men are in deep sleep and flatter themselves as if there was no hell, or at least that God will not deal so harshly with them as to damn them. Psal. 36:2. He flattereth himself in his own eyes, until his iniquity be found to be hateful. They need to be told of the terrors of the Lord, that they may flee from wrath to come: A little matter will not scare men, their hearts be as hard as a stone, as hard as a piece of the nether milstone, and they will be ready to laugh at the shaking of the spear. Ministers must give them no rest in such a condition: they must pull them as brands out of the burnings. It is well if thunder and lightning will awaken them. They had need to fear that they may work out their salvation with fear and trembling. Ministers are faulty when they speak

to them with gentleness, as Eli rebuked his sons. Christ Jesus often warned them of the danger of damnation: Mt. 5:29-30. It is better that one of thy members should perish, and not that thy whole body should be cast into hell. Mt. 7:13. Broad is the gate and wide is the way that leadeth to destruction, and many there be that go in thereat. Mt. 13:42. The angels shall cast them into a furnace of fire, there shall be wailing and gnashing of teeth. So also, Mt. 22:13. Mt. 25:41, 46. This for our imitation. Christ knew how to deal with souls, and Paul followed His example. Men need to be terrified and have the arrows of the Almighty in them that they may be converted. Ministers should be Sons of Thunder. Men had need have storms in their hearts, before they will betake themselves to Christ for refuge. When they are pricked at the heart, then they will say, What must we do to be saved? Men must be fired out of their worldliness and sloth. Men must be driven as Lot was out of Sodom. Reason will govern men in other things; but it is fear that must take them diligently to seek salvation. If they be but thoroughly convinced of their danger, that will make them go to God and take pains" (Solomon Stoddard, Defects of Preachers Reproved, 1723)

Among fundamentalists in general and fundamental Baptist churches in particular, the preaching is growing softer and weaker with each passing decade. There are still exceptions, but the Bible-believing church that has a bold, uncompromising preaching ministry is no longer the rule.

This happened to Southern Baptists and evangelicals 70 years ago, and it is happening to Independent Baptists and fundamentalist Bible churches today.

Many people have written to me to describe the downgrade in preaching. Consider a couple of examples:

> "Another issue that I see is the church letting up on preaching and teaching about hell and the consequences of living without a close relationship with the Lord. In the fifties, when I was a preteen, the airwaves were filled with hellfire sermons. These taught me a right fear and reverence for a Holy God that was not only loving and merciful but also righteous and would one day judge me. It seems to me that we have accepted a lot more worldly philosophy into the pulpit than we would like to admit."

"Churches need to preach harder against moderation in the home with respect to media, fashion, respect, associations and language. Stand firm on the Bible's standard and stop apologizing for the Truth."

Preachers are toning down the message to fit the growing mood of compromise and worldliness. They are bending to the will of the people. Oftentimes the church members are being influenced by New Evangelicals and worse on the radio and in the bookstores and on the Internet and have become accustomed to soft, "non-judgmental," "self-esteem building" preaching. They have unconsciously adopted the "don't be so negative" philosophy. They don't want to hear preaching against rock music and television and wicked video games and immodest dress or anything else that they love. They don't like it when the preacher warns about popular but compromised Christian leaders, whether it is Franklin Graham, James Dobson, Rick Warren, David Jeremiah, Jim Cymbala, or Max Lucado. They don't want to hear any warnings about their heroes.

Instead of educating and warning about such things, many preachers have backed off.

It is increasingly rare to hear ringing rebuke of worldly music, lukewarmness, worldly dating with its moral temptations, public school education which is an illicit yoking together with unbelievers, immodest and unisex dress, worldly entertainment, unfaithfulness to the services and to prayer meetings and other godly responsibilities, etc.

At the very time when the pop culture is getting ever more filthy, preachers are toning down their warnings.

And even when some rebuke is still made, it is often done in vague generalities or in an apologetic tone so that its effect is greatly diminished. Or the preacher will include a joke or a lighthearted comment at just the right time to soften the blow, so to speak, so that the people won't get upset. When we look at Scripture, we never find jokes or lighthearted comments in the midst of reproof and rebuke. I don't think a joke or lighthearted comment is always out of place in the pulpit, but it is out of place when it is used to lighten the effect of reproof.

In the 1990s I was invited to preach at a Baptist Bible Fellowship state meeting. I didn't want to go, but the host pastor urged me to accept the invitation, because he wanted to "let the flag of separation fly." He knew my ministry and wanted to sound out some corrections. Knowing the compromise of the BBFI by that time, I expected that my messages wouldn't be well received, and I wasn't wrong. I preached against contemporary music and some other things, and I preached on the characteristics of Southern Baptist preaching, which is the type of preaching I had grown up with and which had almost zero spiritual power. The characteristics are things like avoiding controversial issues, speaking in generalities, and dealing plainly only with those sins of which the congregation was not generally guilty, such as abortion and homosexuality. The BBF preachers didn't express anything to me personally one way or the other about my messages, as I recall, although they bought almost none of my books and materials; but the host pastor said that he had never seen preachers so upset at a series of messages. The other preacher at the conference was well received, because though he is a skilled Bible preacher, he avoided rebuking the very things that his preacher friends at the conference were guilty of. The things he did preach on were things that the crowd could "amen." Many preachers are geniuses at this type of thing, and though they can sound very bold and forthright and very much the warrior, they know how to be bold without being very offensive to that particular congregation.

Though not popular, plain rebuke is necessary, because we are sinners, even after we are saved, and there are fierce enemies that perpetually seek to turn us from truth and righteousness.

To warn people of things that are wrong and to call them to turn from such things is an act of Christian love. Christ said, "As many as I love, I rebuke and chasten" (Re. 3:19). The Bible says that parents that don't discipline their children don't love them (Pr. 13:24), and the same is true for church leaders.

When a preacher seeks to fulfill this obligation in the love of Christ, he is often labeled unloving and Pharisaical, but that is a slander. It is to misunderstand the nature of biblical preaching and the importance of correction. For a preacher to reprove and rebuke in Christ's love is God-like rather than Satan-like.

The rebuke must take different forms depending on the character and condition of the people. At times it will be mild; at other times it must be sharp (Titus 1:13). The same is true for child discipline. The discipline has to fit the character and actions of the child, and the message has to fit the character and actions of the church.

Biblical preaching is *TO EXHORT*. This is from the Greek word "parakaleo," which means "to call near, to invite, to implore or console." It is also translated "beseech," "comfort," "intreat." It means to plead with and encourage and invite people to come to the truth, to call them to the truth. The preacher must therefore reprove and rebuke plainly and also call sweetly. Sound preaching is a Spirit-led mixture of these elements and is not composed of only one or the other.

A biblical exhorter and reprover will not turn a blind eye to sin, unfaithfulness, and lukewarmness (e.g., members not faithful to services, men not attending prayer meetings, men not helping with church set up, teens loving the world, lack of Bible studiousness).

That the preaching is to be with reproof, rebuke, exhortation means **the preaching must be very *PRACTICAL*.** It must get down into the daily lives of the people. The preacher must learn to apply God's Word to every part of the people's lives. He must not preach and teach in generalities. He must ask himself before God, "What does this teaching mean for my people's marriages, child training, jobs, schooling, friends, entertainment," and he must apply it to these things. A great deal of the preaching I have heard has been vague and not properly applied. It might be good teaching as far as that goes, but it lacks the practical, life-changing power that it should have because it is not carefully applied to the people's daily living situation.

Biblical preaching is to preach *WITH LONGSUFFERING*. The preacher must be patient toward the people like God is. The preacher is to have a patient and persevering spirit when he is opposed and when his preaching is not immediately heeded. "If thou do not see the effect of thy labours presently, yet do not therefore give up the cause; be not weary of speaking to them. While God shows to them all long-suffering, let ministers exhort with all long-suffering" (Matthew Henry).

Preaching with longsuffering is a matter of preaching with compassion for the people. We are to care for Christ's sheep (1 Pe. 5:2). We are to speak the truth in love (Eph. 4:25).

This does not mean that the preacher is to be endlessly patient, for Christ Himself is not endlessly patient. In His messages to the seven churches in Revelation 2-3, Christ called the churches to repentance and warned some of them of dire consequences if they did not repent. The preacher must be wise enough to know when it is time to be patient and when it is time to rebuke and when it is time to discipline. Only the Spirit of God can give this wisdom, and He gives it in answer to prayer.

Biblical preaching is to preach *WITH DOCTRINE*. The preacher must be a teacher. Preaching must not be composed merely of exhortation and reproof. It must be full of sound doctrine. It must build the people up in the faith. It must educate them so that they become effectual Bible students. They must be taught to rightly interpret the Scriptures. They must be shown the *why* of obedience as well as the *way* of obedience. They must be given a solid foundation for obedience, which is the doctrine of God's Word. We see the example of this in the New Testament Epistles such as Ephesus. The first three chapters consist of doctrine, while the last three chapters consist of exhortation and reproof. Preaching with doctrine is an essential aspect of sound preaching. This flows from the preacher's study life. The preacher who is a serious student, not only of the Bible but of life in general, will have a rich preaching and teaching ministry. He is ever learning new things that enrich his ministry, making it more effectual, more interesting. Preaching with doctrine requires expository preaching so that the Lord's people learn to understand the Bible as a whole and how that each book fits into the whole.

Biblical preaching *PROTECTS FROM APOSTASY* (2 Ti. 4:3-4). These verses dealing with apostasy are connected with the previous verses about preaching. It is biblical preaching, with its doctrine, exhortation, reproof, and rebuke, that can protect the church from end-time apostasy. No matter how dark the time, God has given the churches everything they need to stand. Biblical preaching is rejected by compromisers and apostates as judgmentalism and Phariseeism, but biblical preaching can stem the tide of apostasy in the lives of those who receive it.

Requires a Plan to Teach the Whole Word of God

Christ commanded this (Mt. 28:19-20).

Paul practiced this (Acts 20:27).

All Scripture is necessary for spiritual perfection (2 Timothy 3:16-17).

This is why we say that the church should not merely *have* a Bible Institute; the church should *be* a Bible institute.

This requires an effective Bible teaching plan that involves each service and ministry.

Requires Expository Preaching

Teaching through books of the Bible requires expertise in expository teaching.

Topical preaching has an important place in the ministry, but expository preaching is also essential for a discipling church.

There are many benefits of expository preaching:

First, the people learn how to understand the Bible as whole and how that each book fits into the whole. The Bible is one Book, and each of the 66 books has its own important message and its own significant place in the canon of Scripture.

Second, through good expository preaching, the people learn how to interpret the Bible in context, which is absolutely essential for a right understanding.

Third, they learn the definition of biblical words.

Fourth, they learn the major doctrines of God's Word.

Fifth, they learn Bible history, geography, and customs. The best way to learn these things is within the context of studying the historical books.

Sixth, they learn about the key people of the Bible.

Seventh, they learn how to deal with difficult passages in context.

Even when I preach topically, I try to take major passages dealing with that topic and exegete them instead of taking individual verses from all over the Bible. This method allows the Bible to speak for itself more effectively, and it avoids the error of taking verses out of context. For example, my book *Holiness: Pitfalls, Struggles, and Victory,* consists of an exegesis of major New

Testament passages on that subject. My course *New Testament Prayer* does the same thing.

In training our preachers, I focus on helping them become effective expository preachers. I have found that few preachers are very good at this.

What we tend to do, even if preaching from a passage, is to take a couple or a few words or subjects from that passage and then preach them topically.

What we want to teach our preachers to do is to let that one passage speak. Just let it speak whatever message and whatever lessons are there. Don't run here and there to other passages very much. Focus on exactly what that particular passage is saying.

For example, if preaching on Romans 1:8-10, the main subject is prayer, but when preaching expositorily, you don't preach on prayer as a topic by going to many other passages about prayer. You stay with this one passage and preach *what this one passage says about prayer*. Likewise, you don't choose a word or phrase such as "the gospel of his Son" in verse 9 and preach on that topically. There is very little in this immediate passage about the gospel. You stay with the one passage and bring out what that one passage teaches. You only go to other passages to help illuminate the passage at hand, and you should do that sparingly. You preach expositorily by letting that one passage speak.

We teach preachers to exegete a passage by the following simple plan: (1) Choose the passage. If you are preaching a topic such as the gospel, you choose the passage prayerfully and wisely. If you are preaching through a book, you first outline the book so you will have the overview before you. Then you must decide how large a segment of that book to preach for each message, depending on your purpose and how much time you are allowed or how much time you want to devote to that book. You can preach verse by verse, segment by segment, or chapter by chapter. (2) Identify the main subject of the passage you are preaching. (3) Study and describe the context of the passage. (4) Define any difficult words. (5) Identify and list the main lessons of the passage. (6) Apply the teaching of the passage to the people's daily lives.

For example, consider Romans 1:8-10 again. The main subject is Paul's prayer for the church at Rome. In considering the context, the preacher could say something about that church and Paul's relationship to it and possibly give the outline of the book. The main lessons are as follows: (1) Paul prayed to God through Jesus Christ. (2) Paul prayed with thanksgiving, (3) Paul prayed without ceasing, (4) Paul prayed always, (5) Paul prayed by making requests rather than demands, (6) Paul prayed by the will of God, (7) Paul prayed by making specific requests. If the preacher wanted to get more detailed in his examination of the passage, he could deal with lessons about God being a witness, serving God in the spirit of the gospel, etc.

We teach the preachers to always look for lessons about God and Christ. This is the main purpose of the Bible. We must always aim to see the Lord Himself in the pages of Scripture and draw closer to Him through our study of the Bible.

One way to practice exegesis is to take a verse or short passage and find as many lessons from it as possible. I love to study the Bible this way, because I learn so many new things. It focuses my attention. It helps me meditate on God's Word. You find lessons from the passage by considering the context, by doing word studies, by comparing Scripture with Scripture (the *Treasury of Scripture Knowledge* is the preeminent tool for this), and by meditating on the verses. I begin by doing my own study and finding as many lessons as possible on my own, using dictionaries and lexicons and the *Treasure of Scripture Knowledge*. Then I turn to commentaries.

The Benefit of Multiple Preachers

We build a church that is strong in God's Word by raising up multiple preachers. Currently we have four main preachers who serve together as a leadership team, plus we have 11 preachers in training.

This is a great advantage because our people benefit from the variety of gifts, insights, and experiences.

We try to give opportunity for as many preachers as possible to minister to the church.

In our main service, we have two preachers. The first one preaches 20 minutes on the gospel, focusing on the needs of our visitors. The second preacher preaches about 45 minutes and focuses on building up the saints.

On Wednesday prayer meeting, we usually have two young preachers deliver 15 minute messages, and we have mid-week prayer meetings in other parts of the city where some of the preachers minister. This is for training, and it is for the edification of the church body.

The young preachers also preach in village works.

We deal with this in the chapter "A Discipling Church Trains Preachers."

Training the People to Be Effectual Bible Students

There are exceptions, but most of the time over the years when I have asked pastors, "How many of your people are serious Bible students," they reply, "Not many."

An Independent Baptist pastor recently challenged his people to read the Bible one minute a day. One minute! And that is a church that considers itself a strong Bible-believing church. What a dishonor to God to offer Him a mere 60 of the 86,400 seconds of my daily schedule for His holy Word. What an incredibly shallow age we live in! No wonder so many "conservative" churches are moving quickly toward a contemporary stance. The foundation is mere sand.

In my experience in preaching in hundreds of churches, most members are like the man I talked with recently. He a faithful church member of long standing in a Bible-believing church, and as he was driving me to the airport, I inquired about his Bible study habit. He told me that his Bible reading is "hit and miss" and that he has no Bible dictionary, concordance, or commentary, has never learned to use such tools, and knows little to nothing about the principles of Bible interpretation.

Another church member told me that he reads two or three verses a day and meditates on them for a while.

We want all of our people, from teens to senior citizens, to be serious Bible students. This is a fundamental aspect of a solid New Testament church.

People who aren't serious Bible students will not know God very well.

Parents who aren't serious Bible students aren't the type of parents that can train and disciple their children.

Young people who aren't serious Bible students will never find God's will, because God's will is found in God's Word.

We use the *Effectual Bible Student*, which shows how to establish a daily Bible reading/study habit, how to use Bible study tools, and how to interpret the Bible. This is available on DVDs and as a free eVideo download from the Way of Life web site, www.wayoflife.org.

We make all of the essential Bible study tools readily available in the church's bookstore.

We challenge the people to commit themselves to devoting the time that is necessary to learn God's Word. It requires serious commitment.

I think of a young man who approached me at a Bible conference and told me that he wants to learn how to be a real Bible student. When I began to explain what was required, he told me that his schedule is pretty full and he didn't think he would be able to devote as much time as I was suggesting. I told him that he needs to forget being a good Bible student, then, because there are no shortcuts and God requires first place in our lives.

Public Bible Reading

We read a chapter of the Bible each week in the main church service.

Bible Memorization

We memorize at least one verse of Scripture each week as a church.

The young people memorize large numbers of Scripture. Recently one of our young women memorized 1 John on her own initiative.

We encourage the parents to help their children memorize Bible verses.

Pastor Kerry Allen has published 150 salvation verses that can be used for a Scripture memorization program for children and has posted it on the web for free download. See the following forwarding link: www.wayoflife.org/memory-cards.pdf

Exhorting and Challenging the People

We make a large effort to exhort and challenge the people about their relationship with God's Word.

Challenging them about personal Bible reading

We urge the church members to read the Bible through each year, and we offer a Bible reading plan for that.

Each week we have the people raise their hands if they have read the Bible faithfully that week.

For those who are weak readers, we urge them to read one chapter per day instead of trying to read three or four and getting bogged down and not getting much out of the reading.

We emphasize Bible reading constantly in our own ministry. The wife of one of our preachers was illiterate when God called her husband to preach, but she learned to read so she can read God's Word. I give accounts of people I know and have read about who learned to read in order to read the Bible, and after some time she took the exhortation to heart and learned to read alongside of her young children.

Learning to be an effectual Bible student should begin in childhood. Children should be taught to have a habit of daily Bible reading. We describe how to do this in the book *Keeping the Kids*.

Challenging them about their knowledge of God's Word

It is helpful for church members to be challenged about their status as Bible students. It is possible to sit in church for years and think that one knows something about the Bible, but oftentimes it is a pipe dream.

We challenge people with the *Bible Knowledge Test*, which is available as a free eBook at www.wayoflife.org.

Challenging them to get a Bible Institute level of Bible knowledge and then to continue learning

I am convinced that a Bible Institute level of education is *the beginning* of being of full age by the definition of Hebrews 5:12-14. To understand the Bible, one must learn the principles of Bible interpretation. He must understand Bible geography, Bible culture, Old Testament history, the law of Moses, the priesthood, the sacrifices, the tabernacle, the covenants, the life of Christ, Acts and New Testament history, Bible theology, the defense of the faith (apologetics, cults, false teachings), Bible prophecy, and other things. These are fundamental elements of understanding the Bible.

I am not saying that it is necessary to attend a formal Bible college. Many churches today operate part-time Bible institutes. Further, with the tools available for self-study, a Bible Institute education and more is within the reach of most English-speaking Christians who are willing to do the necessary work. Way of Life currently publishes 30 serious study courses, as listed in the chapter on "Recommended Materials."

Challenging the people to meditate in God's Word day and night (Ps. 1:2)

It's not enough to read the Bible and study the Bible; I must fill my mind with Scripture and meditate on it continually.

The Bible must become my worldview.

The Bible must renew my mind and transform my life (Ro. 12:2).

Only then will I really know God and His will and be equipped to serve Him in this present world.

Re-evaluating Services and Programs

The church is at liberty in regard to services and programs (such as Sunday Schools), but it is easy to get into a rut and follow tradition year after year, even decade after decade, without stepping back to re-evaluate things.

The Bible tells us what to do (e.g., preach the gospel to every creature, baptize and disciple every believer, prayer, Bible teaching), but it doesn't tell us how to do this in a practical sense. Things such as Sunday morning and evening services, Sunday Schools, Training Unions, Bible Institutes, and mid-week prayer meetings are simply tools that can be used toward doing what God has told us to do.

The silence of the Bible is not law, but liberty. This is clear in Romans 14. The liberty Paul is talking about in this chapter pertains to things not clearly taught in Scripture, such as diet (Ro.

14:2-4). There are no laws about diet in the church age other than not eating blood (Acts 15:20). Beyond that, there is complete liberty (1 Ti. 4:4-5). In such matters, each individual believer and each church is free to follow the Lord's leading. The Bible's silence is not law; it is liberty.

We try to re-evaluate things continually, and we feel at liberty to change anything that is not clearly spelled out in Scripture. We are bound by the clear teaching of Scripture, not by the Scripture's silence.

We consider our changing situation; we consider our goals and needs; and we try to learn from what other Bible-believing churches are doing.

Following are some examples of ways that some churches veer from tradition a bit:

- Extended Sunday morning/afternoon services. Some churches have services on Sunday morning followed by a meal and an afternoon service.

- One general Sunday School class instead of graded classes

- Afternoon Sunday Schools. Sunday Schools were born in the 19th century in England as evangelistic ministries. They were held on Sunday afternoons and were not held in church buildings. Metropolitan Church of London, England, still follows this pattern.

- Sunday afternoon Bible classes

- The church's preacher and staff members invite visitors home for lunch after the morning service.

- A meal is provided for visitors after the Sunday service. A former church where we were members ministered to a lot of single military servicemen from a nearby base, and the pastor started hosting a simple home-cooked meal after the morning service to encourage them to stay behind. The women of the church volunteered to prepare the meals, and the family or families that provided the food that week stayed behind and ate lunch with pastor and the servicemen. This was a very fruitful ministry for many years.

- Monthly prayer and fasting Sunday. One church has a focus on prayer and fasting on one Sunday a month. The members are encouraged to fast that day until after the evening service. The

Sunday school and teacher training times are used for prayer that day.

- A Bible training program on Sunday evening before the regular service
- Bible Institute classes on weekday evenings
- Prayer meetings before the services
- Saturday evening prayer services
- Saturday discipleship meetings for men and women
- Weekday evening visitation program preceded by a simple meal. This allows the people to come to the church directly from work, eat, then go out on visitation.

We need to evaluate everything prayerfully and be ready to change methods when we can find a better way. I'm not talking about "church growth" and "seeker-sensitive" methods, such as using the world's music and toning down the reproof of God's Word to make visitors feel comfortable. I'm talking about evaluating things by Scripture and not feeling limited by tradition outside the bounds of Scripture.

For example, I've always thought that the typical Sunday School program of the average Baptist church doesn't accomplish much. It is too rushed, for one thing, because the time is limited to about 45 minutes, and that time is used for announcements, singing, offerings, and other things in addition to Bible teaching. I've often come away thinking that very little of biblical and spiritual substance was accomplished.

As a church leader, I feel at liberty before the Lord to examine this type of thing and to change it.

Following are some of the things we consider when evaluating the church's programs and services:

Are we accomplishing our goals?
Are we doing everything the Lord has instructed us to do?
Are we having a real spiritual impact?
Is everything bathed in prayer?
Do we have enough Bible teaching and discipleship?
Have we appointed the right teachers and workers?
Are we giving opportunity for new preachers and workers to be trained and to gain experience?
We often change things.

For example, during the mid-week prayer service, we have a half hour of testimonies, a half hour of preaching, and then we divide into prayer groups. I started this plan years ago based on 1 Corinthians 14:26 to give the members opportunity to share a verse that has blessed them or a testimony or a prayer request. We limit the testimonies to a few minutes, because some of the folk tend to be longwinded if given the opportunity. At first there would be services when only one or two people wanted to say something, but now we never have enough time for the testimonies.

Some years ago I realized that the Wednesday evening preaching time could be used to train our young preachers, so we started having two 15-minute sermons instead of one half hour one. This gives the young preachers another opportunity to preach, and the people are blessed by the variety of messages.

A few months ago I halted that program for a while because I wanted to use that half hour to teach a series of messages on prayer.

And we don't have the traditional order of service in our main weekly meeting. Typically, a church's song service is chopped up by announcements, offerings, etc. I prefer to have an uninterrupted song service so the people can get their hearts into it, so we start with the greeting and opening prayer, followed by a half hour of uninterrupted singing. After that we have the public Bible reading, Bible memorization, announcements, offerings, etc., followed by the preaching.

And we don't have one sermon in our main weekly service, we have two. The first one is a 20-minute gospel message by one of our young preachers. The second is a message geared to the saints by one of the older preachers. We started having two messages in order to give the young preachers more opportunity to gain experience and to make sure that we don't forget the visitors. We always have a lot of unbelievers in the service, and we found that many times the preacher focused exclusively on building up the saints and didn't address the visitors.

After the main weekly service, we have a refreshment time. We started this years ago with the goal of encouraging visitors to stay behind so our people can get to know them and deal with them further about salvation. We have instructed and trained the people to pay attention to the visitors and not just to sit around and fellowship with their friends. We have found this to be very effective. In the winter we serve hot tea and cookies, and in the summer we serve Tang or Kool-aid and cookies.

We have a lot of variety in our song services, as we explain in the chapter "A Discipling Church Is Careful about Music."

We don't want to be locked into tradition just for tradition's sake.

One-on-One Discipleship

We use portions of the One Year Discipleship Course as a one-on-one discipleship program.

The more mature church members teach the new converts and new additions to the membership.

The program has the following objectives:

> *Discipleship* - The first goal is to give some basic beginning teaching to every new church member.
>
> *Training potential teachers* - The second goal is to provide a means for training new teachers and an opportunity for the people to develop spiritual gifts. The program provides opportunities for serious ministry, including opportunities for the more mature young people. It has been said that the best way to learn is to teach.
>
> *Multiplying the ministry* - The program takes some of the teaching workload from the leaders.
>
> *Fellowship* - Another goal is to help develop closer relationships between church members.

The program is set up in the following way:

The first step is to select some church members who have grown in Christ and proven themselves faithful and who possess some basic ability to teach at a private level. These can include older teens that meet the standards. The basic requirements are that the teachers have a good testimony, that they are faithful and submissive to authority, that they agree with the church's doctrine and practice, and that they have read the Bible through at least once.

After the potential teachers have had an opportunity to study the material on their own, the church leaders set up training sessions to go through the course, hitting the high points of the lessons and providing teaching tips. During the training sessions, the potential teachers present a portion of a lesson to the leaders and the other trainees, after which they are critiqued.

When the teachers are deemed ready, they are prayerfully assigned a student, female students being assigned to a female teacher and male students to a male teacher.

The next step is for the teachers to set up appointments with their students to meet with them privately and to go through the material.

The leaders should try to attend some of the first lessons to provide further training and to make sure that the teacher is effective.

The leaders must monitor the program to make sure that the teachers are actually meeting with their students and making good progress and to see if there are any problems. A bi-weekly or monthly teacher's meeting can be held to facilitate this follow-up.

Another option is to appoint two-person teams for discipling. This is what we do in our missionary church. A more mature and knowledgeable Christian is teamed with a younger or newer Christian. Both team members participate in the teaching, but the older team member is responsible to help develop the newer one. As the second members of the teams mature and prove themselves, they can become the leaders in new teams.

Men's Discipleship Meetings

Several years ago I started a men's discipleship meeting an hour before the main morning service. When I started it, I didn't know who would come. That is usually our men's only day off (if they get a day off), and to come an hour earlier than they had been in the habit of coming would be a major thing. But almost all of men attended right from the start. At first it was just for members, because I had some things I wanted to deal with them about, but now we open the meeting to visitors.

A couple of years ago we decided to get rid of the Sunday School class for boys ages 13-15 which met at the same time as the men's discipleship meeting, and we invited those boys to attend the men's meeting. We based this partly on the Jewish system of Bar Mitzvah, which means "son of the commandment." At age 13, a Jewish boy is considered a man for the purpose of attending the synagogue and reading the Scripture. The 13-year-old is thought to have come of age in the sense that he is accountable for his own sins before God. We want our boys to identify with the men and to be around the men as much as possible, and we have seen good fruit by this plan.

Women's Discipleship Meetings

The women in our church have weekly two-hour meetings when they get together for prayer and Bible study.

Youth Ministry

We work hard to disciple all of our youth and to build them up to be strong in God's Word. The younger preachers spend a lot of time with them.

We have monthly youth meetings that are attended by nearly all of our youth. The church leaders take turns leading that meeting, so it varies each month. Usually we have one game, which is a quiz from a Bible passage they have been assigned to study. Mostly the youth meetings consist of serious Bible teaching and Scriptural memorization.

Once a year we have an extended youth meeting for three or four full days. Following is a description of the one in January 2017:

> We had our annual youth conference this week with more than 100 in attendance. These young people are the joy of our hearts and our hope for the future of the Lord's work here, and we are focusing like a laser on serious youth discipleship and training future workers and leaders.
>
> The conference was three days, 10am to 8pm. We had one Bible quiz, and the rest of the time was devoted to preaching, teaching, singing, and a missionary play. I preached six times on evidence of salvation, a testing mindset, a first love for Christ, and the believer's eternal inheritance. And there were

seven other preachers, including two young men ages 17 and 18 who preached their first messages to a congregation.

It is cold and damp here in January, and the church auditorium has no heating, so everyone is bundled up in their winter gear, but they are gung ho!

The vast majority of our young people (those who are baptized members of the church) are true disciples of Jesus Christ. They are seeking God's will, making decisions based on God's Word, and separating from the world from the heart. In most cases, they don't have much or any encouragement from their parents, and in a great many cases they are actively resisted by their Hindu families. Twelve of our young men are preachers. The young people are learning to be Bible students. They memorize at least 60 verses a year.

Nani is an example of the type of discipleship the young people are exhibiting. She is in her last year of high school and is at the top of her class in that part of Nepal, but she attended the conference though it meant missing several classes and a test. She is putting the Lord and His business first and trusting His promise in Matthew 6:33. She has led some young ladies to the Lord who are with her at the conference. Two of them have endured mental and physical persecution for their faith in Christ. Last year Nani memorized the five chapters of 1 John plus about 60 other verses.

Bookstore

We operate a bookstore that is open after the church services. This is an important ministry of providing Bibles, hymnals, and sound doctrinal materials to the congregation.

Bible Conferences

Our Bible conferences are not two or three nights of special meetings. They are three or four full days of meetings, and we have seen great growth in our people when they come apart from the world for extended periods under God's Word.

We have taught things such as the highlights of Hebrews, the highlights of Romans, the Tabernacle, Dispensationalism, Bible apologetics, Bible Archaeology, Bible prophecy, and Holiness.

Bible College

We have a full-time Bible college to train preachers and church workers. This is for our own people. There are only a couple of other churches that we accept students from, and they are completely likeminded. The students that do attend from other churches join our church during their training, but they return to their home church upon graduation unless their church agrees for them to stay in special circumstances.

The class time consists of 12 hours per week, plus chapel.

This school has been a major part of building churches that are strong in God's Word. Church leaders, preachers, preacher's wives, and teachers must have solid training, and it is the church's responsibility to provide it.

The graduates raise the biblical standard of the entire congregation. They also go out as teams to start new churches.

Recommended Materials

• *Way of Life Literature* publishes a Bible training curriculum currently consisting of 32 courses that churches can use to educate and disciple preachers (and the congregation as a whole) and that preachers can use for self-study.

- Acts
- Baptist Music Wars
- Bible History and Geography
- Bible Times & Ancient Kingdoms
- The Bible Version Issue
- Defense of the Faith
- The Discipling Church
- The Effectual Bible Student
- First Corinthians
- The Four Gospels
- Genesis
- Give Attendance to Doctrine
- Hebrews
- A History of the Churches from a Baptist Perspective

- Holiness: Pitfalls, Struggles, Victory
- How to Study the Bible
- James
- Job
- Keeping the Kids
- Mobile Phone and the Christian Home and Church (Youth Discipleship)
- Music for Good or Evil (9 video presentations)
- The New Testament Church
- Pastoral Epistles
- The Pastor's Authority and the Church Member's Responsibility
- Proverbs
- Psalms
- Revelation
- Romans
- Sowing and Reaping: A Course in Evangelism
- An Unshakeable Faith: A Christian Apologetics Course
- Understanding Bible Prophecy

These courses contain about 9,000 pages of material plus 150 PowerPoint presentations with roughly 15,000 slides.

- The following new courses are scheduled for publication in 2017:

  The Bible's Teaching on Marriage
  Daniel
  God the Trinity
  Isaiah
  New Testament Prayer
  Preaching God's Word
  World History

- *Fairhaven Baptist College online classes*
  https://www.youtube.com/channel/UCN4N_GXiQ6LmKUzT15aA7LQ/featured

In 2016, Fairhaven Baptist College in Chesterton, Indiana, began offering some of its courses online via YouTube. Registration is required, but to view the courses for non-credit is free.

- *Faith Bible Institute*

http://fbiclass.com/index.html

This three-year institute is taught by John Yates, senior pastor of Rowland Baptist Church of Monroe, Louisiana. Any church can use the courses, which are available on DVD, but the requirement is that at least 10 students be enrolled. The program consists of a detailed survey of every book of the Bible, plus studies on theology, prophecy, creationism, personal evangelism, and discipleship. We would warn that the church itself is moving in a contemporary direction.

A Discipling Church Is Strong in Prayer

Outline
The Bible's Strong Emphasis on Prayer
The Power of Prayer
Keys to Effectual Prayer
The Practicality of Prayer
A Praying Church

The discipling church that will be standing until Christ comes is a praying church.

Actually, we could have *started* these studies by emphasizing the importance of prayer, because prayer is the spiritual dynamo of a church.

The Bible's Strong Emphasis on Prayer

Prayer is mentioned at least 415 times in Bible, 129 times in the New Testament.

The great saints in the Bible were praying people (e.g., Enoch, Abraham, Hannah, David, Jeremiah, Daniel, Nehemiah, Paul, Lydia).

Prayer is one of the four foundational characteristics of the first church in Jerusalem ("they continued steadfastly in the apostles doctrine and fellowship, and breaking bread and prayer," Acts 2:42).

Prayer is to be first of all (1 Ti. 2:1-2).

Prayer was a major emphasis of Christ's teaching (e.g., Mt. 6:5-13; 7:7-11)

The apostle Paul mentioned prayer 25 times in his epistles.

James said that effectual fervent prayer availeth much (Jam. 5:16).

John and Jude mentioned prayer.

Nothing is more important in the Christian life and ministry than prayer.

The Power of Prayer

God invites us to pray; He exhorts us to pray; He commands us to pray. Surely He wants to answer. I expect the Lord to answer unless He shows me it is not His will to answer that particular prayer.

Prayer changes things. "The effectual fervent prayer of a righteous man availeth much" (James 5:16).

Elijah's prayer stopped the rain in Israel for three years (Jas. 5:17).

Moses' intercessory prayer for Israel changed the course of history (Ex. 32:7-14).

Through prayer, we have seen people healed of sicknesses. When I was in intensive care with acute pancreatitis in 2014, my vital signs and organs were deteriorating quickly. The first four days was a fog of pain and misery. I was taken off of all food and liquids and fed only through an IV. I could only breathe with the assistance of oxygen. The doctors said they had done all they could, but I wasn't improving. But as soon as we sent out a notice and began receiving word that people were praying, I began to heal. We received calls and emails from 1,000 people in 37 countries. When I was still on oxygen, some men in the church gathered around my bed and prayed, and within 15 minutes my oximeter reading went from 60 to above 90 and I could breathe normally without supplementary oxygen. The next day I walked out of the hospital.

Through prayer we have seen people delivered from demons. One young man was learning about the gospel when he decided to attend a charismatic church. When the people prayed for him, he became demon possessed! On a bus ride afterwards, he forced the passengers to shout praises to Jesus, warning that if they didn't participate, he would kill them. Through prayer he was delivered of the demons and called on the Lord to save him. He attended Bible School and became a preacher.

Through prayer, the Maoist insurgency in Nepal was turned back. The insurgency gained strength year by year, from 1996-2006, and the Maoists vowed to turn Nepal into a communist state. More than 19,000 people died in the fighting and terrorism. They vowed to close the churches and turn the public schools into a Maoist indoctrination system. There was nothing to stop them.

The king was overthrown; the army was powerless to stop the Maoist advance; the political parties were inept and hopelessly divided in the face of the threat. Nothing but earnest, believing prayer can explain the fact that the Maoists gave up their goal and joined the political process within a democratic system. Recently the former leader of the violent insurgency said the country must make progress "by development, not by revolution." That is a major answer to prayer.

The Neglect of Prayer

In spite of the emphasis on prayer in Scripture, we are witnessing a dearth of prayer in the typical Bible-believing church. There is a lot of entertainment and lots of activities, but not a lot of serious prayer.

> "I reviewed my consultation notes of dozens of churches I visited over the past few years. Most of them were in a slow decline. Perhaps more than any single factor, the absence of dynamic corporate prayer ministries was the contrasting element. I could not find one declining church that had an ongoing prayer ministry specifically for the lost. Perhaps these dying churches have not because they ask not" (Thom Rainer, *Effective Evangelistic Churches*, p. 77).

Recently I attended a mid-week prayer meeting at an Independent Baptist church, and the prayer time consisted of four minutes of silent prayer.

Even when a church has serious prayer meetings, it is typical that most of the people don't care enough for spiritual things to attend.

We must double down on prayer, but it must be biblical prayer.

Some churches are participating in ecumenical prayer, joining hands with various types of churches to "bring America back to God," but God requires oneness of belief (1 Co. 1:10). Biblical prayer is not ecumenical.

Keys to Effectual Prayer

My maternal grandmother was a prayer warrior, and her prayers were doubtless instrumental in my dramatic conversion at age 23. She taught me some practical "secrets" of answered prayer. Since then I have learned by experience the importance of the things she taught me, such as the following:

Faith (Mr. 11:24). By comparing Scripture with Scripture, we know that this does not mean that I can have anything I pray for if I only have faith. Other Scriptures emphasize that prayer must be according to God's will (e.g., 1 John 5:14-15). But Christ greatly emphasized the role of faith in answered prayer. He emphasized this in the case of the demon possessed child that the disciples were unable to cast out (Mt. 17:18-20). Christ often reproved the disciples for "little faith" (Mt. 6:30; 8:26; 14:31; 16:8).

We have seen great things done by believing prayer.

When we returned to Nepal in 2001, we didn't try to raise any missionary support. I didn't travel on deputation. We decided to trust the Lord who had called us. We still had a house in the States with a mortgage, and our expenses basically doubled upon arriving in Nepal, but every need was met. When we needed a van, someone gave us the money to buy a new one. This is the way we have operated our missionary work ever since. I don't travel on deputation. I don't mention money in our prayer letters and don't ask for any specific thing. We only mention what we are doing and planning and trust the Lord to meet the needs, and He does that and more.

When we started a full-time Bible college in 2013, we basically had none of the things we needed. We didn't have a building, teachers, equipment, dorm parents, etc. But we were sure that it was the Lord's will, and we started making plans and moving ahead, and the Lord supplied *everything*, not all at once, but step by step.

When we started planning to produce a K-12 video school for Nepal in mid-2015 toward a start date of January 2016, again we had almost none of the things we needed, including qualified teachers, a curriculum, video editors, high grade computer and video equipment, camera operators, building, etc. We were confident that it was the Lord's will, so we moved ahead. My wife estimated that we would need at least $100,000. She suggested we mention this in the prayer letter, but I decided against that. The Lord knows where we are and what we are doing. Before the year was out, a man gave us $100,000. It wasn't designated for the school. It was for our ministry in general, but we immediately knew what it was for.

We have lived like this for all of our Christian lives. It is how Way of Life Literature was built. It's how we have planted churches in Nepal. It's how we raised our children. *Believing* prayer in God's will is sufficient for every need and every ministry.

Fervency ("fervent," Jas. 5:16; "striving" Ro. 15:30). Effectual prayer is fervent, passionate, earnest, zealous. It is engaging in spiritual warfare. It is not halfhearted or frivolous.

It is Epaphras "labouring fervently for you in prayers" (Cl. 4:12).

It is Hezekiah weeping in prayer (Isa. 38:5).

Persistence (Lu. 18:1). Christ taught His people to ask, seek, and knock in prayer, and the verbs are in the continual tense: ask and keep on asking, seek and keep on seeking, knock and keep on knocking (Mt. 7:7). Persistence is required for many reasons. For one, God tests our faith, as He did Abraham (Jas. 1:3). Also, persistence is required because prayer is spiritual warfare. Daniel had to wait 21 days for an answer to prayer because of demonic opposition (Da. 10:12-14). Most great answers to prayer have required time and persistence.

Fasting (Mt. 17:21). There is a study on fasting in the *One Year Discipleship Course,* published by Way of Life Literature. When we started the first Baptist church in Nepal, we had gospel meetings in our living room and many people attended, but no one was willing to turn from their idols and face the wrath of a Hindu society and potential prison time. After we had a period of fasting and prayer, people began to repent and turn to Christ in saving faith. Most of those first converts are still walking with the Lord today. One is a pastor. Another is a pastor's wife.

Prayer partners. Paul taught the importance of this by his frequent, earnest requests for prayer (Ro. 15:30; Eph. 6:19; Col. 4:3; 1 Th. 5:25; 2 Th. 3:1). Your first prayer partner should be your husband or wife; pray together for each of your children from the time before they are born; don't keep problems to yourself; that is often an act of pride, because we don't want others to know of our imperfections; ask Christian friends to pray for you; be faithful to prayer meeting and ask the church to pray for your situation.

Praying in God's will (1 John 5:14-15). We can pray for anything good and right, but we need to focus our prayers on things that are *clearly* God's will. Then we can have confidence in prayer. We see this in Paul's prayers. He focused on evangelism, the salvation of souls, church planting, and spiritual power and blessing.

When God has revealed that He wants to do a particular thing, and when I pray for that thing, I can have complete confidence that it will be done. Examples of this include the following: praying for laborers for God's harvest (Luke 10:2), praying for protection from evil men (Ro. 15:31), praying for government leaders that we might lead a quiet and peaceable life in all godliness and honesty (1 Timothy 2:1-4), praying for spiritual wisdom (Col. 1:9), praying to walk worthy of God's will (Col. 1:10), praying for spiritual fruit (Col. 1:10), praying to know God (Col. 1:10), praying for strength for the Christian life (Col. 1:11), praying for God's Word to have free course and to be glorified (2 Th. 3:1).

Focusing prayer on such things is powerful because God is totally inclined to answer. We can't be sure of a positive answer when we pray for money or health or new carpet or a new auditorium, but we can be sure when we pray for things that are revealed in Scripture as God's will.

In a study of 576 growing churches, Thom Rainer found that focused prayer was a key factor. In this case, the focus was on evangelism.

> "Focusing the church's attention on intercession for the lost has brought the Lord's blessings time after time. One pastor shared the thought that, 'Praying for the lost did more to refocus our church than any single factor. We became a church with an outward focus after being an inwardly focused church for years.' ... Most churches that are effectively reaching the lost have broken out of the 'rut' of prayer-as-usual and have experienced wonderful results brought about by effective emphasis on praying for the lost. ..." (*Effective Evangelistic Churches*, pp. 69, 74).

The Practicality of Prayer

There are many ways that we need to double down on prayer.

A private prayer closet. We suspect that the reason why it is so difficult to get the Lord's people to attend real prayer meetings is that so few have an effectual private prayer life. Christ mentioned a prayer closet in Matthew 6:6. This refers to a quiet, private place where the individual meets with God. Effectual congregational prayer begins with effectual private prayer. God's people must be prayer warriors in their private lives. They must engage in intercessory prayer for their families, their church leaders, their friends in Christ, their nation, the unsaved. The churches must teach and exhort the people to have private prayer closets. Mothers with young children can find it difficult to have a private time with the Lord, but it can be done when the children are sleeping, either before they wake in the morning or during a nap time. And the mother must discipline the children to be quiet at times. This is for their good and for her mental well-being (and that of their visitors).

Prayer partners. It is a powerful and effectual thing to agree together in prayer before the Lord for particular requests. Paul earnestly sought prayer partners. In nearly every epistle, he pleaded with the brethren to pray for him and with him, and he shared exactly what he wanted them to pray for.

Prayer by husbands and wives. The husband's first prayer partner should be his own wife. We see husbands and wives praying together in 1 Corinthians 7:5 and 1 Peter 3:7. In the latter verse, the husband is warned that mistreatment of the wife can result in his prayers being hindered.

Prayer at family devotions. The family's prayer should not be routine and ritual. The parents need to lead the children in how to pray and what to pray for. Praying for specific things and seeing God answer is a powerful witness to the children.

Serious prayer meetings. In our church, we emphasize the importance of all of our people attending the prayer services. For the mid-week prayer service, we have multiple prayer meetings at various places in the city to facilitate attendance. We have a half hour of testimonies, a half hour of preaching, and we then divide into groups of two or three or four and pray for at least a half hour. When a group finishes praying, they remain in their places in silence or talking very quietly until everyone is finished and the pastor closes the meeting in a final prayer. This way the prayer service isn't disrupted or disturbed by people going in and out and talking in the halls. The church women meet once a month for a special prayer meeting that lasts three or four hours. That's three or four hours of prayer, not three hours of talking and a few minutes of prayer. Most of the women attend this very serious prayer meeting. The Berean Bible Baptist Church in metro Manila has a prayer and fasting Sunday once a month. That day the people are encouraged to fast until after the evening service. The Sunday Schools and training times are devoted exclusively to prayer. The pastor told me that they see special answers to prayer after each one of those days.

Group prayer. There are many ways to pray in small groups. Each individual in the group can pray, one by one. Or one person can lead the group in prayer. Or someone can start and conclude the prayer time and those who want can pray in between. When someone leads in public prayer, the rest should agree in their hearts and say "Amen" at the end. "All the people should swell the loud 'Amen!' at the close of every prayer, for this is also the rule of Scripture and the example of Heaven. 'Amen' comes from the Hebrew verb to be firm or to be sure. It means 'truly' and 'let it be so'" (Peter Masters, *The Power of Prayer Meetings*). See 1 Corinthians 14:16 which says that New Testament worshipers practiced this. They did the same in the Old Testament (1 Chr. 16:36; Neh. 8:6).

Prayer before services. Some churches have a brief prayer meeting before some or all of its services. I have always sensed special blessing in my preaching when ministering in churches that practice this.

Prayer chains. A prayer chain is a pre-arranged plan to inform church members of special prayer requests. One person contacts another who contacts another, by pre-arranged plan.

24-hour prayer. For this, members of the congregation sign up to pray at a certain time during a 24-hour period with the goal that someone will be praying at all hours.

Prayer before special meetings. These used to be called "cottage prayer meetings" and they were common in some parts of America in the first part of the 20th century. They were still common in the 1960s and 1970s. But they have gone by the wayside in most churches. Special meetings are not preceded by special prayer, and the result is a lack of spiritual power. We tend to depend more on advertising, enthusiasm, decorations, special music, and the dynamism of the speaker.

Pelham Baptist Church in South Carolina, was pastored by Harold B. Sightler from 1942 until 1952. Consider the following testimony about the power of prayer for revival and evangelism:

> "In 1946 only three people were baptized at Pelham, and so in early 1947 a week of prayer meetings were held at night at the church, prayer only, for revival and salvation of souls, with no preaching or singing. People began to get saved, and the church grew. The prayer meetings continued, and by 1949 were being held on Sunday nights after church in a pasture. These often drew a hundred people and sometimes lasted until one o'clock in the morning. A rock altar was built around a tree. Each represented a person being prayed for by name" (James Sightler, "Observations on Dr. Harold B. Sightler's Early Ministry and the Heritage of Tabernacle Baptist Church," http://tabernacleministries.org/Church/history.php4).

In 1898, the Chicago Avenue Church pastored by R.A. Torrey began an organized prayer meeting for each Saturday night from 9-10pm. It was attended by an average of 300. During those prayer meetings, Torrey had the idea to go on evangelistic tours, and we are told that tens of thousands came to Christ in subsequent years.

For more on a praying church we recommend the course *New Testament Prayer*, scheduled to be published in 2017 by Way of Life Literature.

A Praying Church

Metropolitan Tabernacle of London, England, during Charles Spurgeon's ministry (pastored 1854-1882) is an example of a mighty prayer church. Thousands were saved with changed lives as evidence.

The preaching was splendid and the church was very aggressive in evangelism (e.g., street preaching, aggressive tract distribution, 27 Sunday Schools and Ragged Schools ministering to over 8,000 children with 612 teachers), but the converting, life-changing power was in the prayer.

> "Spurgeon regarded the prayer meeting as 'the most important meeting of the week.' He often said that it was not surprising if churches did not prosper, when they regarded the prayer meeting as of so little value that one evening in the week was made to suffice for a feeble combination of service and prayer meeting'" (Wonders of Grace: Original testimonies of converts during Spurgeon's early years, p. 14).

> "A.T. Pierson, who ministered at Tabernacle during Spurgeon's last illness, said, "This Metropolitan Tabernacle is a house of prayer most emphatically ... prayer is almost ceaselessly going up. When one meting is not in progress, another is. ... There are prayer meetings before preaching, and others after preaching. ... No marvel that Mr. Spurgeon's preaching has been so blessed. He himself attributes it mainly to the prevailing prayers of his people" (Ibid.).

A Discipling Church Is a Reproving Church

Outline
Christ's Reproof
Paul's Reproof
The Ministry of Reproof in Scripture
The Blessing of Godly Reproof
Effectual Reproof
Public and Private Reproof
The Ministry of the Body

A ministry of exhortation, reproof, rebuke, and correction toward sin and error are necessary for making true disciples of Jesus Christ.

The ministry of loving reproof and correction is necessary for the type of atmosphere that produces disciples.

But a biblical ministry of reproof is a misunderstood and neglected ministry today.

A ministry of reproof is even thought to be strange and hurtful. A preacher told me recently, "You have a strange ministry." He was referring to my reproof of erring pastors. Actually a ministry of reproof is not strange at all. It is biblical.

To love righteousness is to hate sin, and to love truth is to hate error.

> "Therefore I esteem all *thy* precepts *concerning* all *things to be* right; *and* I hate every false way" (Ps. 119:128).

> "*Let* love be without dissimulation. Abhor that which is evil; cleave to that which is good" (Ro. 12:9).

Christ said, "As many as I love, I rebuke and chasten" (Re. 3:19).

John, the "apostle of love, defined love as obedience. He said, "For this is the love of God, that we keep his commandments: and his commandments are not grievous" (1 John 5:3).

Proverbs teaches us that the parent who does not chasten his child does not love him (Pr. 13:24). The same is true for a church leader. Those who do not reprove and correct the sheep do not love them. It would be like a shepherd who sees the sheep going astray but does nothing about it.

Further, a ministry of godly reproof is a ministry of spiritual growth and protection.

> "Whom we preach, warning every man, and teaching every man in all wisdom; that we may present every man perfect in Christ Jesus" (Col. 1:28).

> "For the commandment *is* a lamp; and the law *is* light; and reproofs of instruction *are* the way of life" (Pr. 6:23).

Far from being harmful, a godly ministry of reproof and correction has the potential for great blessing.

The Ministry of Reproof in Scripture

Reproof and correction is one the purposes for which God gave the Bible (2 Ti. 3:16). To avoid reproof and correction is to cut a lot of truth out of Scripture. Some years back a man published *The Positive Bible*. He had the audacity to "remove the negative things from the Bible." The result was a very small "Bible"!

The terms "reprove," "rebuke," "warn," "admonish," "chasten," "convince," "blame," and "correct" are used more than 30 times in Acts and the Epistles.

These words have similar but different meanings.

"**Admonish**" means to put in mind; to caution; to charge; to reprove gently; to notify of a fault; to counsel against wrong practices; to advise; to instruct. The Greek word translated "admonish" in Romans 15:14 is "neotheteo," which is elsewhere translated "warn" (Acts 20:31). The word "admonish" is used for Jeremiah's warning to the Jewish remnant about not going to Egypt (Jer. 42:19), Paul's warning to the ship's captain (Acts 27:9), admonishing an erring brother (2 Th. 3:15), and God's admonition to Moses to build the Tabernacle exactly according to the divine pattern (Heb. 8:5).

"**Reprove**" means to charge with a fault, to convict, to blame. An example is John reproving Herod for marrying his brother's wife (Lu. 3:19) and Paul reproving Peter for his hypocrisy (Ga. 2:11). To reprove also means to persuade, to give evidence, to convince. The word "reproof" in 2 Timothy 3:16 is the Greek word "elegchos," which is elsewhere translated "evidence" (Heb. 11:1). To reprove is to convince someone of his sin or error (1 Co. 14:24; Tit. 1:9). To reprove means to shine the light of God's Word on the deeds of darkness (Eph. 5:11-13). The Spirit of God has come to reprove the world of sin (John 16:8).

"**Rebuke**" means to reproach; correct; chide, scold, reprimand. Nehemiah rebuked the elders (Ne. 5:7). The judges of Israel were to rebuke sin (Amos 5:10). Christ will rebuke the nations when He returns (Is. 2:4). Jesus rebuked Peter (Mr. 8:33). The Christian is to rebuke his brother when he trespasses against him (Lu. 17:3). Sinning elders are to be rebuked (1 Ti. 5:20). The Word of God is to be preached with rebuke (2 Ti. 4:2; Tit. 2:15). Some are to be rebuked sharply (Tit. 1:13). Christ rebukes those He loves (Re. 3:19). One's attitude toward rebuke reveals his spiritual condition (Pr. 9:7-8; 13:1).

Admonish, reprove, and rebuke are similar in meaning. All of these terms refer to correction and warning. Rebuke is the strongest. Reprove and admonish are usually a little milder, a little less forceful. Admonition and reproof ignored or rejected leads to rebuke.

Christ as Reprover

Christlikeness is compassion and gentleness and patience, but it is also firmness, even toughness, in regard to God's holy laws. The Lord said, "As many as I love, I rebuke and chasten: be zealous therefore, and repent" (Revelation 3:19).

Consider how forceful Christ can be in reproof to His own people (not to speak of His millennial rod of iron and the issue of eternal judgment for the unbeliever):

> "But when he had turned about and looked on his disciples, he rebuked Peter, saying, **GET THEE BEHIND ME, SATAN**: for thou savourest not the things that be of God, but the things that be of men" (Mark 8:33).
>
> "Afterward he appeared unto the eleven as they sat at meat, and **UPBRAIDED THEM** with their unbelief and hardness of heart, because they believed not them which had seen him" (Mark 16:14).

"But he turned, and **REBUKED THEM**, and said, Ye know not what manner of spirit ye are of" (Luke 9:55).

"Then he said unto them, **O FOOLS** and slow of heart to believe all that the prophets have spoken" (Luke 24:25).

"Remember therefore from whence thou art fallen, and repent, and do the first works; or else **I WILL COME UNTO THEE QUICKLY, AND WILL REMOVE THY CANDLESTICK** out of his place, except thou repent" (Revelation 2:5).

"But this thou hast, that thou hatest the deeds of the Nicolaitans, **WHICH I ALSO HATE**" (Revelation 2:6).

"So hast thou also them that hold the doctrine of the Nicolaitans, which thing I hate. Repent; or else I will come unto thee quickly, and **WILL FIGHT AGAINST THEM WITH THE SWORD OF MY MOUTH**" (Revelation 2:15-16).

"Behold, I will cast her into a bed, and them that commit adultery with her into great tribulation, except they repent of their deeds. And **I WILL KILL HER CHILDREN WITH DEATH**; and all the churches shall know that I am he which searcheth the reins and hearts: and I will give unto every one of you according to your works" (Revelation 2:22-23).

"Remember therefore how thou hast received and heard, and hold fast, and repent. If therefore thou shalt not watch, **I WILL COME ON THEE AS A THIEF**, and thou shalt not know what hour I will come upon thee" (Revelation 3:3).

"I know thy works, that thou art neither cold nor hot: I would thou wert cold or hot. So then because thou art lukewarm, and neither cold nor hot, **I WILL SPUE THEE OUT OF MY MOUTH**" (Revelation 3:15-16).

Five times in the Gospels, Christ expressed disappointment and reproof by saying that the disciples were of little faith (Mt. 6:30; 8:26; 14:31; 16:8; Lu. 12:28).

Christ "looked round about on them with anger" (Mark 3:5); called Israel a "generation of vipers" (Ma. 12:34) and a "faithless and perverse generation" (Mt. 17:17); called the Jewish leaders "hypocrites ... blind guides ... fools and blind ... serpents" (Mt. 23:13-33); sharply upbraided the cities in which He did mighty works (Mt. 11:20-24). He called Herod a fox (Lu. 13:32). He twice made a whip and drove the moneychangers and sellers out of the temple (Joh. 2:15-17; Mr. 11:15-17). He commanded that holy things not be given to dogs and pigs (Mt. 7:6).

Christ is the example that church leaders are to follow. To see compromise, sin, and error in the church and not deal with it effectively is not the Christ-like way.

The apostle Paul exemplifies the right "balance" in ministry. He said, "Brethren, be followers together of me, and mark them which walk so as ye have us for an ensample" (Php. 3:17). See also 1 Corinthians 4:16; 11:1. On the one hand he was as gentle as a nurse with the believers (1 Th. 2:7). On the other hand, he was firm and unyielding about discipline (1 Co. 5; 2 Th. 3:6-14). He was a strong reprover (e.g., 1 Co. 6:5; 15:33-36; Ga. 3:1), and he taught the preachers under his watchcare to be the same (2 Ti. 4:2; Tit. 1:13; 2:15).

We see the ministry of reproof in Paul's attitude toward the sin and error in the church at Corinth. He was kind and patient, but he did not overlook sin, error, and carnality. He dealt with it head on. He exhorted, reproved, and rebuked. He did whatever was necessary to effect repentance and change.

> "Now I beseech you, brethren, by the name of our Lord Jesus Christ, that ye all speak the same thing, and *that* there be no divisions among you; but *that* ye be perfectly joined together in the same mind and in the same judgment. For it hath been declared unto me of you, my brethren, by them *which are of the house* of Chloe, that there are contentions among you" (1 Co. 1:10-11).
>
> "And I, brethren, could not speak unto you as unto spiritual, but as unto carnal, *even* as unto babes in Christ. I have fed you with milk, and not with meat: for hitherto ye were not able *to bear it*, neither yet now are ye able. For ye are yet carnal: for whereas *there is* among you envying, and strife, and divisions, are ye not carnal, and walk as men?" (1 Co r. 3:1-3).
>
> "If any man defile the temple of God, him shall God destroy; for the temple of God is holy, which *temple* ye are. Let no man deceive himself. If any man among you seemeth to be

wise in this world, let him become a fool, that he may be wise" (1 Co. 3:17-18).

"But I will come to you shortly, if the Lord will, and will know, not the speech of them which are puffed up, but the power. For the kingdom of God *is* not in word, but in power. What will ye? shall I come unto you with a rod, or in love, and *in* the spirit of meekness?" (1 Co. 4:19-21).

"It is reported commonly *that there is* fornication among you, and such fornication as is not so much as named among the Gentiles, that one should have his father's wife. And ye are puffed up, and have not rather mourned, that he that hath done this deed might be taken away from among you. For I verily, as absent in body, but present in spirit, have judged already, as though I were present, *concerning* him that hath so done this deed, In the name of our Lord Jesus Christ, when ye are gathered together, and my spirit, with the power of our Lord Jesus Christ, To deliver such an one unto Satan for the destruction of the flesh, that the spirit may be saved in the day of the Lord Jesus. Your glorying *is* not good. Know ye not that a little leaven leaveneth the whole lump?" (1 Co. 5:1-6).

"I speak to your shame. Is it so, that there is not a wise man among you? no, not one that shall be able to judge between his brethren? But brother goeth to law with brother, and that before the unbelievers. Now therefore there is utterly a fault among you, because ye go to law one with another. Why do ye not rather take wrong? why do ye not rather *suffer yourselves to* be defrauded?" (1 Co. 6:5-7).

"Flee fornication. Every sin that a man doeth is without the body; but he that committeth fornication sinneth against his own body. What? know ye not that your body is the temple of the Holy Ghost *which is* in you, which ye have of God, and ye are not your own?" (1 Co. 6:18-19).

"Ye cannot drink the cup of the Lord, and the cup of devils: ye cannot be partakers of the Lord's table, and of the table of devils. Do we provoke the Lord to jealousy? are we stronger than he?" (1 Co. 10:21-22).

"For in eating every one taketh before *other* his own supper: and one is hungry, and another is drunken. What? have ye not houses to eat and to drink in? or despise ye the church of

> God, and shame them that have not? What shall I say to you? shall I praise you in this? I praise *you* not" (1 Co. 11:21-22).
>
> "Brethren, be not children in understanding: howbeit in malice be ye children, but in understanding be men" (1 Co. 14:20).
>
> "If therefore the whole church be come together into one place, and all speak with tongues, and there come in *those that are* unlearned, or unbelievers, will they not say that ye are mad?" (1 Co. 14:23).
>
> "Be not deceived: evil communications corrupt good manners. Awake to righteousness, and sin not; for some have not the knowledge of God: I speak *this* to your shame. But some *man* will say, How are the dead raised up? and with what body do they come? *Thou* fool, that which thou sowest is not quickened, except it die" (1 Co. 15:33-36).

Paul's ministry of reproof to the carnal church at Corinth worked repentance and change (2 Co. 7:8-11). A sound ministry of reproof and discipline has the same power today.

We see a ministry of reproof in James' epistle.

> "Ye adulterers and adulteresses, know ye not that the friendship of the world is enmity with God? whosoever therefore will be a friend of the world is the enemy of God. Do ye think that the scripture saith in vain, The spirit that dwelleth in us lusteth to envy? But he giveth more grace. Wherefore he saith, God resisteth the proud, but giveth grace unto the humble. Submit yourselves therefore to God. Resist the devil, and he will flee from you. Draw nigh to God, and he will draw nigh to you. Cleanse *your* hands, *ye* sinners; and purify *your* hearts, *ye* double minded. Be afflicted, and mourn, and weep: let your laughter be turned to mourning, and *your* joy to heaviness. Humble yourselves in the sight of the Lord, and he shall lift you up" (Jas. 4:4-10).

James did not countenance worldliness and carnality. He dealt with it in the most direct manner. He called the worldly saints adulterers and adulteresses. He called them the enemies of God. He called them sinners and double minded. He called them proud.

There is no beating around the bush here. There is no speaking in vague generalities. James' audience knew exactly what he meant and whom he was talking about.

This is the example for every church leader. Yet today it is common for preachers to accept worldliness as the status quo and to allow it to spread throughout the congregation. Instead of reproving the worldly members after the fashion of James, church leaders put worldly people into positions of ministry and allow them to influence the entire church body. Within a generation the spiritual character of the church is destroyed because of church leaders who won't exercise the biblical ministry of reproof.

We see a ministry of reproof described in Paul's instruction to Titus.

> "One of themselves, *even* a prophet of their own, said, The Cretians *are* alway liars, evil beasts, slow bellies. This witness is true. Wherefore rebuke them sharply, that they may be sound in the faith" (Tit. 1:12-13).

Titus was ministering on the island of Crete. He was establishing churches and training and ordaining elders.

But the national character of the Cretians was affecting the churches. Paul taught Titus what to do, and he was to exercise a sharp ministry of reproof.

Discipline must fit the character of the individual or church. It's like chastening a child. Each child is different and must be dealt with differently. If a child obeys, he is not spanked, but the stubborn, self-willed child must be dealt with more forcefully.

This is true in the church. If there is a Cretian character, the chastening must be firmer and sharper. The Cretians tended to be liars (deceitful, dissembling), evil beasts (backbiters, gossips, hurtful), slow bellies (lazy, idle, living for their physical appetites). Because of their exceedingly poor character and slowness to obey God, the churches on Crete needed to be dealt with more sharply than churches in other places.

Sharp rebuke is contrary to the teaching of humanistic psychology, but God knows human nature and His Word instructs us how to deal wisely with stubborn insubordination.

We see the ministry of reproof in 2 Thessalonians 3:6-15.

> "Now we command you, brethren, in the name of our Lord Jesus Christ, that ye withdraw yourselves from every brother that walketh disorderly, and not after the tradition which he received of us. For yourselves know how ye ought to follow

us: for we behaved not ourselves disorderly among you; Neither did we eat any man's bread for nought; but wrought with labour and travail night and day, that we might not be chargeable to any of you: Not because we have not power, but to make ourselves an ensample unto you to follow us. For even when we were with you, this we commanded you, that if any would not work, neither should he eat. For we hear that there are some which walk among you disorderly, working not at all, but are busybodies. Now them that are such we command and exhort by our Lord Jesus Christ, that with quietness they work, and eat their own bread. But ye, brethren, be not weary in well doing. And if any man obey not our word by this epistle, note that man, and have no company with him, that he may be ashamed. Yet count *him* not as an enemy, but admonish *him* as a brother."

This is a description of a strong reproving ministry of God's Word exercised in the New Testament church.

Paul is giving a commandment, not a suggestion (2 Th. 3:6). This type of ministry is required of God in every congregation.

The passage deals with church members who are disorderly and do not work, but rather are busybodies (2 Th. 3:11). But it would apply to any type of disorderly conduct that is unlawful for God's people to engage in.

The church is not to overlook this type of thing. It must be dealt with plainly and as severely as necessary to bring it to a stop.

Disorderly conduct is to be dealt with in a variety of ways. First, there must be *teaching*. The saints must be patiently instructed about the importance of good labor (2 Th. 3:7-9). Compare Pr. 6:6-11; 13:4; 14:23; Acts 20:34-35; Eph. 4:28; 1 Th. 4:11-12. Next, there is to be *exhortation* (2 Th. 3:12). The church is to be exhorted to do what God commands. Then there is to be *reproof and rebuke* of those who disobey (2 Th. 3:11). Finally, there is to be *discipline* if the reproof is not taken to heart and there is no repentance (2 Th. 3: 6, 14). We, see, too that brotherly love is to permeate a ministry of reproof and correction (2 Th. 3:15), which is one of the things that sharply distinguishes godly reproof with a cultic, Diotrephes type of reproof.

Paul is describing the ministry of reproof and correction that must characterize every New Testament church. The church is not to overlook disorderly conduct. It is to deal with it with every spiritual tool that God has provided.

The Blessing of Godly Reproof

"*As* an earring of gold, and an ornament of fine gold, *so is* a wise reprover upon an obedient ear" (Pr. 25:12).

Wise reproof that is received well is a great blessing. I have personally witnessed this many times over the years.

Following are a few examples:

In one of my classes in Bible School, a student frequently harassed the teacher from his (the student's) Ruckmanite thinking. Finally one day as we were leaving class I reproved him about disturbing the class and showing dishonor to the teacher. I reminded him that he had not been given authority to teach that class, and the rest of the students were not there to hear his opinions. He was a large, gruff man, and I approached him in some fear, but he was humble and apologetic.

On another occasion I confronted a young relative about dating a worldly man who was contributing to her backsliding. We were sitting in our living room, and initially she ran out of the room crying. But she repented and today is married to a godly man.

I reproved one of our church men who consistently absented himself from our men's discipleship meetings. We had exhorted him previously about faithfulness, but he had not changed. Now I said, "It appears to me that you are either unsaved, lazy, or you don't like me and therefore don't want to attend my classes." I also said that if I had missed something, please let me know. After saying nothing for some time, he replied, "I am lazy." I then exhorted him about his need to be zealous in his service for Christ and a good example to the church and to his own family. He has been faithful ever since.

I once reproved a young mother in our church about letting her daughter disobey her instructions and commands. I said, "If you are disciplining her properly, the evidence will be obedience. If she doesn't obey, she isn't disciplined. It's that simple." The mother took this to heart, and today her child obeys her and obeys other adults.

My wife and I discipline our grandkids when they stay with us, if necessary, which has been extremely rare. We never let them get away with disobedience or disrespect, and they know that we mean business. One of our grandsons was acting a bit rebellious one day, and my wife reminded him that she had her spanking stick handy. She was referring to a short rod, but it so happened that a seven-foot stick was standing in a corner of the room for some project she was doing, and the grandson thought she was talking about that. He was just a little guy and he was standing near that corner of the room, and after looking that huge stick over from the floor to the ceiling he was immediately in a better mood!

Of course, it doesn't always turn out this way. When the ear is not obedient, the reproof won't be fruitful in that individual's life and might even result in trouble for the reprover, but God is glorified either way, because the reprover has obeyed God and honored His Word (Pr. 15:23).

This is true for every aspect of discipline. It doesn't always result in blessing in an individual's life, but it always results in glory to a holy God and the purification of the church (1 Co. 5:7-8).

The same is true for preaching the gospel (2 Co. 2:14-16). The preaching of the gospel is a sweet savour unto God, whether the person believes or does not believe. In the case of the unbeliever, God is glorified because His Word is preached and the offer of salvation is made and His goodness is evident even in the offer.

The preacher of the gospel and the reprover of sin and error obeys God's Word, and leaves the result to Him.

Effectual Reproof

There are many things that are necessary for effectual reproof. To engage disobedience and error is no simple matter, and it must be done by those who are properly qualified and prepared.

1. The reprover must be filled with goodness.

"And I myself also am persuaded of you, my brethren, that ye also are **full of goodness**, filled with all knowledge, able also to admonish one another" (Ro. 15:14).

He must have a respectable Christian testimony. He must not be a hypocrite. If the people to whom I minister see me doing things that are wrong, they will lose respect for me and my reproof will lose effectiveness. I've not always done right in this, but I know that a good testimony is necessary for a fruitful ministry of preaching God's Word. And I am thankful that in spite of my failings, the Lord has given me a good testimony in the eyes of those who know me.

I once challenged a church member about her dress and asked her if she would read my book *Dressing for the Lord*. She replied, "I will read the book because of my respect for you." A national preacher once said, "Brother Cloud can reprove us because we know he loves us and we know how long and faithfully he has ministered among us."

If there are glaring sins and failings in an individual's life, he is incapable of reproving those things. For example, if a pastor's children do not know and serve the Lord, no one will pay much attention to him when he tries to teach them about how to raise children. And if he is divorced, they probably won't listen very well to his warnings about divorce.

Being filled with goodness includes mercy and care. The one being reproved must know that the reprover cares for him.

This is why we can effectually reprove the young people in our church. They respect our Christian lives and they know that we care for them. Even when I have had to "rebuke them sharply" at times because of their sin and stubbornness, they have received it, or at least most of them have. Otherwise, the reproof could frustrate them and drive them away.

2. The reprover must be filled with knowledge.

> "And I myself also am persuaded of you, my brethren, that ye also are full of goodness, **filled with all knowledge**, able also to admonish one another" (Ro. 15:14).

The reprover must know God's Word and know how to properly use God's Word; the better you know God's Word, the more fruitful you can be in helping others. Many saints remain ignorant year after year; therefore, they are ineffectual and unfruitful.

The necessity of being filled with goodness and knowledge reminds us that the young believer or even the young preacher should be extra careful about reproving. He doesn't have the maturity to be as highly respected as an older saint; therefore, his reproof will not be received as well as that of an older saint.

I think of a little church in Tennessee where I taught Sunday School. One of the members was a rough old "hillbilly" with several children that he was not training properly. I decided to teach about child training, though I wasn't even married yet. After the first class, he said, "You don't know what you are talking about," and if I remember correctly he stopped attending the classes. He was right that I didn't know what I was talking about experientially. I was only about two years old in the Lord. I was still "wet behind the ears!" At the same time, he should have been more respectful toward God's Word. He lost most of his children to the world. In fact, some of his children went to prison.

3. The reprover must be wise.

> "*As* an earring of gold, and an ornament of fine gold, *so is* **a wise reprover** upon an obedient ear" (Pr. 25:12).

Consider some characteristics of wise reproof:

There is a right time and situation to reprove.

> "He that passeth by, *and* meddleth with strife *belonging* not to him, *is like* one that taketh a dog by the ears" (Pr. 26:17).

Reproof should be given when it is your business to reprove.

Since the pastor is responsible for his flock, it is his business to reprove them when necessary. He can't say it is not his business. How can a shepherd say that the sheep are not his business? And how can the sheep say the shepherd has no business meddling in their lives?

The Lord has given the God-called preacher the authority to reprove in season and out of season (2 Ti. 4:2), but this doesn't mean it is wise to get involved in every situation that comes to his attention.

Some situations will work themselves out without the input of a pastor, and he must have the wisdom to know these things.

When at all possible, the reproof should be made face to face rather than by email or text.

Reproof shouldn't be given when the individual is severely distracted, such as during a tragedy.

Reproof shouldn't be given early in the morning or some other very inconvenient time. One time a friend started reproving me about something he felt I was doing wrong, but he did it first thing in the morning before I even had my cup of coffee. Not wise! To reprove someone when he or she is preparing for something and is therefore distracted and under pressure is usually not wise. For example, if you want to try to correct something the preacher has said, don't do it just before he is scheduled to preach. Be wise.

And the reprover must decide whether the reproof should be private or public. Paul reproved Peter publicly (Ga. 2:11-14), but there is also a time for private reproof. In general, public error should be dealt with publicly, and private error should be dealt with privately. Paul reproved Peter publicly because Peter's hypocrisy was public and he was influencing others (Ga. 2:13). I am often criticized for reproving preachers publicly about their ministries, but I only do this when the ministry in question is public and that preacher is influencing people outside of his own congregations.

There is a right person to reprove.

The Bible teaches us to consider the character of the individual that is to be reproved.

In a nutshell, we should reprove when we are dealing with a receptive heart.

> "He that reproveth a scorner getteth to himself shame: and he that rebuketh a wicked *man getteth* himself a blot. Reprove not a scorner, lest he hate thee: rebuke a wise man, and he will love thee" (Pr. 9:7-8).

There are levels of reproof. I will give a certain type of reproof to the insubordinate and another type of reproof to the subordinate. When I am pretty confident that a person isn't going to respond positively, I will still sometimes give a reproof because God tells me to (Eph. 5:11; 2 Ti. 4:2). But I won't dwell on it or pursue it.

Consider Proverbs 26:4-5.

> "Answer not a fool according to his folly, lest thou also be like unto him. Answer a fool according to his folly, lest he be wise in his own conceit."

Verse 4 means not to answer a fool in like manner to his folly. Don't respond to anger with anger, to mocking with mocking, to berating with berating, etc. But verse 5 says we should answer a fool according to his folly in the sense of what his folly deserves and requires. To give no answer can make him wise in his conceit, because he takes no answer to mean there is no answer to his folly. I sometimes follow this method in regard to email communications from obstinate people. Sometimes I ignore them totally; sometimes I reply briefly. But I aim not to get carried away with their foolishness by getting into name calling and mudslinging and character attacks. I'm not always successful, but this is my aim, because I know that to answer a fool in like manner to his folly is unwise and accomplishes nothing and takes me down to the level of the fool.

Consider Titus 3:9-11.

> "But avoid foolish questions, and genealogies, and contentions, and strivings about the law; for they are unprofitable and vain. A man that is an heretick after the first and second admonition reject; Knowing that he that is such is subverted, and sinneth, being condemned of himself."

Here we see how to deal with the heretic, who is a person that has made a choice to cleave to error. He is "subverted." There is something wrong with him. God's Word instructs us to admonish such a person *once or twice*, and then reject him. The heart of the heretic is not receptive to the truth, and it is therefore a waste of time to pursue him.

For example, one night I accompanied some relatives to distribute gospel tracts and to witness to people in a park in my home town where a lot of people congregate on weekends. Some of my relatives played musical instruments and sang to attract a crowd, and the rest of us witnessed to them. A Church of Christ man accosted me with one objective, and that was to debate about baptism. I showed him from Scripture how that it is the gospel that saves (Ro. 1:16) and that baptism is not the gospel (1 Co. 15:3-4), but he didn't hear a word I was saying. He focused on his false interpretation of Acts 2:38. In a short while, I said, "You are wasting my time. I am here to preach the gospel to needy sinners, and you are of the devil, because you are hindering me from doing that. If you believe baptism is the gospel, go to the other side of the park and preach your gospel. Goodbye." I turned away from him and ignored any further attempts to harangue me with his heresy. I was careful not to say, "The Lord bless you," because we are not to bless false teachers (2 John 10-11).

A ministry of reproof deals wisely with people according to their character.

There is also a right way to reprove.

The reprover must have "the spirit of meekness" (Ga. 6:1). He must put himself in the place of the person he is reproving and exercise the "royal law" to do unto others as he would have them do unto him (Jas. 2:8). He must reprove with the attitude that he, too, is a sinner who is susceptive to backsliding.

The reprover must seek God's help and wisdom to know how to deal with every situation, because each situation is different. Consider Christ's dealing with Peter in Matthew 16:21-23 versus His dealing with Peter in John 21:15-18. We see the difference between sharp rebuke and gentle but persistent exhortation. After Christ's denial, the Lord knew that Peter was already deeply reproved by his own conscience and that he had wept bitterly (Mt. 26:75), so the Lord focused on questioning Peter about love. Christ got to the heart of the matter, which was Peter's self-love and lack of love for Christ. This is why Peter, rather than John, was sifted by the devil. Christ's persistence in asking Peter three times if he loved him pressed the issue into Peter's conscience. It was extremely effectual and fruitful. Peter spent the rest of his life loving Christ and feeding the sheep. His epistles are extremely powerful and searching. He had indeed been converted (Lu. 22:32).

The reprover should know the difference between *attitude* and *action*. Both my attitude and my action must be right. Sometimes we are so careful to keep a right attitude that we don't do the right action, or we do the right action with the wrong attitude. For example, consider a young woman who wants to serve in some ministry in the church, but her hair is too short. On one hand, hair length is a relatively small thing, but that doesn't mean that it is of no consequence. Paul addressed it and taught that hair length is an issue of authority. The woman's long hair is her God-given glory and is a sign of her submission to the man's authority, whereas the man's short hair is the sign of his submission to God (1 Co. 11:3-5). Paul said that even angels are affected by this issue (1 Co. 11:10). The right attitude in this context is to deal with the young woman kindly and patiently and to keep this issue in the right perspective in my own heart. I must remember that hair length is not necessarily a spiritual thermometer. A woman with short hair might love the Lord much more passionately than a woman with long hair, and a man with longer hair might love the Lord more passionately than a man with short hair, and love for the Lord is the most important issue. But keeping my *attitude* right does not mean that there is no *action* to take. In the previous case, the young woman needs to be instructed and guided in this matter so that she will come to understand the issue and not want to be an offense and stumbling block by her appearance. And the action includes enforcing the church's standards for workers, even in external appearances and even in matters that are considered by many of "small" consequence.

We must exercise special wisdom in reproving an elder, referring to an elder in age as well as to a leader. An elder is not to be rebuked, but to be entreated as a father (1 Ti. 5:1). Paul is talking particularly about the fact that younger people are not to rebuke elders but rather must deal with them in an entreating manner. (In contrast, an elder, referring to a pastor, is to be rebuked if he sins, 1 Ti. 5:19-20.)

4. The reproof must be repetitious (Phi. 3:1; 2 Pe. 1:12).

The wise repetition of reproof is a major part of the process of discipleship.

Human nature demands repetition in instruction and reproof. We don't learn all at once, but a little at a time. We forget and have to be reminded of what we have already learned. Thus biblical reproof must permeate the church's ministry and must incorporate repetition.

We see the principle of teaching by repetition throughout the Bible. But effectual repetition does not mean saying exactly the same thing repeatedly. It is dealing with the same subject in different ways, coming at it from different directions, presenting it in different contexts, emphasizing different aspects.

For example, consider Bible study. The leaders produce good Bible students by repetition. It isn't enough to preach this once a year or mention it in a sermon once in awhile. It isn't even enough to offer a course on Bible study. Bible study and every other major aspect of discipleship must be constant themes that are woven throughout the church's ministry. The leaders must explain the reasons why the people need to study the Bible. They must exhort the people to study the Bible. They must teach the people how to study the Bible. They must rebuke those who do not study the Bible. They must do all of these things all of the time.

The same is true for teaching prayer, holiness, faithfulness, separation, modesty, etc.

Public and Private Reproof

Both public and private reproof are necessary for an effectual ministry of reproof. Here we are talking about reproof in the congregation.

There must be **PUBLIC REPROOF** (2 Ti. 4:2).

A preaching ministry that includes clear and practical reproof and rebuke is a very essential part of a disciplined church. It is a necessary part of the atmosphere that produces true disciples.

Not everyone will respond properly to such preaching, but those who have a heart for God will grow in this atmosphere.

Public reproof is necessary for spiritual protection.

Public reproof is a major part of keeping the church disciplined, a major part of producing disciples.

Yet preaching with reproof and rebuke is becoming a neglected ministry. In many churches, the preaching is getting softer, and the result is a weakening of the spiritual climate of the church and the inevitable breaking down of the walls of separation from the world.

Once I interviewed a father about his grown children who were serving the Lord and asked him if he had any suggestions for other parents. The first thing he said was that after he was saved, the Lord had led him to a good Bible preaching church, and he determined as a young father that he was going to obey what the pastor preached. He tried to do whatever the preacher preached from God's Word, and this resulted in good fruit in his family. Of course, we don't blindly follow a preacher, but when the preacher is preaching God's Word, it is right and wise to obey (Heb. 13:17). This church is a church where the preaching is given with plenty of reproof, rebuke, and exhortation, as well as sound doctrine, and those who submit to such a ministry are sanctified thereby.

An example of something that requires the ministry of reproof is the believers' responsibilities before God such as being faithful to services and being faithful to prayer meetings. It is God who requires faithfulness, and the preacher must uphold God's requirements (e.g., Acts 2:42; 1 Co. 4:2; Heb. 10:25).

Consider the prayer meetings. The members of the first church "continued in prayers" (Acts 2:42). But today it is typical that only a small percentage of church members attend prayer meetings, and this should be a matter of teaching, exhortation, rebuke, and even discipline, but many pastors are content with small participation in the sense that they do little or nothing to change the status quo.

I think of a large church in Florida that announced a women's prayer meeting before the service, but my wife was the only one in attendance!

I think of two fairly large churches, but the special prayer meetings before the services are ill attended.

In fact, as I travel in my Bible conference ministry, I am almost always shocked by the pitiful number of men who attend such meetings compared to the number who attend the service itself. Typically, the prayer meeting is only about 15 minutes, so it is not a major sacrifice for the men to attend. Some are unable to attend, of course, but many simply don't make the effort.

If a man can't get off work and is therefore unable to attend, though he wants to, that is one thing, and we are patient with that type of thing. But in many cases, it is a matter of rank disobedience and lack of spiritual zeal.

I always rebuke men for this sin. I think of a church in North Carolina where I preached a Bible conference. There were just a few men in the prayer meeting, but there were probably 30 men in the services.

I don't believe that a preacher has a right to ignore this type of blatant disobedience to Scripture.

I think of a church where I preached a Bible conference that ran from Wednesday to Sunday. The attendance on Wednesday, Thursday, Friday, and Saturday evenings was about 50, if I remember correctly. I was therefore shocked on Sunday morning to see something like a couple hundred people in attendance. I began my message that morning by reproving those who had neglected the services. I said, "Where were you the last three nights? Didn't you know that the church was having a Bible conference?" I was preaching a series on Revelation 2-3, and these people had demonstrated a powerful example of Laodicean lukewarmness! I thought that would be the last time I was invited to preach there, but in fact I have been invited back two or three times.

I think of another church where I preached a Bible conference. This church had not had a Bible conference in something like 25-30 years. The services were well attended and the response seemed to be good, but I noticed after a couple of nights that there weren't many teens and young single people in attendance, and when I inquired about the matter I was told that the young people were at a softball league tournament. I couldn't believe it. The first Bible conference in decades and the adults let the young people skip out for a softball game! The next evening, I rebuked the church for this great compromise. The day before this reproof, the pastor had been excited about the meeting and had even asked me if I could come back *every year* for a conference. But after the reproof about putting sports before Christ, I was never invited back.

But we refuse to accept this type of thing, and we have learned how to deal with it in our own church work. Ninety-five percent of our people are faithful.

We don't want to rebuke our people. We get no joy out of that. The last thing we want to do is hurt them. We no more want to hurt our church members than to hurt our own children and grandchildren, but reproof and correction are matters of obedience to God and blessing for those who need it.

Our desire is that our people be true disciples of Christ, and we are willing to do whatever is necessary from our side to see that happen.

If God requires a steward to be faithful and if He has given us the example of faithfulness in the members of the first church, who am I as a church leader to require less?

The public process of perfecting disciples requires teaching, exhortation, reproof, rebuke, and discipline, in that order.

As with child training, chastening must precede rebuke and scourging or spanking (Heb. 12:5-6). The word "chasten" is from the Greek "paideuo," which is elsewhere translated "learn" (1 Ti. 1:20), "instruct" (2 Ti. 2:25), and "teach" (Tit. 2:12). This is the foundation of proper discipline. The parent patiently teaches the child the difference between right and wrong and makes him to understand what is required of him.

Likewise, discipleship begins with **teaching**. You don't reprove and rebuke and correct and discipline until first you have carefully instructed the church member as to what he is supposed to do. The same is true for child discipline. To reprove before proper teaching will produce confusion rather than good fruit.

So, in regard to producing faithful church members, we begin by patiently and persistently teaching our people about faithfulness and why they should be faithful and the blessings of faithfulness. This instruction includes the ministry of our *One Year Discipleship Course* which has a lot of teaching on this subject.

Together with teaching and instruction is **exhortation**. We exhort our people to be faithful. We weave this teaching and exhortation into the preaching and teaching ministry.

Only after teaching and exhortation is there **reproof and rebuke**. Those who do not obey and persist in unfaithfulness must be reproved.

Ultimately, there is **discipline**. If an individual persists in disobedience in the face of teaching, exhortation, reproof and rebuke, we do not allow him to be a member of our church.

Of course, there are many other elements necessary for producing faithfulness to Christ, including much prayer, compassion and patience.

Take another issue, that of loving God's Word. According to Scripture, the believer is to have an intimate relationship with God's Word from the time he is a babe in Christ (1 Pe. 2:2). He is to delight in it and meditate therein day and night (Ps. 1:2). He is to study it diligently and rightly divide it (1 Ti. 2:15). He is to become skillful in the use of it (Heb. 5:12-14).

God requires this of His people; therefore, the church leaders must require it.

Again, the process of requiring a right relationship with God's Word begins with teaching.

We teach our church members about every aspect of Bible study. We teach them how to have a daily Bible study time. We teach them how to use Bible study tools and how to interpret the Bible for themselves. Our teaching on this subject is extensive and includes two courses, a basic one entitled *The Effectual Bible Student* and a deeper one entitled *How to Study the Bible*.

Then we exhort them to read the Bible and study the Bible and love the Bible. We weave this theme into the messages.

Finally, we reprove and rebuke those who refuse to obey God in this matter.

Other examples of things that commonly need to be reproved are husbands not being the spiritual leaders of their homes, husbands not loving their wives, husbands neglecting their children, wives not honoring and obeying their husbands, wives not being keepers at home, parents not disciplining their children, young people not honoring and obeying their parents, employees not being good workers, lying and dishonesty, laziness, not paying one's debts, putting one's work and business before God, putting education above seeking God's will, and neglecting the duty of being an ambassador for Christ.

There must also be **PRIVATE REPROOF**.

> "Whom we preach, warning every man, and teaching every man in all wisdom; that we may present every man perfect in Christ Jesus" (Col. 1:28).

Note that this is a ministry to "every man." Public reproof is not enough. There must also be individual, private reproof.

This is very necessary, and it can be very effectual.

I often talk briefly to individuals when they are late or miss services or other things in order to exhort them. I inquire as to their situation (such as where they were during the service) and then exhort them according to their situation and need.

We sometimes meet privately with members after church services to exhort them.

We also visit homes to encourage and exhort the people. Last year we used one evening every week to visit the homes of the church members. The church leaders visited each home together, and after we talked with the family and inquired as to their situation and needs, each of the preachers delivered a word of exhortation.

As with dealing with children, you don't rebuke church members until it is necessary, and you don't rebuke them more than necessary.

Usually the public teaching and exhortation and reproof and the private exhortation is enough.

But if the individual persists in disobedience, the leaders must get increasingly firm.

The Ministry of the Body

Another essential part of the ministry of reproof that produces a church of disciples is the ministry of the body itself.

The following are some of the Bible's teaching about the "one another" ministry of the New Testament church. Note that admonishing is one of the ministries that the members are to exercise toward one another.

> "And I myself also am persuaded of you, my brethren, that ye also are full of goodness, filled with all knowledge, able also to ADMONISH ONE ANOTHER" (Ro. 15:14).
>
> "BEAR YE ONE ANOTHER'S BURDENS, and so fulfil the law of Christ" (Ga. 6:2).
>
> "Let the word of Christ dwell in you richly in all wisdom; TEACHING AND ADMONISHING ONE ANOTHER in psalms and hymns and spiritual songs, singing with grace in your hearts to the Lord" (Col. 3:16).

"But as touching brotherly love ye need not that I write unto you: for ye yourselves are taught of God to LOVE ONE ANOTHER" (1 Th. 4:9).

"Wherefore COMFORT ONE ANOTHER with these words" (1 Th. 4:18).

"Wherefore comfort yourselves together, and EDIFY ONE ANOTHER, even as also ye do" (1 Th. 5:11).

"But EXHORT ONE ANOTHER daily, while it is called To day; lest any of you be hardened through the deceitfulness of sin" (Heb. 3:13).

"Not forsaking the assembling of ourselves together, as the manner of some *is*; but EXHORTING ONE ANOTHER: and so much the more, as ye see the day approaching" (Heb. 10:25).

Our goal is to build the congregation up in Christ so the members are able to minister effectively to one another. This does not replace the ministry of the leaders and preachers and teachers; it works together with that ministry and is under the direction of that ministry.

Note that the Bible doesn't say that the members are to rebuke one another. They are to teach, encourage, comfort, exhort, and admonish. The rebuking should be done by the preachers and leaders.

Exhort means to encourage; to challenge; to cheer. The word translated "exhort" is from the Greek "parakaleo," which means "to call near." This Greek word is also translated intreat" (Lu. 15:25), "desire" (Ac. 8:31), "beseech" (Ac. 13:42), "comfort" (Ac. 16:40), "call for" (Ac. 28:20), and "pray" (Ac. 16:9).

Admonish means to put in mind; to caution; to reprove gently; to warn or notify of a fault; to counsel against wrong practices; to advise; to instruct. The Greek word translated "admonish" in Romans 15:14 ("neotheteo") is elsewhere translated "warn" (Acts 20:31). It is used for Jeremiah's warning to the Jewish remnant about not going to Egypt (Jer. 42:19), Paul's warning to the ship's captain (Acts 27:9), the admonition of God's Word about sin (1 Co. 10:11), admonishing an erring brother (2 Th. 3:15), God's admonition of Moses (Heb. 8:5).

I often hear of the operation of this ministry in our church. I hear of one brother or sister encouraging another, teaching another, exhorting another, comforting and helping another, and it is a great blessing to the church family.

Our more spiritual young people exercise this ministry toward the weaker ones.

We give instruction about this ministry, and we encourage it.

A Discipling Church Maintains God's Standards for Ministers and Workers

Outline
Arguments against Standards
Reasons for Maintaining Standards
Standards Our Church Maintains
Implementing and Enforcing Standards
Are Standards Contrary to Compassion?
Standards and Foundation Building
Some Things That Can Weaken Standards and Discipline
A Matter of Faith

Spiritual standards for leaders and workers is something that is emphasized in Scripture. Two entire chapters are devoted to describing the high standards for church leaders (1 Timothy 3; Titus 1).

And the standards are high for every worker:

"it is required in stewards, that a man be found faithful" (1 Co. 4:2)

"faithful men" (2 Ti. 2:2)

"whom we have oftentimes proved diligent in many things" (2 Co. 8:22)

Maintaining high biblical standards for leaders and workers is a major tool in raising the spiritual climate of the church. The leaders and workers set the tone for and give the example for the entire congregation. If a church compromises on this, it is already on a downward slide. It is better to err on being a little too strict.

I recall the pastors, deacons, teachers, and workers of the church in which I grew up. One of the deacons allowed his teenage children to build a collection of rock & roll records in the 1960s and this is one of the major avenues whereby I became addicted to this sensual music and influenced by its licentious philosophy. My parents wouldn't let me have rock & roll records at home, but that was no problem because I just visited my buddy, the deacon's son.

My teachers never guided the conversation to the things of Christ. They conversed only of worldly things, and one of my teachers told off-color jokes. They did not challenge us to love Christ in our daily lives and turn away from our worldliness, and had they attempted to do so, we would not have listened because their lives did not back up such a message.

When appointing leaders and teachers, churches need to care about the people that will be influenced by them. It is one thing to recognize that "no one is perfect," but it is another thing to ignore godly biblical standards and appoint people to positions who are going to undermine the ministry through their carnal thinking and the spiritually careless way in which they live.

I recall a Sunday School teacher in a fundamental Baptist church that was training pre-teen girls. She wore her hair short like a man's, wore pants contrary to the church's position, was stubborn and carnally opinionated, and habitually neglected the mid-week prayer service for other activities. What a poor example she was to her class! She was teaching the holy things of the Bible, but her life undermined what she was teaching. Some of the other teachers in this church were just as worldly, and it is no wonder that a large percentage of the young people loved the world more than Christ.

I think of another church in which the wife and children of one of the teachers forsook church services for sporting activities. That man should not have been allowed to teach. It was a bad example for the church and it had the potential to ruin young lives who might have been negatively influenced by his family's compromise and poor example.

This neglect of biblical standards for workers pulls down the spiritual atmosphere of the church.

Arguments against Standards

There is great pressure on pastors today to lower standards, and many are bending to the pressure.

Some of the arguments against maintaining high standards are as follows:

"We must reach the heart and not focus on externals."

This is true, but proper biblical standards *do* focus on the spiritual qualifications, as we will see. Further, externals are important, because that is what man sees. The Bible says that the Lord looks on the heart, but the same verse says that man looks on the outward appearance (1 Sa. 16:7). One's heart condition is reflected in "externals." When we talk about "standards," we are not talking about a mere external rule. We are not talking about Phariseeism that produces whited sepulchers. We are talking about a true and close walk with Christ that *produces evidences in* external obedience (John 8:47; 10:27-28; 14:23; 1 John 2:3-4) and separation from sin and error (Ps. 119:128; Ephesians 5:11; 1 John 2:15-17).

"We cannot force obedience."

This is true, but we can and must reprove, rebuke, and exhort (2 Ti. 4:2), even though this often comes across like "force" to the rebellious. Further, we are to chasten and discipline, both in regard to children and to church members. God chastens every son that He receives (Heb. 12:6-7). It could be said that chastening and discipline is a type of "force," but whatever it is called, it is Scriptural! Further, maintaining standards for workers is not forcing obedience, because no one is forced to serve in the church's ministries. It is a privilege to serve, not a right or something one can demand. It's like a driver's license. I must meet the qualifications.

"We don't have enough workers."

One preacher said, "It is the old dilemma, do we have a youth program led by men who are less than we want them to be in order to reach the children from our large families, or do we shut it down because there are no mature men to lead them?"

There are almost never enough workers in a church to do all that should be done and could be done, but that is no excuse to lower the standards of God's Word. Far better to have one qualified musician or Sunday School teacher than a dozen unqualified ones.

We can't have God's power and blessing if we don't obey His Word. We are often too hasty; we outrun God; we pick unripe fruit. We must build a solid biblical and spiritual foundation rather than building on sand, and building something solid requires time and patience. How much time? As much as it takes!

"We want to help people to grow by being in a ministry."

God's principle is that they *first be proven faithful*, then use an office (1 Ti. 3:10).

I have ignored this principle at times, and I have always lived to regret it. God's way is best.

"I get in the flesh when I try to maintain standards."

The preacher needs to put the standards in writing and teach the people and then simply enforce them. He needs to train up men and women of God who will stand with him in this matter, and he obtains such people by enforcing standards from the beginning of the ministry. Then, whatever workers the church has, are workers who stand with the preachers on these issues.

It is not an issue of fighting in the flesh. It is an issue of standing firm for God's Word because I love God and fear Him more than the people, and I want to build a good spiritual foundation for the house of God, and I love the people enough to enforce the discipline of God's Word.

If a preacher can't do God's work without getting in the flesh, he should not be in the ministry. The people need strong leaders who stand firm for God's Word.

Reasons for Maintaining Standards

1. God requires it.

The Word of God says that "it is REQUIRED in a steward that a man be found faithful" (1 Co. 4:2). That is God's requirement, not man's, and the church leader who does not require that which God requires is a rebel. To be found faithful would encompass faithfulness to church services and functions and fellowship (Acts 2:42; Heb. 10:25; 1 Ti. 3:15), faithfulness in doctrinal purity (Acts 2:42; 1 Ti. 1:3; Jude 3), faithfulness in right relationship to the leaders (1 Th. 5:12-13; Heb. 13:17), faithfulness in separation from the world (Eph. 5:11), faithfulness in modesty (1 Ti. 2:9), etc.

2. The workers represent the church and affect its testimony.

The community knows who the church workers are, and if they don't live as they should, they will bring reproach upon Christ. Visitors judge the entire church on the basis of its workers and ministers. This is the theme of Titus 2. Here God instructs every age group in the church: old men, old women, young women, young men. And the focus is on how that their lives affect the testimony of the Lord. See Titus 2:5, 8, 10.

3. Having standards for church workers is an important part of raising the level of standards for the entire church.

It is not possible for a church to have worker-type standards for every member, but it is possible to require specific standards for those who serve in a ministry. A person doesn't have to teach Sunday School or participate in the music ministry, etc., but if he does, it is not unreasonable for the church to require him to meet specific standards.

One of the ways that new members learn how to live for Christ is by observing the church leaders and workers, and if they do not live right, the entire church is affected. If the Sunday School teachers, for example, are not required to maintain high spiritual and moral standards, the students will learn from their poor example, but if Sunday School teachers are required to maintain standards, the students will tend to follow their example and grow in Christ.

4. Having standards for church workers is a challenge to the believers.

They understand that if they want to serve the Lord in any capacity beyond merely attending, they must live a godly, faithful Christian life. I recall how I was challenged when I was a new believer. I wanted God to use my life, and I wanted to prepare for His service. The Bible school I wanted to attend had many standards, and this was one of the motivations for me to cut my hair, quit smoking, give up rock, stop watching Hollywood movies, and do other things in preparation for the Lord's service. The standards challenged me. They were biblical standards of Christian living, and I am thankful that they were maintained.

Standards Our Church Maintains

Following are the fundamental qualifications that our church requires of every teacher and worker (those who do any type of ministry in the church, including ushering, taking the offering, musician, singer, giving announcements, public Bible reading, operating the bookstore, working with the sound system):

1. The individual must have a good Christian testimony (Php. 2:15-16). This testimony will be evident in the home, on the job, at school, etc. This includes an honest reputation (e.g., paying debts, not stealing, not lying). This includes separation from the world (including worldly music, whether secular or "Christian," worldly television and movies, worldly things on the Internet, worldly video games, worldly literature, etc.) (Eph. 5:11; Jas. 4:4; 1 Joh. 2:15-17).

2. The individual must *agree with the church's doctrinal position* (1 Co. 1:10; Acts 2:42; 1 Ti. 1:3).

3. The individual must be in submission to and have a good attitude toward God-ordained authority: church leaders (1 Th. 5:12-13; Heb. 13:17), husbands (Eph. 5:22), parents (Eph. 6:1-3), and government (Ro. 13:1). God has established authority. "The powers that be are ordained of God" and those who resist God-ordained authorities are fighting God and will be judged by God (Ro. 13:1-2). Disobedience to and disrespect toward God-ordained authority is lawlessness and anarchy, and it has no place in the house of God and the kingdom of Christ (Col. 1:13; 1 Ti. 3:15). A stubborn spirit toward authority is a lawless spirit. God's Word says, "stubbornness is as iniquity and idolatry" (1 Sa. 15:23). Before a woman can serve in a ministry, we want to see that she is in submission with a godly attitude toward her husband. Likewise, a teen toward his or her parents.

4. The individual must be *faithful* (Pr. 29:15; 1 Co. 4:2; Heb. 10:25). We look for a good level of faithfulness and dependability in those who serve in ministry. God requires it, and practicality requires it. "Confidence in an unfaithful man in time of trouble *is like* a broken tooth, and a foot out of joint" (Pr. 25:19).

5. The individual must *dress modestly* according to the church's standards (1 Ti. 2:9).

6. The individual must have the *ability and gifting to do the assigned task* (Ro. 12:3). Having a love for the Lord and a good testimony is not enough for specific positions of service. One must have the ability and gifting for that particular task. Not everyone is gifted in music, teaching, working with children, ushering, finances, etc. When it comes to church business, I have often wondered why it is so common for the wrong person to be put into a certain position. God's people should exercise practical wisdom and strive for excellence.

Implementing and Enforcing Standards

Following are some of the ways that standards are implemented and enforced:

Education

Education is the fundamental tool for setting up and maintaining biblical standards in a congregation.

Education through the church covenant. When we started a new church in 2003, the first thing we did was write out the standards for workers, the reasons for the standards, etc., to use as a teaching tool. As the Lord has given us converts, they are required to study the church covenant and agree with it before they are received as members. As a consequence, every member understands from the very beginning that we have these standards and is instructed as to their biblical foundation and purpose.

Education through the preaching/teaching ministry. We frequently emphasize the biblical principles of God's requirements for those who exercise public ministry. This theme is woven throughout the church's teaching ministry. I emphasize this in our men's weekly discipleship meeting. My wife emphasizes it in her Titus 2 ministry to the women (Tit. 2:3-5).

Starting where you are

If you have only one person qualified to teach a Bible class, lead singing, play a musical instrument, work as a deacon, etc., then that is where you start.

I am convinced, and I have experienced in our ministry, that if we hold the Lord's standards and use only those people who are qualified for a particular position (and the qualifications are not the same for all positions of service), that this produces more qualified workers.

This is the slower path, and that can be frustrating, but it is the solid path. It is the way of building on rock rather than sand. As already stated, every time I have gotten in a hurry and have ignored the principle of 1 Timothy 3:10 ("let these first be proven"), I have regretted it.

Christ has plainly instructed us about what happens to a house constructed on sand, and we are seeing the fruit of that everywhere among Baptist churches today. They are collapsing because of a weak foundation.

Enforcement

A law that is not enforced is no law. Having rules without enforcement is anarchy.

We cannot enforce God's laws in the world today, but we can enforce them in His house and spiritual kingdom (1 Ti. 3:15; Col. 1:15).

We urge preachers not to back down. Don't let the people rule the leaders. Don't let the sheep rule the shepherd. Don't let the younger generation pull down the standards of God's Word.

Are Standards Contrary to Compassion?

I wrote to a pastor friend recently about this issue, and he responded as follows:

> "Thanks for your insights. ... When I remember where [our youth man] has come from and how far he has come, I am encouraged that he is moving in the right direction. Needless to say, he has some semi-neo friends and family who want to see him compromise, so it is a battle. In our area we face overwhelming odds in that we suffer from a scarcity of separatist workers and when we do find one he goes off to Bible college and we never see him again. It is the old dilemma: do we have a youth program led by men who are less than we want them to be in order to reach the children from our large families, or do we shut it down because there are no mature men to lead them? ... I note that he took on board your criticisms and appears to be willing to move in a

biblical direction. I will speak to him about the issue of dress at the youth activity. I was shocked to see how his wife dressed. ... there is certainly more work to be done with them. Pray for me to be strong, truthful with them, and loving at the same time. It is so easy for me to crush some of these rosebuds trying to get them to open up to the Lord."

I replied as follows:

Thanks for the feedback. I truly understand your dilemma. We never have enough workers and never will.

But I believe that we sometimes use this as an excuse for not upholding the clear standards of God's Word. The Lord is the one who *requires* faithfulness. "Moreover it is required in stewards, that a man be found faithful" (1 Corinthians 4:2). That's God's requirement, and who am I to require less? To be "found faithful" is a general principle, and the term is full of biblical meaning.

To be found faithful would encompass faithfulness to church services and functions and fellowship (Acts 2:42; Heb. 10:25; 1 Ti. 3:15), faithfulness in doctrinal purity (Acts 2:42; 1 Ti. 1:3; Jude 3), faithfulness in right relationship to the leaders (1 Th. 5:12-13; Heb. 13:17), faithfulness in separation from the world (Eph. 5:11), faithfulness in modesty (1 Ti. 2:9), etc.

Holding high biblical standards for workers isn't a matter of crushing rosebuds. We don't want to crush rosebuds. We passionately want to develop them and see them blossom for the Lord, and that is what we are doing. I love the Messianic prophecy, "A bruised reed shall he not break, and the smoking flax shall he not quench: he shall bring forth judgment unto truth" (Isaiah 42:3). Christ is so gracious and kind and patient, and it is our passion not to quench the smoking flax or crush the little bud.

But being patient with the smoking flax and the little bud is a different thing from maintaining standards for church workers. I want to wait for the flax to flame up and for the bud to flower (according to God's standards, not mine) before it is put into the ministry. Serving in ministry is not a right; it is a privilege reserved for those who are fit in their Christian lives for that high calling.

I was glad to meet your youth man. He is on the right path and moving in the right direction, and you are having a good ministry into his life. I will repeat, though, that as for me and my house, we would never let him lead our young people at this stage in his life.

My compassionate, Christlike wife would have been even more discouraged than I was if she had seen that youth outreach. A man whose wife doesn't know how to dress modestly and who would allow her to dress immodestly at a youth activity isn't ready to work with youth. As we know, the fundamental principle of modesty pertains to the heart. Modest dress is a reflection of a modest heart; and this young couple hasn't settled those heart matters solidly enough so that it affects their external behavior. They are not yet the examples they should be.

It is better to have one qualified helper than ten unqualified or questionable, borderline ones.

Youth workers who are still holding on to the world in many ways, who are still biblically weak, who haven't yet gotten fundamental issues nailed down, will produce the same poor fruit in the congregation's children, youth, and families.

Christlikeness is compassion and gentleness and patience, but it is also firmness, even toughness, in regard to God's holy laws. The Lord Himself said, "As many as I love, I rebuke and chasten: be zealous therefore, and repent" (Re. 3:19).

Paul exemplifies the right "balance" in ministry. He said, "Brethren, be followers together of me, and mark them which walk so as ye have us for an ensample" (Php. 3:17). See also 1 Corinthians 4:16; 11:1. On the one hand, Paul was as gentle as a nurse with the believers (1 Th. 2:7). On the other hand, he was firm and unyielding about discipline (1 Co. 5; 2 Th. 3:6-14). He was a strong reprover (e.g., 1 Co. 6:5; 15:33-36; Ga. 3:1), and he taught the preachers under his watchcare to be the same (2 Ti. 4:2; Tit. 1:13; 2:15).

Paul's ministry of reproof to the carnal church at Corinth worked repentance and change (2 Co. 7:8-11). A sound ministry of reproof and discipline has the same power today.

Standards and Foundation Building

A fundamental issue in regard to standards is the matter of foundation building. We must build the right foundation, regardless of how long it takes.

When we started a new church plant in 2003, I thought things would go faster than they have. We had quite a bit of help from the beginning and we had some experience and we had more freedom than ever from the government and society, but it turned out that it has taken 13 years to get the right foundation so we can more aggressively plant other churches from this base as we have envisioned from the beginning.

How long does this take? It takes as long as it takes. The work is the Lord's, and we can't go faster than He goes.

Some preachers talk about being out "in the bush," but no one is really farther out "in the bush" than we are. The culture we work in is 100% pagan. We almost never get anyone from other churches, properly trained or otherwise. In the 25 years of our church planting work, I can probably count on my fingers the numbers of members we have received from other churches. By God's grace, we have been able to build our own workers from the material God has given us out of darkest paganism. And holding high standards for workers is one of the methods we use.

Things That Can Weaken Standards and Discipline

Following are some of the things that can weaken discipline and the maintenance of biblical standards:

Fear of man and pressure from man

One of the most difficult things for a preacher is to enforce God's Word in the face of one's friends and relatives in the church, sometimes even in the face of one's own wife.

Some people will actually try to draw close to the preacher and will flatter him with the goal of having him treat them with more leniency. I have seen this many times, and rare is the preacher who is not susceptible to this type of thing.

Sometimes the pressure is real, and sometimes it is only perceived. The devil can create fears when there is nothing to fear. The preacher might have the idea that if he disciplines (meaning any type of discipline) a member, that other people will get upset, but that might not be the case. It is always good to talk directly with people about any matter that is bothering you. It brings light into the situation and displaces the devil, who always works in the darkness.

The more relatives there are in the church family, the greater the danger. I am referring to church members who are related to one another. If a member is an uncle or an aunt or a niece or a grandchild of other members, it often becomes more difficult for the preacher to enforce the rules of God's Word in that individual's life, because he worries that his actions might cause offense to the relatives.

As the preacher gets older and if his children and grandchildren are in the church, which they often are, the danger becomes ever greater that he will either (1) "lighten up" on the standards that he previously enforced, or (2) treat his own family differently than he treats other members of the church. He might allow a son to be in a ministry even though that son would not have been qualified for the same ministry 20 years earlier. He might allow a grandchild to get away with a level of worldliness and still remain in some ministry. In this way, *many* churches have compromised and gone contemporary.

The fear of man is something that must be faced by every preacher on a regular basis. It is not something that you will get victory over once and for all. Each case is a new test of whether the preacher will fear God or man.

See 2 Timothy 1:7 - "For God hath not given us the spirit of fear; but of power, and of love, and of a sound mind."

(1) We see that there are fears. Timothy had them and needed to be exhorted about them. Paul had them (2 Co. 7:5). I have them (e.g., thinking about the future of the work, thinking about my inability and weakness, fear of man, fear of dangers like an earthquake). The bravest soldiers have fears. A battle-experienced Army Ranger said, "Courage is not being fearless, but courage is moving forward in spite of the fear" (*The Warfighters*, Season 1, Episode 3).

(2) We see that fears do not come from God. You can be sure that your fear is not of God. The only fear that comes from God is the fear of God and the fear of sinning against God.

(3) We see that in God there is victory over fear. We can overcome fear by faith in God. He gives power, love, and a sound mind, but we must seek these things from Him day by day. Seek power every time you are weak; seek love every time you are selfish; seek a sound mind every time your mind is disturbed.

(4) There are two great promises that have often helped me to overcome fear: Psalm 138:3; 1 Peter 5:8.

(5) The promises of God are mighty weapons (2 Co. 10:4-5). Unbelievers don't have these powerful resources. They are not found in psychology, religion, alcohol, drugs, not even in the closest friends and relatives.

Fear of being overbearing and unreasonable

The preacher must always test himself to make sure that he is not being overbearing and unreasonable. Because of our fallen nature, it is easy to abuse one's authority. A wise preacher is going to be examining himself by God's Word even as he ministers God's Word to others. But it is also true that the devil can falsely accuse the preacher of being overbearing and "too hard" when he is only preaching God's Word and enforcing it as God has commanded.

Becoming weary in well doing

Twice we are told in the New Testament "be not weary in well doing" (Ga. 6:9; 2 Th. 3:13). Obviously, then, becoming weary in well doing is a very real possibility.

One of the exhortations to be not weary in well doing is stated in the context of church discipline (2 Th. 3:6-13).

The potential to become weary in well doing explains why many preachers get "soft" in their old age. They soften up on some aspects of discipline. Discipline is a real battle, and it is a never-ceasing battle because even the best of saints has a fallen nature, and the preacher can get weary in the battle.

This is why team ministries are important. It is good for men of various generations to work together in the ministry. The youth supply energy and zeal, while the elderly supply mature wisdom. It is very sad that it is so rare that men can get along well enough to minister in such teams and that the older preachers have to be put out of the ministry to make room for the younger guys.

The old men tend not to want to share the authority of the ministry with the younger men, so they can't get along. I have seen this many times. I think of one pastor who built and oversaw a large church and ministry, and when he got old he would tell younger men that he was going to prepare them and then turn the ministry over to them, but he couldn't bring himself to let go of the reigns, and the young men would get discouraged and leave. By the time the old warrior finally did step down, the ministry was only a shell of what it had been.

In Scripture we see Paul the aged and his Timothys and Tituses working together to the end. Paul wrote his final epistle to Timothy when he was in prison awaiting death, and they were still coworkers in the Lord's work. Paul was still working together in harmony with Erastus and Trophimus and other younger men (2 Ti. 4:20).

Knowledge of your own failings

Every man knows "the plague of his own heart" (1 Ki. 8:38). Every honest preacher knows that he is not worthy to preach God's Word to others and to lead churches. The apostle Paul called himself the chief of sinners (1 Ti. 1:15). When the preacher thinks of his own failings before God, he can draw back from preaching God's Word as he should and exercising discipline as he should.

The preacher must remember that he is ministering before God and will give account to God (2 Ti. 4:1-2). He must honor God by being faithful in the ministry, not for his own glory, but for God's glory.

The preacher must examine himself and confess his sins and walk in the light so that he does not become disqualified (1 Co. 9:27).

Anxiety and impatience

It is an easy thing for the preacher to become anxious about some need or situation and therefore not wait on God to supply. If he needs a pianist or a song leader or a Sunday School teacher or a Bible Institute teacher, etc., he can be tempted to act impulsively and appoint someone who is not qualified.

But the solution to this is to walk by faith in God.

A Matter of Faith

I see the issue of standards as an issue of faith like everything else in the Christian life and ministry.

We teach people to put God first and be faithful to services, and God will take care of them. But they have to take the step of faith.

We teach couples to put God first and to live on one salary so that the wife and mother can be a keeper at home as God's Word instructs. We teach the couples that God will take care of them if they obey Him. But they must take the step of faith.

That is a principle that runs throughout the Christian life, and it is based on Matthew 6:33--"But seek ye first the kingdom of God, and his righteousness; and all these things shall be added unto you."

The preacher must put God first and honor His Word and trust Him and wait for Him to supply.

I constantly cast this business onto the Lord on the basis of one of my favorite prayer promises (1 Pe. 5:7). It is the Lord's harvest, His Word, His church, and His standards. I have often prayed, "Lord, you *must* raise up workers. You see what we are working with. You see our lack. We want to move ahead and get more done in your great harvest fields according to your command, but you *must* give us qualified workers if you want that to happen. We can't create that type of heart. We are waiting on you, Lord. You told us to do this work, but we can't move if you don't move."

When we started church planting again in 2003, that is what I told the Lord. "I am ready to do it, Lord, but we *must* have help. I am just one weak man. We *can't* do this alone."

I know you can't *boss* the Lord, but Abraham, Moses, and other men of God have taught us that you can get a lot from the Lord if you are pressing and persistent in things clearly pertaining to His will and if you reason with Him on the basis of His own Word. I learn from Scripture that this is the essence of the prayer of faith and that God is pleased with it. In my ministry He has always answered this cry, beginning when we started the first church in the early 1980s.

I think of a man who was translating for me. I needed him. He was the best translator I had and the only one who was available for that particular teaching project. But he was becoming very independent minded and was not doing what we told him to do. I feared to deal with him firmly about the matter, lest he quit, but I finally determined to require his faithfulness and obedience, because God requires it and because his lack of faithfulness and obedience was harming the ministry, and I was going to trust the Lord with the result. In this case, he submitted and has had a good attitude ever since, but I knew that if he had quit, the Lord would have taken care of the matter according to His own will.

We must have the spirit of Esther who said, "Go, gather together all the Jews that are present in Shushan, and fast ye for me, and neither eat nor drink three days, night or day: I also and my maidens will fast likewise; and so will I go in unto the king, which *is* not according to the law: **and if I perish, I perish**" (Es. 4:16).

When Abraham went to Mt. Moriah with Isaac, he believed that God would work things out, even if it meant raising Isaac from the dead (Heb. 1:17-19).

A Discipling Church Is Properly Educated

Outline

Widespread Ignorance
Suggestions for Educating the Church

A discipling church is a church that is properly educated in all matters necessary to Christian life and ministry.

In this chapter we are talking about education beyond education in the Bible itself, education that encompasses every issue that affects Bible-believing people and churches.

The church that will be standing when Jesus comes is the church that loves truth, teaches truth, and exalts truth. The church is the pillar and ground of the truth, so truth must be central to its existence (1 Timothy 3:15).

Widespread Ignorance

The average Independent Baptist church is not such a church. There is widespread ignorance about important issues such as contemporary rock & roll philosophy or "cultural liberalism" (that mocks strict holy standards of Christian living as legalism), modern textual criticism, Roman Catholicism, Protestantism, New Evangelicalism, Purpose Drivenism, the Southern Baptist Convention, self-esteemism, kingdom now theology, replacement theology, charismaticism, reconstructionism, ecumenical evangelism, emerging church, C.S. Lewisism, Christian counseling psychobabble, Modernism, Neo-orthodoxy, Darwinian evolution, theistic evolution, contemporary music, contemplative prayer, Christian hedonism, and organic churchism.

Thousands of churches have been established around the world by fundamental Baptist missionaries, but what is their character? How solid is their spiritual foundation? Are they well-grounded, properly-taught congregations, or are they shallow and largely ignorant of important issues facing God's people today? Are the parents properly educated by the church so they can train, disciple, and protect their children? What is happening to the second generations in these churches?

Around the turn of the century, my pastor rented a table at the Southwide Baptist Fellowship annual conference for two or three years running. He offered solid Bible study books such as the *Way of Life Encyclopedia of the Bible and Christianity* and *Things Hard to Be Understood* and seriously-researched books on issues such as music, New Evangelicalism, and evangelism. Though the books were deeply discounted, there was little interest by the hundreds of preachers in attendance.

I see a direct connection between this and the spiritual downfall of a great many of these very churches, including the host church, Highland Park Baptist Church, which turned into a rock & roll Southern Baptist congregation before going defunct.

A couple of decades ago, those same churches would have said that they rejected New Evangelicalism, but even the pastors had only a vague idea of New Evangelicalism's history and principles, were uneducated about contemporary music, etc., *and they weren't interested in studying such issues*. And for the most part the people were more ignorant by far than the preachers.

In light of the fact that every Independent Baptist church is inundated with New Evangelical philosophy from every direction (e.g., Christian bookstores, Christian radio, Internet, friends, neighbors, relatives, graduates of compromising schools), it is no surprise that churches that were not properly educated and spiritually fortified against error are either in the evangelical contemporary camp today or are heading in that direction.

I think of a pastor who showed a video presentation in his church by Steve Anderson, who holds a wide variety of heresies, such as replacement theology, denial of the imminency of the Rapture, believing that Christ suffered in hell for sinners, and calling for the death of homosexuals. When challenged by a church member as to why he would use Anderson's materials, the pastor said that someone sent him the DVD and that he didn't have a clue about the man's ministry. Why would a pastor bring the influence of a preacher into his congregation without making the effort to know who he is?

A preacher friend told the following sad testimony about the condition of many Independent Baptist preachers:

> "Some years ago I started asking preachers questions when we sat around talking or when we drove down the road. Questions such as what doctrine was especially precious to them at that moment, or what book of the Bible they love the most this week, or what good book they are reading, or which one has helped them grow the most, or what authors are the most challenging to them spiritually, or what they think about this or that verse (and I pick the hardest ones to ask about). If they are driving, I take my Bible and read to them some passage I am meditating on and ask them to explain it to me. Most of them are out of their depth within ten seconds. Some of them stare at me with open mouth and shake their head. Most of the IB pastors have never read anything deeper than Rice or Hutson."

In the 1990s, I had a book table set up at a Bible conference, and a missionary proclaimed during his sermon, "We don't need more books; we need more preaching."

That was a statement of rank ignorance, but it expressed a philosophy that permeates some Independent Baptist circles.

Good preaching is essential. I believe in preaching. I have preached thousands of sermons in more than 550 churches in dozens of countries, on university campuses, in our missionary church planting work, in jails, etc. But good books are also essential. I love good books; I need good books. Good books help me preach more effectually.

Paul was a preacher, but he said to Timothy, "The cloke that I left at Troas with Carpus, when thou comest, bring with thee, and the books, but especially the parchments" (2 Timothy 4:13).

This downplaying of the importance of godly education didn't characterize preachers of the past. Consider two examples:

> "What has exceedingly hurt you in time past, nay, and I fear to this day, is want of reading. I scarce ever knew a preacher who read so little. And perhaps by neglecting it you have lost the taste for it. Hence your talent in preaching does not increase. It is just the same as it was seven years ago. It is lively, but not deep: there is little variety; there is no compass of thought. Reading only can supply this, with meditation

and daily prayer. You wrong yourself greatly by omitting this. You can never be a deep preacher without it any more than a thorough Christian. O begin! Fix some part of every day for private exercises. You may acquire the taste which you have not; what is tedious at first will afterwards be pleasant. Whether you like it or no; read and pray daily. It is for your life; there is no other way; else you will be a trifler all your days, and a petty, superficial prayer" (John Wesley to John Trembeth, August 1760).

"Only Heaven will determine which was the most important in my earthly ministry--my preaching or the distributing of books." (Peter Cartwright, circuit riding preacher).

Thank the Lord for the preachers who are serious students, but countless times I have witnessed pastors, missionaries, and evangelists walk by a book table, take a cursory look, and walk away. For the most part, they don't walk away because they are already well educated in the issues facing the churches and already know the things we publish. And usually they don't walk away because they have no money. We find a way to purchase the things we want and the things we hold valuable. Charles Spurgeon counseled his Bible college students to "sell your shirt and buy books." No, these preachers more typically walk away because they have no passion for godly and continual education. They are satisfied to put together a little three point sermon outline, backed by a few illustrations which are never fact checked and many of which are pure fantasy.

The members of the average church walk into a Christian bookstore or listen to Christian radio or surf the Internet and are grossly unequipped to distinguish between sound and unsound authors and are thus in great danger of being influenced in a wrong direction. They are unequipped to discern the compromise represented by the nationally-syndicated personalities on Christian radio. They are unequipped to deal effectively with the error that permeates Internet blogs. They are unequipped to deal with the contemporary worship phenomenon. They don't know Darlene Zschech from Annie Oakley.

A pastor once accompanied me to a LifeWay bookstore, and as I pointed out various authors and the spiritual/doctrinal danger they represent, he exclaimed, "I don't know anything about these people!" He *should* know something, because his people are in danger of being influenced by them, either by book or the Internet, but the problem is that he isn't a student.

I frequently hear from preachers who say, "I don't know anything about Darlene Zscheck or Hillsong or the Gettys or these other people you talk about." There is no excuse for this in a day when these people are influencing members of Independent Baptist churches throughout the world.

Yet many of these same pastors know a lot about professional sports, conservative politics, fishing, and hunting. It's a matter of priorities.

Some church members put their own pastors to shame. I was told recently about a woman in a church who works six days a week but she has gone through the entire 20 titles in our *Advanced Bible Studies Series* (totaling more than 6,000 pages). I know of several church members who have read the entire *Way of Life Encyclopedia of the Bible and Christianity*. Many people in the congregations educate themselves with materials such as *O Timothy* magazine, *Foundation* magazine, and the *Fundamentalist Digest* even though their own pastors have no interest in such education.

Suggestions for Educating the Church

Following are some ways a church can be sufficiently educated to be standing until Christ comes:

The education of the church begins with the pastors. They must be serious students, both of God's Word and of everything associated with the protection of the flock. The more studious a pastor is, the richer his preaching/teaching ministry can be. When a pastor is studious, his enthusiasm for study spreads to the congregation.

Use solid teaching material. The people won't be properly trained or challenged by shallow material. The church's teaching ministry must have some serious depth.

Establish a good bookstore and lending library. Put someone in charge of it who has an enthusiasm for reading and study and who has read the materials himself or herself. The pastors should be in charge of deciding what materials are stocked. Many times I have found that a church or Bible college bookstore is overseen by someone who is not properly familiar with the issues that need to be addressed and is not aware of dangerous and compromising authors that should be avoided. See the chapter "Suggested Materials for a Discipling Church."

Promote good material from the pulpit. Encourage reading and study. Make suggestions about books that the people should read.

Educate the children and young people to love learning and to be readers, beginning with a passion for studying the Bible itself. We must teach them how to discriminate in their reading and study. How to choose the right things to read, and how to judge what they are reading by God's Word. We need to teach them how to use their time wisely. We deal with this in *The Mobile Phone and Christian Home and Church* in the chapter on "The Youth."

Way of Life Literature provides an education on a large number of issues facing Bible-believing churches today. In addition to our regular catalog of materials that are sold, we publish more than 80 free eBooks and many free eVideo series. People can download these and put them on their smart phones, tablets, and computers.

A Discipling Church Has an Atmosphere of Charity

Outline
The Heart of God
The Presence of Charity
The Priority of Charity
The Type of Charity That Is Needed
The Goal and Effect of Charity
The Efficacy of Charity
The Driving Force behind Charity

"And above all things have fervent charity among yourselves: for charity shall cover the multitude of sins" (1 Peter 4:8).

Charity is a "fundamental" and an "essential" of a New Testament church.

The Heart of God

Love is the essence of God's character. He does not merely *have* love; He *is* love (1 Joh. 4:8). Love is *of* God (1 Joh. 4:7). All love flows from Him. When parents long for their children to love one another, that is just a little snippet of God's Father heart. Love is the essence of God's commandments (Ro. 13:8-10). Love is the royal law (Jas. 2:8). God's kingdom is a kingdom of love (Isa. 11:9).

The church should be the outpost of Christ's kingdom, like a Greek colony. The sending city was called a "metropolis" (*mater* = mother, *polis* = city). The Greek cities trained their children in the work of commerce, and sometimes one son was chosen by lot from every family in the sending city to establish the new colony. The colony was ruled by a charter written by the sending city. The colony kept the gods of the sending city. Fire was sent to the new colony from a public fire that was kept burning in each city in one of the temples, signifying the spiritual tie between the sending city and the colony. By their colonies, the Greeks spread their language and culture all across that part of the world.

We see many lessons from this for the churches. They are outposts of Christ's heavenly kingdom, and each member is an ambassador of that kingdom. The churches should be training their children for the Father's business and sending them out to start new colonies. Each new church, generation after generation, should reflect the spiritual character of the original church.

The Presence of Charity

Peter takes for granted that believers have charity. It is a product of Christ living in you. If there is no charity, there is no Spirit of Christ, and if there is no Spirit of Christ, there is no salvation.

> "Now if any man have not the Spirit of Christ, he is none of his" (Ro. 8:9).

> "Seeing ye have purified your souls in obeying the truth through the Spirit unto unfeigned love of the brethren, *see that ye* love one another with a pure heart fervently" (1 Pe. 1:22).

The fervent love that covers a multitude of sins is first of all the love of God that provided the perfect atonement of Christ's blood.

Charity is not born in us full blown. We are to "increase in love" (1 Th. 3:12). In 2 Peter 1:5-7, we see that charity is the product of spiritual growth.

The Priority of Charity

Charity is to be "above all things." It is the heart attitude that makes the ministry effectual. "Probably to the absence of love in the Church is due, more than to anything else, the defections from the Church. It is largely in the power of love to make others what they should be, to draw them into the Church if they are not in, and when they are, the quick eye of love should detect the first signs of wandering, and the gentle power of love restrain. The atmosphere of heaven is love, and when that is the atmosphere of the Church, God will be honored in the beauty of a piety which otherwise he seeks in vain" (*Pulpit Commentary*).

There are a thousand things that God's people are instructed to do, but above all is the necessity that there be fervent charity.

Charity must permeate our discipline.

"When a church is infiltrated with false doctrine [or sin], it is not long until punitive church discipline must be exercised. In Galatians 6:1, the Holy Spirit reminds us that punitive discipline is intended to bring the offender to repentance and restoration. And it is so important that those who are exercising it, do it in love with the view to help a brother, being conscious of the fact that were it not for the grace of God they would be the ones who would be having to be disciplined. We impress our church family with the fact that to discipline a brother with a censorious self-righteous attitude makes us as guilty of heinous sin as the one whom we are disciplining. Most churches would have to have a baptism of love before they could begin a New Testament church discipline program. I always have a serious question about any member who seems concerned that we hurry to discipline a brother. Love waits long, is patient, and does not rejoice in iniquity. We have dealt with some folk as long as three and four years before withdrawing fellowship" (James Crumpton, *New Testament Church Discipline*).

The Type of Charity That Is Needed

We are to "have fervent charity."

"This expression occurs in non-biblical Greek to describe a horse at full gallop and a runner straining for the tape at the finish line of a race" (Thomas Constable).

God wants wholehearted, passionate service in all areas of our lives; He hates lukewarm. The world accepts enthusiasm in sports and politics and many things, but not in "religion."

God's love is not an emotion, it is an expression. It is not something we feel, it is something we do.

> "by love serve one another" (Ga. 5:13)

> "be kindly affectioned one to another in brotherly love" (Ro. 12:10)

> "forbearing one another in love" (Eph. 4:2)

> "as good stewards of the manifold grace of God" (1 Pet 4:10)

You cannot work up a feeling of fervent charity, but you can focus on caring for the brethren and ministering to them and dealing in a godly way with sin. You can stop being selfish and sitting around having a pity party and focusing your attention on your own condition and needs, and focus instead on others. And this produces right feelings. "We cultivate charity by doing acts which love demands. It is God's merciful law that feelings are increased by acts done on principle" (*Biblical Illustrator*). I need to think about what I can do to help my brethren, to encourage them, and challenge them, and be busy doing those things.

It is the fervent love that causes one to want to cover sins and help people get victory over sin rather than to judge them and criticize them and gossip about them. Charity is sympathetic, caring. Consider how you feel toward those you love the most, such as a child, a grandchild, a special friend. God's love is like a father pitying his children. It is the love of David and Jonathan (1 Sa. 20:17). Charity compels you to help those you love. You are patient with them; you aren't quick to condemn; you want to carry them along, to see them grow and get victory, to be restored when they fall.

The environment of fervent love is the environment in which God's children can best grow. This is how God looks upon and treats His redeemed. It is how the church leaders are to live and act. It is how every member of the church is to live and act.

These are the churches that will be standing until Christ comes. These are the churches that are most fruitful with real spiritual fruit rather than mere external conformity. It is love that wins the heart to a passionate relationship with Christ; we love him because he first loved us (1 John 4:19). Fervent love will win our children to Christ and win them to full discipleship.

If charity can cover sin, how much more can it cover things that aren't sin (e.g., frustrating habits, being slow to order food, slow to make decisions, misplacing things, not talking much, the pastor who had a distracting cow lick). "I knew a pastor in Texas who told me that he had a lock of hair right on top of his head which would always stand up no matter how he combed it. He said that the choir threatened to quit because of it. They sat behind him and could always see that hair come up sometime during his sermon. They actually became angry with him because of that lock of hair. Every time he went for a haircut he had the barber cut it off because he did not want to offend his choir. Imagine that type of thing! If they had had love in their hearts, that lock of hair wouldn't have bothered them one bit" (J. Vernon McGee)

The Goal and Effect of Charity

It shall "cover the multitude of sins."

What does it mean to cover sins? Charity doesn't ignore sins or condone sins. Shakespeare wasn't right when he said that "love is blind." And John Wesley wasn't right in saying, "He that loves another, covers his faults, how many soever they be. He turns away his own eyes from them; and, as far as is possible, hides them from others" (John Wesley).

Covering sins doesn't mean ignoring sin; it means dealing with sins in a godly way. We learn this by comparing Scripture with Scripture. We are never taught to ignore sin; we cover sin, first of all, by dealing with it in a godly way: by kindness, tenderheartedness, forgiveness (Eph. 4:32). This is the starting point and the continual duty. This is 70 x 7 forgiveness (Mt. 18:22).

We deal with sin, further, by patience, by giving people time to grow, by giving God time to work in their lives (1 Th. 5:14). This is a necessary part of preaching ("with all longsuffering," 2 Ti. 4:2).

We deal with sin by reproving and rebuking those who persist in disobedience (2 Ti. 4:2).

We deal with sin by restoration, which involves everything necessary to restore someone who is backslidden (Ga. 6:1).

This is how Christ covered the sins of the churches in Revelation 2-3.

This is how Paul covered the sins of the church at Corinth.

This is how the first church I joined helped me as a young Christian.

Dealing with sin in a godly way is the essence of love. "It wishes the well-being of the whole man--body, soul, and spirit, but chiefly spirit. And the highest love is the desire to make men good and Godlike" (*Biblical Illustrator*).

"... this also we wish, *even* your perfection" (2 Co. 13:9).

A Multitude of Sins

A "multitude of sins" are the sins that are committed daily by sinners. Though we are saved, the old man is still present and there are daily sins. Consider Ephesians 4 - lying, every type of deception, anything less than complete honesty (v. 25), stealing, including stealing time from an employer (v. 28), laziness (v. 28), bitterness, wrath, clamour, evil speaking (v. 31).

This shows the total error of any type of sinless perfection doctrine. There are multitudes of sins in the Christian life that must be dealt with.

There are sins unto death that cannot be covered (1 John 5:16-17). This is sin that is especially grievous before God and is not repented of. David almost committed this sin (2 Sa. 12:13).

The Efficacy of Charity

It can cover a multitude of sins.

We need fervent charity in the home: husbands loving their wives (if you love your wife you won't let yourself be bitter against her and be too demanding of her and be uncaring about her), wives loving their husbands (if you love your husband you will honor him and submit to him), parents loving their children (if you love your children you will not neglect them, you will not fail to train and discipline them), children loving their parents (if you love your parents you will honor and obey them; you will not want to hurt them). We need to find ways to show love, find ways to build one another up in Christ. We need to think about this and plan for this.

We need fervent charity in the church: *By the members for the pastors* ("to esteem them highly in love for their work's sake," 1 Th. 5:13); if you love your pastor it is easy to honor and obey him; you will give him the benefit of the doubt; you will honor God by honoring the authority God has given some men; but you will not follow him blindly; that is cultic. *By the members toward one another* ("exhorting one another," Heb. 10:25).

The Driving Force behind Charity

"But the end of all things is at hand: be ye therefore sober, and watch unto prayer" (1 Pe. 4:7).

Both passages dealing with covering sin are prefaced by prayer. Compare James 5:16-20.

Little prayer results in little spiritual power, which results in little love.

A Discipling Church Is Zealous for Biblical Separation

Outline
The Necessity of Spiritual Wisdom
A Testing Mindset
The Principle of Spiritual Safety
Warnings and Education
A Stricter Basis
Zeal for God's Word and against Error
Forthright Reproof of Error
Romans 14
Christian Unity
The Centrality of the Church

The discipling church is a church that is careful about separation because it is an essential protection against spiritual danger.

The church that will stand until Christ comes will be stricter about separation these days than ever before, because the dangers are greater and the technology has made it easier to connect with the dangers.

Some time ago I received the following question from a reader:

"I have read a lot of your writings about separation. I fully agree that among many Independent Baptist Churches, there is an utter lack of teaching on this subject and that God's people are being destroyed for lack of knowledge, especially in this area. But there are a couple of related issues that I have seldom, if ever, heard addressed: (1) What does it actually mean to separate? The church across town adapts CCM; do we refuse to participate in anything they do? Do we not attend their revival meetings? We don't allow their pastor and staff to speak at our church, I assume. Do we treat the people there as lepers and have nothing to do with them? Are we still friendly with their members? (2) When does separation need to occur? How much disagreement is necessary before separation needs to occur?"

Any question on separation that needs to be answered can be answered from the principles of God's Word. Holy Scripture is able to make God's people "perfect, throughly furnished unto all good works" (2 Timothy 3:16-17).

Following are some practical Bible principles on separation:

The Necessity of Spiritual Wisdom

Separation requires spiritual wisdom.

> "Trust in the LORD with all thine heart; and lean not unto thine own understanding. In all thy ways acknowledge him, and he shall direct thy paths" (Pr. 3:5-6).

> "Consider what I say; and the Lord give thee understanding in all things" (2 Ti. 2:7).

> "If any of you lack wisdom, let him ask of God, that giveth to all *men* liberally, and upbraideth not; and it shall be given him" (Jas. 1:5).

The practice of separation is not a matter of following a simple list of dos and don'ts. This is true of separation from the world as well as separation from compromise and false teaching.

There are questions of who to separate from and when to separate and how to separate that can be answered only within the context of each developing situation.

The previous questions fall into this category.

> "(1) What does it actually mean to separate? The church across town adapts CCM. Do we refuse to participate in anything they do? Do we not attend their revival meetings? Do we not allow their pastor and staff to speak at our church? Do we treat the people there as lepers and have nothing to do with them? Are we still friendly with their members? (2) When does separation need to occur? How much disagreement is necessary before separation needs to occur?"

Practical spiritual wisdom is required to answer such questions, and God gives this wisdom to those who walk in obedience to His Word. He has promised to direct the paths of the individual who leans not to his understanding but who knowledges Him in all his ways (Pr. 3:5-6). He has promised wisdom to those who ask in faith (Jas. 1:5-7).

A blanket answer cannot be given to such questions. For example, at what stage should we separate from a church that is gradually adapting CCM? This type of thing does not happen overnight. It happens gradually. And the exact point at which to separate is something that the Lord must give wisdom about to those who are involved in that particular situation. Many factors must be weighed in such a decision.

A Testing Mindset

The heart and soul of discipleship and separation is a testing, vigilant mindset. This is the path of spiritual growth and protection.

Consider some Bible passages that instruct God's people to have this mindset:

Psalm 119:128 - "Therefore I esteem all *thy* precepts *concerning* all *things to be* right; *and* I hate every false way."

The Psalmist esteemed all of God's Word to be right. This is the foundation for a testing mindset. The believer has an absolute standard of truth. Christ said the Scripture is truth (John 17:17). It cannot be broken (Joh. 10:35), meaning it is correct and authoritative in every point. Peter said the Scripture is a light in a dark world that we are to take heed thereto (2 Pe. 1:19).

The Psalmist rejected *every* false way. If something is contrary to God's Word, the believer should reject it as false.

The Psalmist hated every false way. The child of God should be passionate about this. The Psalmist's hatred of false ways was a reflection of his love for God and God's truth. He was not on the fence. He cast his vote for God's Word in every matter, and he stood zealously opposed to anything that is contrary to God's Word. He did not make excuse for error; he hated it. He did not treat error as a small thing.

Isaiah 8:20 - "To the law and to the testimony: if they speak not according to this word, *it is* because *there is* no light in them."

The Old Testament saints were to test everything by the Scripture that they had. If anything is contrary to God's Word, it is darkness.

Psalm 1:1-3 - "Blessed *is* the man that walketh not in the counsel of the ungodly, nor standeth in the way of sinners, nor sitteth in the seat of the scornful. But his delight *is* in the law of the LORD; and in his law doth he meditate day and night. And he shall be like a tree planted by the rivers of water, that bringeth forth his fruit in his season; his leaf also shall not wither; and whatsoever he doeth shall prosper."

The way of discernment is the way of spiritual protection, blessing, and fruit. Today it is popular to say that careful testing of everything by God's Word is "Phariseeism" and "legalism." It is condemned by modern churches, but it is praised by God.

The foundation for testing is a strong knowledge of God's Word (Ps. 1:2). It is necessary to know God's Word, but not only to know it, to delight in it. It is necessary to read and study it, but also to meditate therein day and night. This is the description of a child of God who loves God's Word above honey, above fine gold (Ps. 19:10). He is not only intellectually satisfied with God's Word; he is delighted with it. He really and truly loves it. Only this type of relationship with God and His Word will protect the individual from error and spiritual danger.

The Psalm 1 man of God measures everything by God's Word and rejects every counsel and every way that is contrary to God's Word.

1 Thessalonians 5:21 - "Prove all things; hold fast that which is good."

The believer is to prove *all things* by God's Word. There is nothing in this world that should not be proved by God's Word: doctrine, philosophy, all areas of church practice, and every aspect of the Christian life. "All things" includes music, dress, attitude, entertainment, education, relationships.

The believer is to hold fast only that which is good by the standard of God's Word.

Hebrews 5:12-14 - "For when for the time ye ought to be teachers, ye have need that one teach you again which *be* the first principles of the oracles of God; and are become such as have need of milk, and not of strong meat. For every one that useth milk *is* unskilful in the word of righteousness: for he is a babe. But strong meat belongeth to them that are of full age, *even* those who by reason of use have their senses exercised to discern both good and evil."

A testing mindset begins with skill in God's Word. The believer can't test things unless he first knows God's Word well. Every believer is to be so skillful in God's Word that he can teach it to others and that he can discern good from evil. Every believer must set out to gain skill in God's Word, and this is no simple, easy matter. It requires good instruction and hard work and daily commitment and persistence. The Bible is not a small, simple book, and there is no shortcut to learning it well. This passage is one reason why I am convinced that the equivalent of a Bible Institute education is the *beginning point* to be able to understand the Bible and to study it effectually. The effectual Bible student must have an understanding of the Bible as a whole and how each book and section fits into the whole. He must understand Bible words. He must know Bible theology. He must know Bible history, Bible times, and Bible customs. He must understand principles of Bible interpretation and methods of Bible study. He must know Bible prophecy.

The professing believer who is unskillful in God's Word is disobedient to God's command, is unfruitful in the ministry he should be exercising, and is not walking as a disciple of Christ. He is a babe and has not made spiritual progress. He lives perpetually on milk and is totally dependent on a teacher. The author of Hebrews refused to accept this carnal condition as a status quo. He reproved them sharply for their carnality and laziness.

The mature Christian is skillful in God's Word and constantly uses God's Word to test everything in life "to discern both good and evil." This is his worldview, his mindset, his way of life. Studying the Bible is not a mere intellectual exercise. It is a whole life exercise.

By walking in a testing mindset, the believer exercises his spiritual and moral senses and grows stronger.

Acts 17:11 - "These were more noble than those in Thessalonica, in that they received the word with all readiness of mind, and searched the scriptures daily, whether those things were so."

The Bereans are called "noble." The Greek word "eugenes" is translated "nobleman" in Luke 19:12. In God's eyes, the true nobleman is the person who loves the truth and tests everything by His Word. Such "noblemen" are despised in this present world, but they will rule with Christ in glory in the next.

The Bereans received Paul's preaching with all readiness of mind. They did not reject things without hearing them. They did not take someone's word for what Paul taught. They heard him for themselves. The Bible warns, "He that answereth a matter before he heareth *it*, it *is* folly and shame unto him" (Pr. 18:13).

They searched the Scriptures daily. This is the authority and wisdom for testing things. They were zealous and persistent. They were willing to work at it day after day. Bible study was not a mere passing interest.

They tested everything by Scripture. They did not believe every word like the fool (Pr. 14:15). They did not test things by their opinions and feelings and traditions and old wives' tales. Scripture is able to make the man of God "perfect, throughly furnished unto all good works," which means that nothing else is needed (2 Ti. 3:16-17). There is no need of Catholic tradition or purported authorities such as the *Book of Mormon* or *Science and Health with a Key to the Scriptures* (Christian Science) or extra-biblical revelations such as dreams and visions and prophecies. The Bible is the sole authority of faith and practice.

Every Christian must be a Berean. The very foundation for the kind of Christian life that pleases the Lord is an intimate relationship with the Scriptures after the fashion of the noble Bereans. We must test everything by God's Word.

1 Corinthians 14:29 - "Let the prophets speak two or three, and let the other judge."

This instruction was given for the time then existing, which was a transitional time. The New Testament canon had not been completed. The apostles were still alive. The apostolic gifts of tongues and prophecies were still operating. Yet 1 Corinthians 14 contains principles for the entire church age. The churches today don't have prophets as in the first churches, but they do have prophecy in the sense of preachers who "speak unto men to edification, and exhortation, and comfort" (1 Co. 14:3).

When the Word of God is preached, it is to be tested. Preachers are not to be followed blindly and "unquestioningly." God's Word is their only authority, and the preacher is under this authority. If he teaches contrary to God's Word, his teaching should be rejected.

This ministry of testing requires teams of preachers and ministers. Beginning with Christ's apostles and the establishment of the church at Jerusalem, we see a team ministry in the New Testament churches, with one man as the senior or head pastor. Compare Acts 13:1; 14:23; 15:13-22; 20:4; Php. 1:1. When there is a team of ministers, one man cannot easily lead the flock astray. There is strength and protection. When Paul said, "let the prophets speak two or three, and let the other judge" (1 Co. 14:29), he was referring to the other preachers. When he said, "For ye may all prophesy one by one," he was referring to preachers, to ministry gifted men, not to every member of the congregation. This is the context.

This ministry requires an educated, spiritual congregation. Every believer is taught to exercise this ministry.

2 Corinthians 10:3-5 - "For though we walk in the flesh, we do not war after the flesh: (For the weapons of our warfare *are* not carnal, but mighty through God to the pulling down of strong holds;) Casting down imaginations, and every high thing that exalteth itself against the knowledge of God, and bringing into captivity every thought to the obedience of Christ."

A testing mindset is an essential part of spiritual warfare and spiritual protection. We live in a dark, fallen world. It is a world that has exalted itself against God. The Christian life is not a playground; it is a battleground. Every believer has a fierce, relentless enemy that "walketh about, seeking whom he may devour (1 Peter 5:8). Those who drift through the Christian life carelessly will not stand. They will be led astray in their thinking.

The chief battleground is the imagination. The devil wants to corrupt the mind with error in order to lead the individual astray from the truth. "Imaginations" is from "logismos," which is elsewhere translated "thought" (Ro. 2:15). "It refers to all the plans of a wicked world" (Barnes). The world is filled with false philosophy. The enemies of Christ boast in their reasoning power. Their chief authority is human thinking, but man's best thinking cannot discover ultimate truth and the knowledge of God.

The way of protection is to measure every idea and principle by God's Word and to cast down every error. Note the repetition of "every." Biblical testing is a constant, thorough ministry.

The truth is found in the knowledge of God. The main purpose of the Bible is to reveal the true God. The better the believer knows God personally and understands His character and ways and thinking, the better he can protect himself. The fullness of God is known in Jesus Christ and in the gospel of Christ. Everything that is contrary to Christ and His gospel is wrong.

The believer has mighty weapons. They are such things as the infallible Word of God, which is quick and powerful (Heb. 4:12), the indwelling Spirit of God (1 Joh. 2:20), fasting (Mt. 17:21; Es. 4:16), and prayer (Eph. 6:18). Satan's false imaginations cannot stand against these mighty weapons.

The Bible believer has the power to cast down every wrong imagination. This means he can discern its error and reject it and be protected from it and protect others. The believer has the ability to test every philosophy because God's Word gives him the wisdom to do so. He can get to the heart of a false philosophy by the power of God's Word (Ps. 119:99, 104, 130). The apostle Paul took on the exalted imaginations of the Greeks in Athens and refuted them and thereby won some of them to the truth (Acts 17:18-34). The man who led me to Christ did not know anything about the philosophies I had been studying (Hindu, New Age, mind science), but he knew God's Word well and was able to take God's Word and destroy these philosophies as I explained them to him. He tore down high things such as reincarnation, universalism, Christ as a guru, allegoricalism, the innate goodness of man, and spiritual enlightenment by following one's heart.

Casting down error requires training and skill. This is no simple ministry. Every church should train its people for this work by making them effectual Bible students and by teaching them all things that are necessary, such as apologetics and world history. The church's Bible training must not be mere rote learning so that the people can repeat things back to the teacher. God's people must be trained to think biblically. They must not just memorize God's Word and know some doctrine. They must learn how to understand God's Word and apply it to daily life.

The power to cast down error is of Christ - "mighty through God." The believer does not have the power to confront sin and error and false gods and false religion and philosophy in his own ability. The power is of Christ. The wisdom is of Christ. The believer must walk in close fellowship with Christ and seek His help. Some have taken it upon themselves to war against error by the power of the flesh (e.g., human reasoning, philosophical argument, the power of personality and intellect), but instead of conquering error they have been conquered by error. I think of a pastor's son who became an atheist by studying the writings of men like Richard Dawkins, thinking, apparently, that he was strong enough to refute them.

This warfare begins in this present life, but it will be perfected when Christ returns and establishes His kingdom. Then every high place will be torn down and every thought will be brought to the obedience of Christ throughout the world. God's people currently have the power to bring souls to Christ and to protect themselves and their homes and churches from error, but they don't have the power to completely destroy Satan's strongholds. When He comes, Christ will humble the pride of man and tear down every idol (Isa. 2:10-22). He will bind Satan, the god of this world, and cast him into the bottomless pit (Re. 20:1-3) and eventually cast him into the lake of fire (Re. 20:10). Christ's governors will rule every nation with a rod of iron and bring them into obedience to God's will.

Philippians 3:17 - "Brethren, be followers together of me, and mark them which walk so as ye have us for an ensample."

Colossians 2:8 - "Beware lest any man spoil you through philosophy and vain deceit, after the tradition of men, after the rudiments of the world, and not after Christ."

1 Timothy 4:1 - "Now the Spirit speaketh expressly, that in the latter times some shall depart from the faith, giving heed to seducing spirits, and doctrines of devils."

1 John 4:1 - "Beloved, believe not every spirit, but try the spirits whether they are of God: because many false prophets are gone out into the world."

In all such verses we see a testing mindset. The believer is to be aware that there is spiritual danger, false teachers, the potential for deception and spoiling, and he is to test everything by the New Testament Scripture.

Revelation 2:2 - "I know thy works, and thy labour, and thy patience, and how thou canst not bear them which are evil: and thou hast tried them which say they are apostles, and are not, and hast found them liars."

Christ praised the church at Ephesus for testing everything by God's Word. Regardless of the slander of this present age, this is a ministry that well pleases Him.

Note the clear, strong language used to describe false teachers: "evil," "liars." This is not the language of "hatred" and "mean-spiritedness." It is the language of a genuine love for and zeal for the truth.

2 Timothy 3:13 - "But evil men and seducers shall wax worse and worse, deceiving, and being deceived."

2 Timothy 4:3-4 - "And they shall turn away *their* ears from the truth, and shall be turned unto fables. But watch thou in all things, endure afflictions, do the work of an evangelist, make full proof of thy ministry."

Matthew 24:4-5 - "And Jesus answered and said unto them, Take heed that no man deceive you. For many shall come in my name, saying, I am Christ; and shall deceive many."

These verses describe the progression of the church age as one of increasing apostasy, ending in an explosion of apostasy at the end of the age after the translation of the church.

God's people need a Christian worldview that encompasses this doctrine of apostasy. They need to understand that the closer we draw to the return of Christ, the greater the spiritual danger and the greater the need for vigilance against danger.

This is the mindset I was given as a new Christian. The man who led me to Christ took me into a Christian bookstore to buy me a Bible and a Strong's Concordance, and he made the point of warning me to be cautious and discerning. He told me that there are dangers in Christian bookstores because there are many false teachers and that protection requires testing everything with Scripture. I began my Christian life with this mindset.

This is the only mindset that will protect an individual, home, and church today.

This is the foundation of effectual separation.

The separatist church builds up its members so that they can exercise the essential ministry of discernment. The church that does this will not be led astray.

The average Independent Baptist Church is like Highland Park Baptist Church in Chattanooga, Tennessee. It was the second largest church in America in the early 1970s, but it didn't teach its people to exercise a discernment ministry. The people were not plainly informed of error. They were not educated about such things as Baptist conventionalism, New Evangelicalism, charismaticism, Reformed theology, and the Jesus People Movement with its Christian rock and charismaticism and antinomianism. They were not taught to judge everything by Scripture. Lee Roberson, Highland Park's pastor for 40 years, said, "Stay out of controversy in the pulpit--stay out of it and stay on the main line. I think that helped me a lot. I tried to avoid personalities and stay on the main line: preaching the gospel, emphasis on winning people to Christ, emphasis on developing the spiritual life, dying to self, the fullness of the Spirit, the second coming--kept on the positive side, kept negatives away from the people" (James Wigton, *Lee Roberson--Always about His Father's Business,* pp. 78, 243).

Testing and plain warning was considered "negativism." Those who tried to test everything by Scripture were considered divisive trouble makers.

As a result, Highland Park quickly went in the way of New Evangelicalism and the contemporary philosophy when new leaders came. The people, including the deacons, were not of a testing mindset and were not properly educated and prepared for what they would face.

Lee Roberson's philosophy of ministry is very influential among Independent Baptist churches, and there are many good elements. Winning people to Christ, dying to self, the fullness of the Spirit, the second coming are all wonderful and important things. But that isn't enough. A gardener must deal with weeds and pests. A shepherd must deal with wolves. And a preacher must deal with error, every type of error facing his people.

Consider the following examples of exercising a ministry of vigilance and testing:

> "I was just looking at a missionary email of a young man going to China. We support one young family from the local church mission organization he is with. I've been impressed by what I had seen of several young people coming from this church. I had read all their doctrinal statements and was content in that regard. I decided to look more closely at the church and more importantly the pastor and leader. I read in the church statement of introduction something that alarmed me. It said, 'We sing the old hymns, spiritual songs and choruses as well as songs written recently.' Red flags went up while praying that I wouldn't be upset. After working my way through to video songs played at the church, lo and behold, here is the young missionary in question singing Don Moens song, 'Our Heart Our Desire.' There was also a trio of ladies singing a David Crowder Band song 'How He Loves.' They were dressed appropriately and yet singing this stuff. Wow, I'm blown away at how the termites are eating up the house in IFB churches. I cannot support this kind of thing and I have to drill deeper in investigating the beliefs of missionaries that request our time and support. No matter what organization or how good their doctrinal statement, one can't assume they aren't involved in CCM. The Mission, I mention, is Vision Baptist Mission in Alpharetta, Ga. The pastor is a veteran missionary and they have so much going for them except this huge fly in the ointment. Keep on warning."

> "I'm going through the song leader's copy of *Living Hymns* and marking the hymns we will NEVER sing (like the two Gaither ones). I'm using your Directory of CCM artists book to check some hymn writers I am not familiar with, and I've googled a few names I didn't know. The song, 'Because He Lives,' is one that I had to make clear to a church member that we wouldn't sing it and why. He had no problem with it once he understood. He is one that really wants to do right."

The foundation of effectual biblical separation is a testing mindset.

The Principle of Spiritual Safety

"Be not deceived: evil communications corrupt good manners" (1 Co. 15:33).

Biblical separation is an issue of protection, and it is better to err on the side of safety. It is better to be too strict on separation than not strict enough.

In 2016 a pastor wrote as follows:

"I love you and appreciate your stand. The July *O Timothy*, which I have just recently read, has been very challenging for me personally. I have made some changes to my associations even in the last couple of months and am sad that it was necessary but grateful that I have removed the influence."

Certainly when it comes to contemporary music, I strongly suggest that churches err on the side of safety. To use CCM is to build bridges to the very dangerous world of CCM, and those bridges will bring negative influences.

In the free eVideo presentation *The Transformational Power of Contemporary Praise Music*, we have documented how that CCM influences churches. It does this by its "judge not, loosen up" philosophy, and it does this by its sensual, seductive music, both of which (the philosophy and the music) are very attractive to the flesh. See www.wayoflife.org/free-evideo/index.php

When churches that are opposed to CCM join hands in ministry with churches that are messing around with it, the influence of CCM impacts the people in all of the churches that are associating together.

This is the principle that we follow in our ministry. We refuse to join hands in ministry with churches that are messing around with CCM. We won't join them for youth activities or Bible conferences or missions conferences.

I will meet with a pastor of a church that is messing around with CCM and eat a meal with him, but I won't associate with him in ministry. I won't invite him to preach to our people, and I won't accept an invitation to preach in his church.

When it comes to associations, we must think of our own people and the effect that our associations will have on them. For example, I was invited to teach at an Independent Baptist Bible college that was a joint project supported by a wide variety of IFB missionaries. Declining that, I was later invited to preach at one of the graduation services at that school. Some teachers used CCM and some didn't. Some cared about modest dress and others didn't want to be "strict" or "legalistic" on that issue. One of the teachers was a recent graduate of a rock & roll Southern Baptist college. One of the prominent churches involved in the venture operates a Christian bookstore that sells CCM and charismatic junk. If I were to accept such an invitation I would be sending a message to our own people and to others that this school is OK and the men who operate it are safe, but I don't believe this. I know some of these men and like them at a personal level and appreciate many things about them, but I believe they are compromisers, and I believe that within one generation their churches (and their children) will be out-and-out New Evangelicals or worse.

I don't want our people to be influenced by these people insofar as I can help it.

It is a matter of spiritual safety. We want to build walls of separation to protect our people from compromise.

1 Corinthians 15:33 teaches us to draw the line of separation at the safest place.

Warnings and Education

Biblical separation requires clear warnings and proper education.

See Romans 16:17 - "mark them."

We see this throughout the New Testament. There is a lot of marking of and warning about false teachers.

See 1 Corinthians 15; Galatians; Ephesians 4; Colossians 2; 1 Timothy 4; 2 Timothy 3; 2 Peter 2-3; 1 John 2, 4; 2 John; Jude.

Many churches falsely label warnings as "negativism," but this is a big part of the New Testament Epistles, and it is a matter of spiritual protection.

The church that will be standing until Christ comes is a church that flies the flag of separation by emphasizing separation in the preaching/teaching ministries.

A Stricter Basis

Biblical separation is much stricter than the separation that is practiced in the vast majority of churches today.

This is true for separation from the world.

> "Wherefore come out from among them, and be ye separate, saith the Lord, and **TOUCH NOT** the unclean *thing*; and I will receive you" (2 Corinthians 6:17).

> "Having therefore these promises, dearly beloved, let us cleanse ourselves from **ALL** filthiness of the flesh and spirit, perfecting holiness in the fear of God" (2 Corinthians 7:1).

> "And have **NO** fellowship with the unfruitful works of darkness, but rather reprove *them*" (Ephesians 5:11).

> "Abstain from **ALL** appearance of evil" (1 Thessalonians 5:22).

> "Pure religion and undefiled before God and the Father is this, To visit the fatherless and widows in their affliction, *and* to keep himself **UNSPOTTED** from the world" (James 1:27).

> "Love not the world, neither the things *that are* in the world. If any man love the world, the love of the Father is not in him. For **ALL** that *is* in the world, the lust of the flesh, and the lust of the eyes, and the pride of life, is not of the Father, but is of the world. And the world passeth away, and the lust thereof: but he that doeth the will of God abideth for ever" (1 John 2:15-17).

This is also true for separation from false teaching and compromise. It is stricter than the separation that is practiced by most churches.

> "Now I beseech you, brethren, mark them which cause divisions and offences contrary to the doctrine which ye have learned; and avoid them" (Romans 16:17).

> "Be ye not unequally yoked together with unbelievers: for what fellowship hath righteousness with unrighteousness? and what communion hath light with darkness?" (2 Co. 6:14).

"Now we command you, brethren, in the name of our Lord Jesus Christ, that ye withdraw yourselves from every brother that walketh disorderly, and not after the tradition which he received of us" (2 Th. 3:6).

"If any man teach otherwise, and consent not to wholesome words, *even* the words of our Lord Jesus Christ, and to the doctrine which is according to godliness; He is proud, knowing nothing, but doting about questions and strifes of words, whereof cometh envy, strife, railings, evil surmisings, Perverse disputings of men of corrupt minds, and destitute of the truth, supposing that gain is godliness: from such withdraw thyself" (1 Ti. 6:3-5).

"I give thee charge in the sight of God, who quickeneth all things, and *before* Christ Jesus, who before Pontius Pilate witnessed a good confession; That thou keep *this* commandment without spot, unrebukeable, until the appearing of our Lord Jesus Christ" (1 Timothy 6:13-14).

"But shun profane *and* vain babblings: for they will increase unto more ungodliness. And their word will eat as doth a canker: of whom is Hymenaeus and Philetus; Who concerning the truth have erred, saying that the resurrection is past already; and overthrow the faith of some" (2 Ti. 2:16-18).

"A man that is an heretick after the first and second admonition reject; Knowing that he that is such is subverted, and sinneth, being condemned of himself" (Titus 3:10-11).

"Whosoever transgresseth, and abideth not in the doctrine of Christ, hath not God. He that abideth in the doctrine of Christ, he hath both the Father and the Son. If there come any unto you, and bring not this doctrine, receive him not into *your* house, neither bid him God speed: For he that biddeth him God speed is partaker of his evil deeds" (2 John 1:9-11).

The doctrinal basis of separation is much narrower than commonly taught.

Paul taught Timothy to separate even on the basis of the wrong interpretation of prophecy. The heretics he was warning about taught that "the resurrection is past already." They were interpreting prophecy allegorically! They were not denying the resurrection; they were spiritualizing it, which is exactly what amillennialists do with prophetic events. Typically, the interpretation of prophecy is not considered a "cardinal" doctrine and is not considered a matter of separation, but Paul's position was different, and Paul's position is right.

The modern evangelical philosophy is often stated by the dictum, *"In essentials unity; in non-essentials liberty; in all things charity."*

This was the rallying cry of the Moravians, who had a wonderful missionary zeal but retained such Romanist heresies as infant baptism and an ordained priesthood and who promoted Christian unity above the absolute truth of God's Word.

The "in non-essentials liberty" principle was adopted by the fundamentalist movement of the first half of the 20th century. Fundamentalism focused on a unity built around "the fundamentals of the faith" while downplaying "minor issues." The pragmatic objective was to create the largest possible united front *against* theological modernism and *for* world evangelism.

> "Historic fundamentalism has always been characterized by a core of biblical, historic, orthodox doctrines. ... Most fundamentalists would be content with terms like 'major doctrines' or 'cardinal doctrines' to describe their consensus. ... [T]here are other doctrinal distinctives that some may claim for themselves as fundamentalists. But to make these beliefs articles of fundamentalist faith would cut the movement's channel more narrowly than history will allow" (Rolland McCune, *Detroit Baptist Seminary Journal*, Fall 1996).

This has been a hallmark of the Southern Baptist Convention, as well. In describing why he is glad to be a Southern Baptist, Pastor Ben Simpson says, "I'm captivated by the commitment to unity in the essentials and mission of Christ while allowing diversity in the nonessentials and methodology" ("Two Divergent Views from Young Pastors," Baptist Press, April 14, 2011).

This dictum has been an integral philosophy of New Evangelicalism. Influential evangelical leaders such as Chuck Swindoll promote this philosophy. Swindoll writes:

> "There was a time in my life when I had a position that life was so rigid I would fight for every jot and tittle. I mean, I

couldn't list enough things that I'd die for. The older I get, the shorter that list gets" (*Grace Awakening*, p. 189).

This reminds us that once you buy into the principle of "in non-essentials liberty," your list of "non-essentials" tends to grow ever longer as your associations broaden.

The Promise Keepers movement promoted this philosophy as a basis of its broad unity. The *Promise Keepers Ambassador* booklet listed the following as examples of issues that must be ignored for the sake of unity: eternal security, the gifts of the Spirit, baptism, pretribulation or post-tribulation prophecy, sacraments or ordinances."

Many Independent Baptists are now buying into this heresy.

The Independent Baptist Friends International conferences which have been held annually since 2010, hosted by Clarence Sexton of Crown College, are based on the premise that such things as the Bible text issue, dress, music, Calvinism, modes and candidates of baptism, and separation from the SBC should not hinder associating together for the sake of world evangelism.

Before the 2012 conference, Pastor Sexton said:

> "There is AN IRREDUCIBLE BODY OF TRUTH (e.g., who God is, what His Word is, what He says about salvation, the local New Testament church). There are a number of things that are in THIS IRREDUCIBLE BODY OF TRUTH. And I believe that all over the world that God will raise up circles of friends. They have the truth; people need the Lord; and they are going to work together. ... This should happen in every state, on every continent, among every people group" (Sexton, "On the High Road with a High Vision of God," YouTube.com, April 9, 2012).

Sexton's "irreducible body of truth" refers to the "essentials."

Clayton Reed of Southlake Baptist Church, Southlake, Texas, and head of Global Church Planters, in his paper on "Ecclesiastical Separation," says we should not separate over non-fundamentals. He quotes John Rice in saying that we should work with those who disagree on baptism, tongues, prophecy, election, association with SBC. Reed concludes, "We ought to join every willing, warm-hearted Christian in advancing our Lord's kingdom while it is day."

There is no support in Scripture for the "in non-essentials liberty" doctrine. It is a man-made heresy created to further pragmatic objectives (e.g., unity, evangelism).

The Bible principle is **the ALL THINGS principle**.

Consider the Old Testament law. Its requirement was summarized in Deuteronomy 27:26, which Paul cited as follows:

> "Cursed is every one that continueth not in **ALL THINGS** which are written in the book of the law to do them" (Galatians 3:10).

The Psalmist preached the all things principle.

> "Therefore I love thy commandments above gold; yea, above fine gold. Therefore I esteem **ALL THY PRECEPTS** concerning **ALL THINGS** to be right; and I hate **EVERY FALSE WAY**" (Psalms 119:127-128).

Observe that the reason the Psalmist esteemed all of God's precepts was that he had a passionate relationship with and a high view of God's Word, loving it above gold.

Observe that the Psalmist did not merely hate those things that were contrary to the "essential" doctrines of God's Word. He hated *every* false way.

There is no "non-essential" principle in the New Testament, either.

The Lord Jesus Christ commanded His disciples to teach their converts "to observe **ALL THINGS** whatsoever I have commanded you" (Mt. 28:20).

The apostle Paul reminded the elders at Ephesus that the reason he was free from the blood of all men was that he had preached **THE WHOLE COUNSEL** of God (Acts 20:27).

The more plainly and fervently you preach the whole counsel of God, the less likely it will be that you will join hands in ministry with those who hold different doctrines.

In 1 Corinthians 11:2 Paul said to the church at Corinth,

> "Now I praise you, brethren, that ye remember me in **ALL THINGS**, and keep the ordinances, as I delivered them to you."

This passage deals with hair length and the Lord's Supper, which are widely considered to be "non-essentials," yet Paul praised the church for remembering him in ALL things.

In light of this clear Bible teaching, I reject the contemporary philosophy that rebukes those who make an issue of hair length rather than rebuking those who flaunt their "liberty" in this matter. When God's Word speaks, our liberty ends. When the Word of God says it is a shame for a man to have long hair and when it says that long hair is the woman's covering and glory, that is the end of the matter and it is our part simply to honor God by obeying His Word.

Paul instructed Timothy to "keep this commandment **WITHOUT SPOT**, unrebukeable, until the appearing of our Lord Jesus Christ" (1 Ti. 6:14). A spot is a small, seemingly insignificant thing.

That particular epistle contains commandments about such things as the woman's role in ministry (1 Ti. 2:12). This is widely considered a "non-essential" today, but Paul taught Timothy to have an entirely different approach toward such teachings.

I challenge anyone to show me where the Bible instructs the believer to treat some doctrine as "non-essential" for any reason whatsoever.

We know that not all doctrine has the same significance and weight, but none of it is "non-essential."

Consider the following issues that are widely treated as "non-essentials" --

Modesty is considered a non-essential, but in reality it is a fundamental doctrine, because the Bible has a lot to say about it. (In the book *Dressing for the Lord*, we exegete 25 key Bible passages on this topic which contain principles that can be applied to any nation or culture.) The Bible has spoken on the issue of modesty, and we will not treat this as a "non-essential."

Sacred music, another so-called non-essential, is actually a fundamental doctrine. Music is dealt with in two prominent New Testament epistles (Eph. 5:19; Col. 3:16), and hundreds of other Scriptures deal directly with music. The largest book in the Bible is a song book. Music is one of most powerful forces in modern society. It is at the heart and soul of worldliness and compromise and apostasy today. It is a major element in the building of a one-world church. To treat music as some sort of non-essential is spiritual folly.

Unconformity to the world is a fundamental doctrine. Many Scriptures directly and plainly teach the doctrine of separation from the world (e.g., Romans 12:2; Ephesians 5:11; Titus 2:12; James 1:27; 4:4; 1 John 2:15-17; 5:19; Proverbs 4:14-15).

Worship in spirit and truth is a fundamental doctrine (John 4:23).

Preservation of Scripture is a fundamental doctrine (1 Pe. 1:25).

"Whosoever will" election is a fundamental doctrine (as opposed to "sovereign" election). "Whosoever believeth" is repeated seven times in five New Testament books. The Bible clearly teaches that everyone is invited to be saved and everyone *can* be saved.

Repentance and proper evangelism practices are fundamental doctrines. (I am convinced that "quick prayerism" is damnable, and I refuse to minister together with those who practice it.)

Baptism is a fundamental doctrine, and the Bible's teaching on the method of baptism is as clear as its teaching on the purpose of baptism. This is why I declined an invitation a few years ago to preach at a Bible Presbyterian seminary. I cannot treat election or baptism as "non-essentials."

Pastoral humility is a fundamental doctrine (1 Peter 5:1-3).

Church discipline is a fundamental doctrine (1 Corinthians 5).

Separation from compromising brethren is a fundamental doctrine (e.g., 2 Th. 3:6).

Reproving compromising preachers is a fundamental doctrine (Ga. 2:11-15).

When it comes to spiritual compromise, little is big. The Bible warns that a **LITTLE LEAVEN** leaveneth the whole lump.

If error is not stopped early, it cannot be stopped at all.

This is why I warn about independent Baptists that are getting soft on separation and are messing around with contemporary worship music and recommending the writings of "conservative" evangelicals.

When I see that a preacher and a church are committed to a path of "small" compromise, that is when I separate.

Again, I would rather err on the side of being too strict than not strict enough.

We need to be stricter about separation, because that is what we are taught in Scripture, and a strict program of separation is a matter of spiritual protection.

Zeal *for* God's Word and *against* Error

Biblical separation requires a zeal for all of God's Word and a zeal against error.

> "Therefore I esteem all *thy* precepts *concerning* all *things to be* right; *and* I hate every false way" (Psalm 119:128).

> "That thou keep *this* commandment without spot, unrebukeable, until the appearing of our Lord Jesus Christ" (1 Timothy 6:14).

The zeal of loving all of God's Word, even the spots, and hating everything that is contrary to God's Word is a heart attitude. It is love for God. It is the fruit of the Spirit, who is called the "Spirit of truth" four times (Joh. 14:17; 15:26; 16:13; 1 Joh. 4:6). The fruit of the Spirit is in all goodness and righteousness and truth (Eph. 5:9).

A zeal for truth is missing in New Evangelicalism. While New Evangelicals profess a love of truth, there is little zeal to defend it against error. Typically, the New Evangelical has more zeal against those who warn of error than he does against the error itself.

A genuine zeal for the truth is also missing among an ever-increasing number of Independent Baptists.

A zeal *for* God's Word and *against* error will keep the believer and the church rightly separated. Before I knew much about separation, it was a zeal for truth that produced separation and protected me.

When I first arrived in South Asia as a missionary in 1979, I was invited to preach in various evangelical, ecumenical forums, such as Campus Crusade for Christ and a national church fellowship. At the time, I knew very little about evangelicalism and ecumenism, but I loved every jot and tittle of God's Word and "hated every false way." This mindset soon got me in trouble with the ecumenical crowd. For example, I got in trouble for saying that one of their main pastors was unqualified because he had three wives. Eventually, they rejected my ministry and even demanded that I leave the country, so we went our separate ways.

I didn't yet understand biblical separation. In fact, those experiences were a major part of my education in separation, but a zeal for the truth kept me separated even before I well understood what was happening.

Forthright Reproof of Error

Biblical separation requires forthright reproof of error, and forthright reproof of error will keep you separated.

> "Preach the word; be instant in season, out of season; reprove, rebuke, exhort with all longsuffering and doctrine" (2 Timothy 4:2).
>
> "And have no fellowship with the unfruitful works of darkness, but rather reprove *them*" (Ephesians 5:11).

Obedience to God's Word requires reproof of sin and error. It is not enough to be against something. I must reprove it.

The church must let the flag of truth fly. When I was a hippie, I wanted everyone to know it, and I showed it by my dress and hair. My long hair was a "freak flag." I didn't have to say anything.

Likewise, the church must let its flag of separation fly. This is done by forthright preaching that deals plainly with sin and error. It is also done by the display of literature that deals with issues of separation.

Many churches seem to be ashamed of biblical warning and separation. They prefer to hide the more "negative" parts of a biblical ministry for the sake of the visitors. If asked, they say they believe in warning and separation, but they won't display materials that are "against" things or that name the names of compromisers and false teachers. Visitors will not see anything against such things as rock music, Contemporary Christian Music, Southern Gospel, immodest dress, New Evangelicalism, Christian "psychology," or compromising Baptist churches.

But it is the church that maintains a ministry of reproof that will stay separated and stay protected.

I think of preacher friends who have been willing to reprove their alma maters. Almost invariably this results in them being blacklisted, but it also keeps them and their people separated from compromise.

On the other hand, compromising preachers know how to narrow their message and tone down and generalize their reproofs so that they can maintain a larger tent of fellowship and ministry.

Romans 14

Some try to use Romans 14 to support the philosophy of "in non-essentials liberty," but Romans 14 does not say that some Bible doctrine is non-essential. It says that we are to allow one another liberty in matters in which the Bible is silent! The examples that Paul gives to illustrate his teaching are diet and the keeping of holy days. Those are things about which the New Testament faith is silent. There is no doctrine of diet in the New Testament, so it is strictly a matter of Christian liberty.

The only "non-essential doctrine" is a doctrine *not* taught in Scripture. When we are dealing with such things as diet or holy days, or the order of service, or the time and the day of prayer meetings, or the number of deacons, or to use or not use musical instruments, or to have or not have a Sunday School or formal youth ministry, or the time and frequency of the Lord's Supper, or to have or not have a bus ministry, or how much to support missionaries, or a thousand other such things, we are dealing with tradition rather than the clear teaching of God's Word, and each church must make up its own mind in these matters.

These are the types of things that are "non-essentials."

What doctrine should we be willing to stand for? Jude instructs every believer to "earnestly contend for the faith once delivered to the saints" (Jude 3). Since he did not delineate what part of the faith is to be defended, the obvious meaning is that we should defend whatever aspect of the faith is under attack at a particular time.

The fact is that once an individual adopts the "non-essentials" philosophy, his list of "non-essentials" tends to grow as time passes and as his associations broaden. It is a slippery slope.

Christian Unity

Aren't we supposed to strive for unity? Indeed, but we must interpret this according to the Bible and not according to modern thinking.

We see the basis of true Christian unity in passages such as the following:

> "Now I beseech you, brethren, by the name of our Lord Jesus Christ, that **YE ALL SPEAK THE SAME THING**, and that there be no divisions among you; but that ye be perfectly joined together in **THE SAME MIND** and in the same judgment" (1 Corinthians 1:10).

> "Only let your conversation be as it becometh the gospel of Christ: that whether I come and see you, or else be absent, I may hear of your affairs, that ye stand fast in one spirit, **WITH ONE MIND** striving together for the faith of the gospel" (Philippians 1:27).

This is genuine Christian unity. It is not unity in diversity. It is not a unity based on shared compromise. It is based on shared truth. It is a unity practiced by those who believe the same thing.

Many will argue that this type of unity would be very narrow, and I agree, but it is what the Bible requires. Anything else is a man-made unity based on human thinking and pragmatism rather than God's Word.

The Centrality of the Church

It is important to note that the previous verses on unity are found in the context of epistles written to churches: the church at Corinth and the church at Philippi.

It is the church that is the pillar and ground of the truth (1 Ti. 3:15), and in the context this is the "church" that has pastors and deacons (1 Ti. 3:1-14).

One of the major reasons why men have compromised the Bible's teaching on unity and have broadened the basis of unity is because they aren't content with the church. They want to build schools and associations and denominations and missions and other structures that operate beyond the bounds of the New Testament church, regardless of how formal or informal.

Within a local church, we can practice biblical Christian unity by having, and indeed enforcing, one mind in doctrine and practice. Our church, for example, has a lengthy statement of faith and covenant, and no one can join who is not likeminded. We enforce this "one mind" position on the authority of God's Word.

Beyond the church, we can fellowship with, associate with, and minister with other Christians insofar as we share "one mind" in the truth.

If I am content with the local church and am not trying to build something beyond that, I am not tempted nearly so much to compromise the truth for the sake of a "broader unity" and a "bigger tent."

The conclusion is that we must draw the line of separation at a very strict place, because God requires it.

We deal with this topic more extensively in *Bible Separation: Its Doctrine and Practice*, available from Way of Life Literature.

A Discipling Church Is Careful about Music

Outline

The Transformational Power of Contemporary Music
The Difference between Contemporary Music & Old Protestant Hymns
The Danger of the Internet
The Necessity of Education
An Effectual Vetting Process
The Power of Incrementalism
The Power of a Good Song Service
The Bounty of Sacred Music

A church that will be standing in 20 years is a church that is very careful about music.

We have mentioned music in other chapters, but we also want to include it as a separate category because it has played such a key role in the downfall of formerly sound churches.

The Transformational Power of Contemporary Music

It is impossible to use contemporary music without ruining the biblical stance of the church.

There are three reasons why this is true:

First, because this music is patterned after the world and brings the influence of the world into the congregation.

Second, because using this music builds bridges to the one-world church and brings the one-world church philosophy (e.g., judge not, be tolerant, lighten up, ecumenical fellowship is good) into the congregation.

Third, because using this music creates a fleshly addiction which changes the congregation's musical appetite and weakens its spiritual power.

These things are clearly forbidden in Scripture. See 1 Corinthians 15:33; Galatians 5:13; Ephesians 5:11; James 4:4; 1 Peter 2:11; 1 John 2:15-17.

Contemporary Christian Music is the heart and soul of the one-world church, and it is impossible to build bridges to contemporary music without bringing dramatic changes to a church's philosophy and character.

The music itself is patterned after the world; it is worldly rather than sacred in character. As a result, it is sensual and addictive, because this is what the world's party music is designed to be.

This is true even of the most "conservative" of contemporary musicians, such as Keith and Kristyn Getty and Stuart Townend, whose music is used widely today in fundamental Baptist churches. Their music is used in Majesty Music's *Rejoice Hymns* and in Bob Jones University's *Hymns Modern and Ancient*.

Getty/Townend are unapologetic one-world church builders who have ministry associations with Roman Catholics.

Keith Getty collaborated with Catholic Margaret Becker in the song "Jesus Draw Me Ever Nearer." In an interview Becker said, "One of my missions has been to say, let's not label ourselves, let's not put up walls between each other." ("US singer to make an appearance at Cross Rhythms '95," *CR Magazine*, June 1, 1995). Getty also collaborated with Roman Catholic Máire [pronounced Moya] Brennan in writing "With the Early Morning." Brennan says, "Christians fighting Christians, Catholics and Protestants! It breaks my heart, because we're all stemming from the same rock" ("Back to the Rock of Ages: Máire Brennan Talks to Christina Rodden," rootsworld.com).

In July 2012 the Gettys and Townend appeared on WorshipTogether.com's *NewsongCafe* with Roman Catholic Matt Maher to promote ecumenical unity.

Maher ministers at Our Lady of Mount Carmel Parish in Tempe, which is devoted to Mary as the Queen of Heaven. A sign at the front of the church says, "Mary, Mother of Life, pray for us." Maher calls himself a "musical missionary," a missionary for Rome, that is. *Christianity Today* says "Maher is bringing his music--and a dream of unity into the Protestant church" ("Common Bonds," CT, Oct. 27, 2009). He says, "I've had co-writing sessions with Protestants where we had that common denominator, and I've seen in a very radical way the real possibility of unity." He says, "I look at it like the Catholic church is my immediate family, and all my friends from different denominations are extended family."

Maher's wife is Methodist, but they are raising their son "in the Catholic Church," while also taking him to Methodist services "so he can experience both traditions" (Religion News Service, May 17, 2013).

This is the perfect recipe for building the end-time, one-world "church," and Getty/Townend are right in the middle of it.

In these ecumenical settings, in which Getty/Townend are comfortable, fundamental doctrinal differences are so meaningless that they are not even mentioned. Spiritual abominations such as the papacy, the mass, infant baptism, baptismal regeneration, veneration of Mary, and prayers to the saints are ignored. Jude 3 is despised and Romans 16:17 disobeyed for the sake of creating unity through contemporary Christian music.

Therefore, while the Getty's doctrinal statement might be conservative, their associations are as radically one-world church as Michael W. Smith, Amy Grant, Darlene Zschech or any other contemporary artist.

The Gettys aren't even conservative in their musical stance. Their web site tells us that they "fuse the music of their Irish heritage with THE SOUNDS OF NASHVILLE, their newly adopted home." There is nothing conservative or spiritual about this syncretism, for Nashville represents the very heart and soul of worldly music today and the Gettys are comfortable with that.

While the Getty's "modern hymns" are fairly conservative in rhythm, the Gettys are not opposed to rock & roll. They themselves rock out pretty hard at some venues. And while they don't write hard rock worship songs, they don't speak against this, either. In fact, Keith Getty said that he is glad for edgy, rocking renditions of his music by artists such as Newsboys, Ricky Skaggs, Owl City, Alison Krauss, and Natalie Grant, because "it is an honor" for him that popular modern musicians record them, and "it's also interesting to hear their interpretation of it and useful for the song because it helps the song get played more" ("The Gettys Exclusive: Famed Hymn Writers Talk Irish Christmas Tour," *Christian Post*, Dec. 2, 2014).

Regardless of how sincere Getty/Townend are, and regardless of how "conservative" they might appear in contrast to some of the other contemporary Christian musicians, and regardless of how fervently they speak about "the truth," these are not friends of a Bible-believing stance.

Any bridge that Bible-believing churches build to contemporary music is a bridge to the end-time one-world "church."

Contemporary Southern Gospel Music

Contemporary Southern Gospel is just as dangerous as Contemporary Christian Music. It is the music of a large number of Independent Baptist churches in the southeastern part of America.

When we talk about "contemporary Southern Gospel," we are not talking merely about gospel music with a country-twang or merely about a gospel quartet.

We are talking about *contemporary in sound and philosophy*. We are talking about the Gaithers and those who have been influenced by them.

The philosophy of contemporary Southern Gospel is the philosophy that music is neutral and the world's music can be used for the glory of God.

During a concert tour in New England in 1986, Bill Gaither admitted that he had changed his musical style due to the influence of the "world's culture." This is a clear example of the Bible's warning that "evil communications corrupt good manners" (1 Co. 15:33). Gaither said he believes there is a place for Christian rock, expressing his philosophy of music in these words: "God speaks through all different kinds of art forms and musical styles and musical forms" and the "format itself is not necessarily spiritual or non-spiritual" (*FBF News Bulletin*, March-April 1986, p. 3).

Gaither has used every type of pop and rock in his music. During the disco craze in the late 1980s, the Gaither Trio even recorded a disco album (*Calvary Contender*, August 15, 1989).

Bill Gaither has mentored many of the popular Christian rockers, including Sandi Patty, Russ Taff, Michael English, Carman, and the members of Whiteheart (*CCM Magazine*, July 1998, p. 20).

Today, Southern Gospel is filled with rock & roll. When I attended the National Quartet Convention in 1999, the dress of the attendees was fairly conservative, but the music itself was anything but conservative. If you stripped away the words, the music is that of the world. Every quartet used a strong back beat, bass guitar, drums, and heavy dance syncopation. It is the "Nashville sound." Some of the lyrics were Christ-honoring, but the worldly music distracted greatly from the message. It is confusion, and it is spiritually dangerous.

The philosophy of contemporary Southern Gospel is the philosophy of "judge not" and "ecumenism."

In his autobiography *It's More Than the Music*, Gaither said that one of the fringe benefits of playing their concerts in "neutral, nonchurch environments" was that people from "all church denominations" attended. "Before long, Baptists, Methodists, Presbyterians, charismatics, Catholics, and Pentecostals were all praising the Lord together. Subtly, the walls between denominations began to crumble..." (p. 115).

Gaither's "Hymns for the Family of God" was purposefully "nondenominational" and included devotional readings from a wide variety of Christians, including heretics such as Deitrich Bonhoeffer (one of the fathers of Neo-orthodoxy), Malcolm Muggeridge (a liberal Roman Catholic who did not believe in Christ's virgin birth or bodily resurrection), and Robert Schuller, who has wickedly redefined the gospel in terms of his humanistic self-esteem theology.

The Gaithers provided the music one evening at Indianapolis '90, a large ecumenical charismatic gathering I attended with press credentials. One-half of the 25,000 participants were Roman Catholic. A Catholic mass was held each morning, and Catholic priest Tom Forrest from Rome brought the closing message. At an earlier conference in 1987, Forrest said that purgatory is necessary for salvation. Roughly 40 denominations were present in Indianapolis. The Gaithers were perfectly at home in this unscriptural gathering and entertained the mixed multitude with their jazzy music.

The ecumenical philosophy has permeated contemporary Southern Gospel. During the presentation of *Singing News* awards at the 1999 National Quartet Convention, one of the speakers thanked the leaders of the Convention for "THEIR ABILITY TO BRING TOGETHER CHRISTIANS OF ALL DENOMINATIONAL LABELS BY THE MEANS OF MUSIC." I was there with press credentials and heard this statement.

There isn't two cents worth of difference between the world of contemporary worship music and the world of contemporary Southern Gospel. It is fleshly music that gets the people emotionally addicted to honkytonk, ragtime rhythms and even pure rock & roll.

About 20 years ago I preached at a church in Cowpens, South Carolina, and the music was raucous honkytonk Southern Gospel powered by a white-haired grandmother pianist that would put any 1920s bar room rag timer to shame. After the service, the elderly pastor asked me what I thought of the music, and I replied, "It is boogie woogie." He exclaimed, "I don't want boogie woogie." I said, "That's what you've got, pastor." I never heard from him again.

Southern Gospel brings a congregation into association with the likes of the Gaithers and the National Quartet Convention. Anyone who is hooked into Southern Gospel is holding hands with and playing footsie with ecumenists and is on a fast road to full-blown ecumenism.

Consider the 2016 Burlington Revival in North Carolina that was supported by large numbers of Independent Baptist churches: "C.T. Townsend's brother, Brian, is a full-blown contemporary pastor in Georgia that C.T. has verbally supported. CT's father-in-law married Brenda Ruppe of the Ruppe family, who were featured singers on the Gaither Homecoming specials. Her daughters formed the singing group 'The Sisters' and sing contemporary Southern Gospel music and have very immodest clothing in some of their photo shoots. I know we are not guilty because of family ties, but we become guilty when we promote our worldly families and their music, which C.T. has done publicly for years without any reproof of his relatives."

Having been born and raised in the South, saved in the South, educated in the South, and begun preaching in the South, I have watched as Baptist churches there have grown ever weaker over the past 30 years, and one of the major reasons is the influence of

Southern Gospel and the worldly, ecumenical baggage that it carries.

I refuse to have anything to do with it. Even 20 years ago, I wouldn't have preached at the church in Cowpens had I known what the music was like. And I feel much stronger about this today.

The Difference between Contemporary Music and Old Protestant Hymns

The danger of contemporary music is nothing like the danger of using Protestant hymns.

I have never known of a Baptist church becoming Lutheran by singing Luther's hymns or even becoming Roman Catholic by singing one or two old hymns written by Catholics (though I don't recommend the latter), but I have known of dozens of churches that have become contemporary by messing around with contemporary music, EVEN THOUGH THIS PATH INVARIABLY STARTS IN A "SMALL" AND "CAUTIOUS" MANNER.

The Unique Danger of the Internet

The age of the Internet has dramatically increased the danger of using the wrong music.

In the age of the Internet, it is impossible to use materials by contemporary musicians without building bridges that the church members will inevitably cross, particularly young people.

They are going to Google "Getty/Townend," etc., and many of them are going to be influenced by them, and some are going to be influenced deeply.

The Necessity of Serious Education on the Music Issue

It is impossible to keep the church's music safe without serious and continual education.

Pastors must be educated. There is no excuse for a pastor to be ignorant about the music issue. It's not that difficult to learn to read music and to gain some basic understanding of music itself.

But at the very least the pastor must educate himself about the basic differences between sacred and worldly music. And he must be familiar with the history and character of contemporary Christian music. A lot of education is available for those who are willing to access it, and much of it is available for free. It is not possible for a pastor to give this responsibility to someone else until he first understands the basics himself so he can check on and oversee the church's music program in an educated manner.

We have produced the following materials on this subject and have made all of them available for free download from the Way of Life web site:

Music for Good or Evil. This video series, which is packed with photos, video and audio clips, has eight segments. I. Biblical Principles of Good Christian Music. II. Why We Reject Contemporary Christian Music. It is worldly, addictive, ecumenical, charismatic, shallow and man-centered, opposed to preaching, experience-oriented, and it weakens the strong biblicist stance of a church. III. The Sound of Contemporary Christian Music. In this section we give the believer simple tools that he can use to discern the difference between sensual and sacred music. We deal with syncopated dance styles, sensual vocal styles, relativistic styles, and overly soft styles that do not fit the message. IV. The Transformational Power of Contemporary Worship Music. We show why CCM is able to transform a "traditional" Bible-believing church into a New Evangelical contemporary one. Its transformational power resides in its enticing philosophy of "liberty" and in its sensual, addictive music. We use video and audio to illustrate the sound of contemporary worship. V. Southern Gospel. We deal with the history of Southern Gospel, its character, its influence, and the role of the Gaithers in its renaissance. This section is packed with audio, video, and photos. VI. Marks of Good Song Leading. There is a great need for proper training of song leaders today, and in this segment we deal with the following eight principles: Leadership, preparation, edification, spirituality, spiritual discernment, wisdom in song selection, diversity. One thing we emphasize is the need to sing worship songs that turn the people's focus directly to God. We give dozens of examples of worship songs that are found in standard hymnals used by Bible-believing churches, but typically these are not sung properly as "unto God." VII. Questions Answered on Contemporary Christian Music. We answer 15 of the most common questions on this subject, such as the following: Is rhythm wrong? Isn't this issue just a matter of different taste? Isn't the sincerity of the musicians the important thing? Isn't some CCM acceptable? Didn't Luther and the Wesleys use tavern music? What is the difference between using contemporary worship hymns and using old Protestant hymns? VIII. The Foreign Spirit of Contemporary Worship Music. This presentation documents the frightful spiritual compromise, heresy, and apostasy that permeate the field of contemporary praise. Through extensive documentation, it proves that contemporary worship music is controlled by "another spirit" (2 Co. 11:4). It is the spirit of charismaticism, the spirit of the "latter rain," the spirit of Roman Catholicism and the one-world "church," the spirit of the world that is condemned by 1 John 2:16, the spirit of homosexuality, and the spirit of the false god of *The Shack*. The presentation looks carefully at the origin of contemporary worship in the Jesus Movement of the 1970s, examining the lives and testimonies of some of the most influential people.

See http://www.wayoflife.org/publications/video/music-for-good-or-evil.php

The Baptist Music Wars. This book is an up-to-date warning about the transformational power of Contemporary Christian Music to transport Bible-believing Baptists into the sphere of the end-time one-world "church." We don't believe that good Christian music stopped being written when Fanny Crosby died or that rhythm is wrong or that drums and guitars are inherently evil. We believe, rather, that Contemporary Christian Music is a powerful bridge to a very dangerous spiritual and doctrinal world. The book begins by documenting the radical change in thinking that has occurred among independent Baptists. Whereas just a few years ago the overwhelming consensus was that CCM was wrong and dangerous, the consensus now has formed around the position that CCM can be used in moderation, that it is OK to "adapt" it to a more traditional sacred sound and presentation technique. The heart of the book is the section giving eight reasons for rejecting Contemporary Christian Music (it is built on the lie that music is neutral, it is worldly, it is ecumenical, it is charismatic, it is experienced-oriented, it is permeated with false christs, it is infiltrated with homosexuality, and it weakens the Biblicist stance of a church) and the section answering 39 major arguments that are used in defense of CCM. There are also chapters on the history of CCM and the author's experience of living the rock & roll lifestyle before conversion and how the Lord dealt with him about music when he was a young Christian. 285 pages.

See www.wayoflife.org/free-ebooks/baptist-music-wars.php

The Directory of Contemporary Worship Music. This directory contains information on influential contemporary worship musicians who are creating the music that is being used ever more frequently by Baptist, fundamentalist, and very conservative evangelical churches. Contemporary worship music is a dangerous bridge both to the world and to the "broader church" with all of its ancient and end-time heresies, and the *Directory of Contemporary Praise Musicians* contains more documentation of this than has ever before been gathered into one volume, to our knowledge. The *Directory* documents the history of contemporary praise music from its inception in the Jesus People movement and its intimate association with the charismatic movement in general as well as with its most radical aspect, the "latter rain apostolic miracle revival." The documentation contained in the *Directory* proves that Contemporary Christian Music is a jungle of end-time apostasy and that it is controlled by "another spirit" (2 Co. 11:4). The music itself feeds the charismatic-ecumenical mystical experience. 570 pages.

See www.wayoflife.org/free-ebooks/directory-of-contemporary-worship.php

What Every Christian Should Know about Rock Music. Forty years ago, we published *Mom and Dad Sleep While the Children Rock in Satan's Cradle* to exhort parents and pastors to educate and protect their young people from the great spiritual enemy of rock & roll. Since then, churches have grown strangely quiet about this danger. It must be the "frog in the pot" phenomenon. Rock permeates society, and we have grown accustomed to it, even though the music and the culture it has helped create have grown ever more wicked. Today our warning about rock is just as fervent as it was 40 years ago, though the content is updated for a new generation. The power of rock to produce rebels and to build the one-world church has not lessened. Homes and churches that don't give clear and persistent warnings about rock music in all of its forms should not be surprised if their young people are worldly and tend toward New Evangelical and emerging church thinking. This book lays out nine things that every Christian should know about rock music. 1. It represents a moral revolution. 2. It preaches a philosophy of narcissism and licentiousness. 3. It is permeated with blasphemy. 4. It is the music of false christs. 5. It is condemned by the Bible. 6. It is a fulfillment of Bible prophecy. 7. It is at the heart of the one-world church. 8. It is addictive. 9. The only sure protection is to avoid it. 70 pages.

See: www.wayoflife.org/free-ebooks/what-every-christian-should-know-rock-music.php

Rock & Roll's War against God. This is an examination of rock music and its evil influence on society. Chapters include "My Experience with Rock Music" (the author's testimony), "What Every Christian Should Know about Rock," "The History of Rock," "The Roots of Rock" (blues, jazz, black spirituals, and Southern Gospel), "The Pioneers of Rock" (the lives of pioneer rockers, the influence of 50s and 60s rock on society, etc.), "The Character of Rock Music," "Rock and the Occult," "Rock and Spirituality," "Rock and Violence," "Rock and Love," "Rock and Voodoo," "Rock and Drugs," "Rock and Suicide," "Rock and Insanity," "Rock Musicians as Mediums," "Rock and Pagan Religion," "Death Metal Rock," and "How Rock Rebels Are Produced." 785 pages.

See www.wayoflife.org/free-ebooks/rock-rolls-war-against-god.php

A Plea to Southern Gospel Music Fans. The book deals with this subject extensively with the most up-to-date research. It is also a multimedia report with 67 links to audio and video clips that illustrate the points, particularly the musical and vocal styles. 150 pages

See www.wayoflife.org/free-ebooks/a-plea-to-southern-gospel-music-fans.php

The music people must also be educated. The previous materials are a good starting point for educating the church's music people.

The whole church must be educated. Education on the music issue should permeate the church's ministry. If only the leaders understand the issue, the church will change when the leaders change. The parents must be educated so they can lead the way in their homes. The young people must be well educated on this issue, since the character of the youth determines the future of the church.

An Effectual Vetting Process

Clear standards must be in place and all music used in the church must be vetted by someone who has been properly educated.

Contemporary music usually enters the church through the specials and the choir numbers.

The Power of Incrementalism

The move to contemporary music never happens overnight. It doesn't come full-blown. It happens as a process of incrementalism. It happens by pushing the boundaries just a little at a time. But the pushing is always in the direction of the contemporary.

The best position on music is to draw the line at the very safest place. If it is questionable, leave it alone.

The Power of a Good Song Service

It is not enough to avoid contemporary music and to eschew charismatic praise and worship. That's important but it is actually a minor thing.

A discipling church will work hard at using sacred music as the powerful instrument for sanctification and worship that it is.

We put a lot of work into the song services.

Training good song leaders

The song services are too important to be given into the hands of just anyone who happens to be available. Like everything else, we pray for God to raise up the right people for this ministry.

We look for those who have the spiritual qualifications required of all church workers, plus they need to understand music and, ideally, have some ability to play a musical instrument. We also look for leadership ability. The song leader must be a leader. He might not be a pastor, but he is the leader of the song service.

I spend a lot of time and effort training song leaders. The material I use for this can be found in the report "Marks of Good Song Leading" at www.wayoflife.org.

Teaching the people the purpose of the song service

One major thing we teach the song leaders is the purpose of the song service so they can in turn teach the people.

The purpose is two-fold according to Ephesians 5:18 and Colossians 3:16, which is to sing to God (worship) and to sing to one another (edification of the body).

The lyrics of the songs can be categorized by these two things.

We teach the song leaders that the songs are the message. The song leader's job is not to preach mini messages before or after each song to explain it. His job, rather, is to draw the people's attention to the song's message and to teach them to sing from their hearts with understanding. Some songs are sung directly to God, and some songs are sung to themselves and to the other brethren.

The song leader will explain any words that the people might not be familiar with (such as "beulah" or "seraph"), point the people's attention to the basic theme of the song, and then encourage the people to sing with understanding.

Concentrating on the song service

We want the people to concentrate on the song service without distraction. For this reason, we sing for a half hour or more without interruption. We open with a greeting by one of the leaders and the opening prayer, then the song leader leads the congregation in an extended song service. This way the people can get their minds and hearts in tune with the service and sing with understanding. After the song service, we have the announcements, Bible reading and memorization, offering, etc. Then we have the preaching.

A ministry of the body

The church is a body, and we do our best to include as many of the Lord's people as possible in the ministry.

In addition to our mid-week testimony time, once a month we devote the entire song service to choices by the people. The people raise their hands and wait to be recognized, so everything is done decently and in order, and then the individual either quotes or reads a Bible verse and tells what song he wants to sing. We sing the first two stanzas of the songs so there is opportunity for more people to have a choice. This is another opportunity for the people to have more direct participation in the services.

Sometimes we have an actual worship service. In this service we only sing songs that are directed to the Lord, such as "Holy, Holy, Holy," or songs that are partially directed to the Lord, such as the last stanza of "Day by Day" and the chorus to "Living for Jesus" and "I'm Pressing on the Upward Way." We teach the people to meditate on the words and to direct the message of the hymn to the Lord as a prayer from their hearts.

A lot of instruction is required for these types of things to be effective.

The Bounty of Sacred Music

There is no end to the variety of sacred music available today.

There are many dozens of sacred music hymnbooks, both new and old.

Another sacred music resource is the Psalters in which the Psalms are rephrased and sung by meter.

A Discipling Church Is a Hard Working Church

Outline
The Effect of Social Media on God's Work
Hard Work Is Essential for Success
Hard Work Is Commended in Scripture
Hard Work Is Required of Church Leaders
Hard Work Is Required of the Body

A discipling church is a hard working church. Everything about building and maintaining such a church involves a lot of old-fashioned labor.

I am convinced that many churches don't accomplish nearly as much as they could, because neither the pastor nor the people are really hard workers. There is a *lot* of time wasted on vanity that could and should be spent on valuable things. Many pastors are not real hard workers and are not good managers of their time, and as a consequence they don't teach their people these things.

In fact, I know of a number of pastors who seem to be in retirement mode and actually work very little.

I don't know how many people have asked me, "Brother Cloud, how do you accomplish all that you do? You have written 200 books, publish a monthly magazine, write daily articles for your news service, start churches, operate a full-time Bible college, and travel all over the world. How?" A fundamental part of the answer to that question is that I have been a very hard worker since the day I was saved. Before that I drifted around, hitchhiked, worked some and then drifted, without direction and clear purpose. But as soon as I was saved, I was excited that I had found God and had discovered my purpose in life, and I didn't want to waste any more time. I wanted to spend the rest of my fleeting life pursuing God's calling with diligence. My wife is also a *very* hard worker, and together we have accomplished a lot, and we have taught a lot of people how to be hard workers.

You aren't going to see us sitting around doing nothing, just loafing. We enjoy spending time together and we have dates, but we discuss profitable things, and we find this very enjoyable. We get together with friends, but we guard our time so that those occasions don't get out of hand and interfere with more important business. And usually the time with friends is spent more profitably than just playing games, though we do some of that.

I got a shock in 1988 when my most influential Bible mentor died unexpectedly at age 58. I had written to him that year and had challenged him to put more of his good teaching into print, and he described his plans for that, but he died that very year before he could accomplish those things. This event spurred me to be even more conscious than ever of using my time wisely.

And the older we get the harder we work, because we are increasingly conscious of the brevity of life. You never know when you will lose your health. It can happen in a moment.

Hard Work Is Essential for Success

It is impossible to build anything profitable without hard work. That's true in the physical realm as well as in the spiritual. It is true for building successful businesses, winning ball games, and fighting wars.

I recently watched a documentary about the life of Bill Gates, founder of Microsoft. The biography emphasized that Gates has been a very hard worker since childhood. When he was small he read an entire set of encyclopedias. When he was building Microsoft, he would work two and even three days straight without sleep, and he required a strong work ethic of Microsoft employees.

All of the things necessary to build a discipling church require hard work. Hard work is necessary to build up the people in God's Word (from the pastor's private study to the preaching and teaching to the operation of a Bible Institute), to build up homes, to disciple the youth, to build up the church in prayer and discipline, to get the gospel to every creature. All of these things require a lot of work.

The Effect of Social Media on God's Work

Something I have observed with increasing concern is the dramatic effect of social media on God's work.

Computers, mobile devices, electronic technology can be a wonderful benefit to the Lord's work. I have always been on the cutting edge of these things. I got my first computer in 1982. Way of Life was one of the first Independent Baptist ministries to have a web site. I got video projectors and iPhones and iPads and digital cameras as soon as they appeared. These are such great tools for the ministry!

But the average church member, even the average pastor and missionary, I fear, wastes a ton of time on nothing because of these things, particularly on social media.

When we first came to Nepal in 1979, you couldn't easily communicate with friends and family back home. Even to make a foreign call was time consuming and very expensive. We had to go downtown to the telegraph office and book an overseas call and sit on old wooden benches to wait for the operator to make a connection. There was no Internet, texting, Skype, Facetime, Facebook. Letters were slow and undependable. As a consequence, you dug in and paid full attention to the missionary work. You didn't run back home every few months. You didn't take frequent "furloughs." You didn't talk all the time to your friends back home.

That isn't true now. "Back home" is always with you. There is no real separation. Over the past few years, people have become addicted to being online constantly and communicating constantly with their friends. They post photos of every meal. They post selfies of every outing. They describe everything they do throughout the day.

Some of this can be spiritually valuable, but a huge amount of it is just empty vanity.

The Bible says, "In all labour there is profit: but the talk of the lips *tendeth* only to penury" (Proverbs 14:23).

This verse contrasts profitable labor with the talk of the lips. Some talk of the lips is profitable, if you are talking about profitable things (Ps. 37:30; Pr. 15:23; Eph. 4:29; Tit. 2:8; 1 Th. 5:11). But talk that is lacking this profitability tends to penury or poverty. There is poverty of money and poverty of spiritual blessing and fruit. I am convinced that a large number of God's people are poor in spiritual growth and blessing and fruit because they waste so much time on vanity. Some are even poor in finances because they waste time that could at least be spent making money.

Many visit missionary works to help, but they usually spend an inordinate amount of time on social media. They don't put their hearts into the missionary work as they could and should. Often they don't even try to make friends with the national people, remaining within their social media world.

> "Whatsoever thy hand findeth to do, do *it* with thy might; for *there is* no work, nor device, nor knowledge, nor wisdom, in the grave, whither thou goest" (Ec. 9:10).

Hard Work Is Commended in Scripture

The Bible emphasizes the importance of and blessing of hard work. The "yankee work ethic" was a product of the Bible's influence on western society.

The Bible condemns the sluggard (Pr. 6:6-11). The sluggard isn't careful about the use of time. If he doesn't have an overseer, he doesn't do much on his own initiative. He doesn't have long range plans, and he doesn't stay busy accomplishing those plans. He wastes time ("a little sleep, a little slumber, a little folding of the hands"). He is a loafer; he is not known as a diligent, self-motivated worker. The sluggard could be studying the Bible, reading profitable books, preparing for a ministry, helping in a ministry, but instead he relaxes every chance he gets and plays video games, talks about nothing, goofs off on social media, and surfs the Internet with no clear direction. He is not above watching others work and even wasting their time by talking to them when they are trying to concentrate on their own business.

Don't ever sit and watch someone else work! If you don't have any real work of your own, at least ask how you can help with someone else's project!

The Bible commends diligence (Pr. 10:4; 12:24; 22:29; 27:23-27).

Believers are labourers together with God in His harvest (1 Co. 3:9).

We are to pray that God will send forth "workers," not slackers, into His harvest (Lu. 10:2).

Believers are always to abound in the work of the Lord (1 Co. 15:58).

The Bible teaches us to redeem the time (Eph. 5:16).

Rightly interpreting the Bible requires labor (2 Ti. 2:15).

Effectual prayer requires labor (Col. 4:12).

Widows approved for support are those who have "diligently followed every good work" (1 Ti. 5:10).

Christian growth is to be pursued diligently (2 Pe. 1:5-7).

Paul commended individual believers for their labor (Ro. 16:6, 12).

Hard Work Is Required of Church Leaders

Like everything else, the church's work begins with the leaders. They have more work to do than anyone else in the church, and they must provide an example to the congregation.

Hard working men are the only kind of men we ordain, and they have to prove this *before* ordination.

> Paul showed the example of laboring night and day (Acts 20:31; 1 Th. 2:9; 2 Th. 3:8).
>
> Ruling requires diligence (Ro. 12:8).
>
> It is the elders who labor in the Word of God who are worthy of support (1 Ti. 5:17).
>
> Church leaders are to be diligent in protecting the saints from backsliding (Heb. 12:15).
>
> The workers Paul chose were those who were diligent in many things (2 Co. 8:22).

In addition to study, visitation, preaching, and teaching in the capital city church ministry, our national preachers make multiple weekly village preaching trips over rough mountain roads. The trips are from three to 14 hours one way. One of our preachers, for example, ministers in services in the capital city on Saturday from 10am to 2pm, then heads out on a grueling four-hour road trip to his village where he preaches and ministers Saturday evening and Sunday. He returns to the city and heads out again on Monday to other villages several hours away. Recently when he returned to the city from those weekly journeys, he turned around and traveled

20+ hours on a bus to a village in eastern Nepal to carry a special offering to a preacher whose house had burned down. When I tried to discourage him from making that trip, arguing that he needed to rest, he begged me to let him go! And this is a married man with three children.

Hard Work Is Required of the Church Body

The Lord's work must be done by all members of the body.

> "From whom the whole body fitly joined together and compacted by that which every joint supplieth, according to the effectual working in the measure of every part, maketh increase of the body unto the edifying of itself in love" (Eph. 4:16).

In the typical church, a relatively few people do the bulk of the labor, but this is a mixed multitude rather than a discipling church. In a discipling church all or almost all of the members contribute their part -- "that which every joint supplieth."

We train all of the people to be diligent workers. We reprove laziness and slackness. A lazy person will not be comfortable in our church.

We train our Bible college students how to work hard.

We train the parents to teach the children how to work hard.

We train the young people how to work hard.

A Discipling Church Builds Godly Homes

Outline

The Home and the Church Working Together
The Church Training Parents
The Church Preparing Singles to Be Parents
Suggested Materials

The discipling church, the church that will be standing until Christ comes, is a church that builds godly homes.

The Home and Church Working Together

The church and home must work together to produce disciples. These two divinely-appointed institutions should work together to evangelize, train, and disciple children for God's glory. The church builds up the homes, and the homes raise the children.

The home was the first human institution established by God. He created the first marriage and blessed it and instructed it to be fruitful and multiply (Ge. 1:26-28).

One of God's purposes in marriage is to seek a godly seed (Mal. 2:15).

Consider the teaching of Psalm 127:

> "Lo, children *are* an heritage of the LORD: *and* the fruit of the womb *is his* reward. As arrows *are* in the hand of a mighty man; so *are* children of the youth. Happy *is* the man that hath his quiver full of them: they shall not be ashamed, but they shall speak with the enemies in the gate" (Ps. 127:3-5).

We see, first, that children are an heritage of the Lord (Ps. 127:3). Children belong to God. He is in control of conception (Ge. 29:31; 30:22; Ruth 4:13; Ps. 139:13, 16). God forms man's spirit (Zec. 12:1). He owns every soul (Eze. 18:4). He is the "God of the spirits of all flesh" (Nu. 16:22) and the "Father of spirits" (Heb. 12:9). Every soul comes from God and returns to God (Ec. 12:7, 13-14).

Second, children are to be fashioned as arrows for the glory of God (Ps. 127:4). The image of fashioning an arrow tells us that effectual child training requires hard work, skill, and patience. Fashioning an excellent arrow by hand in the time when this Psalm was written was difficult and exacting work. Likewise, there is no quick and easy path in child training, no simple program. The job requires 100% commitment on the part of the home and the church.

We have two courses on this: *Keeping the Kids* and *The Mobile Phone and the Christian Home and Church*. Both are packed with practical teaching on child training and discipleship, but so few parents and pastors are interested in being this focused and working this hard at the task. In a church of 200, I might sell 10 or 15 copies of these books, and these are some of the best churches we have today, in my estimation.

We are losing the battle for the youth because we are barely in the battle. The spiritual malaise is breathtaking.

The church is the house of God, the pillar and ground of the truth (1 Timothy 3:15). It is tasked with being the headquarters of world evangelism and discipleship in this age.

In the New Testament epistles, we see the church and the home in harmony, working together to accomplish God's will.

Families are addressed through the church epistles (e.g. Ephesians 5:22 - 6:4; Colossians 3:18-21; Titus 2:4-5; 1 Peter 3:1-7). A major part of every church's task is to build up the homes by this teaching.

Church families are to hear what the Spirit says to the churches (Re. 2-3).

The Church Training Parents

Churches must build and train the parents so they can build godly homes and raise their children for Christ.

This must be an ongoing process.

It must be emphasized in the preaching.

There should be special classes on this subject.

The older women are to teach the younger women (Titus 2:3-5).

The church must teach about the husband-wife relationship, the father's role in the home, the mother's role, how to have family devotions, child discipline, holiness, and separation from the world.

Pastor Ken Shaver shares how that he trains the families in Cumberland Baptist Church, Hopkinsville, Kentucky:

> I preach and teach, and I strongly believe, that God keeps His word; and I believe God when He says, 'Train up a child in the way he should go: and when he is old, he will not depart from it' (Proverbs 22:6).
>
> The Bible very clearly says that it is the parents' responsibility to teach and train their children. 'And, **ye fathers**, provoke not your children to wrath: but bring them up in the nurture and admonition of the Lord' (Ephesians 6:4). 'And these words, which I command thee this day, shall be in thine heart: And **thou** shalt teach them diligently unto **thy** children, and shalt talk of them when thou sittest in thine house, and when thou walkest by the way, and when thou liest down, and when thou risest up' (Deuteronomy 6:6-7)
>
> Working within this biblical framework, what can a church do to help the family? I would like to consider several things.
>
> *First of all, churches should also make much of the family.* There are several biblical ways that we can and should do this. At Greater Cumberland Baptist Church, where I have been the pastor since starting the church eight years ago, we take a month each year and preach and teach with a special emphasis on the family. We have named this time 'The Family Crusade.' The Sunday School hour, the morning service, the evening service, and our Wednesday Bible study are all used as times to take the Word of God and show the families a biblically-based way to have a God-honoring home. There is much advertising and promotion (many people are interested in how to have a better family), and a special theme is given. For example, the themes for the last two years at our church were 'Having a Healthy Home' and 'Helping the Home.' Some of the topics were, 'The Joy of Family,' 'Training the Next Generation,' 'Dealing with Difficulties,' and 'Signs of a Healthy Home.' [Some of Pastor Shaver's sermons on the home can be found at the church's web site, http://www.visitgcbc.com/menu/id/20/Audio%20Sermons]
>
> *Secondly, churches can take time during the year to have sermons or lessons on the practical side of parenting.* The roles

and responsibilities of family members is a worthy focus. When I first became pastor here, my four children were all in their teens and the church naturally attracted families with teens. As a result of this, my focus fell more on dealing with teenagers and how to help them establish their own relationship with their Heavenly Father; how to have personal devotions; how to have an effective prayer time; how to be a witness for Christ; how to deal with setbacks in the Christian life. These are all areas where we would spend time in the Word of God. I believe we would be amazed at how many in our churches do not have a good grasp of these basic issues.

After a few years, we had many, many newborns in the church and we concentrated more on helping the family with issues they would face with young children. Areas such as dealing with a child's will and consistency as a parent were points of focus.

Additionally, and I cannot understate the importance of this, the families should be shown how to have family devotions. Family devotions are such an important but neglected part of the Christian family. It is a time to draw together as the family draws closer to the Lord. As best as I can recall, every year we have taken a portion of a service, usually one where I was preaching on the family, and actually have had family devotions so that the families can see how it can be done. In the Shaver family, devotions consist of a moment of Scripture memorization, a time of singing, a time of Bible reading (sometimes we also read a Christian biography or story like *Pilgrim's Progress*), and a short period of prayer. We always have tried to include all the family, maybe one reading, one picking out a song, one praying, and everyone quoting Scripture. We also do not try to make it an in-depth Bible Study, although as our children grew older, we would spend a few weeks on issues like modesty, biblical principles for entertainment, and other relevant things. Additionally, we would work very hard at keeping it light and upbeat. In our home, we just tried to take a few minutes to focus on the things of God and to draw closer together. There are many good family devotion books available, but most of the time we would just take a different chapter of the Bible and take turns reading it.

> One of my greatest joys as a pastor is to have a parent bring their child to me and let their child share the fact that they trusted Christ during their family devotions. This shows me that Dad and Mom are taking home what they are learning at church as impacting their family.
>
> *Finally, another help I believe the church can provide is to make opportunities for families to serve the Lord together.* We have families who work in the bus ministry together, have services in nursing homes together, sing together, clean the church together, visit shut-ins together, and even work in children's ministries together. I believe it is good for the children to work alongside of their parents and to see their parents serving the Lord. Several years ago, I had the privilege of speaking for a friend of mine during a missions conference. While I was up on the platform in front of the choir, the pastor brought to my attention that right behind me were three generations of adult men singing as choir members. What a source of encouragement that was for me.
>
> The local church has the opportunity and the responsibility to help the family be all that God wants it to be. I can say from first-hand experience that it is a great privilege to serve the Lord as a family (Pastor Ken Shaver, Greater Cumberland Baptist Church, Hopkinsville, Kentucky).

A major emphasis should be to build up the men to take their spiritual responsibilities seriously. It is the father who is to take the headship and oversight of his family. The fathers are instructed to bring up the children in the nurture and admonition of the Lord (Eph. 6:4). The father doesn't do all of the work of raising the children, but he is in charge of all of the work and he oversees all of the work, and he must have a very active role.

One pastor wrote, "We have various times when our fathers are asked to teach or to speak so that their own children may know that their father is a voice to be listened to within the congregation."

Pastor Mike Sullivant, Pembina Valley Baptist, Winkler, Manitoba, says, "One thing we have found helpful is having a men's retreat. Last year we had 87 men. We go for two and a half days of fishing, but we have five teaching sessions. It has been so helpful for the men and the families. We have had men saved. We have had men look around and see that Christian men are real men who can enjoy masculine things."

The Church Preparing Singles to Be Parents

We spend a lot of time and effort preparing our young people and single adults for marriage. The time to begin learning how to be a good husband, wife, and parent is before you get married.

When we teach on marriage and child training, we are not addressing the married couples only. We are addressing the single people to prepare them for marriage.

We don't need a "home church," so to speak. We need a church that ministers *to* the home and works together *with* the home.

(For more about the home church see *The House Church Movement*, which is available as a free eBook from www.wayoflife.org.)

Suggested Materials

Following are some suggested materials for building good Christian homes:

God's Wisdom for Marriage and the Home by Scott Markle, https://www.amazon.com/Wisdom-Marriage-Pastor-Scott-Markle/dp/1609575547/ref=tmm_hrd_swatch_0?_encoding=UTF8&qid=&sr=

How Can I Except Some Man Guide Me? by Pastor Kerry Allen. This child evangelism course includes a Bible memory program with 150 salvation verses.

https://www.wayoflife.org/memory-cards.pdf (forwarding link)

Keeping the Kids: How to Keep the Children from Falling Prey to the World by David Cloud, www.wayoflife.org

Marriage and Child Discipline (a course scheduled for publication by Way of Life Literature in 2017)

The Mobile Phone and the Christian Home and Church by David Cloud, www.wayoflife.org

Music for Good or Evil, a video course with eight presentations, by David Cloud, www.wayoflife.org

A Plea to Southern Gospel Music Fans by David Cloud, a multimedia report with 67 links to audio and video clips that illustrate the points, particularly the musical and vocal styles, www.wayoflife.org

Training Your Children to Turn out Right by David Sorenson, www.northstarministries.com

A Discipling Church Disciples Youth

Outline
Youth are Leaving
Church and Home Working Together
Not a Youth Ministry but a Ministry Geared To Youth
Be Careful about Salvation
Be Serious
Discipling Rather Than Entertaining
Effectual Bible Students
Enjoying the Christian Life
Finding God's Will
Separation from the World
Ministry Opportunities
High Standards
Youth Discipling Youth
Living by Faith
Walking in Vigilance
Finding a Marriage Partner
Parents Serving the Lord with Their Children
Youth and the Church Services
Suggested Materials

The church's youth and the people who are won to the Lord from outside are the future of the church. A pastor once told me, "I used to think that the youth are the future of the church. I no longer think that. I now think that those we win to Christ are the future of the church."

It appeared to me that he had changed his thinking because of a general lack of good fruit among the church's youth.

I am convinced that *both* our youth and those we win to Christ are the future of the church. In light of God's promises, there is no reason why we can't win our children to Christ and train them as true disciples of Christ.

Youth Are Leaving

Yet most churches are losing their youth.

Ken Ham, founder of Answers in Genesis, warns, "A mass exodus is underway. Most youth of today will not be coming to church tomorrow" (*Already Gone*, p. 22).

The latest research shows that a frightful percentage of Sunday School children drop out of church in adolescence.

After analyzing 25 different surveys, Barna Research found that 61% of young adults who were active in church as children and teens "spiritually disengage" by their twenties ("Teenagers Embrace Religion but Are Not Excited about Christianity," Jan. 10, 2000, www.barna.org).

In 2005, Answers in Genesis contracted a survey of young adults between the age of 20 and 29 and found that two-thirds of teens who regularly attend "conservative" or "evangelical" churches are gone by college age.

Our own survey in 2005 found that 50% of youth are leaving the churches, and this is a survey of very conservative independent Baptist congregations.

Church and Home Working Together

The church and home must work together to produce disciples. These two divinely-appointed institutions should work together in perfect harmony to evangelize, train, and disciple children for God's glory. The church builds up the homes, and the homes raise the children.

Therefore, a major part of discipling young people is the church's ministry to the families.

A young person in a weak family, either unbelieving or spiritually lukewarm, is handicapped. He can serve the Lord, but it is more difficult than if he were in a godly home that is helping and encouraging him.

A great many churches are failing in this. They are not building the types of homes that can properly train their own children. And the churches themselves are not effectively discipling the youth. As a result, they are dying.

We deal with this in the chapter "A Discipling Church Builds Godly Homes."

One pastor wrote,

> "I came to this church finding the second generation barely holding on to the foundations their parents put in place and a third generation that is nowhere to be found. Why? I believe that the Bible was not given a priority and many false assurances of salvation were given at an altar for emotion's sake and not Christ's sake. We must preach the Bible more thoroughly. We need to trust our young people with the Bible and teach them how to properly use it in their everyday lives. We teach fundamentals of math, grammar, spelling and history, why not a systematic study of the Bible geared toward young people?"

This statement describes the condition in a great many churches, and it also identifies two fundamentals of what needs to be done, which is to be careful about salvation and to help the young people to become true Bible students.

Not a Youth Ministry but a Ministry Geared to Youth

The church doesn't need a youth ministry; it needs a biblical ministry geared to youth.

All too often, a typical youth ministry isolates the youth from the adults, the children from the families, and creates a Christian version of the world's youth culture. Typically such a ministry is a large part entertainment and a very small part New Testament discipleship. It is fun and games with a veneer of biblical spirituality. A typical youth activity consists of a little devotional message sandwiched between a whole lot of goofing off.

This type of thing is nowhere ordained in Scripture. But the Bible does instruct the churches to warn and teach every man in order to present every man perfect in Christ Jesus (Col. 1:28), and this applies to young people as well as older people.

The New Testament Epistles address young people specifically and directly (e.g., 1 Timothy 4:12; 2 Timothy 2:22; Titus 2:6), so it is obviously not wrong for a church to have a ministry to youth.

We see in Titus 2 that every age group of saints has its own particular situation and spiritual challenges, and these should be addressed.

A biblical ministry to youth is *all about* discipleship. This is the plan we follow, and we have seen great fruit from it.

Be Careful about Salvation

The most fundamental thing in youth discipleship is to be careful about salvation, because you can only disciple a born again believer.

I am convinced that the average church youth group has a lot of unsaved young people, and I am not referring to the visitors. They have grown up in the church. They know how to act when they need to. They know what to say if asked, "Do you know the Lord?" They have "believed in Jesus" all their lives. But while their mouths profess love for Christ, their daily lives give testimony that they actually love the world.

We are extremely careful about baptizing young people and receiving them into the church's membership. We don't look for a profession; we look for a conversion.

We have dealt with this in the chapter "A Discipling Church Begins with Caution about Salvation."

But what is often lacking is a clear conversion experience and a clear born again testimony.

I'm not talking about sinless perfection. I'm talking about supernatural, life-changing salvation. A young person who loves the world is either lost or seriously backslidden. The Bible says he is the enemy of God (James 4:4). In the context of James' sharp reproof toward those who love the world, we are taught that such a person needs to experience a radical spiritual revival (Jas. 4:7-10). James did not ignore the worldliness of the people he was addressing, and pastors and youth workers must not ignore the worldliness of young people today. We must not accept worldliness as the status quo.

Worldly young people must not be allowed to be comfortable in their sin. They must not be allowed to think that they are right with God. They must not be allowed to serve in a ministry.

Be Serious

Children and youth ministries must be far more serious than they usually are.

Answers in Genesis found that "Sunday school is actually more likely to be detrimental to the spiritual and moral health of our children" (*Already Gone*, p. 38). They found that students who regularly attend Sunday School are "more likely to become anti-church through the years." This is because "Sunday school actually didn't do anything to help them develop a biblical worldview." The education is typically entertainment-oriented and irrelevant to children's daily lives.

This was what I experienced as a child in Sunday School and Vacation Bible School. I learned a lot of Bible stories but they appeared distant and mythical and didn't seem to have anything to do with my personal life. When I was confronted by the Bible through a well-equipped believer in 1973 at age 23, I was amazed that the Bible was so practical and actually spoke to the things I was thinking about and doing. That was *not* the way the Bible was presented when I was in Sunday School, and this is a shame.

Teachers must avoid trivializing the Bible and not connecting the Bible to real life. Children's ministries can be enjoyable without being silly and without trivializing the things of God.

Many children's ministries present Bible lessons almost as fairy tales.

For example, Noah's Ark is often depicted as a silly-looking cartoon thing that could not possibly have held all of the animals or survived the raging storms.

David is depicted as a little boy when he killed Goliath, whereas he was actually a young man.

Jesus is depicted as an effeminate, long-haired individual, whereas He was an ordinary-looking, short-haired Jewish man, a carpenter, a man who chased the money-changers from the temple.

Avoid mindless children's songs (such as "let the sun shine in, face it with a grin, smiler's never lose and frowners never win," or, "This little light of mine...").

We believe that cartoons should be avoided for the most part, as they tend to trivialize spiritual things by their very character.

Teachers should test everything by the principle of holiness and soberness. They should ask themselves, "Is this helping the children to take Christ and God's Word seriously?"

Discipling Rather Than Entertaining

The church must disciple the young people, not entertain them.

In the average church, as much as or more time is spent on sports and entertainment than serious Bible training, but there is no authority in God's Word for churches to entertain the saints. Few people are deficient in entertainment today. Life is too short to do everything, so the churches must focus on the most important thing in life, which is the Word of God. We must redeem the time.

In our youth ministry, we don't have sports. Other Independent Baptists in our town occupy themselves with sports. But we made a purposeful decision to avoid this in order to keep the focus of our young people on Christ and God's Word.

Our monthly youth meetings consist of an hour and a half or more of singing and testimonies and Bible teaching, with perhaps 15 minutes for a game, usually a Bible quiz. The preaching and teaching gets down into the daily lives of the young people. We deal with things such as having the right friendships, how to handle social media and modern technology, how to make wise decisions, how to find a mate in God's will, the importance of right counsel, and Bible principles for measuring entertainment.

Multiple times a year we have three- to four-day conferences during which we teach the Bible for 12 or more hours, and there are usually *no* games. Yet the vast majority of our young people love these meetings, because they know Christ personally, have surrendered themselves to Him (Romans 12:1), and have been taught to delight in God's Word.

In these conferences we have taught through Romans and Hebrews. We have taught on the Tabernacle, Dispensationalism, Herod and the Roman Empire, Ur of the Chaldees, Holiness, Evolution, Creation Science, and Archaeology. We memorize verses and give tests on the material.

Effectual Bible Students

We want every one of our young people to become serious Bible students.

We focus on this continually, teaching, exhorting, and rebuking when necessary.

This starts with the children.

The parents and the church should lead them in memorizing Scripture, beginning when they are very small. Children are capable of doing much more than they are typically challenged to do if they have a good teacher. Our oldest daughter memorized 100 verses by age seven, and one of our granddaughters memorized 65 verses by age three.

Make sure that they learn to *understand* the Scriptures rather than memorizing mindlessly and learning by mere rote.

Train the children to have a daily Bible reading habit. This starts with reading a verse or two daily and then extending the portion as they grow older. We give examples of this in *The Mobile Phone and the Christian Home and Church*.

As soon as they are able to read well enough, get them their own Bible dictionary and teach them how to use it. We published the *Believer's Bible Dictionary* specifically for teens, though it is a serious Bible dictionary for any age. I give my grandchildren this dictionary at age eleven.

As soon as they are able to understand it, which is early teens, we use the *Effectual Bible Student* course to train the young people. This can be used by saints of any age, but I designed it particularly with young people in mind.

This training program consists of 12 hours of video instruction plus an accompanying printed manual.

It has four major parts.

First, the *Effectual Bible Student* teaches the spiritual qualifications for effectual Bible study.

Second, the *Effectual Bible Student* teaches how to have a daily Bible study time. It is absolutely fundamental that the individual establish a time and a place and develop a daily habit of meeting with God. If the individual is not willing to carve out time for God on a daily basis, he will never learn God's Word and will not make a lot of progress in his Christian life.

Third, the *Effectual Bible Student* teaches how to understand the Bible by means of fundamental principles of interpretation.

Fourth, the *Effectual Bible Student* teaches how to use the major Bible study tools. We focus on the effectual use of the following study books: *Strong's Concordance, Treasury of Scripture Knowledge, Believer's Bible Dictionary,* and select Bible commentaries. We urge each of our young people to obtain these tools and use them every day. The youngest teenager should be able to learn how to do this at a basic level.

We suggest that the young person develop his Bible study habits first using books rather than electronic programs. Books are less distracting while you learn the fundamentals of Bible study. It is important to unplug at times and to be able to concentrate fully on the Lord and His Word.

After learning the basics of Bible study, the student must go on to learn the background to the Bible and Bible customs and geography.

Our multimedia courses *Old Testament History and Geography* and *Bible Times and Ancient Kingdoms* can help the Bible come alive to the serious student.

The Bible is a thrilling book, the most thrilling book on earth. The more you learn how to study it and the more you study it, the more you get out of it, and the more you get out of it the more you enjoy it.

Enjoying the Christian Life

The church must challenge young people to enjoy the Christian life and teach them how.

Young people need to be taught that Jesus Christ and the Bible are the most thrilling things in life. To know Christ *is* life! There is absolutely nothing boring about the Christian life as God intends it to be lived. God made life to be wonderful, and by redemption we can enjoy the life that was lost through the fall.

Christ came that we might have life and have it more abundantly (John 10:10). The God who made Eden for Adam and Eve has given us richly all things to enjoy (1 Timothy 6:17). The Psalmist says, "... the LORD will give grace and glory: no good thing will he withhold from them that walk uprightly" (Psa. 84:11).

And, "Oh that my people had hearkened unto me, and Israel had walked in my ways! ... He should have fed them also with the finest of the wheat: and with honey out of the rock should I have satisfied thee" (Psa. 81:13, 16).

God is the God of bounty to His people. He is the God of corn. One corn seed typically produces a stalk bearing two cobs, each with an average of 500 kernels per cob. Thus, it multiplies itself 1,000 fold and more in one generation. If you replant the 1,000 seeds from one corn stalk and each grows to maturity--each stalk bearing two cobs with an average of 500 kernels per cob (2,000 X 500)--you get one million kernels of corn. That's just the second generation. And if you plant those one million kernels and each stalk grows to maturity, you get a billion corn seeds in just three generations! This is an example of the blessing with which God has filled the world for man's benefit. "Such is the tremendous reproductive power of DNA, especially in primary producer plants that must generate sufficient food-web biomass so all consumers--including we humans--can survive" (Kenneth Poppe, *Exposing Darwinism's Weakest Link*, p. 33).

The believer has an eternal inheritance that he begins to enjoy in this present life.

The abundant life is not found in worldly things. It is found in walking in intimate fellowship with the Creator and enjoying life with Him at the center of it. He is life. He is the key to life. He is the most interesting part of life. He is the purpose of life.

Consider some things that enrich the life and bring great enjoyment:

Bible Study

We don't want our young people merely to study the Bible as a religious ritual. We want them to delight in the Bible.

Bible study is the most interesting, thrilling thing in my life, and it has been for the 43 years I have been saved. I was thrilled with Bible study from the first day I was saved, and I am more thrilled with it today than ever.

The church needs to teach the young people that the Bible is the world's most fascinating and amazing book, and they must seek to gain a thoroughgoing biblical worldview.

What benefits are there to Bible study?

1. In the Bible you see God. That is the first purpose of the Bible. I see Him on every page, in every verse. I continually learn new things about His glorious Person and character: His holiness, His majesty, His omnipotence, His omniscience, His unchangeableness, His infinity, His eternality (He "inhabiteth eternity"), His truthfulness, His grace, His patience, His gentleness, His tender mercies, His meekness and lowliness of heart, His kindness, His goodness, His peace.

2. In the Bible you see God's glorious salvation for sinners through the cross of Christ, which is the central act of human history.

3. In the Bible you see yourself and come to understand yourself better and better.

4. In the Bible you find the key to understanding all of life ("in thy light we see light," Ps. 36:9). It gives the right worldview. It shows how the world began, where man comes from, what he is, what his purpose is, why the world is like it is, how marriage originated, why men and women are different, why men are different than animals. The Bible is the key to understanding every discipline: social studies, history, economics, politics, government, psychology, every aspect of science, etc.

5. In the Bible you find God's will. The Bible contains the mind of Christ (1 Co. 2:16).

6. In the Bible you see the past and understand history from God's perspective.

7. In the Bible you see the future.

There is no other book that reveals the future. All prophecies outside of the Bible are vague and false. For example, astrological forecasts are typically vague, such as, "You are going to meet someone who will be important in your life." And if they aren't vague, they are usually wrong. A famous British astrologer named Naylor, whose predictions appeared in the *Sunday Times*, said, "In this column, for years, I have constantly laboured these points: Hitler's horoscope is not a war-horoscope ... there will be no war" (August 27, 1939). Edgar Cayce predicted the arrival of Armageddon in 1999. Jeanne Dixon predicted that Russia would beat the U.S. to the moon, that World War III would begin in 1958, and that there would be a cure for cancer in 1967. The royal astrologer for Nepal's King Birendra did not see his death in 2001.

Instead, the astrologer saw an earthquake for that time, which didn't occur.

But the Bible's prophecies are clear and precise, for the most part. They do contain typology but the key to the interpretation of the prophecies is given in Scripture itself.

Consider Christ's first coming. Hundreds of years before Jesus was born, his life was written in Scripture. His birthplace of Bethlehem was named (Mi. 5:2). His rejection by the Jewish nation was foretold (Isa. 53). Every detail of His death was foretold, including the beating, the mocking, the piercing of His hands and feet, His experience of dying, the words He spoke from the cross (Ps. 22) and His burial in a rich man's tomb (Isa. 53:9).

Bible prophecy is a wonderful, important part of the Christian life and an important part of youth discipleship.

Bible prophecy is interesting. Even lukewarm believers like to study Bible prophecy.

Bible prophecy strengthens the faith of young people that the Bible is God's Word. It is one of the great evidences of the Bible's divine inspiration.

Bible prophecy enables young people to see the future and to have a "long view" of life rather than a short-sighted view. By prophecy, young people can "seek those things that are above" (Colossians 3:1-4), and this is a life-changing thing.

Bible prophecy enables the believer to see his eternal inheritance. Paul prayed that the saints would understand "the riches of the glory of his inheritance in the saints" (Eph. 1:18). A large portion of the Bible describes Christ's millennial kingdom and the believer's eternal inheritance in the new heaven and new earth. Dozens of entire chapters of Scripture are devoted to this. God wants His people to know the future. The more we focus our attention on this, the less worldly-minded we will be.

Bible prophecy prepares the believer for his future in Christ's kingdom as a part of Christ's bride. We teach our young people that the Christian life and service in the church are the preparation for the future. It really matters how we live and what choices we make. By pursuing diligent Christian growth, the believer prepares for his entrance into Christ's kingdom (2 Peter 1:5-11). By being rich in good works, the believer lays up treasures "against the time to come" (1 Timothy 6:17-19). By faithful service and obedience to Christ, the believer earns the privilege of ruling with Him (Revelation 2:26-27; 3:21).

Good music (Eph. 5:19)

Note that sacred music is associated with Spirit control. It has the power to change the mood and attitude as it did Saul's (1 Sa. 16:16).

Music is powerful, either for evil or for good. What music do you love? What music do you have on your phone? What music do you share with your friends?

I enjoy a wide variety of wholesome music, not only Christian music, but good classical, semi-classical, marches, etc. It enriches my life. God has given us all good things to enjoy (1 Ti. 6:17).

The report "Suggested Sacred Music Recordings" can help the young person find good Christian music.

www.wayoflife.org/database/sacred-music-sources.html

Good sermons

A Bible college student recently told me, "I don't listen to music much but I listen to a lot of sermons on my cell phone." There are thousands of sermons on SermonAudio, including many dozens of sermons published by Way of Life.

Good videos

Video is a powerful technology that can be used for good or evil, and there are countless wholesome movies and videos that can be used for recreation, education, and edification.

We have published dozens of multi-media Bible teaching videos, including *Music for Good or Evil; Biblical Separation; Israel: Past, Present, and Future; The Glorious History of the English Bible; The Emerging Church; The New Age; The Effectual Bible Student; The Trojan Horse.*

I have personally benefited greatly from creation science videos. In the report "Creation Science Videos" at the Way of Life web site we describe many excellent and helpful titles.

www.wayoflife.org/fbns/creationscience-videos.html

Recently my son finished editing a new video by Dr. Shem Dharampaul about Raymond Damadian, M.D., the inventor of the

MRI, and his faith in Christ and rejection of evolution. *Behind the MRI: Dr. Raymond Damadian* can be viewed and downloaded at the following site:

http://mrimovie.ca/

I have benefited from and enjoyed many educational and historical documentaries. Nature series by BBC, such as *Planet Earth, The Blue Planet, African Wildlife, Nature's Great Events,* and *The Frozen Planet,* are powerfully entertaining and educational, even though the producers are evolutionists and some evolutionary nonsense creeps into the series.

God made nature as a revelation of Himself and as object lessons for mankind, and there is great benefit in studying it. See 1 Ki. 4:33; Job 12:7-9; Ps. 8:3; 19:1-4; Pr. 6:6; 30:24-28; Isa. 40:26; Ro. 1:20. One reason I love photography is that it allows me to capture little slices of God's creation. It helps me to look at things more thoughtfully.

Good conversation with the right friends ("with them that call on the Lord out of a pure heart," 2 Ti. 2:22)

Young people need to pray that the Lord will give them good friends. This is what I did as a new Christian. My old friends left me because of my zeal for Christ and the Bible, and I asked the Lord for new ones. The first one was a young man named Richard who had come to Christ about a year before I did. He was a diligent Bible student and helped me greatly the first year of my Christian life. We talked some about the world or our past lives, but we talked a lot about the thrilling things we were learning in Christ. I plainly recall, for example, the night he showed me some of the wonders of Psalm 119.

Since then, God has answered my prayer for good Christian friends a thousand times over.

Pray for friends, and God will answer that prayer if He knows that you will spend your time with them pursuing edifying things rather than worldly or vain things.

Reading and Learning

Churches should challenge the young people *to be studious*, to be students of the Bible, first, and then students of life in general as God made it.

Everything you learn can enrich your life, marriage, and ministry.

God made man's amazing mind, and He did not make it to waste on laziness and vanity.

Youth is the best time to learn. Your mind is sharper and your memory better than it will ever be. As you get older, you will gradually lose the mental powers of your youth.

We teach our young people that everything you learn *that is wholesome* can enrich your life, ministry, and marriage.

Parents and pastors and teachers should have a passion for learning so they can impart this to the youth.

The English reader has access to the greatest wealth of literature that's ever been available at any time in history.

Young people need to learn to read and to enjoy reading. It's been said that the man who does not read is no better than the man who cannot read. I read the equivalent of a couple hundred books a year, and it is an enriching thing both to my personal life and to my family and ministry.

Even secular society recognizes the benefits of reading. For example, the Barbara Bush Foundation for Family Literacy works to "help parents and children build brighter futures through literacy." Dorothy Bush Koch, daughter of U.S. President George H.W. Bush and his wife Barbara, says,

> "When I was growing up, my mother, Barbara Bush, read to me every night. I remember reaching out to turn the pages when I was very small, caught up in the wonder of each story and the vivid pictures that filled my imagination. I was so fortunate to be raised in a household filled with books and—as you might imagine to be the case in the Bush home—plenty of conversation. By filling my days with loving words and ending each one with a bedtime story, my mother not only helped me form wonderful childhood memories, but also cultivated vital language and literacy skills that prepared me for success in school—and in life" (Dorothy Bush Koch, "What my mother Barbara Bush taught me about learning," *Fox News*, Jan. 18, 2017).

Parents reading to children is so important to intelligence development that the American Academy of Pediatrics urges doctors and nurses to use pediatric visits to discuss with mothers the importance of reading.

A recent article by Charles Chu, "The Simple Truth Behind Reading 200 Books a Year" on betterhumans.coach.me, gives the following advice:

> "Somebody once asked Warren Buffett about his secret to success. Buffett pointed to a stack of books and said, 'Read 500 pages like this every day. That's how knowledge works. It builds up, like compound interest. All of you can do it, but I guarantee not many of you will...' ... [I]n these last two years I've read over 400 books cover to cover. That decision to start reading was one of the most important decisions in my life. ... Reading 200 books a year isn't hard at all. ... The average American reads 200-400 words per minute. Typical non-fiction books have 50,000 words. ... 200 books [requires] 417 hours. ... a single American spends 608 hours on social media and 1642 hours on TV. That's 2250 hours a year on TRASH. If those hours were spent reading instead, you could be reading over 1,000 books a year! ... If you want to read, make sure (1) you remove all distractions from your environment and (2) you make books as easy to access as possible. ... If your goal is to read more, you can't be picky about where you read or what mediums you use. I read paper books. I read on my phone. I listen to audiobooks. And I do these things everywhere -- on park benches, in buses, in the toilet. Wherever I can. Make your reading opportunistic. If you have a chance, take it. If you don't have a chance, find one."

Young people need to learn to capture what they read by reading thoughtfully, underlining or highlighting important things, and jotting down thoughts.

Of course, the fundamental thing in learning is know the Bible, God's Word, well and to test everything by it (1 Th. 5:21). This is the heart of a proper worldview (Heb. 5:14). It is the opposite of the simple person who is gullible and easily misled (Pr. 14:12).

The child of God must use the Word of God to resist the world's wrong thinking and wrong ways in every area of his life. He must cast down every wrong imagination (2 Co. 10:4-5). He must refuse to allow the world to mold him into its image (Ro. 12:2).

A child or youth who loves to read and is left to his own choices and devices without a good knowledge of God's Word and a thorough-going biblical worldview is a sheep among wolves.

Once you have the key to learning, which is the Bible, and once you know the Bible well enough to see everything through its lens, then you can learn to study with discrimination.

Parents and churches must teach young people how to choose the right things to study.

Wise Christian parents will carefully oversee their young people's reading matter to weed out anything that would be a detriment to their spiritual and moral health and will help the young people to develop their own ability to discriminate. We live in a fallen world, and reading and learning is not without its very real dangers.

Of course, God requires that His people separate from every evil thing and keep themselves unspotted from the world (Jas. 1:27; 1 John 2:15-16). It is not spiritually profitable to read unwholesome literature and watch unwholesome videos and engage in any type of unwholesome endeavor.

Magic is something that is clearly off bounds (De. 18:10-12), yet many of the most popular juvenile books today delve into magic. These include *Harry Potter*, *The Finkleton* series, *Enchanted Forest Chronicles*, *Tales of Magic*, *The Dark Is Rising*, and *Percy Jackson and the Olympians*.

Science fiction is another danger-filled genre. It was created in the late 19th and early 20th century as a product of an evolutionary worldview that denies the Almighty Creator. Science fiction takes the reader into a cold, strange world without God. Oh, there might be "a god," a "force," but it is definitely not the God of the Bible, and the prominent names in this field are Darwinists and Atheists. Science fiction and the superhero genre have grown ever darker, stranger, more sensual and godless, and many people are living a dark fantasy world because their minds and hearts have been captured by unsound authors. (See the report "Beware of Science Fiction" at www.wayoflife.org.)

In guiding children and young people in their reading, it is important to guide in the way of substance and value.

Fiction, even wholesome fiction, is rarely the best choice. I see at least three problems with fiction. First, it is addictive. Second, rarely is it intellectually challenging. Third, it rarely provides anything of godly, real substance for one's life. Living on a diet of fiction is like living on junk food, at best. As a child, I devoured countless works of fiction, such as the Hardy Boys, the Bobbsey Twins, and Nancy Drew, but it was the reading equivalent of a mindless video game. At the time when my mind and memory were the sharpest, I wasted countless hours on the literary equivalent of marshmallows. A couple of marshmallows are OK; a diet of marshmallows is foolishness.

Not long ago I wrote the following to a grandmother who was discussing gifts for her grandchildren:

> I like to focus on non-fiction. Truth is as interesting as fiction, and truth is better for kids, I believe. It is easy to get addicted to fiction. Following are some of the things I have gotten for my grandkids:
>
> Christian Heroes four sets
> Heroes of History (Janet and Geoff Benge, age 8 and up) 5 sets of 5
> DK Readers - Thomas Edison
> DK Readers - Wright Brothers
> DK Readers - George Washington
> Moonwalk: First Trip to the Moon (Step 5)
> The Titanic (Step 4)
> Lives and Signers of the Declaration of Independence
> To the Top: Climbing the World's Highest Mountain (Step 5)
> Hellen Keller (Step 4)
> Volcanoes (Step 4)
> Hungry Plants (Step 4)
> Quakes (Step 5)
> Michael Faraday by Charles Ludwig (age 12-15)
> Sower Series (age 9 and up)
> Galileo and the Magic Numbers by Sidney Rosen (12 and up)
> Galen and the Gateway to Medicine by Jeanne Bendick (9 and up)
> The Story of the Romans illustrated by Helen Guerber (11 and up)
> Heroes of the Revolution
> Exploring the World of Biology
> Building Blocks of Life Science (Gary Parker)
> Tools of the Ancient Romans
> Complete Book of Maps and Geography
> Pioneers Go West (Landmark Books)

Meet Abraham Lincoln (Landmark Books)
Landing of the Pilgrims (Landmark Books)
The Story of Thomas Edison (Landmark Books)
Louise Braille (Margaret Davidson)
Helen Keller (Margaret Davidson)
Wright Brothers (Quentin Reynolds)
Secrets of the Woods (William Long)
Moonwalk: First Trip to the Moon (Step 5)
American History by Noah Webster
The following two titles are historical fiction but they recreate the times pretty well -
The Beggars's Bible by Louise Vernon (age 9 and up)
The Bible Smuggler by Vernon Will (age 9 and up)
Also the following from Creation Moments:
Bugs Big & Small God Made Them All
God Made the World & Me-Preschool
Dinosaur Activity Book
Science Activities for Illustrating Bible Lessons
Creation Curriculum Lessons Grades 1-4
God's Design for Life: The World of Plants
Animals of the Bible
Noah's Ark-Preschool Activity Book
Mineral Book
Q & A about Weather and the Bible
Guide to Animals
Astronomy Book

When you have a good Bible foundation and have learned to avoid evil and to read and study with spiritual discrimination, then you can wisely and safely study life and learn from every part of life.

The KJV translators were great scholars because they were great students. *John Bois* could read the whole Bible in Hebrew at age five. His godly father and mother taught him to love education. His mother Mirable read the Bible 12 times and the unabridged *Foxes Book of Martyrs* twice. As a student at Oxford, Bois studied in the library from 4am to 8pm. In the pursuit of perfecting his linguistic skills, he read 60 grammars. He studied in his horse cart on the daily trips from Boxworth to Cambridge, letting his horse find the way. Even in old age, John Bois spent eight hours a day in study.

Carolus Linnaeus, who classified living things, was so poor as a young man that he had to stuff paper in his shoes when they wore out, but when he won a scholarship, he spent the money on lectures rather than clothes.

Michael Faraday, one of the fathers of modern physics and a strong Christian, was totally self-educated. He had a passion for learning, so his boss let him use his personal library, and Michael would read into the night after working all day. This is a reminder that we must learn how to find answers to questions and not depend on others. Once when I sent out an ad for my book on the house church, a man emailed me and asked what is a house church. He wanted me to find someone who would give him a private summary instead of making the effort to read the book and study for himself, even though the eBook was free.

In learning to be studious, young people need to take their school studies seriously.

Don't be intimated by the ignorant crowd. Use this important time of your life wisely instead of following empty people. I have often regretted how that I wasted my youth, and a large reason that I did so was peer pressure from the foolish crowd that I ran with who encouraged me *not to excel*. Dumb was cool!

But go beyond your required studies. Use your youthful mind to learn good things that will enrich your personal life, your ministry to others, and your service to Christ. Recently I talked with a young man who told me that he took nearly every optional course he could take in high school beyond the required courses, because he enjoyed learning. As a result, he is an unusually well-informed young man who can hold an intelligent conversation on many subjects.

The hours that most young people waste on video games or empty talk or vain social media pastimes should be used instead to learn and perfect skills on one or more musical instruments or any number of other profitable things.

One adult gave the following testimony about why he ordered a children's textbook *The Geography Book: Activities for Exploring, Mapping, and Enjoying Your World*: "As a life-long learner, when I want to learn a new subject I begin with children's books because they assume no prior knowledge of the subject. I will enjoy working my way through the activities as a base for this new subject of study." This comment was posted at Amazon's web site, and it is a good example of how to pursue learning throughout one's life.

Learn to study subjects correctly as opposed to the shallow way of the Internet age. It has encouraged "bits and pieces" research, just reading a few bits and pieces of information rather than entire books or at least entire reports. That's like reading a few verses of the Bible instead of reading by chapter and book. By this habit, it is impossible to understand the information in context. The Internet age has encouraged haste and shallowness, just glancing quickly at *Wikipedia* or the top ten Google returns instead of pursuing serious research.

Photography

Photography is a great tool for your personal life, for your family, and for your ministry. It is challenging and technical. It is educational. It is art. It is fun. It is capturing slices of God's glorious creation. It helps you to study life more carefully and thoughtfully.

Our book *Good Photography Made Simple* can help anyone become a better photographer.

Anything wholesome in God's will

Pastor Buddy Smith is a master wood carver and uses his skills to make money for his own needs and ministry, to finance God's work (he helped fund a church building), and to produce gifts to encourage the hearts of people.

Geologist Bill Kitchens studies agates and has a web site GodMadeAgates.com that features studies about agates and beautiful photos of them. He says, "Agates are treasures of God's grace that, through natural processes, fill voids in rocks around us for people to find, wonder at, and use. ... The appreciation of beauty and the desire to create beauty, and to understand it, are parts of the 'image of God' built into mankind 'in the beginning.'"

Young people must learn to use electronic technology and devices for godly and wise learning rather than for sin and worldliness and vanity.

Delighting in God (Ps. 37:4)

Above all, the wise young person will study God. The creation is fascinating, but the Creator is far more so. If you are trying to enjoy God's creation without putting Him first in your heart and life and without looking beyond the creation to God Himself, you are an idolater.

At the heart of life must be God Himself. True Christianity is not a religion, it is a relationship. It is the most intimate relationship imaginable with the living God. "dear child" (Eph. 5:1), loved (Eph. 5:2), "Christ liveth in me" (Ga. 2:20); the believer is part of Christ's bride (Eph. 5:25-26), a member of His very body (Eph. 5:30).

As a child of God, I can enjoy everything wholesome, but I must love only God. Anything else is idolatry.

The greatest thing man can think of is God Himself. It is good to learn from all of life, but everything was created to point man to God and to teach man about God.

Finding God's Will

The church must teach the young people how to find God's will. This is a thrilling thing because it involves finding the very purpose for which you were created.

Romans 12 is a key passage that contains the four fundamental elements of knowing God's will:

First, personal surrender to God and His will (v. 1).

Second, separation from the evil things of and the wrong ways of the world (v. 2).

Third, renewal of the mind through God's Word (v. 2). This requires effectual Bible study and is absolutely foundational. It requires time (Eph. 5:16 "redeeming the time"). And it requires training.

Fourth, service (vv. 3-8).

We teach these principles continually and weave these principles throughout our ministry to youth.

To train young people in knowing God's will we use the *One Year Discipleship Course,* which is very practical and gets down to where the young people live. The 52 lessons deal with such things as repentance, daily Bible study methods, seeking wise counsel, wise use of money, dress, and tests of entertainment.

Separation from the World

Separation from the world must be emphasized continually. The world's pop culture is devouring multitudes of young people in the churches. It is capturing their hearts. The church must deal effectually with the world's music, social media, video games, dress fashions, friendships, attitude.

Even if you are saved and are studying the Bible and seeking His will, there are still powerful enemies within and without, and victory requires keen vigilance (Eph. 5:15; 1 Pet. 5:8) and strict separation (1 Jn. 2:15-17). David, the "sweet Psalmist of Israel," was a passionate seeker of God, but we know what happened to him when he ceased being vigilant.

Christ warned that the things of the world can choke the Word in the believer's life so that he doesn't bear spiritual fruit (Mk. 4:19; Lk. 8:14). Jeremiah warned about sowing among thorns (Jer. 4:3). This refers to trying to serve the Lord without separating from sin, which is exactly what multitudes of professing Christians are doing in fundamental Baptist churches. Their daily lives are filled with worldly lusts and pleasures by the definition of 1 John 2:15-16, such as sensual music, immodest dress, and worldly entertainment, but they profess Christ and attend church and perhaps even read the Bible and pray. This was the condition of Israel of old. ".. this people draw near me with their mouth, and with their lips do honour me, but have removed their heart from me..." (Isa. 29:13). It is not possible to love God and also to love the wicked world. To love the wicked things of the world is to be the enemy of God (Jam. 4:4).

Young people who want to know and do God's will *must* separate from the world.

Note the strictness of biblical separation: "*all* uncleanness" (Eph. 5:3), "*no* fellowship" (Eph. 5:11).

Separation from the world is strongly emphasized throughout Scripture. See Deuteronomy 7:26; Psalm 101:3; Proverbs 4:14-15, 23-27; 6:25-26; 7:6-10; Romans 12:1-2; 1 Corinthians 15:33; 2 Corinthians 6:14-18; 1 Peter 5:8; James 4:4; 1 John 2:15-17.

Some of the Greatest Worldly Dangers Today

The mobile phone itself

The mobile phone has brought the world into people's lives in the most intimate way. It connects to the Internet, where moral dangers and false teaching are only a click or a tap away.

If a young person wants to serve the Lord and know His will, he must be extremely cautious about modern communication tools.

It is wise to remove all temptations from one's phone. Examples are wrong music, wrong apps, even the web browser if necessary. One young man wrote, "Before I got saved, I listened to rock music, copying it to my memory cards. After I get saved, for some time I couldn't delete the songs. I used to say that I would be able not to listen to them, but I was easily tempted to listen to the things that were already in my phone. I was making provision for the flesh while promising not to fulfil the lusts thereof (Ro. 13:14). So one day I decided to delete them totally from my memory card and from my computer too. I thank the Lord, I have never regretted that decision."

It is wise to use a web browser filter like CleanInternet.

It is wise to have an accountability partner.

Some use Covenant Eyes for accountability. It monitors the individual's Internet usage and emails reports to selected people for accountability. The accountability report lists web sites visited, Internet searches, and the times of day when the Internet is used. It also features a score that ranks the individual's level of objectionable Internet usage. Covenant Eyes also has a filtering service that can be used in combination with the accountability service. Another service of this type is X3 Watch. It provides accountability on computers, cell phones, and tablets. While I have not used this personally, it has been recommended by friends.

Others use a church leader or mature Christian friend as an accountability partner. One single young adult wrote: "I have a friend in Bible college who has the restriction codes to my phone. I cannot access the App Store, I cannot access the browser. I personally deleted every game I had off the phone, deleted Facebook and anything else that I felt 'drawing' my mind away in ways that I thought were a hindrance to my walk with God. A great example of this is FoxNews. The App shows a lot of news, to be sure. The space directly below it has a lot of entertainment news, which was basically nothing but soft porn. I got sick and tired of seeing this and deleted that app as well. If SnapChat or other items are a hindrance, the partner can block those as well by restricting it. Remember that browsers can be downloaded through the App Store, so even if Safari or the base browser is blocked, there are ways around it."

Pop music

Twenty-nine of the thirty most popular YouTube videos in 2015 were music videos, and most are filthy. The total views of the 29 videos was 26 BILLION!

Psy "Gangnam Style" (2.3 billion views)
Justin Bieber "Baby" (1.2 billion)
Katy Perry "Dark Horse" (1 billion)
Taylor Swift "Blank Space" (1 billion)
LMFAO "Party Rock Anthem" (906 million)
Eminem "Love the Way You Lie" (896 million)
Shakira "Waka Waka" (889 million)
Jennifer Lopez "On the Floor" (846 million)
Miley Cyrus "Wrecking Ball" (784 million)

Rock is intimately associated with illicit sex and always has been. Even a mere glance at iTunes proves this. The covers of the albums and the lyrics are filthy, and a child of God seeking purity will not touch the unclean thing (2 Co. 6:17).

Consider the following testimonies by rock & rollers:

> "That's what rock is all about--*sex with a 100 megaton bomb, THE BEAT!*" (Gene Simmons of the rock group KISS, interview, *Entertainment Tonight*, ABC, Dec. 10, 1987).

> "Rock 'n' roll is 99% *sex*" (John Oates of the rock duo Hall & Oates, *Circus*, Jan. 31, 1976).

> "Rock 'n' roll is pagan and primitive, and very jungle, and that's how it should be! ... the true meaning of rock ... is sex, subversion and style" (Malcolm McLaren, punk rock manager, *Rock*, August 1983, p. 60).

> "The THROBBING BEAT of rock provides a vital sexual release for adolescent audiences" (Jan Berry of Jan and Dean, cited by Ken Blanchard, *Pop Goes the Gospel*).

"The great strength of rock 'n' roll lies in ITS BEAT ... it is a music which is basically *sexual, un-Puritan* ... and a threat to established patterns and values" (Irwin Silber, Marxist, *Sing Out*, May 1965).

"Everyone takes it for granted that rock and roll is synonymous with sex" (Chris Stein, lead guitarist for Blondie, *People*, May 21, 1979).

"Rock and roll is fun, it's full of energy ... It's *naughty*" (Tina Turner, cited in *Rock Facts*, Rock & Roll Hall of Fame and Museum).

"Pop music revolves around sexuality. I believe that if there is anarchy, let's make it sexual anarchy rather than political" (Adam Ant, *From Rock to Rock*, p. 93).

"The sex is definitely in the music, and sex is in ALL ASPECTS in the music" (Luke Campbell of 2 Live Crew).

Pop music and rap will steal your heart for the world. At best you will have a divided heart.

Pastor Dave Sorenson tells how that as a teen his heart was captured by rock music that he listened to in his bedroom via a transistor radio that his pastor father let him have.

I was captured by rock music via 45-rpm records at a friend's garage. He was a deacon's son.

Videos

YouTube, music videos, X-rated movies, parents used to keep MTV out of the home, but now MTV and much worse is on the kids' phones!

Video Games

"See then that ye walk circumspectly, not as fools, but as wise, Redeeming the time, because the days are evil. Wherefore be ye not unwise, but understanding what the will of the Lord *is*" (Eph. 5:15-17).

Video games are very addictive and they are great time wasters. Also many of them have very wicked content. Even the more innocent games use rock music as a background, thus addicting young people to the sensual rock rhythms.

If young people are allowed to play video games, they must be carefully chosen and the play time must be strictly limited by the parents.

Video games and addiction

"The more we looked into it the more we found that gaming was taking over the lives of kids."

"Some studies suggest that gaming is absolutely taking over the minds of children all together."

"Virtual life becomes more appealing than real life."

Beware of role playing games. Nothing takes over young people's hearts and minds more than these. They are called MMORPG (massively multiplayer online role-playing games).

The most addictive games in 2015 are the following: Madden, Dota 2, Grand Theft Auto, Tetris, Candy Crush Saga (the company is valued at $7.5 billion), Minecraft, EverQuest (called "never rest" and "ever crack"), The Sims (player has omnipotent control over people), World of Warcraft (called World of War Crack), Call of Duty (the last two are played by more than 100 million players), Halo 3 (called Halodiction), Total War, Pong, Civilization, Diablo 3, Super Meat Boy, Team Fortress 2, Dark Souls 2, Counter Strike, Starcraft 2, Persona 4 Golden, Monster Hunter 3, Elder Scrolls, Angry Birds, Faster Than Light, Peggle, League of Legends, Civilization V, Pokemon.

Even in remote places like Nepal, gaming competition is becoming popular. A report on Nepali gamers in the *Kathmandu Post* (Aug. 29, 2015) was entitled "By Their Bootstraps." Gaming started in Nepal in internet cafes in 2010. The 2015 Colors E-sports Carnival at the Civil Mall had 500 participants competing at *Defense of the Ancients* (DOTA), a multi-online battle game.

Video games and violence

Beware of violent games. One of the most popular is *Grand Theft Auto*. Players assume the role of lawless, destructive criminals who kill innocent bystanders, policemen, and military personnel, "while dealing with only temporary consequences." It has been called a cop-killing training machine. Some of the versions require the player to torture people in brutal ways to advance to new levels. Sexual elements include hiring and killing prostitutes (by means of the player's choice of fist, machete, bat, or gun). Real life murders have been committed by people who were obsessive players of *Grand Theft Auto* and have even admitted to being inspired by the game.

Video games and the occult

Many of the video games are occultic. Consider the current craze, Pokémon Go. Almost overnight it has become the most popular mobile game in American history, increasing the stock market value of part owner Nintendo more than 50%. "Pokémon Go, the newest iteration of the nearly 20-year-old Pokémon franchise, engages players in an 'augmented reality' where they try to find and capture Pokémons hidden throughout the real world. The *Australian Business Review* has suggested that it may be a 'watershed moment' in the development of virtual reality" ("Pokémon Go craze drawing gamers to church," *Baptist Press News*, July 15, 2016). The game "uses the mobile phone's camera to create the perception that the Pokémon characters are actually in front of the players." It is so engaging and addictive that people have crashed their automobiles and walked into dangerous situations. Two men recently fell off a cliff near San Diego while engaged in the game.

Pastor David Brown, First Baptist Church of Oak Creek, Wisconsin, who made the effort to investigate *Pokémon* and apply the test of God's Word to it in 1999, says, "The name *Pokémon* is derived from POCKEt MONster. ... One of the first things I did was to find out who produced the Trading Card Game. Here is an exact quote right from the Web page of the producer - 'The *Pokémon* Trading Card Game is a new collectable Card Game that is made and distributed by *Wizards of the Coast*. The same company that made the best-selling game ... *Magic: The Gathering.*' *Wizards of the Coast* also owns TSR, the producers of *Dungeons & Dragons*. When I discovered who owned the American *Pokémon* Trading Card Game rights, I knew it was not just an innocent card game for elementary school children. [The Pokémon rap mantra says]: 'I will travel across the land/ Searching far and wide/ Each Pokémon to understand/ The power that's inside/ Gotta catch them all.' ... To be sure it is a game, but a game that does not glorify God! When God says something is wrong, it is wrong regardless of what form it is in. Not only that, but many of the kids who play this game *are* seduced into believing the principles that the game subtly teaches" (Dave Brown, "The Problem with Pokémon").

In the official literature, the main characters of the game are described as headstrong, stubborn, quibbling, hormonal, having a fascination with and trying to "score" with the opposite sex, self-centered, vindictive, obnoxious, and prone to cross-dressing!

Pokémon promotes the search for occultic power. The cards are called "energy cards." Players engage in "pretend" occultic warfare. Currently there are 729 species of Pokémon monsters, and 151 of them are sought by Pokémon Go players. Two of them are named *Abra* and *Kadabra*, long associated with magic. The *Abra* card promotes the ability to read minds. The *Kadabra* character has a pentagram on his forehead. What an incredibly dangerous, wicked influence for children! Nintendolife says there are poison types, psychic types, dark types, fairy types, dragon types, and ghost types.

There is nothing innocent about Pokémon. It is a clever attempt at demonic mind-control. For more about the dangers of Pokémon see "The Problem with Pokémon" by David Brown, http://logosresourcepages.org/Occult/more.htm

Even the more innocent games use rock music as a background, thus addicting young people to the sensual rock rhythms.

Video games and wasting time

"How long wilt thou sleep, O sluggard? when wilt thou arise out of thy sleep? *Yet* a little sleep, a little slumber, a little folding of the hands to sleep: So shall thy poverty come as one that travelleth, and thy want as an armed man" (Prov. 6:9-11).

The average gamer spends eight hours per week playing video games. This equates to 416 hours per year.

Last year, a teen told me he wanted to learn to study the Bible on his phone, but when I asked to look at his phone, I found that it was filled with games. I challenged him to get rid of them and to spend that time on Bible study and other profitable things. I told him that until he was willing to put aside wasteful things, he wouldn't make much progress in his spiritual life.

One young Christian lady we know became concerned about how much time she was spending on video games, and she decided to figure it up. She concluded that she was spending three months out of a year playing games! She deleted the games from her iPad and is spending that time memorizing Scripture and other profitable things.

Young people who want to find God's will must learn to be careful about time. "Redeeming the time, because the days are evil" (Ephesians 5:16). We deal with this in the section of the course on "The Youth."

Pornography

> "But I say unto you, That whosoever looketh on a woman to lust after her hath committed adultery with her already in his heart" (Mat. 5:28).

> "I made a covenant with mine eyes; why then should I think upon a maid?" (Job 31:1).

> "For the commandment *is* a lamp; and the law *is* light; and reproofs of instruction *are* the way of life: To keep thee from the evil woman, from the flattery of the tongue of a strange woman. Lust not after her beauty in thine heart; neither let her take thee with her eyelids. For by means of a whorish woman *a man is brought* to a piece of bread: and the adulteress will hunt for the precious life. Can a man take fire in his bosom, and his clothes not be burned? Can one go upon hot coals, and his feet not be burned?" (Prov. 6:23-28).

> "Hearken unto me now therefore, O ye children, and attend to the words of my mouth. Let not thine heart decline to her ways, go not astray in her paths. For she hath cast down many wounded: yea, many strong *men* have been slain by her. Her house *is* the way to hell, going down to the chambers of death" (Prov. 7:24-27).

Consider some frightful facts about pornography and the Internet:

• Pornography makes up nearly 40% of the total content on the Internet.

• Nearly 25% of Internet search queries are about pornography.

• Over 50% of boys and over 30% of girls first viewed pornography before age 13.

• A study in the UK in 2013 found that 50% of 18-year-olds have received nude pictures.

- Nearly 70% of boys and a majority of girls have seen homosexual acts online.
- Nearly 70% of young adult men and about 20% of young adult women view pornography at least once a week.
- About 55% of divorce cases involve one party having an obsessive interest in pornographic websites.

The man is visually oriented in his sexuality, which is why the Bible repeatedly warns of the man's lust of the woman's body (Job 31:1; Prov. 6:25; Mat. 5:28). Women are not naturally inclined to be so visual in their sexuality, though they can become perverted as is happening today.

The heart is a bottomless pit of evil, and pornography will carry the heart deeper and deeper into filth and perversion (Jer. 17:9).

This terrible process is described in Romans 1:21-30. Note that it begins with what is happening with the "imagination" and "heart" (verse 21) and ends with the corrupt of the "reprobate mind" (verse 28).

The only victory is complete abstinence. It requires making a covenant with one's eyes as Job did (Job 31:1).

Young people (and old) must remember that pornography will do the following and more:

- It will enslave you.
- It has the power to carry you into ever deeper and unspeakable regions of moral filth.
- It will pervert your way of looking at women and hinder your ability to have proper relationships.
- If you are single, it will ruin your chance for a truly pure marriage.
- If you are married, it will harm or even destroy your marriage.
- It will hurt your children.
- It will hurt your testimony and result in shame and disgrace.

Sexting

Sending sexy pictures of oneself by text messaging is hugely popular.

A study in the UK in 2013 found that 50% of 18-year-olds have received nude pictures.

Studies have found that many young people consider sexting mere entertainment.

> "As a criminal lawyer, I can tell you that teens (and sometimes even younger children) use the picture taking capacity of most cell phones to take and communicate vile images of themselves. The possibilities for harm are virtually endless. This is not a minor matter. ... I don't think this particular danger can be overestimated."

Snapchat is often used for this purpose. It is used by 60% of smartphone users ages 13-34. It is used to send a photo, video, or drawing that disappears in 1-10 seconds (user determined). The messages are called "snaps" and over a billion are sent daily. "It is popular for 'teasing/sexting' as teens think the pic cannot be saved. But all one has to do is take a screenshot or even a picture of the photo with another phone." There are also unofficial apps and web tools that override snapchat's deleting function. The FBI has warned that Snapchat is being used by pedophiles to lure young victims. Snapchat can also be used for video chatting.

Taking the wrong job

A major reason why young people backslide is that they disobey God and get a job that keeps them out of the church services.

Consider the following two warnings,

> "We lose about 20% of the young sometime after the seventh grade, and generally we lose them because they get jobs that make them work on Sundays. Once they get those jobs, it becomes easy for them to justify staying out of services and they generally do."

> "We have noticed that many who leave get the idea that if God gives them a job that requires them to work during services, then it is O.K. to miss services. If God gives them a job that requires wearing immodest clothes then it must be O.K. to wear immodest clothes. If God gives them a job that plays rock-n-roll music on the PA then that is O.K. They think they are strong enough to take that and keep coming to church unaffected. Usually though, within six months of getting the job they are missing 50% or more of the services and within a year, they are out of the services completely. As the Singles Director, I have stressed the fact the God has His perfect job for us and Satan has his perfect job for us.

However, most of the kids won't wait upon God to provide that perfect job."

If a young person lives by faith, he will not take a job that causes him to disobey God's Word. We tell our young people, "God has a job for you and the devil has a job for you. The devil wants you to make a hasty decision, but it is your responsibility to be wise and wait on God's will."

Consider two biblical principles that apply to employment:

First, the Bible says do not associate with evil or with idolatry (1 Co. 15:33; Ro. 12:2; 2 Co. 6:14-18; Eph. 5:11). Thus, it is not God's will for His people to take a job at a place that would require participation in evil (such as selling liquor or wearing immodest clothing or showing wicked movies or playing worldly music or worldly dancing), to participate in pagan religious rituals, etc. I recall a teenager at one church who got a job working in a movie theater. He was bothered by the unwholesome films that were showing and was thinking about quitting, but he was advised not to quit by the church's worldly youth pastor! The result was severe backsliding. I recall another young man who had a job at a restaurant-bar and was responsible to supervise worldly parties that included drinking and dancing. He did not grow spiritually until he quit that job.

Second, the Bible says do not neglect the assembly (Heb. 10:25). Thus, it is wrong to make any decision that would cause you to become unfaithful in church attendance and overall participation in church life. I recall a young man in our church that was saved out of a druggie lifestyle. He showed promise and was growing in the Lord, then his father asked him to return to his village. In spite of our counsel against it, he went, and from that point he backslid in his Christian life and has not made much spiritual progress. This kind of thing has happened many times.

Friendships with the wrong people

> "And Dinah the daughter of Leah, which she bare unto Jacob, went out to see the daughters of the land. And when Shechem the son of Hamor the Hivite, prince of the country, saw her, he took her, and lay with her, and defiled her" (Ge. 34:1-2).

"Girls need to know that boys should not be any part of their lives until they are old enough to marry. Fathers need to keep their daughters' hearts until they love Christ with all of it."

Many of the people who have written to us on this subject have shared horror stories of girls who have been enticed away from their families by men they met either by phone or texting or Facebook.

This happened to a girl in our church about three years ago. A young man started calling her on her cell phone, and at first she said that she didn't want to hear from him. Her parents and church leaders warned her against talking with him, but she refused to listen. Eventually they ran away together out of wedlock.

A Nepali girl recently told my wife her sad story. A man started calling her and wooing her. He told her that he had passed SLC (high school equivalent), had a good job, and didn't drink. Finally she ran away with him and quickly learned that he was lying about everything. He eventually left her for another woman. With a broken heart she said to my wife, "I shamed my parents; they don't want me back; I ruined my life."

A pastor friend told me about a girl who got a SIM card from another person. An unknown male called that number and started talking to her. She unwisely continued conversing with him on the phone. When she resisted, the guy threatened to commit suicide if she didn't marry him, and eventually she eloped with him.

Don't talk on the phone or Facebook, etc., with a young person of the opposite sex except relatives. Creeps are using social media to trap unsuspecting victims.

Don't make plans to meet the wrong people.

Don't hide anything you are doing from your parents and church leaders. God has given them for your protection.

Ministry Opportunities

Being busy serving the Lord is a major part of finding God's will.

Serving in the Lord's great business is an undeserved privilege and blessing.

The young people in our churches who are serving the Lord are the ones who are happy in the Lord and are growing spiritually.

Discipleship is doing, not sitting. Christ commanded that His people be taught to "observe all things," not merely to know all things (Matthew 28:19-20).

God's will is something you *do* today, not something you sit around and wait for (Ro. 12:1-8). If you do the will of God today, you will be in the will of God tomorrow.

The church must challenge the young people to serve the Lord and give them ministry opportunities while being careful to maintain high standards.

Pastor Bobby Mitchell says,

> "Many times the young people are not really involved in the ministry of the church until they are pressed to do so in their late teens. Too many are just observers and not participators. All that is expected of them is to sit and be entertained instead of training and serving. They are not taught that we exist to glorify God. Practically, they are being taught that the ministry exists to make sure that they are having fun. They are not taught to 'buy in' to the work of the ministry. Eventually, they realize that the world's entertainment is better and they look for fulfillment in getting involved in worldly groups and activities."

We have many ministries for young people and are adding new ones all the time. Some of these are the following:

- taking up offerings
- older young people reading the Bible in our main service and leading in prayer
- older young people leading the church in learning weekly memory verses
- music
- evangelism
- Sunday School
- older young people leading home prayer meetings
- deaf ministry
- the older young people leading services once month
- overseeing the church bookstore
- serving refreshments after services to encourage the unsaved to stay behind and talk about the Lord with the church members
- overseeing the sound system

But we must require high standards for service and not allow worldly, spiritually half-hearted young people to serve in ministries.

Of the young people who serve in ministries, we require the following: a good testimony of Christian living (including separation from the world and a good attitude toward parental authority), agreement with the church's doctrinal position, submission to the church's leaders, faithfulness to the services, modest dress according to the church's standards, and the gifting and ability to do the assigned ministry.

Maintaining such standards lifts up the spiritual character of the entire church.

Maintaining such standards challenges the young people to live right and do right.

Maintaining such standards separates those who are serious about serving the Lord from those who aren't.

We care about all the young people and try to minister to all of them, but we give the most attention to those who demonstrate a heart to grow. In light of Jesus' warning, I'm not interested in wasting *much* time on the lukewarm (Re. 3:16).

Consider the ministry of operating the church's sound system. I've seen a lot of worldly-looking and worldly-acting young people involved in that type of thing. I have seen young men in the sound room or sound booth talking and even playing games during services. This should not happen more than once! Where are the parents? Where are the pastors? Young people need godly oversight. The Bible warns that "a child left to himself brings his mother to shame" (Pr. 29:15), and a young teenager is still a child in a biblical sense.

Children, too, can serve the Lord.

> "Children need to be involved in the work of the church, with their parents being the leading examples of that. Three of my six children are born again. My oldest works in the nursery twice a month and has started a neighborhood Bible study for girls. My other two (a son age 10 and a daughter age seven), are intending to join the choir, and my seven-year-old works in the nursery once a month. When we show our children they have a place in the work of God's kingdom, then they

will gladly seek out the work the Lord has ordained for them to do."

"We have had children as young as two years old dusting the pews when it is their family's turn to clean the church. When we had a remodeling program, the Sunday School room section was the children's responsibility. Yes, it took extra work, but it was worth it. Their offering paid for the fan lights, the paint, the insulation, and the linoleum. One little guy had to be held on the ladder so he wouldn't fall off while he painted 'his' wall. Some of the carpeting and the linoleum were laid by a 14-year-old kid. Our son was taught at that time as a 17-year-old how to install the electric lights, and another young man learned how to put the windows in, etc. The children start helping with our Scripture printing ministry when they turn four. Our granddaughter got sick the night before her birthday because she had waited so long to be four so she could tear apart the Scripture Portion sections, and now the time was finally here and she was sooooo excited."

Children need to be trained to pay attention during the services instead of playing. As soon as they can read, they can join in with the congregational singing. Though they are not yet saved, they need to learn to show honor to God during the services. They can even be taught to take notes of the sermon and discuss it later with their parents.

Children will be children, and they should not be made to hate church because the adults are overbearing and lacking in grace and joy, but they can still learn many things at their age level if they are taught to do so.

I think of a young lady who made her Sunday School class sit facing the wall and not talk during the rest of her class because some of them had acted up. We believe in discipline, but that is not the way to encourage children to love Sunday School!

We must be compassionate, of course, as well as strong for righteousness and truth. This is God's character. If the young people aren't convinced that the preachers love them, they probably will not respond positively to the preaching and standards.

We love our young people and go after them when they are slipping spiritually. We do whatever we can to help them.

When one young man in the church family got addicted to sniffing glue and using other drugs, church folk visited him. Other young men rallied around him. They prayed for him. They got him a job and helped to oversee his daily activities. They were patient with him when he backslid.

When a young man stopped attending mid-week prayer meeting because of his focus on school, we met with him repeatedly. We exhorted him. We prayed with him. We offered to go to his school and talk to the principal to try to get permission for him to leave school early on Wednesdays. But we did not back down from maintaining the church's standards for ministry. When we saw that he was going to put school before God and that he didn't want us to try to get permission for him to leave early, we took away his music ministry. Later he became obedient again and was restored to that ministry and has been faithful and growing ever since.

We have had families join our church specifically because they have seen God's blessing on our youth and have wanted help with theirs. They didn't come to our church for fun and games, but for serious discipleship.

Youth Discipling Youth

An important part of a youth ministry is youth discipling youth.

We are preparing to start a youth discipling youth ministry.

The discipling material is part of the *One Year Discipleship Course*. We have taken several of the 52 lessons from this course.

The plan is that the mature youth will disciple new believers. A teacher will be assigned to one individual and will be responsible for arranging a weekly meeting with that individual for the purpose of going through the material.

By this means close personal attention can be given to each new convert and he or she can be grounded in some basic Bible doctrines and practices.

It gives our young people an opportunity to teach and to grow thereby. The best way to learn is to teach. You learn at a deeper level when you try to teach what you are learning to others.

The teachers are encouraged not just to teach the material but to interact with the student, to find out what he or she is understanding, to answer questions.

This has the potential to develop friends in Christ who spend their time building one another up, talking about the things of God rather than worldly things.

Living by Faith

The church must teach the young people *to live by faith* (Mt. 6:33).

Living by faith is living in obedience to God's Word. It means that I don't do anything that will contradict God's Word, and I won't do anything that interferes with or hinders God's business and God's will.

This is something we emphasize continually. Every major decision must be made by faith rather than by sight. It must be made by seeking God's mind rather than leaning to one's own understanding (Pr. 3:5-6).

Living by faith involves choosing the right friends, the right education, the right job. These decisions must be made in obedience to God's Word. The young person must make the right decision and then trust God to take care of him.

Many young people in Nepal go overseas to work, but we teach our young people to weigh this decision by God's Word rather than strictly by monetary concerns or by pressure from their families. Some of the biblical precepts that discourage this practice are as follows: (1) The importance of church and spiritual fellowship (1 Ti. 3:15). Most of the places where the young people go to work don't have a good Nepali-language church. (2) The danger of evil communications (1 Co. 15:33). Typically in overseas work, the young people are thrown together in close living conditions with unsaved people in a worldly environment. (3) Marital responsibilities (1 Co. 7:3-5; Eph. 6:4). It is impossible for a man to fulfill his God-given responsibilities to his family if he is living in another country. (4) Christ's Great Commission (Mt. 28:19-20). There is freedom for preaching the gospel in Nepal today for the first time in known history, and the need for workers is great. Every Christian young person who goes overseas is one less worker in the great harvest field of Nepal. It is possible to witness to Nepalis who are living overseas, of course, but in our experience they are not as open to the gospel as those who are living in Nepal. The need of Nepal is for sound churches to be established, and that cannot be done if a large portion of the potential workers go to other places.

Young people must choose a job based on God's will and faith. The job must not be the type of job that would cause them to backslide because of a worldly environment. I think of a young man who got a job in a movie theater. He was even encouraged to do so by his worldly youth pastor. The immoral environment caused him to backslide, just as God's Word warns (1 Co. 15:33).

Young people must choose education based on God's perfect will and by faith in God's Word. Some of the young people who have attended our Bible College left secular college to do so. That was a big step, because the society and most families emphasize secular education and pursuing money and prestige. But these young people wanted to learn God's Word and prepare for the Lord's service more than they wanted the things of the world.

One young man was pressured by his father to be educated as an engineer so he could make a lot of money and pay off the huge family debts. When the young man was called of God to preach and began to entertain the thought of attending Bible College, his father was very angry and tried to force him to give up that idea. The young man was confused and undecided. Even when it came time to make the final decision about Bible College, he was faltering in the decision. I told him to read Luke 9:60. "Jesus said unto him, Let the dead bury their dead: but go thou and preach the kingdom of God." This doesn't mean that the child of God is to harden his heart against his parents and dishonor them; it means simply that when God has called you to His service, you must not allow anything to interfere, even your closest relatives. I said to him, "This is a situation in which you must let the dead bury the dead." He took the step of faith and joined the Bible College and has been a tremendous blessing to many.

Every major decision must be made in light of God's Word and living by faith. Many years ago I met a young man in a Bible college in Singapore who was a chess champion. After the Lord called had him to preach and led him to pursue full-time training, he was offered a part-time job writing a chess column for a newspaper. He thought it would be a good way to help support himself, but he found that he couldn't get the chess moves out of his mind. Chess was choking the Word of God. He wisely cut off this activity so that he could meditate effectively upon the Scripture and the things of God.

If the young person obeys God and puts God first, God will always take care of him. It is far more likely that the sun will stop shining tomorrow than that God will fail to take care of those who honor Him.

Walking in Vigilance

The church must teach the young people to walk in vigilance (1 Peter. 5:8).

The young people need to get a worldview that this is a dark world filled with spiritual and moral danger, and the child of God must walk vigilantly.

Both young women and young men are exhorted to be sober (Titus 2:4, 6). This means to be in control of one's mind and life with the goal of protecting oneself from danger and obeying the Lord in all things. Soberness refers to spiritual alertness; seriousness of purpose; prudence; temperance. It is the opposite of being under the control of alcohol or drugs or anything other than God's Spirit. A person can be drunk on pop music, fashion, worldly fads, dating and "puppy love," and many other things, but the sober person will refuse this. Soberness means to test everything by God's Word. It is the opposite of being "simple," which means to be gullible (Pr. 14:15).

Spiritual alertness should permeate the believer's life.

I am thankful for the teachers who taught me to walk in soberness in my Christian life. The man who led me to Christ taught me this, as did the first church I joined. They taught me to love God's Word and to test everything by it.

Finding a Marriage Partner

The young people need to be taught how to find the right marriage partner in God's will.

Our church spends a lot of effort in this, because godly matches in marriage are so very important for the future of the Lord's work. Following are some fundamental Biblical principles toward this end:

Preparation (Pr. 24:27). A good marriage requires that young people prepare their lives by a know-so salvation, by moral purity, by learning God's Word, by spiritual growth, and by learning the basics of family life. The best time to learn about how to build a Christian home is before marriage. The preparation should be done by the church and by the home. The young person needs to build true Christian character by walking with Christ so that he or she will be ready for marriage.

Respect for authority and good counsel (Pr. 20:18; Eph. 6:1-3; Heb. 13:17). We teach our young people not to depend on themselves in regard to finding the right mate but to seek help from authority figures: the parents (particularly saved parents) and church leaders and other mature and godly adults. Wise young people will lean heavily on the counsel of such people. This is the opposite of the world's way whereby young people seek to find a mate by dating and chance, which often ends up in moral shipwreck.

The traditional Jewish practice is for parents, rabbis, and other qualified matchmakers to help the young people choose a spouse. "They very carefully look at compatibility--it is not left to chance. They do their homework on their characteristics, their values, morals and life goals" ("Marriage: Can Messianics Learn from Orthodox Jews?" *Israel Today*, Nov. 2016). The matchmakers propose a *"shidduch* date," which is an opportunity for the couple to talk and get to know one another, and they decide then whether to continue meeting. If they determine to continue, they have more dates until they decide whether or not to get married. The marriages are not "arranged" in the sense of force, because each individual makes the final choice of whether or not to marry. Such marriages are arranged only in the sense that the man and woman desire help from and invite help from older and more mature authority figures. After 35 years of study, Robert Epstein of the American Institute for Behavioral Research and Technology found that "arranged marriages are far more likely to lead to lasting affection than marriages of passion. Those who have had their partner chosen for them by a parent or matchmaker tend to feel more in love with time, whereas those in typical marriages often feel less in love over time" (Ibid.). This is because "those who marry for 'love' are often blinded by passion, and when the pressures and unavoidable challenges of family life crop up, they crumble."

Not dating but courtship. The dating culture is an invention of the rock & roll culture. It forces young people to encounter temptations they are not ready to face and to make decisions on their own they are not capable of making. The biblical pattern is courtship under close parental and pastoral supervision. There is no list of absolute laws for courtship, but some of the basics are as follows: (1) The young people are under the supervision of spiritual authorities and are in submission to those authorities. (2) They do not spend time alone together. (3) They do not touch until the wedding (Pr. 6:27). The closer the wedding comes the more potential there is for a couple to let down their moral guard. (4) There must be no pressure or manipulation by any party. The goal is to know God's will, not to make something happen at man's hands. The girl, especially, should be protected from making a purely emotional decision. I think of a young woman who is a pastor's wife today. When the young man who is now her husband began to show interest, she understood that her heart was easily moved just by his attention. She slowed down the process and drew close to the Lord in order to remain sober minded so that God would be in control rather than her emotions. There are no set rules to courtship, as each situation is different; the elders set the rules and the young people obey. For example, the elders might say that all communication must be done at first through a father or pastor and not directly between the young man and woman. This is for protection. If the Lord gives peace to all parties, the young people can communicate more directly.

Agreement (Amos 3:3; 2 Co. 6:14). It is not God's will for a believer to marry an unbeliever or someone of another religion or a different Christian faith. This is confusion. It is impossible to raise children properly in a divided home. Likewise, for the zealous believer to marry a lukewarm one or for a believer with a vision of reaching the world for Christ to marry someone lacking this vision is confusion. Usually what happens is that the lukewarm and the lack of vision dominates the relationship and pulls the other party down spiritually.

Peace as opposed to confusion (1 Co. 14:33; Col. 3:15; 2 Th. 3:16; Jas. 3:13-18). God's will is the way of peace and righteousness, whereas the devil's will is the way of confusion and sin. A major principle of finding God's will is to seek peace. Among our young people, we have seen God's will done as well as the devil's will. I think of one promising young man and young woman. The young lady received Christ in her early teens, and though her unsaved family persecuted her, she was faithful to the Lord. A young preacher, who showed promise got his eyes on the young lady and began to call her and meet her. When her parents and the church leaders found out about it, they were unanimous that it was not God's will. Both the parents and the church leaders exhorted and warned the young couple to break off the relationship. They pretended to agree, but they continued to talk and meet in secret. The relationship had an immediate negative effect on their spiritual lives, resulting in deception and rebellion toward authority. Finally, they ran off together. They refused to repent before the church. They have not done anything in the Lord's service since then, and they have a poor testimony before believers and unbelievers to this day. In contrast, another young man and woman prepared their lives and waited on the Lord. They leaned on the counsel of their church leaders. When the leaders recommended the young lady to the young man, he prayed about it and agreed that it was the Lord's will. The young lady did likewise. Both sets of parents were 100% supportive. (The parents are believers.) The church was 100% supportive. Everyone had peace, and there was no confusion. Their lovely wedding was a powerful testimony to believers and unbelievers alike of the beauty of waiting for God's will.

Patience (Ro. 8:24-25; Heb. 10:36; Jas. 1:3-4). *Patience* is mentioned 46 times in the New Testament. It is a fundamental part of Christian living. It is a fundamental part of living by faith. God doesn't act according to our human time table, and we must wait on Him. Contrast King Saul, who sinned and lost his position because of his impatience (1 Sa. 13:8-14). Likewise, a great many young people have missed God's will by being impatient in major decisions such as friends, employment, education, and marriage, instead of trusting God and waiting until His will is clear. Patience means the young person will not try to manipulate circumstances like tricky Jacob or Sarah (in the matter of Hagar) or Rebekah (in the matter of deceiving Isaac).

Parents Serving the Lord with their Children

Parents should serve the Lord with their children.

Discipling children and youth requires spending time with them.

Many times I have suggested to preachers that they serve the Lord with their children. I am not talking about playing with the children. I am talking about serving the Lord with them: taking the children with you on visitation, etc.

When I see a preacher who has his sons with him and who has his sons' hearts so that they are with him of their own free will and enjoying themselves, I know that those sons will probably follow in their father's faith in Christ.

Paul Pinkerton of Madison, Alabama:

> "My idea was to be an example and to take them with me as I served the Lord. When I worked in the bus ministry and Sunday School and children's church, I took the kids with me and had them involved. They actually participated in these ministries by leading songs and doing Bible stories and other ways. We wanted them to be able to continue on after they left our home. So many seem to disappear after high school, but I didn't want that for my kids. The best way I could see to do that was to be an example before them and teach them the Scriptures and teach them to serve the Lord. It's not a secret. It's there in the Scriptures, and it has worked out for us real well."

Bob Nichols, missionary to Brazil, says:

> "We always involved our children in the work of the Lord. I try to lead my family to memorize 14 verses a month. We'll go over the verses as a family, and what a tremendous help that's been. Now in Brazil, our church memorizes 10 verses a month, and we try to coordinate the two programs. Our children are always in the work with us. Wherever I go I take them. They play musical instruments and know music. They

go when we preach and when we go soul winning. They're involved in AWANA and discipleship. We try to get them involved in everything. I have had all my boys go through our Bible institute in Brazil, and they've had to go through a discipleship program where they learn to win souls. After they win a soul they are responsible to disciple that person and help them grow in the Lord. All my boys have led music in church. As a matter of fact, our church is set up where on Sunday morning we have a 15 minute time during which the young men can sign up to preach or give a devotion from the Bible. It helps them develop their preaching skills and learn to stand before others. Then we have another young man who leads the congregational music each week. The front row in our church is where we have the young people come and play the guitar. We always have some who are learning to play music, both guitar and piano. Then as the boys got older we gave them more responsibilities. We take missions trips up in the mountains and they are responsible to preach and do door-to-door visitation up there. Then I give the responsibility on a rotating basis each year to my preacher boys to organize a camp during carnival season. I give the young men the responsibility to organize the camp, so that helps develop their skills. They get an appreciation of the planning and all that is involved. They have to program the events of each day, the Bible times, the speakers, the games. They have to order the food and everything. Giving my boys responsibilities like this has helped prepare them for life."

Children and young people need to be mentored by adults. One parent wrote,

"Children seem to be always separated from adults, but they need to be included with them and mentored alongside of them. I have done this with my kids since they were in elementary school and it has been extremely profitable. Church and serving the Lord has always been part of their lives and they always want to go. The more opportunities children have at practicing their faith, the more likely they are to stay with their faith and church."

Youth and the Church Services

Young people must be taught how to act in church services and how to listen to the preaching. Like everything else in the church, this is a matter of proper training.

The following things should be taught to all of the people, but there is a special application of these principles to young people:

1. Sit respectfully and alertly

Things such as leaning on your elbows with your head down and chewing gum send signals that you are not interested in what the preacher is saying. Remember that others are watching you and being influenced by you. Your attitude and bodily posture affects the preacher, those sitting around you, and the entire atmosphere of the service.

Young people should not be allowed to sit together unless they are spiritually-minded and serious about seeking the Lord, because they will distract one another as well as others. We have many spiritually-minded young people in our church who sit together and encourage one another to listen carefully and to take notes from the preaching, but when young people are only in church because they are forced to be there and don't have a heart for the truth, they should not be allowed to sit together. This is for their sake, for the sake of the other young people who are influenced by their example, and for the sake of the entire congregation.

One reader wrote about teenage boys who sit together and play a video game during the service. "As one plays, the boy on either side watches until it is his turn."

Another reader described two young men who played video games on their phones the entire service, even when the congregation was standing and singing. The father of these young men was in the service and sitting on the same pew, but he didn't do anything about the matter.

This is a sad thing, and one wonders about the parents. In the case of a parent who would sit in a church service and allow his children to play games, where is his head! God has given the father the job of bringing up his children in the nurture and admonition of the Lord (Eph. 6:4), but many are like Eli who honored his sons more than God and God's Word (1 Sa. 2:29; 3:13).

And why doesn't the pastor put a stop to this type of thing? What kind of pastor would allow people to play games in the house of God when the congregation is supposedly worshiping God? For a pastor to allow such a thing is not fair to those who are there to worship God and hear His Word. Such a thing is a great dishonor to Jesus Christ who owns the church and walks in the midst of the churches (Re. 2:1). Who does this pastor really honor? Who does he fear?

The adults might be afraid of "losing them" if they apply discipline to their young people, but the fact is that they have "lost them" already. The bodies of such young people might still be in church, but their hearts are solidly in the world.

At least the adults can break up this unholy cabal and make the service conducive for *others* to hear God's Word without the distraction of these foolish boys and their games. And who knows, if this cabal were broken up and these young people were required to sit quietly during the singing and preaching, God might get hold of their hearts and they might repent of their disrespect of holy things and be born again before it is too late.

Along this line, the church must make sure that young people are not hiding out somewhere and playing. I have seen young men in the sound room and sound booth talking and playing games during the services. Only spiritually-minded young people should be involved in such ministries. Otherwise, this is the type of thing that happens.

2. Don't distract others

Examples of things that distract others are talking and writing notes back and forth between persons, texting, and playing video games, making noise (i.e., cracking your fingers, stretching and moaning), picnicking (eating and drinking and passing around candy and gum), playing with babies, children gawking at the people behind them, and children running back and forth in the pew when the congregation stands to sing. Parents need to be aware of what their children are doing and make certain that they are not distracting someone.

Another example is leaving the service to go to the restroom. Parents should make sure that their children don't develop this distracting habit. The child quickly learns that it can control the mother by asking to go to the restroom after the service starts. It is the all-too-common case of the child training the parent. This practice is extremely dishonoring to the Word of God being preached. There is plenty of time to go to the bathroom before and after the services. Of course, if a baby is involved or if an individual has a medical or health problem that requires him or her to leave the service, that is a different matter altogether. But such a person should sit in the back and slip in and out quietly.

One reader wrote, "Some families spread the pew with mounds of candy and other snacks, sticky and otherwise, and the children gorge themselves. Then of course, it's not long before parent or grandparent will take each child, one at a time, back and forth to the restroom to wash sticky hands, etc. And no, they do not sit in the back."

One reader gave the following feedback after reading an earlier edition of this report:

> "The section regarding 'Don't Distract Others' really hit home to me. I prefer to sit up front 'near the action'; however, because of my work, I am on call 24 hours a day, 7 days a week, and there are occasional calls on Sundays, so I sit at the back so that I may slip out should I receive a call. However, I have seen others that sit near the front and walk all the way to the back for one reason or the other, and, upon their return, walk all the way back to the front. It is human custom to watch movement. I have tried my best to train myself to pay attention to the preaching and to not be distracted by people moving around. When I was young, we were taught that in any group, if one had to leave, one sits near the back, and even if one is sitting up front and needs to leave, upon returning, a seat should be taken in the back. I don't know why people aren't taught this (rather basic) group courtesy."

3. Listen well

LISTEN WITH COMPASSION TOWARD THE PREACHER. God uses all kinds of men and not all are dynamic, fascinating speakers. It appears that Paul wasn't (2 Co. 10:10). Jonathan Edwards preached one of the most famous sermons of church history, "Sinners in the Hands of an Angry God," but Edwards was not a great speaker. In fact, he simply read the sermon. The preacher who was instrumental in the conversion of Charles

Spurgeon was not a mighty speaker. Spurgeon described him as a very simple, uninteresting speaker, yet how greatly God used him! Remember that God can use weak men. An example is Solomon. He had some serious issues, but God used him to write three important books of the Bible, including the book of Proverbs, which is the book of wisdom. Our eyes must be upon God and not upon the preacher. Listen to the preacher as you would want people to listen to you. Avoid a critical attitude.

LISTEN PRAYERFULLY. Nothing significant is accomplished apart from prayer (Ro. 12:12; Eph. 6:18; Col. 4:2; 1 Th. 5:17). Pray for yourself. Pray for the preacher. Pray for others who are in attendance.

LISTEN ATTENTIVELY. Listen as if Jesus Christ Himself were speaking. The preacher is to preach as the oracles of God (God's mouthpiece), and the people should listen to him as the oracles of God (1 Pe. 4:11). If you listen carefully and seek something from the Lord, you can be edified even from a seemingly boring message. See also Luke 8:18; Revelation 2:7, 11, 17, 29; 3:6, 13, 22. Lazy minds don't learn and grow. Don't let your mind wander to other things. Don't do something else when you should be listening to the preaching. I have seen people read novels in church! More often they read the hymnal or pass notes or other such things. You won't get anything from the preaching if you don't listen attentively.

LISTEN WITH AN OPEN, SUBMISSIVE HEART. God's invitation is extended throughout the message and not merely at the end. Let God speak to you, reprove, rebuke, and exhort you. Don't think that the preaching is for someone else. Don't make excuses for your sins and faults.

LISTEN WITH FAITH (Heb. 4:1-2). The Word of God is ineffective unless it is "mixed with faith." Some listen to preaching as a form of entertainment. They enjoy it but they don't believe it enough to change how they live. This was how the Jews were listening to the prophet Ezekiel: "And they come unto thee as the people cometh, and they sit before thee as my people, and they hear thy words, but they will not do them: for with their mouth they shew much love, but their heart goeth after their covetousness. And, lo, thou art unto them as a very lovely song of one that hath a pleasant voice, and can play well on an instrument: for they hear thy words, but they do them not" (Eze. 33:31-32).

LISTEN DISCERNINGLY. The Bible warns that we must not put our trust in man (Jer. 17:5). We must carefully test all preaching by the Word of God (Acts 17:11; 1 Co. 14:29; 1 Th. 5:21).

LISTEN STUDIOUSLY (2 Ti. 2:15). Have paper and pen ready so that you can capture something from the message. Write things in your Bible (important things, such as cross references, definitions, important thoughts, what God is saying to you through the message). By the way, you should have your own Bible rather than merely looking on with someone else. Take notes of the important points. Write down things to study later, things to check later, and things to share with others. This will help you remember what is preached. If you are studious during the preaching, you will be a good example to others. I remember with fondness a young man in the first church I joined. He was always there in his place with his big study Bible and his notebook and his pens and pencils, ready to capture something from the preaching.

4. Treat the invitation seriously

Respond to the invitation as the Lord leads, and pray for others.

It is important to be quiet until the last prayer is finished. Some people are so spiritually insensitive that they start preparing to leave during the invitation and final prayer, shuffling around, folding papers, zipping up Bible cases, putting on jackets, digging keys out of purses, etc. This is very distracting to those to whom the Lord might be ministering.

Suggested Materials for Youth Discipleship

The following materials are available from Way of Life Literature, P.O. Box 610368, Port Huron, MI 48061, 866-295-4143, fbns@wayoflife.org, www.wayoflife.org; in Canada contact 4212 Campbell St. N., London, Ont. N6P 1A6, 519-652-2619

Proverbs (Advanced Bible Studies Series course)
Baptist Music Wars
Believer's Bible Dictionary
Bible Times and Ancient Kingdoms
Directory of Contemporary Worship Music

Holiness: Pitfalls, Struggles, Victory
Judge Not: Is It Legalism to Judge Sin and Error?
Keeping the Kids
The Mobile Phone and the Christian Home and Church
Music for Good or Evil (a series of eight video presentations)
One-Year Discipleship Course
Sowing and Reaping: A Course in Evangelism
An Unshakeable Faith: A Christian Apologetics Course
The Way of Life Encyclopedia of the Bible & Christianity
What Every Christian Should Know about Rock Music

A Discipling Church Has a Vision for Evangelism and World Missions

Outline
The Scriptural Emphasis
An Independent Baptist Vision
An Example of That Vision

The heart of the Lord's Great Commission is evangelism and missionary church planting.

Building and maintaining passion for this great work is a major part of a discipling church.

It puts a vision before the people of what God is doing today and encourages them to find their part in this great business.

In a church that is zealous for Christ's Great Commission and makes this a major, major priority--other things being right-- young people tend to surrender to God's calling of "full time ministry." It is God, and not churches, that calls individual young people to be preachers and missionaries and church leaders and pastor's wives, but God does this through the vision of His work being kept before the people.

The Scriptural Emphasis

This is the commandment that Christ emphasized to His disciples after He rose from the dead.

See Matthew 28:18-20; Mark 16:15; Luke 24:48; John 20:21; Acts 1:8; 2 Corinthians 5:20; Philippians 2:16.

This Commission is in effect until the end of the age ("lo, I am with you alway, even unto the end of the world," Mt. 28:20).

This Commission is the theme of the book of Acts.

This Commission is at the heart of Christian discipleship.

This Commission is the purpose for which Christ came (Luke 19:10). Christ died that men might be saved, and His death does not benefit men unless they hear the gospel, which is the power of God unto salvation to those who believe (Luke 24:46-47).

Thus, Christ commanded that the gospel be preached to every person in every nation, and He commanded that those who believe should be baptized and taught to "observe all things whatsoever I have taught you" (Mt. 28:19).

We see in the book of Acts and the epistles that this requires the establishing of sound churches which are the pillar and ground of the truth (Acts 14:23; 1 Timothy 3:15; Titus 1:5).

This is a BIG task that requires a lot of workers, and one of the church's chief jobs is to pray for and train workers for this great harvest.

An Independent Baptist Vision

One of the things that attracted me to Independent Baptist churches as a new Christian in 1973 was the evangelistic, missionary, church-planting zeal: every member being trained for and encouraged to be an ambassador for Christ (2 Co. 5:20); training and sending out missionaries; supporting missionaries directly; meeting missionaries personally; reading their prayer letters and praying for them specifically.

Growing up in the Southern Baptist Convention, I had never met a real missionary that I can recall. And the missionaries we learned about were dead ones like Lottie Moon.

In contrast, Highland Park Baptist Church in Chattanooga, Tennessee, trained and sent out missionaries, gave half of its budget to missions and held massive annual missionary conferences attended by "real" missionaries who testified of the miracles God was performing in lives around the world. This Great Commission vision was one of the chief reasons why Highland Park left the Southern Baptist Convention.

A large Great Commission vision was typical of Independent Baptists of that day.

The first church I joined was small and young and still meeting in a storefront building, but it had a Great Commission vision, and many of the young people surrendered to God's will and trained for His service.

Aggressive evangelism (not shallow Quick Prayerism but biblical evangelism) and church planting keeps spiritual excitement alive in the congregation. It gives a forward-looking vision. It produces new converts to disciple.

An Example of That Vision

The missionary vision is gradually dying among Independent Baptists. Fewer men and women are surrendering, fewer are training, fewer are going to foreign lands to live, fewer new churches are being planted.

And the evangelistic missionary vision in many Independent Baptist churches even in the "heyday" was corrupted by such things as shallow evangelistic methodologies, spiritual and biblical shallowness,

But in our ministry we continue to major on Christ's Great Commission, and we have found that this is something that God greatly blesses. It only stands to reason that God will bless a church that makes a big deal of the things that God loves.

Our people think that aggressive evangelism and church planting are normal!

We keep this fire burning in all sorts of ways: by making it a constant emphasis in every part of the preaching and teaching ministry, by making it a part of our basic discipleship course, by making it a major emphasis of youth discipleship and the youth conferences, by annual missions conferences that challenge the people and impart a fresh and larger vision, by focusing on personal evangelism and leading the people and organizing the people in this work locally, by seeking to reach every person in our entire area with the gospel, by Friend's Days that are geared to evangelism, and by ongoing gospel works in a couple of dozen towns and villages.

We exhort the people and train the people and lead them. We challenge our young people to surrender their lives to Christ's Commission and to find their place in this "program."

I am convinced that a church that is doing its business correctly will see young people dedicate themselves to this task. I believe, in fact, that this is an important measure of a church's spiritual temperature.

Else, why would Christ say, "The harvest truly is great, but the labourers are few: pray ye therefore the Lord of the harvest, that he would send forth labourers into his harvest" (Luke 10:2)?

We have seen the answer to this prayer in our work. Several years ago we started having a young man during our main weekly service to lead the church in prayer that the Lord would raise up labourers for His harvest, and ever since then we have had an increasing number of young people dedicate themselves for this work and desire to train for this work. They want to attend Bible college rather than secular college, though our Bible college has no accreditation and is not a path to any type of secular job. Currently we have 13 young preachers in our church!

This is in contrast to the young people in a great many churches who haven't surrendered to God's will. They are seeking a comfortable life. They want money and prestige. They aren't planning their lives as pilgrims in a strange world but as citizens of this present world.

This is a major emphasis of our ministry to the youth. We want them to find their places in the Lord's great harvest. God is in charge of giving gifts and callings, and He doesn't call every person to be a preacher or missionary, etc., but finding my place in God's calling begins with *unconditional surrender* to His perfect will (Romans 12:1-2). It requires that the child of God surrender to Him and get busy serving Him, and the Lord then leads that individual step by step in His will.

We started a Bible college for the purpose of training laborers for God's harvest. When we started praying earnestly for the Lord to raise up workers for His harvest and the Lord began answering that in the lives of our young people, we knew that we had to train them properly in a full-time setting.

We train and challenge the parents to have a spiritual vision for their children's earthly lives rather than a worldly vision. The parents can't call their children; that is God's business. But parents can live the example before their children of putting God first and living for Him and pursuing His will. And parents can disciple their children and urge them to surrender to God's perfect will, wherever that leads.

We deal with this in the chapter "The Discipling Church Builds Godly Homes."

We seek to prepare young people for marriage and to help them find mates in God's will who are likeminded in the work of the Lord. So many times we have heard of a young person who had a vision for doing God's will in missions but he or she married someone who lacked that vision. Almost invariably, the result is the death of the spiritual vision. (We deal with this in the chapter "A Discipling Church Disciples Youth.")

Suggested materials on evangelism and world missions from Way of Life Literature:

Acts

Sowing and Reaping: A Course in Evangelism

A Discipling Church Has a First Love for Christ

Outline

Consider that the Believer is Part of Christ's Bride
Consider Christ's Warning to the Church at Ephesus
Consider the Crucified Life

Love for God is the first commandment. It is man's chief purpose. It is what God intended when He made man. This command is repeated ten times in Scripture, beginning with the following:

> "And thou shalt love the LORD thy God with all thine heart, and with all thy soul, and with all thy might" (De. 6:5).

Adam rebelled against his loving Creator, but God's plan was to make Christ the head of a new creation as the second man or last Adam (1 Co. 15:45-47). Christ is the man who loves God with all his heart, soul, and might. He is the man who delights continually in the Father and who lived only to please the Father. God's plan is that every believer be conformed to Christ's image. He is the firstborn among many brethren (Ro. 8:29).

First love was what God wanted from Israel.

> "And now, Israel, what doth the LORD thy God require of thee, but to fear the LORD thy God, to walk in all his ways, and to love him, and to serve the LORD thy God with all thy heart and with all thy soul" (De. 10:12).

But Israel did not love God. She rebelled against Him and forgot Him and followed false gods.

> "Go and cry in the ears of Jerusalem, saying, Thus saith the LORD; I remember thee, the kindness of thy youth, the love of thine espousals, when thou wentest after me in the wilderness, in a land *that was* not sown. Israel *was* holiness unto the LORD, *and* the firstfruits of his increase: all that devour him shall offend; evil shall come upon them, saith the LORD. Hear ye the word of the LORD, O house of Jacob, and

all the families of the house of Israel: Thus saith the LORD, What iniquity have your fathers found in me, that they are gone far from me, and have walked after vanity, and are become vain? Neither said they, Where *is* the LORD that brought us up out of the land of Egypt, that led us through the wilderness, through a land of deserts and of pits, through a land of drought, and of the shadow of death, through a land that no man passed through, and where no man dwelt? And I brought you into a plentiful country, to eat the fruit thereof and the goodness thereof; but when ye entered, ye defiled my land, and made mine heritage an abomination. The priests said not, Where *is* the LORD? and they that handle the law knew me not: the pastors also transgressed against me, and the prophets prophesied by Baal, and walked after *things that do not profit*" (Jeremiah 2:2-8).

For this reason, Israel was judged. Her temple was destroyed and she was evicted from her land and scattered to the ends of the earth. Instead of being the head of the nations, she became the tail. She was put under the rule of the Gentiles.

God has preserved Israel, and the time is coming when a remnant will repent of their great sin against God and will be converted and love God forever. This is described by the prophet Hosea as follows:

> "And it shall be at that day, saith the LORD, *that* thou shalt call me Ishi; and shalt call me no more Baali. For I will take away the names of Baalim out of her mouth, and they shall no more be remembered by their name. And in that day will I make a covenant for them with the beasts of the field, and with the fowls of heaven, and *with* the creeping things of the ground: and I will break the bow and the sword and the battle out of the earth, and will make them to lie down safely. And I will betroth thee unto me for ever; yea, I will betroth thee unto me in righteousness, and in judgment, and in lovingkindness, and in mercies. I will even betroth thee unto me in faithfulness: and thou shalt know the LORD" (Hos. 2:16-20).

Israel will call the Lord Jehovah *Ishi*, My husband, and will no longer commit spiritual adultery with false gods like Baal.

While Israel is "put aside," so to speak, God is calling out a people for His name among the Gentiles and building the church as the firstfruits of Christ's new creation.

The relationship between Christ and the church is a relationship of intimate love. It is the restoration of man to the position wherein he loves God with all his heart, soul, and strength.

The church as an entity, and each individual member thereof is the object of Christ's infinite love.

The Christian life is an intimate love relationship with God in Christ. That is the heart and soul and essence of salvation.

Consider the Crucified Life

We see this in Galatians 2:20.

> "I am crucified with Christ: nevertheless I live; yet not I, but Christ liveth in me: and the life which I now live in the flesh I live by the faith of the Son of God, who loved me, and gave himself for me" (Ga. 2:20).

Paul is talking about a relationship of passionate love, first love. A more intimate relationship cannot be imagined, and it is a relationship of love "(who loved me")".

The Christian life is Christ in me. A more intimate relationship cannot be imagined.

It is an intimate relationship of tender love "(who loved me, and gave himself for me")". Christ's incarnation was an act of love. He came willingly and died willingly. It was a choice that He made, and it was a choice that was motivated by love.

Not only does Christ redeem the sinner by His blood, but He actually comes into the redeemed sinner's life to live with him as one and to live His life in that individual.

This is true salvation, and it is an eternal relationship of love, being loved by God and loving God in return. "We love him, because he first loved us" (1 John 4:19).

Consider the Love of the Father and Son

> "21 **He that hath my commandments, and keepeth them, he it is that loveth me: and he that loveth me shall be loved of my Father, and I will love him, and will manifest myself to**

him. 22 Judas saith unto him, not Iscariot, Lord, how is it that thou wilt manifest thyself unto us, and not unto the world? 23 Jesus answered and said unto him, If a man love me, he will keep my words: and my Father will love him, and we will come unto him, and make our abode with him. 24 He that loveth me not keepeth not my sayings: and the word which ye hear is not mine, but the Father's which sent me. 25 These things have I spoken unto you, being *yet* present with you. 26 But the Comforter, *which is* the Holy Ghost, whom the Father will send in my name, he shall teach you all things, and bring all things to your remembrance, whatsoever I have said unto you" (John 14:21-26).

Here we see the evidence of the true believer, which is obedience. This is repeated in verses 21, 23, and 24. This is the strongest emphasis on evidentiary salvation from the lips of Christ Himself. The word of the Almighty Father God is that if an individual loves Christ, that individual *will* keep His words, and this is the individual who is loved of the Father and Son. In other words, this is the individual who is saved.

To say that someone is saved who does not love Christ and does not, therefore, obey His words is to deny the plain teaching of Scripture. Yet I have heard many say this. Once I was talking with a missionary to London, England, who told me that he was seeing many people won to Christ in his street ministry. When I inquired about his church services, he said that not many of those people showed up, and when I commented that if people were truly saved they would want to hear God's Word, he replied, "You can't tell who is saved." Christ exposed that as a lie.

Note that a person must have Christ's words before he can obey them (Joh. 14:21). This is why Christ commanded that the gospel be preached to every person. Saving faith is communicated *by* the Word of God (Romans 10:17), not *without* the Word of God. It doesn't come by dreams and visions. It can't be found through yogic meditation.

Having Christ's words is not merely a matter of possessing a gospel tract or a New Testament or a whole Bible. It is a matter of receiving Christ's words into one's heart and treasuring those words. This is saving faith.

We also see the believer's intimacy with God. Having identified the true believer, Christ describes the believer's amazing relationship with God. The believer is loved by and indwelt by the Father and the Son and the Spirit. The relationship could not be more intimate. The believer's relationship with Christ is likened to Christ's relationship with the Father.

> "I am in my Father, and ye in me, and I in you" (Joh. 14:20).

> "he that loveth me shall be loved of my Father, and I will love him, and will manifest myself to him" (Joh. 14:21).

> "my Father will love him, and we will come unto him, and make our abode with him" (Joh. 14:23)

This is the true Christian life. It is no mere "profession of faith." It is not a "sinner's prayer." It's not moral reformation. It is a love relationship with God. It is impossible that an individual enter into such a relationship and this not be reflected in his life.

> So near, so very near to God
>   Nearer I cannot be
> For in the Person of His Son
>   I am as near as He
>   -- Catesby Paget

The believer's intimate relationship with the Father and the Son is communicated by the Holy Spirit (Joh. 14:16, 26). By the Spirit, each believer can know Christ better than the disciples when Christ was on earth. Then, only a few persons on any one occasion could sit at His feet as Mary did (Lu. 10:39) and at any one meal only one could lean on His breast as John did (Joh. 21:20), but by the Spirit, each believer can draw nigh unto God in the most intimate manner.

Christ reveals Himself to those who love Him (Joh. 14:21). The more the believer loves Christ, the better he knows Him. This is true discipleship. It is human life as God intended it.

Consider the Believer as Part of Christ's Bride

> "Husbands, love your wives, even as Christ also loved the church, and gave himself for it; That he might sanctify and cleanse it with the washing of water by the word, That he might present it to himself a glorious church, not having spot,

or wrinkle, or any such thing; but that it should be holy and without blemish. So ought men to love their wives as their own bodies. He that loveth his wife loveth himself. For no man ever yet hated his own flesh; but nourisheth and cherisheth it, even as the Lord the church: For we are members of his body, of his flesh, and of his bones. For this cause shall a man leave his father and mother, and shall be joined unto his wife, and they two shall be one flesh. This is a great mystery: but I speak concerning Christ and the church" (Eph. 5:25-32).

The Bible uses many metaphors to describe the believer's relationship with Christ, including a branch of the vine and a member of the body, and all of the metaphors describe a most intimate relationship. But the most powerful metaphor is the bride.

The Christian's relationship with Christ is likened unto the marital relationship. But not just any marital relationship; it is a picture of marriage as God intends it to be. Marriage was created by God, and it has many purposes and functions, but chief of these is to teach spiritual lessons about the believer's relationship with God. This was a mystery that was hidden in Old Testament times and is revealed in the New Testament Scripture (Eph. 5:32). In the Old Testament we read about the first marriage, but we don't learn there that Adam and Eve were a picture of and a metaphor of Christ and His bride. But the New Testament reveals that Christ is the second Adam, and the church is His bride.

Salvation is to enter into an intimate, loving relationship with God in Christ. The husband wife relationship, as God designed it, is the most intimate, loving of human relationships, and it points to the believer's relationship with the Saviour. Marriage is two becoming one; it is two hearts united in love; it is two persons sharing life together.

The believer is not just saved in the sense of forgiven and cleansed and made right with God; he is a part of Christ's bride. It is not like a slave who is purchased and merely given freedom. It is much, much more than that. It is a slave who is purchased and made the willing bride of a compassionate, fabulously wealthy man and becomes the object of his affections, joint heir of his riches, co-ruler over his dominions, the honored mother of his children.

The church is all of this, and each individual believer participates in this great reality.

Consider the statements in this passage that describe the intimacy of the believer's relationship with Christ.

Christ gave himself for the church (Eph. 5:25). This refers to Christ's death on the cross to redeem the church, but the emphasis is on His complete personal devotion. He gave *himself*. Everything Christ is belongs to the church. This is seen in Song of Solomon 6:3. "I *am* my beloved's, and my beloved *is* mine: he feedeth among the lilies."

> "But here [Ephesians 5:25] that glorious work is not exactly viewed on the side of its atoning and redeeming efficacy, but on that of the devotedness and love to the assembly which Christ manifested in it. Now we can always reckon upon this love which was perfectly displayed in it. It is not altered. Jesus--blessed and praised be His name for it!--is for me according to the energy of His love in all that He is, in all circumstances and for ever, and in the activity of that love according to which He gave Himself. He loved the assembly and gave Himself for it. This is the source of all our blessings, as members of the assembly" (J.N. Darby).

Christ washes the church toward the goal of perfect holiness (Eph. 5:26-27). Sanctification is not religion; it is relationship. Christ intends to present the church to Himself as His holy bride. Toward this end He died to make the full propitiation (Eph. 5:25), and toward this end He personally cleanses each believer. Sanctification is a most intimate, personal process. "For both he that sanctifieth and they who are sanctified are all of one..." (Heb. 2:11). The new birth and the sanctification of the Spirit are the personal work of the church's devoted Bridegroom. "Not by works of righteousness which we have done, but according to his mercy he saved us, by the washing of regeneration, and renewing of the Holy Ghost; Which he shed on us abundantly through Jesus Christ our Saviour" (Titus 3:5-6). The work of sanctification is sure. It begins in this life, but it will be perfected in the next. The wise believer will yield to and hasten the Lord's sanctifying work.

Christ cherishes the church (Eph. 5:29). The Greek word "thalpo" refers to a mother bird keeping her chicks warm with her feathers. It is used for a mother cherishing her children (1 Th. 2:7). The nurse here is the mother herself. "... or 'the children of her own self'; her own children, and so designs a nursing mother, one whose the children are, has bore them as well as nurses them, and therefore has the most tender concern for them; she lays them in her bosom, and hugs them in her arms, and so warms and cherishes them; gives them the breast, bears with their frowardness, condescends to do the meanest things for them; and that without any self-interest, from a pure parental affection for them" (John Gill).

> "Christ tenderly cares for the assembly here below; He nourishes it, He cherishes it. The wants, the weaknesses, the difficulties, the anxieties of the assembly are only opportunities to Christ for the exercise of His love. The assembly needs to be nourished, as do our bodies; and He nourishes her. She is the object of His tender affections; He cherishes her. If the end is heaven, the assembly is not left desolate here. She learns His love where her heart needs it. She will enjoy it fully when need has passed away for ever" (J.N. Darby, *Synopsis of the Books of the Bible*).

Christ cherishes the church like a man cherishes his body (Eph. 5:29). Christ cherishes each member of His body. We understand this and enjoy this truth by faith in God's Word. The devil attacks with fiery darts of unbelief, trying to cause God's people to doubt His love, but the shield of faith in God's Word can quench every fiery dart (Eph. 6:16).

Christ will present the church to Himself a glorious church (Eph. 5:27). The goal of salvation is that Christ's bride will be glorious and without blemish. Glorious refers to beauty. The Greek word translated "glorious" (*endoxos*) is elsewhere translated "gorgeous" in reference to the attire of royalty (Lu. 7:25). We think of Eve when she came from the hand of God. The genius Creator of all amazing things "made a woman" (Ge. 2:22). Doubtless she was the most beautiful, perfect woman who has ever lived. She was womanhood in perfection. Wrinkles and blemishes entered later and only because of sin. She was not only beautiful physically but beautiful morally, intellectually, socially, and in every way. Adam was delighted in every aspect of her. She delighted and fascinated him!

Christ's objective is to create a bride who is more beautiful, more glorious, more fascinating, and more holy than Eve. Christ's bride is described in Psalm 45, which is a Messianic prophecy.

> "The king's daughter *is* all glorious within: her clothing *is* of wrought gold. She shall be brought unto the king in raiment of needlework: the virgins her companions that follow her shall be brought unto thee. With gladness and rejoicing shall they be brought: they shall enter into the king's palace" (Ps. 45:13-15).

Note that the Psalmist describes Christ's bride as "glorious," just as Paul does. She is clothed in the most splendid clothing. Kings and queens in this present world have clothed themselves in the most exquisite fabrics and fashions that man's skill can devise, but this world has not yet witnessed truly glorious clothing. The clothing of a simple lily is said to be more glorious than that of the fabulously wealthy Solomon (Lu. 12:27), and the God who clothes the lily is the God who will clothe the bride of Christ. The clothing of God's people in Christ's kingdom will also be radiant with light (Da. 12:3; Mt. 13:43).

To understand the believer's relationship with Christ, forget marriage as it is in this present fallen world, and consider marriage as God intended it to be. Consider Adam and Eve in the most lovely paradise imaginable, enjoying everything together, in the bloom of youth, perfect in every sense and faculty, untiring, in a spirit of continual joy and delight, looking at the richness and beauty of life through one another's eyes, sharing the enjoyment of God's communion first and of God's blessings next: a peach's luscious flavor, a rose's beauty, a puppy's cuteness, a sunset's glory.

This is a mere *hint* of the amazing relationship the believer has with Christ, his Saviour and Lord and Bridegroom, and will have with Christ forever.

Every true believer and every true church is a part of this amazing reality. The church's job is to live as the bride of Christ in this present world.

For a church to experience the reality of being Christ's bride it must be a church of disciples. A mixed multitude cannot experience the reality of this relationship.

I wonder if the average "Bible-believing church" today really knows anything of the reality of being the bride of Christ?

Consider Christ's Warning to the Church at Ephesus

> "Unto the angel of the church of Ephesus write; These things saith he that holdeth the seven stars in his right hand, who walketh in the midst of the seven golden candlesticks; I know thy works, and thy labour, and thy patience, and how thou canst not bear them which are evil: and thou hast tried them which say they are apostles, and are not, and hast found them liars: And hast borne, and hast patience, and for my name's sake hast laboured, and hast not fainted. Nevertheless I have *somewhat* against thee, because thou hast left thy first love. Remember therefore from whence thou art fallen, and repent, and do the first works; or else I will come unto thee quickly, and will remove thy candlestick out of his place, except thou repent" (Re. 2:1-5).

Sound doctrine and the right Bible are essential, but this is not enough. Truth alone is not enough. I am guessing that the church at Ephesus had more truth and more *zeal* for truth than the majority of Independent Baptist churches.

Spiritual protection will not come only through a program, a course, a checklist, a principle, or an issue. All of these things are necessary, but they must be accompanied by and permeated with a passionate love for Christ.

We see that the church at Ephesus **had a first love previously**. This describes a church of true disciples who are passionate in their relationship with Jesus Christ. This was no mixed multitude.

First love Christianity is no nominal, half-hearted Christianity. It is born again, converted, "turned upside down, inside out" Christianity so that you love the things you once hated and you hate the things you once loved. Having a first love is a passionate relationship with Jesus Christ, knowing Him personally as Paul did (2 Ti. 1:12), seeking to please Him because He loves me and I love Him, counting former things as dung in comparison with the will of God, considering Christ's Word sweeter than honey and more valuable than gold. Love. Passion. Zeal. Enthusiasm. On fire. This is a first love for Christ.

We see first love Christianity in all of the cases of conversion that are described in the New Testament. The woman at the well had it when she left her water pot and went back to her village to tell the people about Jesus. Joseph of Arimathaea had it when he devoted his own new tomb for Jesus' burial. The 3,000 on the day of Pentecost had it when they publicly professed Christ before a wicked nation and continued stedfastly in the apostles' doctrine and fellowship, and in breaking of bread, and in prayers. Paul had it when his eyes were opened and he immediately began to preach the Christ he previously persecuted. The Ethiopian eunuch had it when he urgently sought baptism and went on his way rejoicing. Lydia had it when she urged Paul and Silas to lodge at her house. The Philippian jailer had it when he washed Paul and Silas' wounds.

A great many members of Bible-believing churches have never had a first love passion for the Lord because they have not been born again.

A great many churches have only a relatively few members who have actually experienced a first love. How can such a mixed multitude be called a New Testament church? If Ephesus, which actually had a first love but had left it, did not please Christ, how much more does the typical church today not please Him which has never had a first love?

First love Christianity is real Christianity, and a first love church is a real New Testament church.

But we see that the church at Ephesus **had left its first love**. Christ uses strong language to describe what had happened. They had "fallen." It was a serious matter. We often think of backsliding as falling into some gross sin, but backsliding actually begins with falling from one's first love.

Christ did not overlook this backslidden condition. He requires first love from His churches. He warned that He would remove their candlestick out of its place. The candlestick signifies the true church of Christ (Re. 1:20). The candlestick church is the church that Christ walks in the midst of (Re. 1:13; 2:1). The removal of the candlestick would mean that Christ no longer owns that church as a true church. It doesn't cease to exist. Often such a church will continue for a long time going through the motions after Christ has removed the candlestick.

This is a very serious matter. It tells us that there is more to a sound church before God than doctrinal correctness. We say, "That is a good church." But is it really? Does it abide in a first love for Christ?

Christ calls the church to repentance. "Remember therefore from whence thou art fallen, and repent, and do the first works..." (Re. 2:5).

Love for Christ is what we must focus on like a laser. This is what we must continually emphasize. We must focus on really knowing Christ, walking with Him, pursuing Him, worshiping Him, pleasing Him. The Christian life is not just knowing something and doing something. It is a passionate relationship with the Creator.

If we sense the ardor for Christ fading in our congregation, it is time for a revival before the ardor grows any cooler. This cannot be a secondary matter. This is the essential of the essentials!

This is what we must emphasize in our preaching, our men's ministry, our women's ministry, our youth ministry, our children's ministry.

We must see Christ everywhere in Scripture (Luke 24:27, 44-45). We can't know God apart from His Word. It is only by Scripture that we can learn rightly of God in creation. For example, Matthew 7:7 is about prayer, but it is also about God. It teaches us that God cares enough and is omniscient and powerful enough to hear every prayer.

We must exalt Christ in our preaching. The preaching must be Christ-centered. The preachers must help the people to see Christ and to know their relationship with Him and challenge them to draw near to Him in love.

We must worship Christ in the services: before we come, preparing our hearts; when we sing, singing unto Him (e.g., "Holy, Holy, Holy" and "Day by Day" last stanza and "Living for Jesus" the chorus); when we listen to the preaching, hearing His voice (1 Pe. 4:11).

We must see Christ everywhere and in everything in our daily lives. He is the Author and Creator of all things. He filled the world with goodness for man's pleasure. He "giveth us richly all things to enjoy" (1 Ti. 6:17). "They that seek the Lord shall not want any good thing" (Ps. 34:10). Everything I have ever enjoyed and appreciated came from God's hand. "Every good gift and every perfect gift is from above" (Jas. 1:17).

We must enjoy life together with God. This is the essence of loving God. It is walking with Him through life. This is how Adam lived in Eden. God brought the animals to Adam, and Adam named them. Adam enjoyed the amazing animals together with God. God made Eve and gave her to Adam in marriage. Everything was centered in God. Man was not enjoying the creation for himself apart from God, which is the essence of idolatry.

This is how Israel will live after she is converted. "And ye shall eat in plenty, and be satisfied, and praise the name of the LORD your God" (Joel 2:26). Note that Israel will enjoy the bounty of Christ's kingdom, but they will enjoy it in continual fellowship with and in continual praise of God.

Consider food. God has given man vast riches of food and materials for food, and he has given man an amazing sense of smell (5 to 6 million odor detecting cells) and taste buds (about 10,000) so he can enjoy every aspect of his food. God could have provided man with a tasteless bean that he would eat for his sustenance, but instead He gave an amazing variety of food. Spices are so desirable that wars have been fought over them, nations have become massively rich selling them, and annual festivals are held in their honor (e.g., vanilla bean festival in Mexico). Food is a blessing from God's hand, but it is to be enjoyed in submission to God's will and in fellowship with Him.

We need continually to look behind and beyond the creation to the Creator. This is one of the reasons why I enjoy photography. It enables me to capture little slivers of God's creation, and it helps me focus my attention better and to look at things more carefully. Photography has helped me see life in a new way.

We must see Christ as the Lord of all things.

Christ is the Lord of beauty, the Artist of artists. Recently I was thinking about how many greens there are in creation. There is not just one nice green color; there are hundreds, and they blend together in beautiful arrangements in "nature." The creation is literally filled with beauty. Consider opals. Len Cram in Australia learned how to grow every type of beautiful opal, proving that they don't take millions of years. He was motivated to do this by his love of opals and his love of the Lord of opals. Geologist Bill Kitchens studies and photographs agates. He says, "Agates are treasures of God's grace that, through natural processes, fill voids in rocks around us for people to find, wonder at, and use. ... The appreciation of beauty and the desire to create beauty, and to understand it, are parts of the 'image of God' built into mankind 'in the beginning.'"

Christ is the Lord of kindness and compassion. Proverbs 19:22 says "the desire of a man is his kindness," and no Man is kinder than Jesus Christ, the Lord of Calvary, the One who became acquainted with grief only so that He could share and heal our grief, the one who became poor to make sinners rich.

Christ is the Lord of music, the Composer of composers, the Musician of musicians, the Singer of singers.

Christ is the Lord of intelligence. He is the infinite Mind, the one vaguely sought by great thinkers (e.g., Greek Logos, Chinese Tao, Hindu Brahma, Buddhist Dharmakaya, New Age pantheism). The child of God does not need to engage in vain speculation about the Divine Mind; he has the mind of God in Scripture (1 Co. 2:16), and he can search the Scripture daily to learn *of* this Mind and *from* this Mind.

Christ is the Lord of practical wisdom (Pr. 8:12-19; Isa. 28:24-28). We must seek His wisdom in every part of life (husband, wife, parent, child, student, tailor, painter, farmer, carpenter, mechanic, engineer).

Young people can love Christ and seek Him as Joseph, Ruth, and Timothy did. How infinitely greater and wiser is that than to seek the vanities of the world!

Your first love is what you love. What stirs your heart? What gets you excited? What do you like to talk about? What are you passionate about? What do you live for? What do you do when you can do whatever you want? What do you spend your money on?

To give the firstfruits of my heart, soul, and strength to anything other than the lovely God is idolatry! God has given us all things to *enjoy* (1 Ti. 6:17), but not to love. He only is to be loved.

A New Testament church is a church of the first love. It is a church that has a first love and zealously maintains a first love.

Building a Discipling Church from the Beginning

Outline
Pray for Help
Establish the Church on Prayer
Have a Good Church Covenant
Build a Strong Foundation
Maintain Biblical Standards for Church Workers
Seek to Build up the Church in Every Area
Don't Accept Backsliding and Carnality as the Status Quo

Following are some suggestions for building a discipling church from the ground up:

Pray for help

I have always prayed earnestly for help in the ministry, and it is something I would urge young preachers to pray for. Pray for help. Pray that God would raise up a ministry team (Acts 13:1). Since we see this in Scripture, we can pray in confidence that it is God's will.

When we started our first church in the early 1980s, I prayed for this. I said, "Lord, I am not able to do this by myself. My wife is a great help, but we can't do this alone. We need a ministry team like we see in the Bible." The Lord answered that prayer and brought two other men alongside, one from India and one from Switzerland, and we worked in harmony for several years in founding that church. The three of us together were much stronger and more effectual than any one of us would have been alone.

I can't imagine trying to start a church alone. At the very least, we need a two-by-two ministry team (Acts 13:1-4; 15:39-40).

There have been times when God doesn't answer the prayer for help. David Brainerd, missionary to the American Indians, prayed for help and traveled far on horseback seeking help, but he remained alone.

But in light of the Bible's emphasis on ministry teams, I believe that this situation is the exception and not the rule.

Establish the Church on Prayer

Prayer is the most powerful spiritual instrument we have, and scriptural prayer will bring God's help into any situation. "The effectual fervent prayer of a righteous man availeth much" (Jas 5:16).

From the very beginning, establish serious prayer meetings, not only mid-week prayer meetings but also before each service, etc. Pray with fasting. Get as many prayer partners as you can.

We discussed this in "A Discipling Church Is Strong in Prayer."

Have a Good Church Covenant

We have included a sample church covenant in this book.

We believe that this is a very important tool.

The covenant is an important tool for preparing candidates for church membership. It is a teaching tool and it is a unifying tool to help the church be of one mind (1 Co. 1:10). We require 100% agreement with the covenant from every member, and if a member ceases to be 100% in agreement, he is no longer qualified to be a member of our church.

The covenant is an important tool to help the church maintain the right standards for teachers and workers. When the standards are written out in the covenant and taught to the people, and when it is required for members to agree 100% with them, this issue is clear and out in the open. Either an individual meets the standards of a particular position, or he doesn't.

Build a Strong Foundation

The most essential thing in building a strong biblical church is to build the right foundation.

This requires being very careful about salvation and church membership, as we have described in "A Discipling Church Begins with Caution about Salvation" and "A Discipling Church Guards the Door to Membership."

Caution and wisdom about salvation and church members is the fundamental of fundamentals in building a strong church.

Don't cut any corners. Don't be in a hurry. Take things step by step. Wait for clear fruit. Require faithfulness from the beginning. Those who aren't ready to be faithful, aren't ready to be church members.

How long does it take to build a strong foundation? It takes as long as it takes. God has to build the work, and the wise church planter will not try to outrun God.

Each place where the gospel is preached is unique. As we learn from the Parable of the Sower, the soils of the human heart are not the same. Church planting differs dramatically from nation to nation and from place to place within nations. In some places, people will be saved more quickly than in others. In some places, people will be more surrendered, more faithful, less focused on personal business, than in others. The Cretians had a national reputation that affected their Christian lives (Titus 1:12-13). Paul did not get the same fruit in every place that he preached. In Athens, the response was small. In Galatia, the false teachers had a lot of success in stealing Paul's converts. Each place is different, and the church planter must get wisdom from God for his unique situation.

If the church planter will be patient and not cut corners in building a good foundation, the time will come when he can grow more quickly and start more churches, which should always be the goal.

When I preached youth discipleship conferences in Australia, South Africa, and the Philippines, several preachers told me that they realized that they had been building a soft foundation by not being careful enough about salvation before baptism and by receiving church members too quickly and by not maintaining the right standards for the workers, and they told me that I had sharpened them in these matters.

One young preacher in the Philippines told me this a year ago. He said he realized that he had been too hasty and the foundation wasn't solid. He had baptized people who gave no evidence of salvation and turned out not to be saved, yet they were now church members. He had received members from other churches that he should not have received, and they caused problems and pulled down the church's spiritual life. He returned to my conference this year and told me that he had worked hard over the last year to correct these problems and to build the right foundation.

Don't get sidetracked from the Work of the Ministry

> "But we will give ourselves continually to prayer, and to the ministry of the word" (Acts 6:4).
>
> "Let the elders that rule well be counted worthy of double honour, especially they who labour in the word and doctrine" (1 Ti. 5:17).

It is so easy for pastors to get sidetracked from the true work of the ministry, and in this way the ministry is neglected and harmed.

They get wrapped up in building projects. They spend an inordinate amount of time messing with the church's equipment.

When a church is young, it might be necessary for a pastor to do pretty much everything, from cleaning the church meeting hall to mowing the lawn. But it is so easy for a pastor to continue to do such things when he could find someone to do them.

Some pastors seem to enjoy this type of thing more than the spiritual ministry, so they aren't in a hurry to relinquish the "deacon work" even when men are available to help. This is not the evidence of a God-called preacher.

I think of a pastor of a church that was several years old, and he was still setting up the rented meeting hall each week, assisted by only one man. He had taught, begged, and reproved the members, but they refused to help. I was amazed, and I told him that if I were in his shoes, next Sunday I would announce to the church that the following Sunday we will be sitting on the floor unless they come and set up the meeting hall, because the pastor is going to obey Acts 6:4.

The prayer of faith is the solution to this problem. Since the Lord has given the preacher a spiritual ministry, and it is a far-reaching ministry that requires much time, he can pray in confidence that the Lord will raise up the necessary helpers to take care of other business.

Another way that a pastor can neglect prayer and the ministry of the Word is to get in the habit of allowing unnecessary disruptions to his devotional and study time. We discussed this in the chapter "A Discipling Church Has the Right Leaders" under the section "The Preacher Must Be Right in His Study Life."

A pastor must teach his people the importance of his study time and exhort them to respect that time and help him guard it. He should explain that there are certain times when he is unavailable except for real emergencies. If they want a pastor who has a rich personal devotional life and a rich preaching/teaching ministry, they will understand, respect, and even encourage this.

There are occasions, of course, when a pastor must interrupt his study schedule, but it should be for a true emergency only. If the preacher allows himself to be at the beck and call of people during his study time, he will get into the bad habit of being hit and miss and not concentrating properly. The preacher must honor God by honoring God's Word and giving it the right priority in his daily life. In case of emergency, the pastor can make some arrangement for being contacted during his study time. Perhaps the people can call his wife, secretary, or a deacon and inform them of the problem, and they can decide whether or not to inform the pastor at that time or to wait until later.

There is a time when a pastor must work a part-time job or perhaps even a full-time job, and we know that Paul had a tent-making ministry, but in my experience an outside job is a great hindrance to most church planting ministries. To build a vibrant discipling church under the Lord's leadership is a full time job and more. A part time preacher simply cannot witness enough, pray enough, teach enough, disciple enough.

I think of a pastor who had lost quite a few people from his membership and took a part-time job to make up for the loss of income. It was supposed to be a temporary plan, but he liked the job and didn't return to the full-time pastorate even when he could have. I felt that his absence had hurt the ministry, and I exhorted him to trust the Lord to supply his needs so he could give his full attention to the church, but he didn't want to do it.

Maintain Biblical Standards for Church Workers

This is an essential part in building a strong church. The workers will have a large influence on the spiritual character of the congregation as a whole. Together with the pastors, they will set the tone; they will be the examples.

We have already mentioned the church covenant in this context. The standards for workers are laid out plainly in our church covenant, and we are careful not to cut corners in this.

The tendency is to bend under the pressure of "the need" and lower the standards for workers, whether it be a musician or a teacher or a youth leader.

By experience, I know that if we hold high biblical standards and use only those people who are qualified for a particular position, this gradually produces more qualified workers. It is the slow path, and that can be frustrating, but it is the solid path.

Every time I have gotten in a hurry and have ignored the principle of 1 Timothy 3:10 ("let these first be proven"), I have regretted it. It is a matter of making the foundation strong before a superstructure is built.

Seek to Build up the Church in Every Area

Beyond this, it is a matter of building a scriptural church in every area: a church that is strong in God's Word, strong in prayer, strong in charity, strong in a disciplined environment, strong for biblical separation, careful about music, zealous for evangelism and world missions. It is a matter of building godly homes, discipling youth, etc.

Don't Accept Backsliding, Carnality, and Unfaithfulness as the Status Quo

God's people and God's churches are susceptible to carnality and backsliding, but we see in the New Testament epistles that the apostles did not accept these things as the status quo.

In the chapter "A Discipling Church or a Mixed Multitude," we examined how the apostle Paul dealt with the church at Corinth. He did not allow the church to settle down into carnality as the status quo. He dealt with the church's sins and errors head on, plainly, publicly, firmly, even sharply at times. He called the church to repentance and discipline. He didn't *suggest* discipline; he *demanded* discipline.

Paul is our example (Php. 3:17). Every pastor must imitate Paul's method of dealing with sins and errors in the churches. The pastor must not be content with carnality, lukewarmness, unfaithfulness, unrepentant sin. He must not accept it, because God does not accept it. He must ever strive for a pure body. He must remove the leaven (1 Co. 5:6-7). Carnality, backsliding, unfaithfulness, sin, and error must be dealt with, in whatever ways are necessary, and these things must never be allowed to become the status quo.

Church leaders have many spiritual tools for dealing with sin, including teaching, preaching, private exhortation and reproof, removing an individual from a ministry, and various other kinds of discipline, including an inactive membership status and withdrawing fellowship.

Church leaders must be gracious and compassionate and patient, but there comes a time when discipline must be exercised so that the church doesn't become an "impure lump."

Restoring the Discipling Church

The church we see in the New Testament is a church of born again disciples of Christ who are committed to serving Christ. We call this a discipling church. We see this in the first church (Acts 2:41-42), and we see it throughout the New Testament. It can be demonstrated from Scripture that a New Testament church has a first love for Christ, has qualified leaders, is careful about salvation and church membership, has a disciplined environment and an atmosphere of charity, is strong in God's Word and prayer, is a reproving church, maintains God's standards for workers, is zealous for biblical separation, is careful about music, is a hard working church, builds godly homes, disciples youth, educates and protects the church from every spiritual danger, has a strong vision for evangelism and world missions, and trains preachers.

Most churches have moved away from the New Testament pattern, beginning with hastiness in evangelism and in receiving members and a weakness in maintaining spiritual standards and exercising discipline, and as a result they are falling prey to all sorts of errors.

Following are some suggestions for moving a mixed multitude congregation to a discipling church position:

Outline

Be Patient
Be Ready to Engage in a Difficult Battle
Be Confident of God's Help
Prepare the Church by Prayer
Prepare the Church by Teaching
Develop a Plan for Maintaining a Regenerate Church Membership
Focus on Those Who Are Real Disciples
Reconstitute the Church around a Strong Covenant
Aim to Incorporate all the Biblical Elements of a Discipling Church

Be Patient

A church doesn't become a mixed multitude overnight and it won't be brought overnight to a New Testament pattern. Impatience can cause more harm than good. The goal is not to harm the church and scatter the sheep; the goal is to strengthen it.

Formulate a clear plan before the Lord and then patiently and steadfastly work toward its implementation. It will be a multi-year plan, not a plan for a few weeks or months.

Be Ready to Enter a Difficult Battle

There is no easy way to change a mixed multitude to a discipling church. The elements of the world, the flesh, and the devil that have become entrenched in the congregation are not going to like it. There are going to be battles.

A pastor must be convinced that a discipling church is what pleases God, and no other type of church pleases Him. He must be 100% committed to doing those things that are necessary to make this happen, because he loves and fears God more than man, and he knows that he will give account to God, and not to man, for his ministry.

In 1962, James Leo Garrett, Jr., called upon Baptist churches to restore discipline, and he acknowledged that it would be a difficult job. He said,

> "Those who would lead in the renewal of discipline must be thoroughly convinced of its terrible urgency" (Garrett, *Baptist Church Discipline*).

Be Confident of God's Help

The Lord has given the pattern of the New Testament church in His Word. This is the only type of church that pleases Him. If His people acknowledge their sin of corrupting or weakening this pattern and seek His help in restoring the church to His will, this impulse is from God's Spirit. It is certain that such a desire does not come from the world, the flesh, or the devil.

God is ready to help those who want to obey Him, not matter how weak and backslidden the situation might be. When Christ called Ephesus to repent of losing their first love (Re. 2:4-5) and

Pergamos to repent of false doctrine (Re. 2:14-16) and Thyatira to repent of worldliness (Re. 2:20) and Sardis to repent of spiritual deadness (Re. 3:1-3) and Laodicea to repent of lukewarmness (Re. 2:15-18), He stood ready to help them in that business. And if God be with us, who can be against us?

Prepare the Church by Prayer

Prayer is the most powerful spiritual instrument we have, and scriptural prayer will bring God's help into any situation. "The effectual fervent prayer of a righteous man availeth much" (Jas. 5:16).

To pray in faith is to pray according to God's will as revealed in Scripture (1 John 5:14). Since we know it is God's will that the church be a discipling church with a regenerate membership, the Lord's people can pray with confidence that God will bring this to pass.

The pastor should ask for prayer partners among his friends. This is what Paul did continually. Compare Ro. 15:30-32; Eph. 6:19; Php. 1:19; Col. 4:3-4; 1 Th. 5:25; 2 Th. 3:1; Phm. 22; Heb. 13:18-19.

He should call for special prayer meetings in which the sin of a mixed multitude can be confessed and God's help can be sought. If only a few show up for these prayer meetings, then it should be recognized that this remnant is the true spiritual core of the church. God can answer two or three as well as fifty (Mt. 18:20).

Prepare the Church by Teaching

The early chapters of *The Discipling Church* can be used for this. These are "A Discipling Church or a Mixed Multitude," "The Disappearance of Discipling Churches," "A Discipling Church Begins with Caution about Salvation," and "A Discipling Church Guards the Door to Membership."

The first lessons in the *One Year Discipleship Course* could also provide teaching toward moving the church away from a mixed multitude. These lessons cover repentance, saving faith, the gospel, baptism, eternal security, position and practice; the Law and the

New Testament Christian, Christian growth and spiritual victory, and the Church.

Develop a Plan for Maintaining a Regenerate Church Membership

The foundation for a New Testament discipling church is a regenerate church membership.

Establish a membership class so that every potential baptismal and membership candidate can be prepared with basic instruction. This gives further opportunity to ascertain if the individual is truly saved. The membership class should include teaching on repentance, saving faith, the gospel, baptism, and the church. The church covenant should also be taught and any questions answered. We assign a mature member to go through the membership class with a candidate.

The candidates should be required to agree with the covenant 100%.

Candidates for baptism should be carefully interviewed by the church leaders (and their wives if the candidates are female). The candidate should receive a unanimous vote by the church leaders. The candidate is then presented to the church with the recommendation of the leaders that he or she be received for baptism and/or membership. The individual is then received by a church vote.

Establish an inactive membership program. This is discussed in the chapter "A Discipling Church Has a Disciplined Environment."

Focus on Those Who Are Real Disciples

If a church has been established on a mixed multitude philosophy, it will have a lot of members who are not real disciples of Christ according to Christ's definition in John 8:31 and 10:27.

Our suggestion to pastors who are trying to change the character of an older church is to focus most of your attention on those who are disciples.

We want all of the people to come along and to press on higher ground, and we should do everything we can toward that end, but oftentimes this doesn't happen. Those who are "settled on their lees" (Jer. 48:11; Zep. 1:12) tend to remain where they are spiritually. They have heard a lot of preaching and teaching, but they haven't responded and haven't obeyed, and this is evidence of a frightful spiritual condition, as Christ said:

> "He that is of God heareth God's words: ye therefore hear *them* not, because ye are not of God" (John 8:47).

Of the rebel, there comes a time when God says, "Let him alone" (Hos. 4:17). See also Matthew 15:14.

The pastor who wants to make an older church a discipling church must keep his focus on those who truly love the Lord and want to obey Him. He must work with them to make them stronger and educate them well in the direction the Lord is leading him, so he will have a core of people who support his vision for the future.

Reconstitute the Church Around a Strong Covenant

It might be best to reconstitute the church around a strong covenant.

We have included a sample covenant in this book.

The covenant should include requirements of membership, standards for leaders and workers, the Lord's Supper, the process of discipline, and the church's statement of faith.

> "Examples of the covenants of other churches may be consulted, but churches would do well to personalize and individualize their covenant so that the congregation as a whole owns it as their covenant, not one imposed upon them. Then, when the church has developed a covenant that expresses their commitment to one another and to Christ as his church, the church would vote to dissolve the present membership and reconstitute around those who sign their names to the church covenant. This would be preceded by several announcements of the proposed signing day. I would even encourage the pastor to send a letter to every member of the congregation with the proposed covenant and the decision of the church to reconstitute around it.
>
> "There is a biblical precedent for such action in Nehemiah 9-10. After a time of renewal and confession in Nehemiah

8-9, Nehemiah records the decision of God's people: 'We are making a binding agreement, putting it in writing, and our leaders, our Levites and our priests are affixing their seals to it" (9:38). After listing all the leaders by name, the text states that the rest of the people joined with them (10:28-29). Their 'binding agreement,' or covenant, specified the areas of their lives that needed specific commitments. In that context, the key issues were avoiding intermarriage with the surrounding pagans, conducting no business on the Sabbath, and supporting the temple worship (10:30-39).

"Contemporary covenants would list the areas of commitment contemporary churches see as central to their life together. The people in Nehemiah's day concluded with a summary statement of their commitment, 'We will not neglect the house of our God.' Adopting a church covenant is one way God's people today can say, 'We will not neglect our church.'

"This biblical example gives a beautiful model for contemporary church covenants. The covenant would be their 'binding agreement,' specifying areas of their commitment to Christ and one another. At the conclusion of a service celebrating the adoption of the covenant, the church leadership could be invited to come and sign their names to a roster attached to the church covenant. Then all who are willing to accept the covenant responsibilities would be invited to come and sign. The same document and roster would be taken to shut-in members who are not able to come but are still committed to the church. Those who sign would become the church's membership. Part of the process for adding subsequent members would involve the signing of the covenant, and existing members would be asked to sign their commitment afresh every year. It could become an annual church renewal event" (*Restoring Integrity in Baptist Churches*, Kindle loc. 331).

Aim to Incorporate All of the Biblical Elements of a Discipling Church

We have dealt with many of these things in this book: right leadership, a disciplined environment, an environment strong in God's Word, prayer, reproof, standards for workers, education, an atmosphere of charity, building godly homes, discipling youth, biblical separation, caution about music, zeal for evangelism and world missions.

Cultural Factors in the Weakening of Churches

Outline
Theological Liberalism
The Public School System
Materialism and Working Mothers
The Rock & Roll Pop Culture
Pop Psychology
The Feminist Movement
Self-Esteemism
New Evangelicalism
Television
The Internet
Conclusion

Following are some of the factors that have weakened the character of Bible-believing churches over the past 70 years and helped create a mixed multitude philosophy.

Theological Liberalism

Confidence in the Bible was weakened by theological liberalism and Darwinian evolution, and this greatly weakened the spiritual power of churches.

Though liberalism took many forms, it was an attack upon the authority of the Bible and it was an application of the theory of evolution to Bible history.

The Northern Baptists became liberal in theology at the beginning of the 20th century. (They were known as the Northern Baptist Convention until 1950, when the name was changed to American Baptist Convention.) For example, in 1918, Harry Emerson Fosdick, pastor of the influential Riverside Church in New York City, published *The Manhood of the Master*, denying that Jesus Christ is God. In 1926, the Northern Baptist Convention voted by a margin of three to one *not* to evict Riverside Church from the convention.

Liberalism entered the Southern Baptist Convention in the first half of the 20th century.

By 1902, J.W. Bailey of North Carolina wrote in the *Biblical Recorder* that there were a multitude of "theologies" in the Southern Baptist Convention. He said, "Theologies change every day. ... [Baptists do not stand for] formulated dogmas."

A Baptist pastorate that was probably largely unregenerate stopped depending on spiritual weapons and turned to carnal weapons such as programs and an efficient organization.

There was an emphasis on "efficiency" and "pragmatism" (using whatever works to produce a desired goal).

> "Efficiency consisted not in purity or obedience, but in system, organization, and rationality in all areas of church activity. ... progressive church leaders held that the church in the modern age needed a polity based not on ancient authority but on science, rationality, and system. They looked to social scientists and efficiency experts such as Frederick Winslow Taylor, who in this era developed management into a science for producing efficient organizations" (*Restoring Integrity in Baptist Churches*, Kindle loc. 2167-2174).

In the 1920s, the Southern Baptist Theological Seminary appointed Gaines Dobbins as a "professor of church efficiency." His 1923 book *The Efficient Church* had a wide influence. He claimed that Christ's ministry in the Gospels was "the perfection of efficiency" and Paul was the "world's greatest efficiency expert in religion."

The churches began leaning to the spirit and wisdom of the times instead of God's Spirit and God's Word. Instead of separating from the world and its unenlightened thinking, they learned from the world.

They bowed to the American spirit of individualism and consumerism. They stopped requiring evidence of salvation and practicing discipline so as not to offend potential members. The churches appeased the people's idolatrous, me-centered desire to shop for a church that met their felt needs. They lowered the spiritual standards, became entertainment-oriented, borrowed the world's music to make Christian music more appealing to the unsaved and carnal, softened the preaching, created "youth ministries" that encouraged the generation gap and were merely Christianized versions of the world's pop culture. By the last half of the 20th century, this spiritual appeasement produced the seeker-sensitive, megachurch movement.

The churches bowed to the influence of the "new morality" and allowed church members to live worldly lives. Such things as dating, pre-marital sex, drinking, jazz, rock, divorce, unisex fashions flooded the weak churches.

The churches bowed to the philosophy of non-judgmentalism and non-dogmatism that permeated society.

The concept of Christians as pilgrims and strangers in a foreign country was replaced by Americanism and flag waving.

The Social Gospel produced an emphasis away from evangelism and church planting. Building God's kingdom on earth through social-justice projects and maintaining good social order began to replace "saving brands from the burning."

In 1910, William Poteat, president of Wake Forest College, told the annual Southern Baptist Convention that Baptists were in the best position to save civilization.

In 1920, Richard Edmonds wrote, "Upon the Baptists of the South may rest the salvation of America and of the world from chaos and from sinking back into the darkness of the middle ages" (*The South, America and the World*).

The Public School System

Few things have done more to weaken Bible-believing churches than the public school system with its anti-God, anti-Bible, evolutionary, socialistic, globalistic agenda. It is a major tool of the "god of this world" in these end times. Christian parents have foolishly turned their children over to the hands of the devil to be brainwashed and sexualized and converted to the devil's agenda.

Public school attendance is a major reason why so few of the young people in the churches are true disciples of Christ, why, in fact, many of them become open enemies of Christ.

The public school system was one of the most negative spiritual and moral influences in my youth, and that was in a day wherein the schools in America were not nearly as degenerate as they are today. I entered grammar school in 1955 and graduated from high school in 1967. As I recall, we weren't taught evolution or communism or multiculturalism or feminism or transsexualism.

In fact, for much of that time, we still had Bible reading and prayer in the schools. But even then the secularized environment and the blossoming rock & roll pop culture and the godless friends were devastating to my Christian profession.

My parents took me to church every time the doors were open, but how can a few hours in a weak church overcome 30 and more hours a week of immersion in the world?

By the time I was in junior high school, the Bible and prayer were kicked out of the nation's schools by fiat of the U.S. Supreme Court. Creationism was replaced by evolution. Biblical morality was replaced with moral relativism. The sexual revolution was glorified.

In 2015, I received the following testimony from a public school teacher:

> "I teach math to twelve- to fifteen-year-old children in public school in a heavily Protestant-churched community in North Carolina. The students are absolutely addicted to cell phones. Many walk around campus plugged into their devices. Music and games are the most addictive. Posting of 'selfies' on Snapchat is very popular. All the immorality that we had to work hard to find when we were young is available to children in a second. Few, if any, are strong enough to resist biting the apple."

The truth of 1 Corinthians 15:33 guarantees that a church populated by kids educated in the public school system will be a weak church with weak Christian homes and weak youth. See also Psalm 1:1; Proverbs 19:27; Jeremiah 10:2; 2 Corinthians 6:14-18.

Pastor David Sorenson makes the following wise comment:

> "I know of no greater passage of Scripture dealing with the matter of Christian education than Psalm 1. There probably is no institution in this country that more embodies the counsel of the ungodly, the way of sinners, and the seat of the scornful than the national public education establishment. With its systemic teaching of evolution which mocks creation, it certainly occupies the seat of the scornful. With its institutionalized sex education (that is little more than sex

encouragement), it certainly is in the way of sinners. As it tacitly ignores the things of God under the guise of separation of church and state, it certainly is the counsel of the ungodly. The objective of Psalm 1:1 is to get our families out of the world and to get the world out of our families" (*Training Your Children to Turn out Right*, pp. 92, 93).

Pastor Kerry Allen comments on 1 Samuel 13:19-20:

> "Children are arrows to be sharpened and shot at our enemy, the devil. Are we foolish enough to believe that if we give our arrows to the enemy, he is going to sharpen them for us? No, rather he will see to it that they are dull and useless against him. Wise warriors will never allow the enemy to tamper with their weapons of warfare" (*How Can I Except Some Man Guide Me?*)

I realize there are situations in which a child must attend public school for reasons that might be out of the parent's control. For example, there are divorced Christians that have to share custody with an unsaved parent. And in some situations, missionaries have chosen to send their children to a public school in a foreign country after weighing all of their options before the Lord. I know of two cases like this that have turned out right, and those children are serving the Lord. *But I must hasten to add that I personally know of only two!*

If children must attend public school, the key to having them turn out right for the Lord is intimate, godly involvement by the parents and a committed relationship with a strong church.

The same thing can be said about secular university. Pastor Mike Sullivant has the following observation:

> "Very few that go off to secular university go on to serve the Lord. I've got one guy that is in engineering, but he lives with a Christian family off campus and comes home every weekend. His family is active in the church and during the summer he comes home to work and is faithful to church and goes to the activities. Pastor Bob Kelly said that the only way that a saved person could go to a secular school and turn out right is that he not be just an ATTENDER of a good church but that he be ACTIVELY INVOLVED in the church. I've seen some of our young people leave here and go to the university in Winnipeg and attend a church but they are not

active in a church, and it seems that it is no better for them than if they weren't going to church at all. I've never seen a non-active one make it without being scorched big time."

Materialism and Working Mothers

Another key factor in the weakening of churches over the past 60 years is the breakdown of the home, and one of the chief causes of this is the frenzied pursuit of wealth and comfort with the accompanying phenomenon of working mothers.

During World War II, women entered the work force in great numbers because so many men were fighting overseas. (This phenomenon had begun in World War I, but it exploded in World War II.) When the war ended, the trend toward working moms did not stop.

Instead of being content with living on the father's paycheck while the mothers attended to the essential business of keeping the home and caring for the children, mothers and fathers both entered the work force.

This was direct and brazen disobedience to God's Word, and it was evidence that many homes and churches were following society rather than Scripture.

> "That they may teach the young women to be sober, to love their husbands, to love their children, *To be* discreet, chaste, keepers at home, good, obedient to their own husbands, that the word of God be not blasphemed" (Titus 2:4-5).

The working mother phenomenon left children without close parental supervision and training, and the devil has filled the void.

Ron Williams, founder of Hephzibah House in Winona Lake, Indiana, has many decades of experience working with troubled children from Christian homes. He issues the following warning:

> "Small wonder many children and young people forge such strong loyalties to peers even though they are an adverse influence on them. In the absence of a full-time mother, a child will naturally seek guidance, companionship and fulfillment from another source. Loyalties that should have been cemented with his parents and family are instead farmed out to evil-charactered peers readily provided by a satanically-dominated world. Mom, your children need you,

not a surrogate hireling. You cannot be replaced by another. God has called you to be a 'keeper at home,' not to stunt your creativity or imprison you in an unfulfilling, demeaning role, but because you have been called to the high and noble office of a homemaker; a responsibility with unmeasureable rewards, heavy demands, great fulfillment, and inestimable blessing for you, your husband, and your children."

If a married woman doesn't have children or if her children are grown or if she can work part time without causing any harm to her family, that is a different situation.

The Rock & Roll Pop Culture

Rock music is the heart and soul of an ungodly global pop culture. It is the soundtrack of the modern youth culture. Originating in America and England, it spread throughout the world.

In most nations today, young people share the same philosophy, have the same values, wear the same fashions, love the same techno gadgets, have the same heroes, display the same attitude.

Rock music and the pop culture that it began to create in the 1950s weakened churches almost immediately and it has been weakening them ever since.

Young people were enticed, addicted, and brainwashed. The Pied Piper of rock reached into the church in which I was raised and captured the hearts of all of the young people. I don't know of any exceptions.

I remember how I was affected by early rock & roll records in 1962, the year I turned 13. I was mesmerized. The feelings produced by the music were so powerful. Church was boring, but *this new world* was amazing! I couldn't wait to quit church and live out my rock & roll fantasies, and I did that at age 17 when I graduated from high school and had my own car.

Rock music is enticing and transformational because it brings the philosophy of self-centeredness, rebellion to authority, and moral license.

The rock culture is not morally neutral. Rebellion against God's holy laws is not a sideline of rock & roll; it is the heart and soul.

From its inception in the 1950s and 1960s, rock has preached rebellion and moral license. The rock philosophy is the philosophy of "do your own thing; don't let anyone tell you what to do." It's the me-first philosophy that lies at the heart of the self-esteem culture.

Rock preaches the ancient lie that the devil uttered to Eve: "God's laws are restrictive; He is keeping you from enjoying life to the fullest; throw off His yoke and live as you please; be your own god."

"**Elvis changed our hairstyles, dress styles, our attitudes toward sex, all the musical taste**" (David Brinkley, NBC News, cited by Larry Nager, *Memphis Beat*, p. 216).

"**I'm free to do what I want any old time**" (Rolling Stones, 1965).

"**It's my life and I'll do what I want/ It's my mind, and I'll think what I want**" (The Animals, 1965).

"**You got to go where you want to go/ do what you want to do**" (Mamas and Papas, 1966).

"**It's your thing/ do what you want to do**" (Isley Brothers, 1969).

"**We don't need no thought control**" (Pink Floyd, "Another Brick in the Wall," 1979).

"**I'm gonna do it my way. ... I want to make my own decision ... I want to be the one in control…**" (Janet Jackson, "Control," 1986).

"**Nothing's forbidden and nothing's taboo** when two are in love" (Prince, "When Two Are in Love," 1988).

"**... the only rules you should live by [are] rules made up by you**" (Pennywise, "Rules," 1991).

"So what we get drunk/ So what we smoke weed … **Living young and wild and free**" ("Young, Wild and Free," Snoop Dog and Wiz Khalifa, 2011).

"**We can do what we want; we can live as we choose**" (Paul McCartney, "New," 2013).

"The whole Beatles idea was to **do what you want**" (John Lennon, cited by David Sheff, *The Playboy Interviews with John Lennon and Yoko Ono*, p. 61).

Little Richard **"freed people from their inhibitions, unleashing their spirit, ENABLING THEM TO DO EXACTLY WHAT THEY FELT LIKE DOING"** (*Life & Times of Little Richard*, p. 66).

At the heart of rock music is sexual liberty, which is brazen rebellion against God's holy law of marriage. Again we quote the rock and rollers themselves as evidence for this:

> "**Everyone takes it for granted that rock and roll is synonymous with sex**" (Chris Stein of the rock group Blondie, *People*, May 21, 1979).

> "**Rock music is sex**. The big beat matches the body's rhythms" (Frank Zappa of the Mothers of Invention, *Life*, June 28, 1968).

> "The sex is definitely in the music, and **sex is in all aspects of the music**" (Luke Campbell of 2 Live Crew).

> "**Rock 'n' roll is synonymous with sex and you can't take that away from it**. It just doesn't work" (Steven Tyler of Aerosmith, *Entertainment Tonight*, ABC, Dec. 10, 1987).

> "**Rock 'n' roll is 99% sex**" (John Oates of Hall & Oates, *Circus*, Jan. 31, 1976).

> "**Pop music revolves around sexuality**. I believe that if there is anarchy, let's make it sexual anarchy rather than political" (Adam Ant, *From Rock to Rock*, p. 93).

> "**Perhaps my music *is* sexy** ... but what music with a big beat isn't?" (Jimi Hendrix, Henderson, cited from his biography '*Scuse Me While I Kiss the Sky*, p. 117).

> "**Rock 'n' roll is sex**. Real rock 'n' roll isn't based on cerebral thoughts. It's based on one's lower nature" (Paul Stanley of KISS, cited from *The Role of Rock*, p. 44).

> "**That's what rock is all about—sex with a 100 megaton bomb, THE BEAT!**" (Gene Simmons of Kiss, *Entertainment Tonight*, ABC, Dec. 10, 1987).

> "**Rock 'n' roll is all sex. One hundred percent sex**" (Debbie Harry of Blondie, cited by Carl Belz, "Television Shows and Rock Music," *The Age of Communication*, Goodyear Publishing Company, 1974, p. 398).

Rock music represents the world of the sexual revolution: shacking up, hooking up, the homosexual agenda (LGBT, Lesbian, Gay, Bisexual, Transsexual), no-fault divorce, polyamory (multiple marriage partners).

The rock world is a sleazy, filthy world. It is impossible for a Bible-believing Christian to watch the Grammys or to read *Rolling Stone* and other rock magazines or even to browse the Walmart pop music department or the pop music section of the Apple iTunes store without seeing the continual flaunting of nakedness and fornication.

The lives of popular rock musicians have been filled with profanity, fornication, adultery, multiple marriages, homosexuality, lesbianism, alcohol abuse, drug abuse, tumult, covetousness, theft, and suicide.

No wonder the rock culture has weakened churches. Very few churches have been strong enough to overcome its pull and its influence on the people.

Pop Psychology

Pop psychology has also greatly influenced society over the past half century and in turn weakened the churches.

Humanistic psychology has greatly undermined biblical morality. It is based on the premise that man is basically good rather than a fallen sinner. It de-emphasizes personal responsibility for one's actions. Man is not a sinner, he is a victim (of his home life, his society, etc.). It has transformed sins into diseases (e.g., drunkenness is alcoholism).

At the heart of pop psychology is self-esteemism, which is exactly what fallen man wants. He wants to be the center of his universe. He wants to follow his heart and chase his dreams, and that is exactly what psychology encourages him to do.

The doctrine of self-esteem was developed by the fathers of the psychological counseling movement and has spread throughout that field and beyond to every level of modern society.

According to the doctrine of self-esteem, man must pursue his own self-love or self-confidence for the sake of psychological wholeness, and anything that damages self-esteem is wrong. The mystical path to the development of self-esteem is psychological counseling. Since absolute rules produce guilt in those who don't live up to them, the pursuit of self-esteem emphasizes the need for "new rules which will allow us more freedom of movement and encourage us to accept ourselves just as we are" (E.S. Williams, *The Dark Side of Christian Counselling*, p. 116).

Atheist Abraham Maslow emphasized the need for self-esteem in books such as *A Theory of Human Motivation* (1943), *Motivation and Personality* (1954), and *Toward a Psychology of Being (1955)*. He taught that a lack of self-esteem can lead to "neurotic trends." Rejecting the doctrine of the fall, he believed that man is basically good and there is "a positive, self-actualising force within each person that is struggling to assert itself" (Williams, *The Dark Side*, p. 114). If it is "permitted to guide our life, we grow healthy, fruitful, and happy" (*Motivation and Personality*, 1970, p. 122).

Dr. Nathaniel Branden has had a massive influence in the promotion of self-esteem through books such as *Psychology of Self-Esteem* (1969), *How to Raise Your Self-Esteem* (1987), and the *Six Pillars of Self-Esteem* (1995). He treats self-esteem as a basic human need that is essential for mental health. He says, "The first love affair we must consummate successfully in this world is with ourselves; only then are we ready for a relationship."

Douglas Groothuis identifies the self-esteem doctrine as New Age in character.

> "Maslow's past-breaking efforts cleared the way for an exodus from the old psychological view of humanity toward a new human that is essentially good and has within himself unlimited potential for growth. A whole host of thinkers--Erich Fromm, Rollo May, Carl Rogers and others--sound this call. In humanistic psychology the self is seen as the radiant heart of health, and psychotherapy must strive to get the person in touch with that source of goodness. ... This is the message at the core of New Age teaching" (*Unmasking the New Age*, 1986, p. 78).

The pursuit of self-esteem puts one into contact with the god of end-times apostasy.

Though fashioned by God-haters such as Abraham Maslow, self-esteem doctrine has been promoted far and wide in Christian circles by a slew of Christian psychologists, with James Dobson leading the way.

Dobson claims that "lack of self-esteem produces more symptoms of psychiatric disorders than any other factor yet identified" (*Dr. Dobson Answers Your Questions about Confident Healthy Families*, 1987, pp. 73-74). His 1974 book *Hide and Seek* was designed "to formulate a well-defined philosophy--and approach to child rearing--that will contribute to self-esteem from infancy onwards." He says, "If I could write a prescription for the women of the world, I would provide each one of them with a healthy dose of self-esteem and personal worth (taken three times a day until the symptoms disappear). I have no doubt that this is their greatest need" (*What Wives Wish Their Husbands Knew about Women*, p. 35). He says, "... lack of self-esteem is a threat to the entire human family, affecting children, adolescents, the elderly, all socioeconomic levels of society, and each race and ethic culture" (*What Wives Wish*, p. 24).

Dobson believes that lack of self-esteem is the cause of every social ill.

> "Thus, whenever the keys to self-esteem are seemingly out of reach for a large percentage of the people, as in twentieth-century America, then widespread mental illness, neuroticism, hatred, alcoholism, drug abuse, violence, and social disorder will certainly occur. Personal worth is not something humans are free to take or leave. We must have it, and when it is unattainable, everybody suffers" (*Dr. Dobson Answers Your Questions about Confident, Healthy Families*, p. 67).

To the contrary, the Bible lays the ills of society at the feet of fallen man and his rebellion against God. Jesus taught that murder, adultery, fornication, covetousness, deceit, theft, and such come from man's wicked heart (Mark 7:21-23).

David Seamands is another pioneer of the Christian self-esteem movement. His hugely popular books *Healing for Damaged Emotions* and *Healing of Memories* seek to heal the believer of "Satan's most powerful psychological weapon" which is "low self-esteem." He aims to take the client back into the past to recover and heal memories of events that injured one's self-esteem.

Seamands has been widely recommended by evangelicals, including James Dobson and George Verwer (Youth With A Mission), who wrote the foreword to *Healing for Damaged Emotions*.

Seamands' mystical path toward self-esteem is "healing of memories" through psychological counseling and New Age techniques. He promotes things as positive visualization, guided imagery, dream analysis, and venting of emotions. Through visualization, the individual is taught to imagine painful past events in perfect detail and to imagine Jesus entering the scenes to bring healing. This is not only vain fantasy; it is occultic and it is a recipe for communing with deceiving spirits masquerading as angels of light.

The self-esteem doctrine downplays and redefines sin.

The very popular and influential Robert Schuller, who was a pioneer in the "Christian" self-esteem movement, defined sin as "any act or thought that robs myself or another human being of his or her self-esteem" (*Self-Esteem: The New Reformation*, p. 14). He defined the new birth as "being changed from a negative to a positive self-image--from inferiority to self-esteem" (p. 68). He even said that Christ was "self-esteem incarnate" (p. 135). Schuller has been praised and promoted by a whose-who of evangelicalism, including Billy Graham, W.A. Criswell, R.C. Sproul, *Christianity Today*, National Association of Evangelicals, World Vision, Promise Keepers, James Dobson, Tony Campolo, Bill Bright, Paul Yonggi Cho, Jack Hayford, Ralph Reed, Bill Hybels, Paul Crouch, John Wimber, Ravi Zacharias, Lee Strobel, Chuck Colson, and Rick Warren, to name a few. (See "Evangelicals and Heretic Robert Schuller" at the Way of Life web site.)

The self-esteem doctrine promotes an unscriptural view of the conscience. While acknowledging that the conscience (an "inner voice") produces guilt and negative thoughts, the proposed solution is not the biblical path of regeneration through repentance and faith followed by a Christian walk of obedience and confession. The proposed solution, instead, is to lower the standards of morality.

The atheistic founders of the self-esteem doctrine hated the holy God of the Bible and His holy law and sought to destroy His authority over men by denying His existence and teaching moral relativism and the pursuit of self. Christian counselors who have borrowed the self-esteem doctrine also tend to downplay the absoluteness of God's law, the necessity of strict obedience, and they replace the biblical means of soothing the conscience with psychological mumbo-jumbo.

Humanistic psychology has had a major influence on modern society, and it has caused the thinking of church members to be corrupted away from biblical thinking. Since most church members were educated in the public school system and are otherwise influenced by psychology, and since most of them are not serious students of God's Word, their thinking is more secular than biblical.

Most churches have not been strong enough to resist the onslaught of humanistic psychology. Most pastors have not properly educated the people or properly warned them. They have not stood plainly against heretical psychological principles. They do not want to "offend" the people and "drive them away."

The result has been weakened churches and mixed multitudes.

Democracy

Democracy is another factor that has weakened the discipline of churches.

The democratic political movement of modern times was birthed in America. The rule of kings was replaced with the rule of the people. Though America is not strictly a democracy; it is a democratic republic, which is a democracy under the rule of law, the emphasis is still on the rule of the people. The Declaration of Independence championed "the right of the people," while the United States Constitution begins with the words, "We the people." President Abraham Lincoln described the U.S. government as one "of the people, by the people, and for the people."

Multitudes of people flocked to America in search of people's rights.

In a great many ways democracy has been a great blessing, primarily in the areas of liberty and economic prosperity. It liberated men from the dictates of autocratic kings and state churches. It created a climate in which churches multiplied and world evangelism prospered. It was the search for liberty and economic prosperity that brought the masses to America's shores and that spread American democracy to many nations.

A danger of this is in transferring the philosophy and attitude of "people's power" from the political realm into the church. The church is not a democracy. It is not "of the people, by the people, and for the people." The believer in Christ is spiritually translated into Christ's kingdom (Col. 1:13), and the church is an outpost of Christ's coming kingdom, and it is obligated to live under His Headship. The church is a theocracy ruled by Christ and His Word. Christ appoints governors, who are called pastors, elders, and bishops, and they have the rule over the church under Christ (Heb. 13:17; 1 Pe. 5:1-2). They don't have have legislative power, because the church's laws are already settled in the canon of Scripture. Rather they have executive and judicial powers.

In the New Testament, we see the congregation participating in decisions, particularly in the selection of deacons (Acts 6:1-6). But this is not "people's power" in that it was done under the direction of and in coordination with the leaders.

What has happened in American churches, in particular, and in churches influenced by them, is the intrusion of the attitude of people's power. Too often, an attitude of "we are the people, and we will decide what we do" has replaced that of "we are the *Lord's* people and we will live strictly by *His* will."

This can best be seen by comparing churches today with those of former times.

Consider the following description of church discipline 150 years ago:

> "The oversight of the members was minute and persistent. Their general conduct, their domestic life, their business, their connections in civil society, their recreations, and even their dress, were all deemed legitimate subjects for the strictest supervision" (J.J. Goadby, *Discipline in Early Baptist Churches*, 1871).

This was a perfectly biblical position, and people in that day commonly submitted to such discipline. The level of democracy and the modern focus on self had not yet ruined church discipline.

But today the attitude on the part of vast numbers of church members is that these things are *not* the business of the church. The attitude is more alongs the line of, "You can't tell me what I can or cannot do, how I dress, what music I listen to, how I conduct my family life and business, whom I associate with. Who do the pastors think they are?"

This thinking is evident in the way that so many churches "hire and fire" preachers, not on the basis of biblical truth and righteousness, but on the basis of the whims of the people, as if pastors exist to do the bidding of the people and to please them. I think of a Baptist church in Tennessee that fired the preacher nearly every year and got a new one. Typically, it took a new preacher about a year to offend the main families in the church!

The Feminist Movement

The feminist movement has had a very powerful influence on modern society and on the churches.

It began in the second half of the 19th century with the push for women's suffrage, political equality (an equal voice and place for women in politics), workplace equality (equal pay for equal work), and female education. The first gathering devoted to women's rights was in 1848 with about 100 people in attendance. It was led by Elizabeth Cady Stanton and Lucretia Mott. Full voting rights were granted to women in America in 1920.

By the early 20th century, the feminist movement was pushing for "reproductive rights," which refers to birth control and abortion. Many 19th century feminist leaders were opposed to abortion, but by the 20th century, feminism was at the forefront of the abortion rights movement which has resulted in the destruction of millions upon millions of unborn children.

The feminist movement has become ever more radical. It has pushed for "non-sexist" or "gender neutral" language (e.g., chairman becomes chairperson). It has often been an opponent of traditional marriage and has been at the forefront of homosexual rights. It has reconstituted goddess theology. Pressure for accommodation of women in all positions, has resulted in the lowering of physical standards for police, firefighters, and the military.

Feminism created the unisex movement and paved the way for homosexual rights. The pantsuit was invented in 1966 by homosexual fashion designer Yves Saint Laurent. Feminist Linda Grant said that the pantsuit "put women on an equal sartorial footing with men and "is what fashion gave to feminism" ("Feminism Was Built on the Trouser Suit," The Guardian, June 3, 2008). The breaking down of the created distinction between male and female in the pop culture has, in turn, greatly encouraged the homosexual movement.

The feminist movement has had an influence in Bible-believing churches because so many professing Christian women are more influenced by feminist thinking than by the Bible. They consider feminine characteristics such as "a meek and quiet spirit" (1 Pe. 3:4) and modesty, shamefacedness, and sobriety (1 Ti. 2:9) to be outdated. As Don Boys points out, "For us to suggest that women be modest in apparel, attitude, and actions as Paul commanded is almost quaint. Moreover, not only do feminists go ballistic but also many closet feminists in our churches are quick to demand the right to wear whatever they choose, even if the Apostle Paul or their husbands disagree" ("Megyn Kelly, Whatever Happened to Modesty?" donboys.cstnews.com, Nov. 17, 2016).

Christian mothers aren't content to be keepers at home (Titus 2:5). They resist the Bible's command that the wife submit herself to her husband as unto the Lord. The Scripture's command that a woman not teach or usurp authority over the man is thought to be outdated (1 Ti. 2:12). They want an equal voice with the men in church affairs. They want their daughters to "follow their hearts," even if that means playing male-dominated sports or pursuing something like a career in the infantry.

They bob their hair and wear pants (as a product of the feminist-influenced unisex fashion movement), and woe be to that preacher who tries to reprove them. It has been a long time since a Baptist preacher published a book by the title of *Bobbed Hair, Bossy Wives, and Women Preachers*! (That was the title of a 1941 pamphlet by Evangelist John R. Rice.)

Rice wrote, "The pulpit is a place for the strongest men that we have. The preacher in the pulpit should speak with an authority that is absolutely forbidden a woman to exercise."

Where are those strong men today?

The feminization effect has resulted in a softening of the preaching and the militant stance of the church. God is a "man of war," but very few preachers are. Christ took on the Pharisees and Sadducees, and Paul took on every heretic that raised his head, but such zeal is foreign to most so-called preachers. Martin Luther took on Rome and called the pope the antichrist and called the pope's bull "all impiety, blasphemy, ignorance, impudence, hypocrisy, lying." Charles Spurgeon took on the Baptist Union and railed against "soft manners and squeamish words" in the pulpit, calling for "dinging our pulpits into blads" [smashing them with forceful preaching]. Gilbert Tennent took on the Presbyterians of his day, lifting his voice in 1740 in the midst of a synod (a regional governing body) to warn that many preachers were unregenerate and calling them "rotten-hearted hypocrites, and utter strangers to the saving knowledge of God and of their own hearts" (Joseph Tracy, *The Great Awakening*, 1842).

This type of boldness is entirely unknown among convention Baptists, and it is exceedingly rare among fundamental Baptists. The protest has long gone out of Protestants, and the "fundamentalism" has largely gone out of fundamentalists.

I am convinced that the feminization of society has resulted in a weakening of even the best churches and a rapidly growing de-emphasis on biblical militancy (being a soldier in Christ's army).

The feminization of the churches can even be seen in a softening of the hymns. There is less forthrightness in the lyrics and less military boldness in the music.

New Evangelicalism

New Evangelicalism has greatly influenced and seriously weakened Bible-believing churches, even many of those who would say that they are opposed to New Evangelicalism.

The weakening came after World War II with the advent of a religious philosophy which its own leaders branded "new evangelicalism."

During the first half of the 20th century, evangelicalism in America was synonymous with fundamentalism. Many historians make this connection, including George Marsden, who says, "There was not a practical distinction between fundamentalist and evangelical: the words were interchangeable" (*Reforming Fundamentalism*, p. 48).

When the National Association of Evangelicals (NAE) was formed in 1942, for example, participants included such fundamentalist leaders as Bob Jones, Sr., John R. Rice, Charles Woodbridge, Harry Ironside, and David Otis Fuller.

By the mid-1950s, though, a clear break between separatist fundamentalists and non-separatist evangelicals occurred. This was occasioned largely by the ecumenical evangelism of Billy Graham. Most of the stronger men dropped out of the National Association of Evangelicals. The terms "evangelicalism" and "fundamentalism" began "to refer to two different movements" (William Martin, *A Prophet with Honor*, p. 224).

The sons of evangelical-fundamentalist preachers determined to create a "New Evangelicalism." They would not be fighters; they would be diplomats; they would have a positive rather than a militant emphasis; they would be infiltrators rather than separatists. They refused to be restricted by "a separatist mentality."

The term "New Evangelicalism" defined a new type of evangelicalism to distinguish it from those who had heretofore borne that label. The term "new evangelicalism" was probably coined by Harold Ockenga (1905-1985), one of the most influential evangelical leaders of the 1940s. He was the pastor of Park Street Church (Congregational) in Boston, founder of the National Association of Evangelicals, co-founder and one-time president of Fuller Theological Seminary, first president of the World Evangelical Fellowship, president of Gordon College and Gordon-Conwell Theological Seminary, a director of the Billy Graham Evangelistic Association, and chairman of the board and one-time editor of *Christianity Today*. In the foreword to Dr. Harold Lindsell's book *The Battle for the Bible*, Ockenga stated the philosophy of new evangelicalism as follows:

> "Neo-evangelicalism was born in 1948 in connection with a convocation address which I gave in the Civic Auditorium in Pasadena. While reaffirming the theological view of fundamentalism, this address repudiated its ecclesiology and its social theory. The ringing call for a REPUDIATION OF SEPARATISM and the summons to social involvement

> received a hearty response from many evangelicals. ... It differed from fundamentalism in its repudiation of separatism and its determination to engage itself in the theological dialogue of the day. It had a new emphasis upon the application of the gospel to the sociological, political, and economic areas of life."

Ockenga did not create the movement; he merely labeled and described the new mood of positivism and non-militancy that was permeating his generation. Ockenga and the new generation of evangelicals, Billy Graham figuring most prominently, determined to abandon a strong Bible stance. Instead, they would pursue dialogue, intellectualism, and appeasement. They determined to stay within liberal denominations to attempt to change things from within rather than practice separation.

The New Evangelical would dialogue with those who teach error rather than proclaiming the Word of God boldly and without compromise and separate from them. The New Evangelical would meet the haughty liberal on his own turf with human scholarship rather than following the humble path of being counted a fool for Christ's sake by standing simply upon Scripture. New Evangelical leaders also determined to start a "rethinking process" whereby the old paths were to be continually reassessed in light of new goals, methods, and ideology.

Dr. Charles Woodbridge, a professor at Fuller Theological Seminary in its early days, a founding member of the National Association of Evangelicals, and a personal friend of men such as Harold Ockenga and Carl Henry, rejected the New Evangelicalism and spent the rest of his life warning of its dangers. In his 1969 book, *The New Evangelicalism*, he traced the downward path of New Evangelical compromise:

> "The New Evangelicalism is a theological and moral compromise of the deadliest sort. It is an insidious attack upon the Word of God. ... The New Evangelicalism advocates TOLERATION of error. It is following the downward path of ACCOMMODATION to error, COOPERATION with error, CONTAMINATION by error, and ultimate CAPITULATION to error!" (Woodbridge, *The New Evangelicalism*, pp. 9, 15).

Each passing decade has witnessed more plainly to the truth of Dr. Woodbridge's observations. Toleration of error leads to accommodation, cooperation, contamination, and capitulation. This is precisely the path that evangelical Christianity in general has taken during the past 50 years, as New Evangelicalism has spread across the world.

The New Evangelical philosophy has been adopted by such well-known Christian leaders as Billy Graham, Bill Bright, Harold Lindsell, John R.W. Stott, Luis Palau, E.V. Hill, Leighton Ford, Charles Stanley, Bill Hybels, Warren Wiersbe, Chuck Colson, Donald McGavran, Tony Campolo, Arthur Glasser, D. James Kennedy, David Hocking, Charles Swindoll, Rick Warren, Bill Hybels, and a host of other men. New Evangelicalism has been popularized through pleasant personalities and broadcast through powerful print, radio, and television media. *Christianity Today* was founded in 1956 to voice the new philosophy. Through publishing houses such as InterVarsity Press, Zondervan, Tyndale House Publishers, Moody Press, and Thomas Nelson--to name a few-- New Evangelical thought was broadcast internationally. New Evangelicalism became the working principle of large interdenominational organizations such as the National Association of Evangelicals, National Religious Broadcasters, Youth for Christ, Campus Crusade for Christ, Back to the Bible, Inter-Varsity Christian Fellowship, World Vision, Operation Mobilization, the Evangelical Foreign Mission Association, World Evangelical Fellowship, the National Sunday School Association, etc. It was spread through educational institutions such as Fuller Theological Seminary, Wheaton College, Gordon-Conwell, BIOLA, and Moody Bible Institute.

Because of the tremendous influence of these men and organizations, New Evangelical thought has swept the globe. Today, almost without exception, those who call themselves evangelicals are New Evangelicals; the terms have become synonymous. Old-line evangelicals, with rare exceptions, have either aligned with the fundamentalist movement or have adopted New Evangelicalism.

Evangelicalism's compromise is seen in its repudiation of biblical holiness. It has broken down the walls of ecclesiastical separation as well as the walls of separation from the world. The old fundamentalism was staunchly opposed to worldliness. The New Evangelical crowd has modified this. The result has been incredible to behold. R-rated movies are given positive reviews in evangelical publications. Evangelical music groups look and sound exactly like the world. Evangelical Bible College campuses have the look and feel of secular colleges. The students wear the same clothes (or lack of clothes) as the world; they drink the same beer and liquor; they dance to the same music; they celebrate the same worldly events; they care about the same worldly concerns.

Richard Quebedeaux documented this more than 35 years ago in his book, *The Worldly Evangelicals*.

> "The Gallup Poll is correct in asserting that born-again Christians 'believe in a strict moral code.' But that strictness has been considerably modified during the last few years ... the monthly question and answer column (patterned after 'Dear Abby') in *Campus Life*, Youth for Christ's magazine, gives the impression that more born-again high school age couples are having INTERCOURSE than is generally supposed. Among evangelical young people, MASTERBATION is now often seen as a gift from God. DIVORCE AND REMARRIAGE are becoming more frequent and acceptable among evangelicals of all ages, even in some of their more conservative churches. This new tolerant attitude toward divorce has been greatly facilitated both by the publication of positive articles and books on the problem by evangelical authors and by the growth of ministry to singles in evangelical churches. ... Some evangelical women are taking advantage of ABORTION on demand. Many younger evangelicals occasionally use PROFANITY in their speech and writing (though they are generally careful to avoid traditional profanity against the deity). Some of the recent evangelical sex-technique books assume that their readers peruse and view PORNOGRAPHY on occasion, and they do. Finally, in 1976 there emerged a fellowship and information organization for practicing evangelical LESBIANS AND GAY MEN and their sympathizers. There is probably just as high a percentage of gays in the evangelical movement as in the wider society. Some of them are now coming out of the closet, distributing well-articulated literature, and demanding to be recognized and affirmed by

the evangelical community at large" (Quebedeaux, *The Worldly Evangelicals*, 1978, pp. 16, 17).

James Hunter in the book *Evangelicalism the Coming Generation* (1987) documents "the evolution of behavioral standards for students" at evangelical colleges:

> "What has happened at Wheaton College, Gordon College, and Westmont College is typical of most of the colleges in this subculture. From the time of their founding to the mid-1960s, the college rules unapologetically prohibited 'profaning the Sabbath,' 'profane or obscene language or behavior,' playing billiards, playing cards and gambling, using intoxicating liquors or tobacco, theater and movie attendance, and any form of dancing—both on- and off-campus" (Hunter, p. 169).

Hunter goes on to observe that these rules have largely been dropped. Further, the worldliness on evangelical college campuses has increased significantly in the years since his book was published.

Describing this moral apostasy in *The Great Evangelical Disaster*, Francis Schaeffer said:

> "How the mindset of accommodation grows and expands. The last sixty years have given birth to a moral disaster, and what have we done? Sadly we must say that the evangelical world has been part of the disaster. ... WITH TEARS WE MUST SAY THAT ... A LARGE SEGMENT OF THE EVANGELICAL WORLD HAS BECOME SEDUCED BY THE WORLD SPIRIT OF THIS PRESENT AGE" (Schaeffer, p. 141).

The apostasy of today's evangelicalism was described by the Alliance of Confessing Evangelicals in the Cambridge Declaration. The declaration, signed by 80 theologians and church leaders, was released on April 20, 1996, at the end of a four-day conference in Cambridge, Massachusetts. The signers included James Montgomery Boice, J.A.O. Preus III, David Wells, Albert Mohler, and Michael Horton, and represented Lutheran, Reformed, Baptist, Congregational, and Independent denominations.

> "Today the light of Reformation has been significantly dimmed. The consequence is that THE WORD

'EVANGELICAL' HAS BECOME SO INCLUSIVE AS TO HAVE LOST ITS MEANING. ... As Biblical authority has been abandoned in practice, as its truths have faded from Christian consciousness, and its doctrines have lost their saliency, THE CHURCH HAS BEEN INCREASINGLY EMPTIED OF ITS INTEGRITY, MORAL AUTHORITY AND DIRECTION. ... As evangelical faith becomes secularized, its interests have been blurred with those of the culture. THE RESULT IS A LOSS OF ABSOLUTE VALUES, PERMISSIVE INDIVIDUALISM, AND A SUBSTITUTION OF WHOLENESS FOR HOLINESS, recovery for repentance, intuition for truth, feeling for belief, chance for providence, and immediate gratification for enduring hope" (*The Cambridge Declaration*, 1996).

The Southern Baptist Convention is an example of the influence of New Evangelicalism. This is the largest "Protestant" denomination in America and it has a reputation of being staunchly and traditionally Bible believing, but when one examines the SBC at the congregational level one typically finds extreme worldliness.

The vast majority of SBC congregations do not preach separation from the world, and the teens in the churches commonly love the world's music, fashions, entertainment, etc. Like the world, they go almost-naked to the beaches, dance to rock & roll, wear whatever immodest fashions are in style, even get excited about occultic entertainment trends such as Harry Potter.

I grew up in Southern Baptist churches, and it was in a Southern Baptist youth group that I first learned to love rock music. The pastor's son and the deacons' sons had all of the latest rock albums, and I listened to them when I visited their homes. Large numbers of those who attended the rock dances at my junior and senior high school were church kids. I don't recall even one kid in our church that had a serious relationship with the Lord. We professed Christ with our lips, but we loved the world with our hearts.

That which is sadly true of the Southern Baptist Convention is true of most other denominations today. Even fundamentalist Bible churches and independent Baptist congregations are following suit. They do not preach or practice separation from the world.

Television

Television's influence on modern society is nearly indescribable. In looking back on my childhood growing up in a Baptist church, attending services at least three times a week, the three major influences that stole my heart for the world were public school friendships, pop music, and television, and the three were intimately associated. We got a television when I was about nine years old (1958), and though the programs were innocent compared to today, they certainly did not encourage me spiritually. We got our television a couple of years after Elvis appeared on the *Ed Sullivan Show*. By the time I reached junior high school, I did everything I could to stay home on Sunday nights, because that was when the most exciting programs were on, such as the *Disney Hour* and *Ed Sullivan*. I don't remember if I was home that Sunday night in 1964 when the Beatles appeared on Ed Sullivan, but I could have been. I was in high school and about that time my parents were having a lot of problems and had pretty much given up on trying to keep me in church. I had already started drinking and carousing with my public school buddies every weekend. There is no doubt that television and movies fed my carnal imagination and, together with rock & roll, inflamed me with a passion for the things of the world.

One of my sisters gives the following testimony:

> "As a little girl, I can remember the television being on constantly. It was my 'friend' and a means of escape from the troubles and insecurities in my life. As I would watch a certain program, I would think, 'If I just had her personality or looks, I would be happy.' Later, when I was older and programming became increasingly wicked, I would stay up late and watch hours of mindless, foolish, empty sitcoms, totally oblivious to the damage it was doing to me. Like a drug, it was altering my mind. When I gave my life to the Lord in 1987, I realized how much of my life had been adversely affected by the media and television. The Lord cleansed my mind as I read His Word and replaced the vain, man-centered philosophies with Truth. We have made the deliberate choice not to have a television in our home today and have purposed to not set any wicked thing before our eyes (Psalm 101:3). A child needs to learn how to

communicate with his family, not just sit in a trance in front of a TV."

Brian Snider had a similar experience growing up. He says,

"I always tell people that 3-4 hours of church a week can't hold a candle to 30-40 hours of television as far as power and influence on a young kid. Church was boring; television was fun."

The following testimony describes the addictive power of television and its negative influence on spirituality:

"I got saved when I was 19 and used to watch television 8-10 hours a day and 26 hours on the weekends. When I started going to church and then through Bible College, where there were no televisions, I realized how much it had influenced the way I thought and perceived life. When we got married we decided not to have a television and have been thankful for it. It was only on deputation when we had more access to TV's and found when we turned them on that hours would easily be wasted, even just watching *FOX News*. Not to mention having to continually turn the commercials off. It got so annoying you either wanted to just leave it alone and not turn it off or miss something if you did turn it off. Unfortunately, leaving it on would win, and being aware of this we solidified in our minds we would not have a TV in our home, or cable for that matter. **Both the programming and the commercials are written by non-Christians who are trying to influence others with their pagan humanistic philosophies and lifestyles.** Cheating, illicit sex, drugs, homosexuality, teens in adult situations, Darwinism, cussing, and all kinds of things Christians shouldn't be setting before their eyes. Numerous times, even on 'conservative' *FOX News*, they had a story on prostitutes and actually showed a video of pole dancers."

Only the Lord knows how many Christian lives, homes, and churches have been spiritually weakened, even ruined, by television.

A few pastors of Independent Baptist churches used to preach against it and warn the people of its evil influence, but their number has decreased dramatically over the past 15 or 20 years.

The Internet/Smartphone

The great power of television has been eclipsed by that of the Internet. Today you don't need a television to access moral filth.

It was the **Internet** (beginning in the 1990s) and the **smartphone** (beginning especially in 2007 with the introduction of the iPhone) that have made the world and apostasy all intrusive. No church today can escape the effect of this technology, from the cities of wealthy nations to the villages of Third World countries.

In the Internet/smart phone generation, church young people can access the pop culture at the touch of a finger. Church people can connect with any song writer and be influenced by his or her music, philosophy, and lifestyle.

Church women can be influenced by popular evangelical teachers such as Beth Moore.

Conclusion

We have described theological liberalism, the public school system, materialism and working mothers, the rock & roll pop culture, pop psychology, the feminist movement, New Evangelicalism, television, and the Internet.

These and other cultural and doctrinal factors have combined to create a perfect storm of end-time apostasy that every church must face.

And the Word of God tells us that this storm will grow stronger as the time of Christ continues to draw near.

> "This know also, that in the last days perilous times shall come. For men shall be lovers of their own selves, covetous, boasters, proud, blasphemers, disobedient to parents, unthankful, unholy, Without natural affection, trucebreakers, false accusers, incontinent, fierce, despisers of those that are good, Traitors, heady, highminded, lovers of pleasures more than lovers of God; Having a form of godliness, but denying the power thereof: from such turn away. ... But evil men and seducers shall wax worse and worse, deceiving, and being deceived" (2 Timothy 3:1-5, 13).
>
> "For the time will come when they will not endure sound doctrine; but after their own lusts shall they heap to themselves teachers, having itching ears; And they shall turn

away *their* ears from the truth, and shall be turned unto fables" (2 Timothy 4:3-4).

The storm of end-time apostasy is amplified and empowered by the technology of our age.

Spiritual protection is available and victory is possible, but it requires that church leaders take everything to a higher, stronger level if they want to be standing for the Word of God in the future.

Evangelism must be more biblical. The door to church membership must be guarded more carefully. Love for Christ must be more fervent. Prayer must be taken more seriously. The church must be more deeply immersed in God's Word. Holiness must be pursued more earnestly. Discipleship must be more scriptural. Discipline and separation must be stricter.

Characteristics of a Discipling Church

It has a first love for Christ.
It has qualified leaders.
It is careful about salvation.
It is careful about church membership.
It has a disciplined environment.
It has an atmosphere of charity.
It is strong in God's Word.
It is strong in prayer.
It is a reproving church.
It maintains God's standards for workers.
It is zealous for biblical separation.
It is careful about music.
It is a hard working church.
It builds godly homes.
It disciples youth.
It educates and protects the church from every spiritual danger.
It has a strong vision for evangelism and world missions.
It trains preachers.

Arguments Against a Discipling Church

The following is a summary of some of the common arguments against the principle of a discipling church that we have developed in this book:

We can't know the heart of the people.

It's true that we can't know the heart perfectly, but the Bible says the heart evidences itself in the life and speech. Christ emphasized this at least four times:

> "By their fruits ye shall know them" (Mt. 7:16).

> "Wherefore by their fruits ye shall know them" (Mt. 7:20).

> "for the tree is known by his fruit" (Mt. 12:33).

> "A good man out of the good treasure of his heart bringeth forth that which is good; and an evil man out of the evil treasure of his heart bringeth forth that which is evil: for of the abundance of the heart his mouth speaketh" (Lu. 6:45).

I have rarely been totally surprised at people's actions. Recently a teenage girl in our church ran off with an unsaved boy, and though no one had prior knowledge of her intimate relationship with this boy, not even her parents, many suspected that she was deceitful and hypocritical even though she was faithful to church services. Pretty much we do know one another by the fruit of our lives, though not infallibly.

If God were not ready to give church leaders insight into the reality of the member's lives, He would not have commanded them to do such things as warn every man and teach every man in order to present every man perfect in Christ Jesus (Col. 1:28). This requires wisdom about the spiritual condition of the individual members of the church, as to where they are and where they need to go.

When it comes to salvation, the Bible teaches that there is clearly seen evidence thereof in the person's life. See John 10:27; 2 Corinthians 5:17; Titus 1:16; 1 John 2:3-4.

On the authority of the clear teaching of God's Word, I am confident that we can usually know who is a true disciple of Christ and who is not. There will the odd Judas who slips in, but that is the exception and not the rule.

Do we have authority to wait for baptism?

Another argument about being careful about salvation and looking for some evidence and perhaps holding off baptism until the candidate has received instruction is that in the Bible we see baptism closely following salvation.

We agree that baptism should closely follow salvation. The only thing we want to know if the person is truly saved and if he or she understands the meaning of baptism.

When we see in our ministry the type of dramatic conversion we see everywhere in Scripture (e.g., woman at the well, Zacchaeus, the 3,000 on the day of Pentecost, the Ethiopian eunuch, Lydia, the Philippian jailer) we baptize such a person as quickly as possible, because this type of conversion is exactly what we are looking for. We quickly baptize the very kind of people that were baptized in the Bible. Show me such a person in your ministry, and I will urge you to baptize him without delay (assuming he has been instructed in the meaning of baptism so that he knows what he is doing).

But we aren't interested in baptizing someone who has made a mere profession of faith without any demonstration of the reality of the new birth.

Could it be that you are going too far in the matter of evidence of salvation?

We don't want to go any further than the Scripture goes, and we don't believe that we have. There is a very strong emphasis on evidence in God's Word, and we have given all of the Scriptures that we believe to be relevant to the issue.

Do you mean to say that a new believer is a strong disciple?

We don't believe that a new believer is necessarily a "strong disciple" or a "100% disciple" or anything like that. We simply believe what the Bible says, that Christ's sheep hear His voice and follow Him (John 10:27), nothing more or less. To hear Christ's voice and to follow Him is a disciple.

At the same time, discipleship is a matter of growing.

Do you mean to say that a new believer is 100% submitted to Christ's lordship?

No believer is 100% submitted to Christ's lordship in every matter and in every area of his life.

To say that a believer receives Christ as Lord and believes on Him as Lord, as the Bible plainly teaches (Lk. 23:42; Ac. 11:17; 16:31; 20:21; Ro. 10:9), is not to say that the believer receives Christ as 100% Lord of all of his life.

We have never said this. As we have shown in the chapter "A Discipling Church Begins with Caution about Salvation," this was a straw man that was invented by Jack Hyles to justify his heresies and unscriptural methodology.

Was Corinth a church of disciples?

Yes, Corinth was a church of disciples. Though many of the members were carnal, Corinth was a church whose members gave clear evidence of a saving conversion experience (1 Co. 6:9-11). It was a church that was zealous for the things of Christ, zealous for spiritual things (1 Co. 14:12), and it was a church that abounded in "faith, utterance, knowledge, diligence, and love" (2 Co. 8:7).

Corinth was carnal, but it was not lukewarm and half dead as so many Baptist churches are today. And Paul dealt with Corinth's carnality forcefully and persistently with every tool at his disposal.

Was Lot a disciple?

Lot was not a New Testament believer, and he should not be used as an example of a New Testament believer.

At the same time, Lot also cannot be used as an example of a believer who shows no sign of spiritual life. Peter says Lot was "just," which only comes by faith in God's promise in Christ. And he gave evidence that he was just. Lot was a carnal believer who made unwise decisions that resulted in sorrow and destruction, but he was "vexed with the filthy conversation of the wicked" (2 Pe. 2:7). And unlike his wife and married children, Lot obeyed the angel and fled Sodom.

Lot is not an example of someone who prays a sinner's prayer but shows no sign of new life in Christ, and Lot is not an example of a worldly teenager that professes Christ but secretly loves the filthy conversation of the wicked.

Do you think your program can produce a perfect church?

No, there is no such thing as a perfect church. Every church I have been a member of and every church I have helped start has been a seriously imperfect church. At best, a church is composed of sinners saved by grace, sinners who still have the "old man" and live in a fallen world. The very best church on earth has to deal continually with sin, carnality, and backsliding. The very fact that a book on "The Discipling Church" has to deal much with discipline proves that we don't believe in a perfect church. We do believe that God wants churches to be right and that He is eager to help us if we set out to honor and obey His Word.

We don't have a program of our own. We are wholly inadequate to know how to operate a New Testament church. What we have tried to do is to follow the Bible's "program" for the church.

Though we do not believe that a church in this present world will achieve any sort of perfection, we do believe that a church that is very careful about appointing leaders and is extra careful about salvation and church membership, that is serious about discipleship and discipline, that aims to be *very* strong in the Word of God, etc., will be a much stronger church than one that isn't.

Do you think that a formula will produce a strong church?

No mere formula will produce a strong church.

A strong church comes by the blessing of God upon an obedient people.

We organize things pertaining to the church in a systematic way for the sake of teaching. A church is not operated by an outline, but an outline can help us understand spiritual principles so that we can apply them in a wise and fruitful manner.

Sample Church Covenant

The following is adapted from the Church Covenant of Fellowship Baptist Church, Kathmandu, Nepal.

The Covenant is for the purpose of maintaining unity in the church. See 1 Corinthians 1:10. Since it is God's will that each church have one mind in doctrine and practice, the covenant must be agreed upon by each person who joins the church.

Church Goals

1. A gospel preaching center (Mark 16:15). Our goal is for the gospel to be broadcast by every means possible, through word of mouth, through literature, through correspondence courses, through radio, through the regular church services, through special gospel meetings, and any other means the Lord shows us. Every believer will be challenged to make this a priority in his life in that he is an ambassador of Christ (2 Co. 5:20).

2. A discipleship center (Mt. 28:19-20; Col. 1:28). Our goal is for new converts to be discipled and encouraged and strengthened in the Lord and prepared to do the Lord's work.

3. A leadership training institution (2 Ti. 2:2). Our goal is to train preachers and church leaders.

4. A missionary center (Acts 13:1-3). Our goal is for this church to be the headquarters for church planting.

5. A church that is an example (2 Co. 9:1-2; 1 Th. 1:6-7). We want to start a church that can be an example to others: in preaching, evangelism, doctrine, standards, music, order, family life and child training, vision and ideas, team leadership, and prayer. We realize that we are only sinners saved by grace and that we will be far from perfect, but by the grace of God we want to be a good example of what a scriptural church should be. This is not for our pride or our glory but for God's glory.

Receiving Church Members

We must be very careful about receiving new members (Pr. 3:5-6; Josh. 9:3-6, 14-15). Our aim is a regenerate church membership. If we are hasty and careless in this matter, the church will grow weak because it will be a mixed multitude of saved and unsaved.

We must not forget that not everyone who says they believe in Jesus is truly saved. The Bible warns that the heart of man is deceitful (Jer. 17:9) and sometimes people pretend to "believe" only in order to try to get something or from some other false motive. The people in Matthew 7:21-23 call upon Jesus and do many works, but they are not saved because they do not know Christ personally. The people in John 2:23-25 "believed," but Jesus knew that they were not believing on Him for salvation; they were merely wanting a king to provide for them and to conquer their enemies. Compare John 6:15, 26). In John 6:66, these same people turned away from Jesus because they were offended at His teaching. Also in Acts 8:12-13, Simon "believed," but he was only believing in order to get power and was not believing sincerely for salvation. See Acts 8:18-23.

The requirement for those who are joining by profession of faith in Christ.

In Acts 2 there were two things that were required of those who joined the church at Jerusalem.

1. They repented of their sin and believed on Christ (Acts 2:38-41).

Paul also preached repentance toward God and faith toward our Lord Jesus Christ (Acts 20:21).

Repentance is to surrender to God's authority. It means to turn around and go in a different direction. It is to turn to God *from* idols (1 Th. 1:9). Repentance is a change of heart, not a change of life. If there is a repentant heart, there is a willingness to change the life. Two examples of repentance are Zacchaeus (Lu. 19:5-9) and the Prodigal Son (Lu. 15:17-19).

Saving faith is to receive the gospel joyfully. It is something that is done freely with the full heart. There is no compulsion. Compare Acts 8:37.

2. They were baptized scripturally (Acts 2:41). They were baptized after they believed and were saved, and they were baptized by immersion as public testimony of their faith in Christ

and as a picture of the gospel: the death, burial, and resurrection of Christ (Ro. 6:3-4).

Requirement for joining from another church.
1. The candidate must have a scriptural testimony of salvation.
2. The candidate must testify that his baptism was scriptural. This involves three things:
   - The baptism must follow salvation.
   - The baptism must be by immersion.
   - The baptism must be performed by a New Testament church that has the authority to baptize. This does not mean that the church must agree with our church in all matters of doctrine and practice. It means that it is a church that has a sound gospel and a sound doctrine of Christ and other such "fundamental" doctrines of the New Testament faith so that it can be called a true church. We will not accept baptism from false groups such as the Roman Catholic Church, Mormon, Church of Christ (who teach baptismal regeneration and salvation by grace plus works), Seventh-day Adventist, or Jehovah's Witness. We will not accept baptism from Protestant denominations that baptize infants. We will not receive members from any church that teaches that a child of God can lose his salvation, because this is a perversion of the gospel.

3. If possible, the church leaders must contact the leaders of the other church to see if the candidate is a member in good standing.
4. The candidate must go through the baptismal/church membership class and agree with the church's covenant and doctrinal statement. We want the body to be completely likeminded (1 Co. 1:10). The individual must read the entire covenant and read each of the Scriptures that are referenced.

Steps for Receiving New Church Members
1. A candidate for church membership must meet with the elders and give account of his salvation and his qualification to be a member. They must make sure that the individual understands salvation and baptism. They must try to ascertain whether or not he has been born again.
2. The elders should agree unanimously on the decision as to whether to receive the candidate for membership. If there is doubt

on the part of a leader, the decision should wait until there is full agreement.

3. If the elders are satisfied with the candidate's testimony of salvation and qualification for church membership, they will recommend him/her to the church for membership.

4. Standing before the church, the candidate must give his testimony of salvation and publicly agree with the church's Covenant and Statement of Faith.

5. The church receives the new member by a vote.

6. The candidate becomes a member after being baptized, and if he has already been baptized scripturally, he becomes a member at that time.

Standards for Workers

Standards for Elders

The standards for elders are found in 1 Timothy 3:1-7, 11; and Titus 1:5-9. These standards emphasize that the pastor must be blameless in his personal Christian life, in his family, and in his reputation before the community. A divorced man cannot be a pastor because he cannot be the example that he should be before the church and the community (1 Pe. 5:3). The pastor's wife and children must also serve the Lord and not have a bad reputation (1 Ti. 3:4, 5, 11; Titus 1:6).

Standards for Deacons

The standards for deacons and their wives are found in 1 Timothy 3:8-11.

Standards for General Workers

The following standards apply to all church workers, including song leaders, Sunday School teachers, those who take up the offerings or greet visitors, read the Bible in the services, etc.

It is important to establish such standards for many reasons.

First, God requires it (1 Co. 4:2).

Second, the workers represent the church and Jesus Christ. The community knows who the church workers are and if they don't live as they should, they will bring reproach upon Christ. Visitors judge the church by those who are prominent in leadership and work. If the workers don't live good Christian lives, the unbelievers judge that Christianity is an empty religion.

Third, the workers are examples to the rest of the church. Having standards for church workers is an important part of raising the level of Christian living for the entire church. It is not possible for a church to have worker-type standards for every member, but it is possible to require a certain level of standard for those who serve in the church. A person doesn't have to teach Sunday School or work in the music ministry, etc., but if he does it is not unreasonable for the church to require him to meet the following standards, which are mere basic standards of Christian living. New members learn how to live for Christ by observing the church leaders and workers, and if they do not live right the entire church is affected. If the Sunday School teachers, for example, are not required to maintain the following standards, the students will learn from their poor example, but if Sunday School teachers are required to maintain these standards the students will follow their example and will grow in Christ.

Fourth, the workers should challenge the other believers (2 Co. 9:2). The members learn that if they want to serve the Lord in any capacity in the church beyond merely attending, they must live a godly, faithful Christian life. I recall how I was challenged by this type of standard when I was a new believer. I wanted God to use my life and I wanted to prepare for His service. I learned that the Bible school I wanted to attend had high standards, and this was a motivation for me to cut my hair, quit smoking, and do other things in preparation for the Lord's service. The standards challenged me to live up to them for the sake of serving Christ.

Following are the standards that this church requires for general workers:

1. Good Christian testimony (2 Co. 8:18). Church workers must have a good testimony so that the name of Christ and the reputation of the church are not injured.

2. Faithfulness (1 Co. 4:2). Church workers must be faithful-- faithful to the church services and activities (Heb. 10:25), faithful to their assigned church duties, etc. There are special circumstances that arise, of course, which the church member should discuss with the leaders. The Bible warns that we should not put our confidence in unfaithful people (Pr. 25:19). If a church

worker must miss a service because of his job or some emergency, he should talk to the leaders and get their permission.

3. Honest reputation (2 Co. 8:21). Church workers must be honest in their dealings with all men and must have a reputation of honesty. The church worker must not steal, must not lie, and must pay his debts.

4. Diligence (2 Co. 8:22). Church workers must show diligence in their Christian lives and in their work for the Lord. A person who is lazy and half-hearted should not be involved in Christian ministry. See also Ro. 12:11; Eph. 4:28; 1 Th. 4:11; 2 Th. 3:10.

5. Separation from the evil things of the world (Ro. 12:2; 1 Joh. 2:15-17; Jas. 4:4). Church workers must avoid such things as unwholesome movies and television programs, using or selling liquor, and worldly partying. They should also not work in places where such things are conducted. Church workers should avoid worldly music such as cinema music, pop music on the radio, and also worldly Christian music produced by other churches. Worldly Christian music is music that sounds like the world's music.

6. Modest dress. The following are six Bible principles that teach us how to dress properly before man and God. Our church requires that the female workers dress in a modest fashion all of the time and not just when they are at church. *First, the Christian's clothing must cover the body properly and not expose the parts of the body which have particular sexual appeal.* Isaiah 47:2 says that for a woman to bare her leg and thigh is nakedness. Thus immodest clothing would include skirts or dresses that show the leg, shorts, slit skirts, low blouses, short blouses that bare the midriff, deep V-necked dresses, backless dresses, halter tops, and any modern swimsuit. Immodest clothing would also include any style that uses flimsy material that can be seen through. *Second, the Christian's clothing does not sensually accent the body.* Tight, clinging attire is as immodest as skimpy attire because the woman's figure is emphasized and accented, and man's attention is directed to that which is forbidden outside of marriage. *Third, the Christian's clothing is not extravagant.* When the apostle deals with modest attire in 1 Timothy 2:9, he mentions "broided hair, gold, pearls, and costly array." The goal of this world's fashion industry is to create a haughty, ostentatious, worldly-wise look, as well as a sexual look. The godly woman will reject such fashions. This means

that a godly Christian woman would not wear an inordinate amount of jewelry or makeup so as to draw attention to herself and not to Christ. We must remember to "let our moderation be known unto all men" (Php. 4:5). We must dress for the Lord's glory and not our own (1 Co. 10:31). Therefore, at Fellowship Baptist Church we ask that women and girl workers not wear lots of makeup, including bright lipstick and bright nail polish. *Fourth, the Christian's clothing is to be sexually distinctive* (Ge. 1:27; De. 22:5; 1 Co. 11:14-15). The woman's attire and appearance is to be distinctively feminine and the man's distinctively masculine. The modern unisex movement is rebellion against Almighty God and His Word, and the Christian should have nothing to do with any fashion associated with it. We believe that this means the woman should not wear pants, because these have historically been man's apparel and it was the feminist unisex movement in the 1960s that popularized pants on women. This also means that men should not wear long hair or earrings or jewelry that is feminine in appearance. *Fifth, the Christian's clothing is to be identified with holiness and godliness and not to be identified with anything that is evil* (1 Th. 5:22; Eph. 5:11). If a clothing style is identified with rebellion against God's laws, with anarchy, with sexual freedom, with blasphemy, with idolatry, with moral decadence, or with any other evil it should not be worn by a Christian. This would prohibit fashions, for example, that have come out of the world of punk and rap, such as long hair on men, tattoos, torn jeans, low slung baggy jeans, and such things. This would also prohibit tattoos with their identification with rebellion and paganism. Church members should not wear anything that would pertain to Buddhist or Hindu culture, such as holy strings or tikka. Sixth, *the Christian's clothing is to mark him or her as peculiar unto the Lord, as one who has been redeemed from all iniquity and who is zealous for good works* (Titus 2:14). God's people are to be separate, peculiar, different, set apart. We must bear His stamp. We must stand out from the crowd because we are walking by heaven's light. We must not fly the world's flag. When God's people are no longer peculiar before the world, they have compromised the Word of God. We must fear God more than man. We must be more concerned about pleasing God than people. We must not draw back from bearing Christ's reproach in this wicked world. He said, "Whosoever therefore shall be ashamed of me and of my words in this adulterous and sinful generation; of him also shall the Son of man be ashamed, when he cometh in the glory of his Father with the holy angels" (Mr. 8:38). Paul said that if we deny Christ, he also will deny us (2 Ti. 2:12).

In order to insure that ladies and girls serving as workers in Fellowship Baptist Church are modest at all times, we ask that kurtas be below the knee. Also skirts or maxis should be long, not too tight, and not made of too thin material. The suruwals also should not be tight. Pants should not be worn under a kurta. A kurta with side slits above the waist is immodest. The slits on kurtas should be well below the waist so that when a woman is walking, sitting, bending, and working the shape of her body is not shown.

7. Sound in doctrine (1 Ti. 1:3). Church workers must agree with the doctrines of the Bible as taught by the church.

8. Godly submission to the pastor-elders (1 Th. 5:12-13; 1 Ti. 5:17; Heb. 13:17). Pastors are not worldly lord's over the church (1 Pe. 5:1-3), but God has given them authority to teach the Word of God, to exhort in the way of righteousness, to lead in the fulfillment of the Great Commission, and to discipline those who err. Thus, as long as the pastors are following the Bible, the church members should submit and be a blessing and seek for unity in the congregation. The pastors should be given the benefit of the doubt.

Standards for Church Music

1. The church music must teach sound doctrine (Col. 3:16). The words of the songs must be right according to the teaching of the Bible. Most Contemporary Christian Music is unacceptable because it represents the ecumenical charismatic philosophy or it presents a vague message that lacks doctrinal clarity and strength.

2. The church music must be holy and separate from the world (Eph. 5:19; Ro. 12:2; 1 Joh. 2:15-16). This means that the church's music will not sound like the pop music played on the radio and the music that the world uses for dancing and drinking and partying. Our church music will not use a backbeat and other forms of dance syncopation, because this has always been associated with sensuality and has been characterized as "the sexy" part of pop music. We believe it is not wise to use drums (except in

an orchestra) and electric guitars in church music, because they are so easily used in a pop music fashion.

3. The church music must not borrow from and build bridges to the world of contemporary Christian music, since it is a major element of building the apostate one-world church and represents a foreign spirit (Ro. 16:17-18; 1 Co. 10:21; Eph. 5:11; 2 Ti. 3:5; Re. 18:4). This is evident by examining the history of this music as well as the lives and beliefs of the contemporary musicians. See the free eBook *The Directory of Contemporary Worship Musicians*. See also the free eVideo presentations "The Foreign Spirit of Contemporary Worship Music" and "The Transformational Power of Contemporary Praise Music." These materials are available from www.wayoflife.org.

4. The church music must not be designed to produce a charismatic style mystical experience (1 Peter 5:8). The objective of charismatic music is to produce an experiential worship, to "feel God," and toward this end contemporary worshipers use music with a strong dance rhythm, non-resolving chord sequences, repetition, and electronic modulation so that people will get carried away emotionally. The Bible tells us to be sober-minded and not to allow anything to capture our hearts other than God and His Word. We are not supposed to open ourselves up unquestioningly to any experience but are to continually test everything by the standard of God's absolute Truth (1 Th. 5:21).

Church Finances

The following are some important lessons from the Bible about the church's finances:

1. The church's work should be supported by the tithes and offerings of the members and not by worldly means such as investments or operating businesses (Ge. 14:20; 28:22; Mal. 3:10; 1 Co. 16:1-2). The tithes and offerings should be taken up each week (1 Co. 16:1). Each church member should give a proportion of what God has given to him (1 Co. 16:2). God has promised to bless those who give cheerfully (2 Co. 9:6-8).

2. The tithes and offerings belong to the Lord (Mal. 3:10). This means that when people give to the church, they are not giving to men but to God. Church members must not think that the church

money is their own money; it is the Lord's. The finances must be used prayerfully and wisely according to God's will. No one can borrow from the church money (not the elders nor the church members), because the money is only for the Lord's business and should never be used for private purposes.

3. The church should not seek help from the unsaved for the Lord's work (3 Joh. 7; Ge. 14:21-23; 2 Ki. 5:15-16). When the offerings are taken, the leaders should explain that it is the business of the church members to support the church. If a visitor wants to give to the offering as the bag is passed, that is his business, but the church should not seek help from the unsaved.

4. Only men with a good Christian reputation should handle the money ("honest report" Acts 6:3; 2 Co. 8:18-19).

5. The money must be handled in a careful and honest manner (2 Co. 8:20-21). This means that everything must be done openly and honestly. The counting of the money should be done by at least two men. Good records must be kept. Regular reports must be given to the church members so everyone understands how the money is being used. If a question is raised about the use of the finances, the leaders should give an answer.

6. Business matters are the type of things that deacons handle (Acts 6:1-6). The first deacons were selected to take care of such matters so that the pastors could be free for the spiritual ministry (vv. 2, 4).

7. The church money is handled on a day-by-day basis by the pastors and deacons, with the pastors having the final word (Acts 4:34-37; 6:3; Heb. 13:17). Money can be used for normal operating expenses up to the amount set by the church. For expenses beyond that, the church must vote on the matter.

8. Major decisions should be made by the pastors and church members working together (Acts 6:1-6). This is the example we see when the first deacons were selected. The elders gave the instructions and set the standards (vv. 3-4); the church made the selection (v. 5); then the elders conducted the ordination (v. 6). This is a good example for how major decisions can be made in a church. It is the elders who must decide what decisions should be brought before the church members for a vote. In our church, when major financial (and other) decisions are made, the pastors first meet with the deacons to discuss the matter and to decide

what to present to the church members. They then meet with the men of the church to discuss the matter. The men are given one week to discuss the matter with their wives who are church members, after which another meeting is held to settle the matter by a vote. By this method, the men take the leadership, but the women are not left out of the process. This method also helps the church avoid hasty decisions.

9. The leaders are stewards and will give an account unto God; they must therefore be very careful about how they handle the money and about the decisions that they make (1 Co. 3:9-15; 4:1-2; Jas. 3:1; 1 Pe. 5:1-5).

10. The church should support pastors that labor in the Word and doctrine (1 Co. 9:13-14; Ga. 6:6; 1 Ti. 5:17-18). It should not support lazy men or men who spend much of their time in secular business, but only men who are zealous for the work of Christ.

11. The main work of the church is to fulfill the Great Commission (Mt. 28:19-20; Mr. 16:15; Acts 1:8). This means the main use of the church money is for preaching the gospel, teaching the Bible, and planting new churches. The church should support church planters and preachers (3 Joh. 5-8; Tit. 3:12-13; Acts 15:3; Ro. 15:24; 1 Co. 16:5-6; 2 Co. 1:16).

Church Discipline

Bible discipline is training and chastening with the goal of conforming the church and its individual members to the will of God. It involves teaching, encouragement, correction and reproof, punishment when required, and restoration. Church discipline involves everything necessary to keep a church pure before God (1 Co. 5:7-8). Discipline is a matter of love—love for God, love for holiness, love for the truth, love for Christ's testimony in the church, love for the brethren, and love for the unsaved who are observing the church's testimony.

A study on church discipline can be found in the chapter "A Discipling Church Has a Disciplined Environment."

Statement of Faith

The Scriptures

The Bible, with its 66 books, is the very Word of God. The Bible is verbally and plenarily inspired as originally given and it is divinely preserved in the Hebrew Masoretic Text and the Greek Received Text. The Bible is our sole authority in all matters of faith and practice. The King James Version in English is an example of an accurate translation of the preserved Hebrew and Greek texts; we believe it can be used with confidence. We reject modern textual criticism and the modern versions that this pseudo-science has produced, such as the American Standard Version, the New American Standard Version, the Revised Standard Version, and the New International Version). We also reject the dynamic equivalency method of Bible translation which results in a careless version that only contains the general ideas rather than the very words of God. Examples of dynamic equivalency versions are the Today's English Version, the Living Bible, and The Message.

2 Samuel 23:2; Psalm 12:6-7; Proverbs 30:5-6; Matthew 5:18; 24:35; John 17:17; Acts 1:16; 3:21; 1 Corinthians 2:7-16; 2 Timothy 3:15- 17; 2 Peter 1:19-21; Revelation 22:18-19

The Godhead

The Scriptures testify that God is a spirit whose nature is light, love, and holiness; He is infinite, eternal, all wise, all powerful, all knowing. There is only one God, but that God is revealed as three distinct Persons: Father, Son, and Holy Spirit. This is the traditional doctrine of the Trinity.

Genesis 1:1; Exodus 3:14; Psalm 115:3; Luke 1:37; Psalm 139:1-16: 145:17; 1 Peter 1:16; Malachi 3:6; John 3:16; Psalm 103:8; John 4:24; 5:26; 1 Thessalonians 1:19; Deuteronomy 6:4; Genesis 1:26; Matthew 3:16-17; 28:19-20; John 14:16; 1 Corinthians 12:4-6; 2 Corinthians 13:14; 1 John 5:7; 1 John 3:16

The Father

We believe in God the Father, perfect in holiness, infinite in wisdom, measureless in power. We rejoice that He concerns Himself mercifully in the affairs of men, that He hears and answers prayer, and that He saves from sin and death all that come to Him through Jesus Christ.

Genesis 1:1; 17:1; Exodus 6:3; Deuteronomy 4:35; Psalm 90:2; 139:7-10; Isaiah 40:28; John 4:24; 1 John 1:5

The Lord Jesus Christ

The second Person of the triune God is the Son, whose name is the Lord Jesus Christ. He existed eternally with the Father. At His incarnation, without change in His deity, the eternal Son of God became a man through the miracle of the virgin birth. Jesus Christ is fully God and fully man. He lived a sinless life, performed miracles to prove that He was the Messiah, died a substitutionary death for all men, was buried, and arose from the grave bodily the third day. Thereafter He ascended into heaven and is presently fulfilling His intercessory and mediatorial ministry. He has promised to return to Rapture the church age saints prior to the Tribulation and to return to the earth to establish His millennial reign at the end of the Tribulation.

Isaiah 53:4-5; Matthew 18:11; 20:28; John 1:1,14; 3:16; 8:58; Romans 3:25-26; 1 Corinthians 15:3; 2 Corinthians 5:14-21; Philippians 2:6-11; Hebrews 2:9-15; 1 Peter 1:19

The Holy Spirit

The Holy Spirit is the third Person of the Godhead (Mt. 28:20; 1 Joh. 5:7). He is eternal (Heb. 9:14). He was active in creation (Ge. 1:2). He fashions men and imparts life to them (Job 33:4). He anointed and empowered Israel's judges, kings, and prophets (Jud. 3:10; 6:34; 11:29; 1 Sa. 16:13). He inspired the Scriptures, imparting the words of God to holy men of old (Joh. 14:26; 1 Co. 2:11-13; 1 Pe. 1:10-12; 2 Pe. 1:19-21). He convicts the world of sin and draws men to Christ (Ge. 6:3; Joh. 16:7-11). He came upon the church age saints at Pentecost to empower them for world evangelism (Acts 1:8). He regenerates those who believe (Joh. 3:5-8) and seals them unto the resurrection (Eph. 1:13-14). He indwells all who are born again, sanctifies them (1 Pe. 1:2), equips and empowers them for service (Acts 1:8; 1 Co. 12), and illuminates their understanding of the truth. He calls and sends missionaries (Acts 13:1-4).

Creation

We believe in the Genesis account of Creation and that it is to be accepted literally and not figuratively; that the world was made in six 24-hour days; that man was created directly in God's own image and did not evolve from any lower form of life; that all animal and vegetable life was made directly and made subject to God's law that they bring forth only "after their kind."

Genesis 1; Nehemiah 9:6; Job 38:4-41; Ps. 104:24-30; Joh. 1:1-3; Acts 14:15; 17:24-26; Ro. 1:18-21; Col. 1:15-17; Hebrews 1:1-3; 11:3

The fall of man

By disobedience to the revealed will of God, man became sinful and subject to the power of the devil. When Adam and Eve sinned, their hearts became fallen and corrupted by sin, and this corrupt nature has been transmitted to the entire human race so that man is not only a sinner by nature and practice, but is guilty and condemned before God and possesses within himself no means of recovery or salvation.

Genesis 2:16-17; 3:1-24; Psalm 51:5; Ecclesiastes 7:29; Isaiah 53:6; Jeremiah 17:9; Mark 7:20-23; Romans 3:9-20; 5:12; Ephesians 2:1-3

The way of salvation

Salvation is by the grace of God alone, which means that it is a free gift that is neither merited nor secured in whole or in part by any virtue or work of man or by any religious duty or sacrament. The gift of God's grace was purchased by Jesus Christ alone, by His blood and death on Calvary. The sinner receives God's salvation by repentance toward God and faith in the Lord Jesus Christ. Though salvation is by God's grace alone through faith, it results in a changed life; salvation is not by works but it is unto works. The faith for salvation comes by hearing God's Word. Men must hear the gospel in order to be saved. The Gospel is defined in 1 Corinthians 15:1-4.

John 1:11-13; 3:16-18, 36; 5:24; 14:6; Acts 4:12; 15:11; 20:21; Romans 10:9-10, 13, 17; Ephesians 1:7; 1:12-14; 2:8-10; Titus 3:3-8; Hebrews 1:3; 1 Peter 1:18-19; 1 John 4:10

The benefits of salvation

We believe that all who put their trust in Jesus Christ are justified (declared righteous by God because of Christ); their sins are pardoned; they are regenerated (born again) and are given spiritual life by the Holy Spirit; they are eternally secure because they are kept by God.

Isaiah 53:11-12; John 10:27-30; Acts 10:43; 13:39; 15:11; Romans 3:21-25; 5:1-2, 9; 2 Corinthians 5:21; Titus 3:7; 1 Peter 1:2-5; 1 John 5:10-13

Sanctification

We believe that sanctification is presented in three phases in Scripture, past, present, and future: that the believer has been sanctified in Christ; that he is being progressively sanctified through the working of the indwelling Spirit, and that he will be completely sanctified at resurrection; that there is no complete eradication of the old nature in progressive sanctification during this present life; that speaking in tongues was not a sign of either regeneration or sanctification; that the New Testament gift of tongues is not in existence today, but ceased with the completion of the Scriptures.

John 17:17; Romans 1:17; 6:1-18; 1 Corinthians 1:30; 6:11; 1 Corinthians 13:8-13; 14:20-22; Ephesians 4:15; 5:26-27; Philippians 1:9-11; 1 Thessalonians 4:3-7; Hebrews 10:10; 1 Pe. 1:15-16

The spirit world

Prior to the creation of man, God made a great host of creatures known as angels (Col. 1:16). They are called "sons of God" in Job 38:4-7 and were witnesses of the creation of the earth. Angels are spirit beings (Ps. 104:4). They do not marry (Mt. 22:30). One of these, perhaps the very highest, was Lucifer. Becoming proud he determined to be like God and led a rebellion of angels against God (Isa. 14:12-17; Eze. 28:11-19). Since then Lucifer is called Satan or the devil and those angels that followed him are devils or demons (Mt. 25:41; Re. 12:9). Some of the rebellious angels are in hell (2 Pe. 2:4; Jude 6), while others are free and are assisting the devil (Mt. 9:34). The angels that did not join the rebellion are called "the elect angels" (1 Ti. 5:21) and "holy angels" (Re. 14:10). They are innumerable (Heb. 12:22). They minister to the saved (Heb.

1:14). Satan is called "the prince of the power of the air" (Eph. 2:2) and "the god of this world" (2 Co. 4:4). Satan has opposed the work of God since creation of man and is the power behind the "rulers of the darkness of this world" (Eph. 6:12). He is the power behind idolatry (De. 32:17; 1 Co. 10:20; Re. 9:20). Satan is currently opposing the progress of the Gospel (2 Co. 11:14-15; 1 Ti. 4:1). The devil was defeated at the cross of Christ (Heb. 2:14). He is not greater than or equal to God (Job 1; 1 Joh. 4:4). He can be resisted (Jas. 4:7) and overcome (1 Joh. 2:13; Re. 12:11). He will be cast into the bottomless pit at the return of Christ (Re. 20:1-3), will be released briefly after the millennial kingdom, and will be cast into the lake of fire to be punished for ever and ever (Re. 20:7-10).

The church

We believe that the church on earth is a congregation of scripturally baptized believers bound together by a common New Testament faith and fellowship in the Gospel of Jesus Christ. The church was established and built by Jesus Christ (Mt. 16:18). The church is the pillar and ground of the truth (1 Ti. 3:15). Each established church is autonomous (self-governing, self-disciplining, self-supporting, self-propagating) and stands on its own feet under its one Head Jesus Christ, which is what we see in Acts and the Epistles. Its officers are pastors (also called elders and bishops) and deacons (1 Ti. 3). Its two ordinances are baptism and the Lord's Supper, which are performed as memorials of Christ's death and resurrection (Acts 2:41-42; 1 Co. 11:23-24). Baptism is for believers only and is by immersion and is called a burial (Ro. 6:1-4). It is not for salvation and is not a part of salvation but it follows after salvation as a public testimony and as a picture of the believer's identity with Christ in His death, burial, and resurrection (Acts 8:36-39; 16:30-33; 18:8). Baptism is not the gospel but it is a picture of the gospel (1 Co. 15:1-4). The church's sole authority is the Bible (2 Ti. 3:16-17). Its Great Commission is the work of world evangelism and discipleship (Mt. 28:18-20; Mr. 16:15; Lu. 24:44-48; Acts 1:8; 13:1-4).

Civil government and religious liberty

We believe that civil government is of divine appointment for the interests and good order of human society; that magistrates are to be prayed for (1 Ti. 2:1-4), honored and obeyed (Mt. 22:21; Ro. 13:1-7; Titus 3:1; 1 Pe. 2:13-14), except only in the things opposed to the will of God (Acts 4:18-20; 5:29); that church and state should be separate, as we see in Scripture; the state owing the church protection and full freedom, no ecclesiastical group or denomination being preferred above another. A free church in a free state is the Christian ideal.

Future events

We believe the Scriptures teach that at death the spirit of the believer passes instantly into the presence of Christ and dwells there in conscious joy until the resurrection of the body when Christ comes for His own (Mr. 9:4; 2 Co. 5:8; Php. 1:23; 2 Ti. 4:6; Re. 6:9-11). At death, the spirit of the unbeliever descends immediately into hell to await the resurrection of the wicked into judgment; there the conscious soul is tormented in fire (Mr. 9:43-49; Lu. 16:22-31). The blessed hope of the believer is the personal, pre-tribulational, pre-millennial appearance of Christ to rapture the church age saints away before the Tribulation (1 Co. 15:51-57; 1 Th. 1:9-10; 4:13-18; 5:1-9; Titus 2:13). This coming of Christ is imminent (Mt. 24:42-44; 25:13; 1 Th. 5:2-4). God's righteous judgments will then be poured out on an unbelieving world during the Tribulation (Da. 12:1; Joel 2:2; Mt. 24:21; Re. 6-18). This is the seventieth week of Daniel (Da. 9:24-27). The climax of this era will be the physical return of Jesus Christ to the earth in great glory to establish the Davidic Kingdom (Mt. 16:27; 24:30-31; 26:64; Re. 1:7; 2 Th. 1:7; Re. 19:11-21; 20:1-4). Israel will be saved and restored completely to their land and kingdom (Isa. 2:2-5; 60; 66:20-24; Joel 3:1-2; 18-21; Zec. 14; Ro. 11:25-29). Satan will be bound, and the curse will be lifted from the physical creation (Isaiah 11:6-9; Re. 20:1-4). Following the millennial kingdom, Satan will be loosed from the bottomless pit, will lead one last unsuccessful rebellion, and will be cast into the lake of fire to be tormented forever and ever (Re. 20:7-10). This will be followed by the Great White Throne judgment of the unsaved dead (Re. 20:11-15) and the establishment of the New Heaven and the New Earth (Re. 21-22; 2 Pe. 3:10-13).

Separation from heresy and apostasy

We believe that the Bible requires separation from all forms of heresy and ecclesiastical apostasy (Ro. 16:17; 2 Co. 6:14-18; 1 Th. 3:6; 1 Ti. 6:3-5; 2 Ti. 3:5; Titus 3:10-11; 2 John 10-11; Re. 18:4). We are commanded to try them, mark them, rebuke them, have no fellowship with them, withdraw ourselves, receive them not, have no company with them, reject them, and separate ourselves from them. The Bible teaches that the course of the church age is characterized by increasing apostasy (2 Timothy 3:1 - 4:6).

Separation from the world

We believe the Bible also requires strict separation from the evil things of the world (Mt. 6:24; Ro. 12:2; 2 Co. 6:3; Eph. 5:11; 1 Th. 5:22; Tit. 2:11-14; Jas. 1:27; 4:4; 4:8; 1 Joh. 2:15-17; 5:19).

Some False Doctrines That Could Be a Danger to the Church

Some Bible facts about false teachers

The Bible has many warnings about false teachers:

1. Jesus warned about false teachers (Mt. 7:15-17).
2. Paul warned about false teachers (Acts 20:29-30; 2 Ti. 3:13; 2 Ti. 4:3-4).
3. Peter warned about false teachers and said that many will follow them (2 Pe. 2:1-2).
4. John warned about false teachers (1 John 2:18-20).
5. Jude warned about false teachers (Jude 3-4).

Some Bible facts about doctrine

1. The Bible is given for doctrine (2 Ti. 3:16-17).
2. We are to continue in the apostles' doctrine (Acts 2:42).
3. Preachers are to give themselves to doctrine (1 Ti. 4:13).
4. No false doctrine is to be allowed (1 Ti. 1:3).
5. Our doctrine is to be uncorrupt (Titus 2:10).
6. We are to separate from false doctrine (Ro. 16:17).

Some common false doctrines

1. The false teaching that salvation is by grace plus works (Seventh-day Adventists, Jehovah's Witnesses, Church of Christ, Roman Catholic Church)

Bible Answer:

a. The Bible says salvation is by grace without works and that works follows after salvation (Ro. 4:1-6; Eph. 2:8-10; Titus 3:4-8).

b. The Bible says that grace and works cannot be mixed together (Ro. 11:6).

c. Grace means a free gift. Salvation is called a gift 16 times in the New Testament. If salvation requires some works, then it is not a true gift. The gift of God is free for the sinner because Jesus Christ purchased it at great price with His blood and death on the cross.

d. The purpose of the Old Testament law was to show man that he is a sinner and that he needs the Saviour (Ro. 3:19-24; Ga. 3:24-26)

2. The false teaching that Jesus is not God (Jehovah's Witnesses)

Bible Answer:

a. The Bible plainly says that Jesus is God

(1) Isaiah called Jesus God (Is. 7:14; 9:6).

(2) Matthew called Jesus God (Mt. 1:23).

(3) Jesus called Himself God (Joh. 5:17-18; 8:58-59; 10:30-33; Re. 1:8).

(4) John called Jesus God (Joh. 1:1; 1 John 3:16; 5:20).

(5) Thomas called Jesus God (Joh. 20:28).

(6) Paul called Jesus God (Acts 20:28; Php. 2:5-6; 1 Ti. 3:16; Titus 2:13).

(7) God the Father called Jesus God (Heb. 1:8-10).

b. In His incarnation the Lord Jesus Christ "made himself of no reputation" and became a lowly servant to God and man (Php. 2:7). The Greek word for "made himself of no reputation" is "kenoo," meaning "to empty, to abase, to make of none effect" (Strong). Jesus did not cease to be God. Php. 2:6 plainly states that He is God, but the Son of God willingly laid aside His glory for the purpose of redeeming man by the cross.

c. There is an order to the Trinity. God the Son submits to God the Father, even though they are equal.

3. The false teaching that God is not a Trinity (Jehovah's Witnesses)

Bible Answer:

a. The term "trinity" is not in the Bible, but the doctrine is (Mt. 28:19; Joh. 14:16, 26; 16:7-15; 2 Co. 13:14; Eph. 4:4-6; 1 Joh. 5:7).

b. The O.T. teaches that God is one in a plurality. Though the Old Testament does not fully reveal the doctrine of the Trinity, it does teach us that God is a plurality. It is left for the New Testament to open up this revelation fully.

(1) Genesis 1:1. The Hebrew word for God here is *elohim*. This is a plural noun, but the verb is singular, teaching that there is one God in a plurality.

(2) Genesis 11:6-7. Here again God is spoken of in the plural and in the singular at the same time.

(3) Deuteronomy 6:4. This verse could be translated, "Jehovah our *elohim* is a united Jehovah." The word "one" refers to a unity. The same word for one is used in Ge. 2:24, speaking of the oneness of a husband and wife. This verse summarizes the Bible's teaching about God. He is one but exists in three Persons.

(4) Psalm 45:6-7. According to Heb. 1:8-9, God the Father is speaking in Psalm 45, and He is referring to the Son as God. Sometimes people ask, "If Jesus Himself was God, why did He address the Father as God?" The answer is that Jesus addressed the Father as God for the same reason that the Father addressed the Son as God—because they are both God!

4. The false teaching that baptism is necessary for salvation (Church of Christ)

Bible Answer:

a. Paul taught that baptism symbolizes the death, burial, and resurrection of Christ (Ro. 6:3-4). It is the blood and death of Christ that takes away our sins, not water or religious rituals.

b. Paul says that baptism is not the gospel (1 Co. 1:17). The gospel is the death, burial, and resurrection of Christ for our sins (1 Co. 15:1-4). Baptism only symbolizes the gospel.

c. The book of Acts teaches us that baptism follows salvation (Acts 8:36-38; 16:30-33; 18:8).

d. Acts 2:38 does not teach that baptism is a part of salvation, because Peter later taught that baptism is a symbol (1 Pe. 3:21). Acts 2:38 teaches that we are baptized *because we have been* forgiven of our sins not *in order to be* forgiven.

5. The false teachings that the Passover is necessary for salvation (Church of Christ)

They say that since Jesus kept the Passover, the believers, too, should keep it. They say that those who do not keep it are false teachers and they cannot be saved.

Bible Answer:

a. The Passover was for the Jews (Ex. 12:45). The church is not Jews (1 Co. 10:32).

b. The Passover was under the Old Covenant of the law, but we live under the New Covenant. Jesus has given us the Lord's Supper instead of the Passover (Luke 22:20; 2 Co. 3:5-18; Col. 2:13-17).

c. The Bible says that salvation is by grace and not by works or law (Ro. 3:19-24; 4:4-8; Eph. 2:8-9; Titus 3:3-8).

d. The Passover required many things (killing the lamb, putting the blood on the door, eating herbs, etc.). Those who have this false teaching today don't practice these things.

e. The apostles never taught the churches to keep the Passover. Instead, they taught the churches to keep the Lord's Supper (1 Co. 11:20-34).

f. Paul taught that the churches are free to keep the Lord's Supper as often as they want (1 Co. 11:26). There is no law about how often we should keep it.

6. The false teaching that infants should be baptized (Roman Catholic, Lutheran, Presbyterian, Methodist)

Bible Answer:

a. Baptism is only for those who believe (Mr. 16:15; Acts 8:36-38). When a child is old enough to believe on Jesus Christ as

Lord and Saviour, then he can be baptized. But an infant cannot do this.

b. No infants were baptized in the New Testament. Some say that there must have been infants baptized in the case of Cornelius since his kinsmen and friends were present (Acts 10:24, 47). Contrariwise, Acts 11:17 says that those who were saved and baptized with Cornelius were those "who believed on the Lord Jesus Christ." Obviously these were not infants. What about the case of Lydia and her household (Acts 16:14-15). Nothing is said about infants in this passage, and it is highly unlikely that this busy merchant woman would have had babies. There is no evidence here whatsoever for the practice of infant baptism. What about the Philippian jailer and his household (Acts 16:30-34). This passage clearly says that Paul spoke the Word of God to the entire household (v. 32) and that the entire household "believed" (vv. 32-33). This could not be said of infants. What about the household of Crispus (Acts 18:8)? Those who were saved and baptized in this family were all believers, for we are told, "Crispus ... believed on the Lord with all his house..." Obviously they were not infants. What about the household of Stephanas (1 Co. 1:16)? Again nothing is actually said about infants being present or baptized. In 1 Co. 16:15 we are told that this household addicted themselves to the ministry. This could not be said of infants.

7. The false teachings of the Pentecostal-Charismatic Movement (Assemblies of God, etc.)

The false doctrine that tongues speaking is for today

Bible Answer:

a. The Bible says tongues were a real language (Acts 2:3-11).

b. The Bible says tongues were a sign to the unbelieving Jews (1 Co. 14:21-22). After Israel rejected God's sign of tongues and Jerusalem was destroyed in 70 A.D. and the Jews were scattered to the ends of the earth, the need for tongues as a sign was finished.

c. Biblical tongues had to be used according to the teaching of the apostles, yet the Pentecostals and Charismatics do not submit to these restrictions:

(1) Women are not allowed to speak in tongues (1 Co. 14:34)

(2) Tongues were to be spoken only by course (1 Co. 14:27)
(3) Tongues must be interpreted (1 Co. 14:27)
(4) There is to be no confusion (1 Co. 14:33)
(5) Everything is to be decent (1 Co. 14:40)
(6) Everything is to be orderly (1 Co. 14:40)

d. Tongues were not spoken by every believer even in the days of the apostles (1 Co. 12:28-30).

e. Biblical tongues were not sought after but were sovereignly given by God (1 Co. 12:11).

f. There is no instruction in the Bible about HOW to speak in tongues. Those who believe in tongues speaking today claim that they can teach people how to do it.

g. The Bible says tongues speaking, prophesying, and words of knowing will pass away (1 Co. 13:8). When the New Testament was completed, there was no further need for these particular gifts.

The false doctrine that healing is promised in the atonement

Bible Answer:

a. The Bible says that not all sicknesses are healed (2 Co. 12:7-10; 1 Ti. 5:23; 2 Ti. 4:20)

b. The Bible says that the physical part of our salvation is for the future (Ro. 8:17-25).

c. Peter says that Isaiah 53:5 refers to spiritual healing of the soul (1 Pe. 2:24-25).

The false doctrine that miracles should be sought

Bible Answer:

a. Jesus warned that it is not good to seek miracles (Mt. 12:39).

b. The miracles performed by the apostles were special (2 Co. 12:12). Not every Christian could perform miracles.

c. Faith does not come from miracles but from God's Word (Ro. 10:17). Multitudes witnessed Jesus' great miracles, but most did not believe.

The false doctrine that the Holy Spirit baptism follows salvation

Bible Answer:

a. Jesus promised the baptism of the Holy Spirit (Acts 1:5) and this was fulfilled in Acts 2 for the Jews and in Acts 10:44-47 for the Gentiles.

b. Since then, every believer receives the Holy Spirit when he believes (Eph. 1:12-14).

c. The book of Acts is a transitional book. Not everything that happened then is the pattern for the rest of the church age.

d. In the epistles, the reception of the Holy Spirit is always mentioned in the past tense (Ro. 8:9-10; 1 Co. 12:13; 2 Co. 1:21-22; 5:5; Eph. 1:13).

The false doctrine that we should exalt the Holy Spirit

Bible Answer:

a. The Lord Jesus Christ foretold what role the Holy Spirit would have in the church age (John 16:13-15). In this passage we learn that the Holy Spirit does not exalt Himself and the Holy Spirit does not draw attention to Himself.

b. There is no example in the N.T. of praying to the Holy Spirit. The Lord Jesus Christ taught us to pray to the Father, not to the Holy Spirit (Mt. 6:6, 9; Joh. 16:23). The Apostle Paul taught us to pray to God the Father through the Lord Jesus Christ by the Holy Spirit (Ro. 1:8; 7:25).

c. There is no example in the New Testament of inviting the Holy Spirit to work. Neither Jesus nor the apostles did that.

The false doctrine that we should not test the Holy Spirit with the Bible

Bible Answer:

a. The Bible warns that there are false spirits and that the devil tries to deceive (2 Co. 11:4; 1 Joh. 4:1). Therefore we must test everything carefully or we will be deceived.

b. The Bible commands us to prove all things (1 Th. 5:21).

c. The Bible commended the Bereans because they tested everything by the Scriptures (Acts 17:11)

The false doctrine that the believer can be rid of his sin nature

Bible Answer:

a. Paul taught that the believer still has the struggle with sin (Ro. 7:14-21; Ga. 5:16-17).

b. John teaches that the believer still has sin (1 John 1:8, 10).

The false doctrine that victory in the Christian life comes through unusual baptisms and experiences

Bible Answer:

a. The Bible does not exhort us to make spiritual leaps through unusual experiences. Rather, it exhorts us to GROW in Christ (1 Pe. 2:1-2; 2 Pe. 3:18).

b. The apostles wrote many epistles instructing the believers about how to deal with sin and spiritual problems, but they never instructed the believers to seek a second baptism or other such special experiences.

The false doctrine that visions and prophecies are for today

Bible Answer:

a. The Bible says the faith was completed in the days of the apostles (Jude 3).

b. The Bible says that the Scriptures are sufficient (2 Ti. 3:16-17).

c. The Bible says that Scripture is more sure than visions (2 Pe. 1:16-21).

d. The Bible says that prophecies will pass away (1 Co. 13:8).

8. The false teaching that death is a sleep and not a journey (Seventh-day Adventists)

Bible Answer:

a. The Old Testament plainly says that death is a journey (Ge. 25:8; 35:18; Nu. 27:13; 2 Sa. 12:23; 1 Ki. 17:21-22).

b. The New Testament plainly says that death is a journey:

(1) Jesus said death is a journey (Lu. 16:19-23; 23:42-43). That Luke 16:19-31 is not a parable is evident by the fact that Jesus named the names of Abraham and Lazarus. He never named names when He was giving parables. Further, even if it were a parable, it would still teach literal truth.

(2) Paul said death is a journey (2 Co. 5:6-7; Php. 1:23; 2 Ti. 4:6).

(3) Peter said death is a journey (2 Pe. 1:13-15).

(4) The fact that the dead saints return with Christ from heaven at the time of the rapture shows that dead saints go to heaven at death (1 Th. 4:14).

(5) John's heavenly visions show that dead saints are conscious in heaven prior to the resurrection and during the Great Tribulation on earth (Re. 6:9-11).

(6) Moses' and Elijah's appearance on the Mount of Transfiguration proves that the dead have conscious existence between death and resurrection. Moses and Elijah, though dead, were allowed by God to appear in time on that mountain and to converse about events which were soon to take place in Jerusalem (Mt. 17:1-3; Lu. 9:30-31).

c. The Bible sometimes speaks of death as a "sleep," but it is the body that sleeps, not the spirit (Jas. 2:26).

d. Ecclesiastes sometimes speaks of death as nothingness (i.e., Ec. 9:5), but this is because Ecclesiastes is written from the perspective of the man "under the sun" (Ec. 1:3, 9, 14, etc), the perspective of man looking at life the way it appears apart from divine revelation. To the natural man who does not have the revelation of the Scriptures, death appears to be the end of things. But other portions of the Bible tell us that this is not the case. Even the book of Ecclesiastes itself, in its conclusion, says that death is a journey (Ec. 12:7).

e. The Old Testament speaks of the "spirit" as the breath once or twice, but usually the "spirit" of man is that non-material part which is separate from the body and which lives on after death (1 Th. 5:23). False teachers make the mistake of refusing to allow the context to define Bible words and instead they put their own preferred definition on the word and force that definition into every context.

9. The false teaching that hell is not eternal torment (Jehovah's Witnesses, Seventh-day Adventists)

Bible Answer:

a. The doctrine of death and hell were not fully revealed in the Old Testament; these were brought to light with the coming of Christ (2 Ti. 1:10).

b. The New Testament plainly teaches that hell and the lake of fire are places of eternal torment:

(1) Jesus said hell is a place where the worm does not die (Mark 9:43-44).

(2) Jesus said the rich man was in torment in hell (Lu. 16:24). This is not a parable, because Jesus named the names of Lazarus and Abraham.

(3) Revelation says those who receive the mark of the antichrist will be tormented forever (Re. 14:10).

(4) Revelation says Satan, the Antichrist, and false prophet will be tormented forever (Re. 20:10).

(5) Revelation says all the unsaved will be cast into the same lake of fire (Re. 20:15), and since the antichrist and false prophet are not burned up but are tormented forever in the lake of fire, it is obvious that other sinners cast there will have the same experience.

c. The Bible says the punishment of the unsaved will be worse than violent death (Mr. 9:42). This proves the punishment is not annihilation, but is eternal torment. Jesus said it would have been better if Judas had never been born (Mt. 26:24). Jesus' words make no sense if Judas was only going to be annihilated.

10. The false teaching that Sabbath worship is for the churches today (Seventh-day Adventists)

Bible Answer:

a. The sabbath, though mentioned in Ge. 2:2-3, was not delivered to man until it was given to Israel in the wilderness (Neh. 9:13-14).

b. The sabbath was given, not to mankind in general, but to Israel alone as a special covenant sign between her and God (Ex. 31:13, 17).

c. Jesus kept the sabbath because He was born under the law to fulfill the demands of the law (Ga. 4:4-5).

d. The apostles and early churches met on Sunday.

(1) On the first day Jesus rose from the dead and first appeared to His disciples (Mr. 16:9). The sabbath is associated with the old creation; the first day is associated with the new creation.

(2) On the first day Jesus met with the disciples at different places and repeatedly (Mr. 16:9-11; Mt. 28:8-10; Lu. 24:34; Mr. 16:12-13; Joh. 20:19-23).

(3) On the first day Jesus ascended to heaven, was seated at the right hand of the Father and was made Head of all (Joh. 20:17; Eph. 1:20).

(4) On the first day the Holy Spirit descended (Acts 2:1). Pentecost was on the 50th day after the sabbath following the wave offering (Lev. 23:15-16). Thus Pentecost was always on a Sunday.

(5) The Christians met to worship on the first day (Acts 20:6-7; 1 Co. 16:2).

e. The New Testament plainly teaches that the Christian is not bound to the sabbath law (Col. 2:16-17).

11. The false teaching that the Prophecies of Matthew 24 and Revelation 6-22 are not for the future but are being fulfilled today (Roman Catholic, most Protestant denominations such as Presbyterian and Lutheran, etc.)

Bible Answer:

a. The timing of the events of Matthew 24 are plainly given:

(1) Jesus said that the prophecy of Matthew 24 pertains to the end of the age and to the time of His return (Mt. 24:3-4). This includes the rule of the antichrist (Mt. 24:15) and the Great Tribulation (Mt. 24:21).

(2) Jesus said the events of Matthew 24 will occur just prior to His return (Mt. 24:29-30).

b. Paul also taught that the antichrist is a real man who will rule the world just prior to Christ's return (2 Th. 2:2-9).

c. The judgments of Revelation are the wrath of God (Re. 6:16; 15:1), whereas Paul said the church-age believers are not appointed to wrath (1 Th. 5:9-10).

12. The false teaching that God is finished with the nation Israel; that the church has replaced Israel (Roman Catholic, most Protestant denominations such as Presbyterian and Lutheran, etc.)

Bible Answer:

a. God's covenants with Israel are eternal (Jer. 31:31-37).

b. Paul said that Israel has been set aside temporarily, and that God will fulfill His promises to Israel after He completes His plan for the church (Ro. 11:25-29).

13. The false teaching that God chooses who will be saved and that only those who are chosen can be saved (Calvinism).

Bible Answer:

a. The Bible says that God wants all men to be saved (1 Ti. 2:3-5; 2 Pe. 3:9).

b. Jesus died for the sins of all men, not just some who are pre-chosen (1 John 2:1-2).

c. God has ordained that every person who believes on Christ will be saved (Joh. 6:40).

d. God has commanded that the gospel be preached to every person (Mark 16:15).

e. The Holy Spirit convicts every sinner and Jesus draws and gives light to every sinner (Joh. 1:9; 12:32; 16:7-8).

f. Believers are the elect of God, but that does not mean that God chooses some to be saved and the others not to be saved. Election is based on God's foreknowledge (1 Pe. 1:2).

14. The false teaching that the believer can only eat certain things (Seventh-day Adventist)

Bible Answer:

a. Dietary laws in the New Testament are a mark of false teachers (1 Ti. 4:1-5).

b. The New Testament believer has liberty in such things (Ro. 14:1-4; Col. 2:16).

15. The false teaching that there should only be one church in each village and city

Bible Answer:

a. This idea has no support in the Bible. In the very beginning there was naturally only one church in a city because there were only a few believers and no need for more than one church, but there is no commandment in the New Testament that says it is wrong for there to be more than one church in a city or town or village.

b. This idea is contrary to Christ's Great Commission and to the autonomy of the church. Jesus commanded all believers to preach the gospel and baptize every nation and individual (Mt. 28:19-20; Mr. 16:15). This commandment was not given just to one church in each area. Believers do not have to ask other churches for permission to preach the gospel and baptize and establish churches. We have authority from Jesus Christ. When God spoke to the church at Antioch to send out missionaries to other places to start churches, they didn't have to get permission from any other church. Likewise, we do not have to get permission from other churches before we can preach the gospel and baptize converts and organize them into a church.

c. This idea is contrary to God's command that each church should have one mind and doctrine (1 Co. 1:10). If other Christians and churches in a city have different doctrine, it is not possible for us to join them. We must establish a church that has the doctrine that we believe to be the sound Bible doctrine and have one mind together as a church before the Lord.

d. If this idea about having only one church in each city is true, how can it be accomplished? Such a principle would mean that one church would be able to forbid other churches to preach, but Jesus said we are not to forbid others (Lu. 9:49-50).

e. If there is only one church in each city, what church would it be? Who will have control to say which church it should be? This is the authority that the Roman Catholic Church and the Greek Orthodox Church falsely claim for themselves. They claim to be the only true churches and they try to forbid others to start churches. This is what the Russian Orthodox Church does in Russia.

Suggested Materials for a Discipling Church

Following are some suggested materials for Christian families and youth ministries.

BEREAN CALL

www.thebereancall.org/

Many helpful books by Dave Hunt. We recommend *Judgment Day: Islam, Israel and the Nations*, *What Love Is This* (Calvinism), *A Woman Rides the Beast* (Roman Catholicism), *Fast Facts on Jehovah's Witnesses*, *Fast Facts on the Masonic Lodge*, *Fast Facts on the Middle East*, *The Seduction of Christianity*, *The Godmakers*, *When Will Jesus Come?*

BETHEL BAPTIST PRINT MINISTRY

www.bethelbaptist.ca/contact.htm, 519-652-2619, info@bethelbaptist.ca

They publish books by Bruce Lackey and many others. I recommend the following books by Bruce Lackey: *Repentance Is More Than a Change of Mind*, *Proverbs for the Family*, *Ten Ways to Study Your Bible*, *What the Bible Teaches about Drinking Wine*, *Cremation, Divorce, and Other Matters*, *Why I Believe the Old King James Bible*. I also recommend *A Closer Look at the Evidence* by Richard & Tina Kleiss (a daily devotional that focuses on facts of life that prove divine creation), *Baptist History* by J.M. Cramp, *Bible Doctrines Affected by Modern Versions* by Paul Freeman, *Bible Wines or the Laws or Fermentation* by William Patton, *Boys and Girls Who Became Great Missionaries* by John Mueller, *Except Ye Repent* by H.A. Ironside, *The History of the Christian Church* by William Jones, *Israel and the Churches* by James Brookes, *The Life and Works of Charles Spurgeon* by Henry Northrop, *Me a Widow?* (by a pastor's wife), *Must Purity Be Sacrificed on the Altar of Unity* by Bert Esselink, *Prayer* by John Bunyan, *The Fear of God* by Bunyan, *Scripture Memorization* by John Charlton, *Prayer* by D.L. Moody, *After C.T. Studd* by Norman Grubb, *The Weapon of Prayer* by E.M. Bounds, *Heroes of Faith on Pioneer Trails* by E. Myers Harrison.

BIBLE TRUTH PUBLISHERS

www.bibletruthpublishers.com/

This is a Brethren publisher and we do not recommend everything they teach on the church, but their books on prophecy and many other subjects are excellent. Some of the books from this publisher that we recommend are the writings and commentaries of H.A. Ironside and William Kelly, as well as *The Bible Promise Book, Concise Bible Dictionary, A Defense of Dispensationalism, Hades and Eternal Punishment, Holiness: The False and the True, Miller's Church History* (though written from a Protestant perspective it is still very helpful), *Outline of Prophetic Events, Self-Esteem: A Scriptural Analysis, Things Which Must Shortly Come to Pass, Types and Symbols of Scripture, The Tabernacle, Priesthood, and Offerings*, and *What They Believe* (Cults).

BLESSED HOPE PUBLICATIONS

www.himknowledgey.org/FRAMES/MainPage.asp

Douglas Snow has an excellent book entitled *Revive Us Again: Chronological Anthology of American Gospel Hymnody*.

FAIRHAVEN BAPTIST COLLEGE ONLINE CLASSES

https://www.youtube.com/channel/UCN4N_GXiQ6LmKUzT15aA7LQ/featured

In 2016, Fairhaven Baptist College in Chesterton, Indiana, began offering some of its courses online via YouTube. Registration is required, but to view the courses for non-credit is free.

FAITH BIBLE INSTITUTE

http://fbiclass.com/index.html

This three-year institute is taught by John Yates, senior pastor of Rowland Baptist Church of Monroe, Louisiana. Any church can use the courses, which are available on DVD, but the requirement is that at least 10 students be enrolled. The program consists of a detailed survey of every book of the Bible, plus studies on theology, prophecy, creationism, personal evangelism, and discipleship. We would warn that the church itself is moving in a contemporary direction.

FUNDAMENTAL BAPTIST MINISTRIES

fundamentalbaptistministries.com

Don Jasmin's book *Why Do Fundamental Schools Go Apostate?* is excellent. He traces the spiritual downfall of two schools founded by D.L. Moody in the late 19th century, and applies the principles to things that are happening in evangelical and fundamentalist schools today. He publishes other good books, including *Great Doctrines of the Faith, Here I Stand, Quotes and More Quotes, Manual in the School of Prayer,* and a three-CD set on *The History of American Fundamentalism.*

FUNDAMENTAL EVANGELISTIC ASSOCIATION

www.feasite.org

They publish *Foundation* magazine and some helpful booklets and tracts. I recommend *An Analysis of Rick Warren's Purpose Driven Life, Biblical Basics for Believers, The Blood of Jesus, God's Song, The Humanist Manifesto 2000, The New Evangelicalism, What About the Church Growth Movement,* and *The World Council of Churches.*

GLORY TO GLORY MINISTRIES

www.glorytogloryministries.com, -- *The First 2,000 Years of Baptist History* by Terry Lee Hamilton is a helpful 100-page curriculum on Baptist history and distinctives.

LIGHTHOUSE TRAILS

www.lighthousetrails.com/

Many helpful books exposing the error of contemplative spirituality, the emerging church, the New Age, Roman Catholicism, etc. I recommend *A Time of Departing* and *For Many Shall Come in My Name* by Ray Yungen, *Faith Undone* by Roger Oakland, *Far From God Near to Rome,* and *Messages from Heaven* (DVD). They also publish biographies and some interesting and challenging accounts of resistance to Hitler in World War II.

LOCAL CHURCH BIBLE PUBLISHERS

www.localchurchbiblepublishers.com

Selection of excellent leather-bound KJV Bibles, including Old Scofield Reference Bible in compact size and large wide-margin size

NORTHSTAR MINISTRIES

www.northstarministries.com/

Dave Sorenson publishes several excellent books, including *Touch Not the Unclean Thing* on the Bible version issue, *Moral Failure: Its Cause and Prevention*, *Training Your Children to Turn out Right*, and *Broad is the Way: Fundamentalists Merging into the Evangelical Mainstream*. He also has a whole Bible commentary set called *Understanding the Bible*.

PERIL OF ISLAM

www.amazon.com/Peril-Islam-Telling-Truth/dp/1932307230

Peril of Islam: Telling the Truth by Gene Gurganus, who was a missionary to a Muslim nation for 17 years, is excellent.

PRAIRIE FIRE PRESS

www.prairiefirepress.com/

America in Crimson Red: The Baptist History of America by James Beller is excellent. They also publish other helpful materials, such as *The Collegiate Baptist History Workbook*, *The History of American Liberty* (DVD). Beller is a graduate of Hyles-Anderson College and speaks there occasionally and we cannot therefore recommend his associations, but his historical research is helpful.

PSYCHOHERESY AWARENESS MINISTRIES

www.pamweb.org/mainpage.html

This ministry publishes material by Martin and Deidre Bobgan exposing the error of Christian psychology, such as *12 Steps to Destruction: Codependency/Recovery Heresies*; *Christ Centered Ministry vs. Problem Centered Counseling*; *Four Temperaments, Astrology, and Personality Testing*; *Hypnosis: Medical, Scientific, or Occultic*; *James Dobson's Gospel of Self-Esteem*; *Manufacturing Victims: What the Psychology Industry Is Doing to People*; and *PsychoHeresy: The Psychological Seduction of Christianity*.

SHEPHERDING THE FLOCK MINISTRIES

www.shepherdingtheflock.com/store/c1/Featured_Products.html

Many excellent books by Pastor Scott Markle. We particularly recommend *God's Wisdom for the Marriage and the Home.*

STARR PUBLICATIONS

www.starr-publications.com

Pastor Randy Starr of Mt. Zion Baptist Church, Brogue, Pennsylvania, has several books available currently: *Head Covering* and *Profiles in Genesis*. His wife Shirley has published *Helpmeets and Homemakers*; *Faithful and Fruitful*; *Helpless and Hurting*; *Powerful and Prestigious*; *Carnal and Conniving*; *Tattoos, Body Piercings, and Cuttings*; and *Dress--The Heart of the Matter* (co-authored with Lori Waltemyer).

SUMNERWEMP.COM

www.sumnerwemp.com/books/index.htm

The book *How on Earth Can I Be Spiritual* by C. Sumner Wemp is a practical study on the Holy Spirit in the believer's life.

WAY OF LIFE LITERATURE

P.O. Box 610368, Port Huron, MI 48061, 866-295-4143 (toll free), www.wayoflife.org; in Canada contact 4212 Campbell St. N., London, Ont. N6P 1A6, 519-652-2619, 866-295-4143

Following are some of the titles:

Advanced Bible Studies Series (Acts, Bible History and Geography, The Bible Version Issue, The Church, Church History, Defense of the Faith, Daniel (scheduled for 2017), Doctrine, First Corinthians, The Four Gospels, Genesis, God the Trinity (scheduled for 2017), Hebrews, How to Study the Bible, Isaiah (scheduled for 2017), James, Job, Marriage (scheduled for 2017), New Testament Prayer (scheduled for 2017), Pastoral Epistles, Preaching (scheduled for 2017), Prophecy, Proverbs, Psalms, Revelation, Romans)

Answering the Myths on the Bible Version Debate
Baptist Music Wars
Believer's Bible Dictionary
The Bible and Diet

The Bible and Islam
Bible Separation: Its Doctrine and Practice
Bible Times and Ancient Kingdoms
The Calvinism Debate
Directory of Contemporary Worship Music
The Discipling Church: The Church That Will Stand until Christ Comes
Dressing for the Lord
The Emerging Church Is Coming
The Future According to the Bible
The Glorious Heritage of the King James Bible
Holiness: Pitfalls, Struggles, Victory
The Hyles Effect
Judge Not: Is It Legalism to Judge Sin and Error?
Keeping the Kids
The Modern Bible Version Hall of Shame
The Mobile Phone and the Christian Home and Church
Music for Good or Evil (a series of eight video presentations)
The New Age Tower of Babel
New Evangelicalism: Its History, Characteristics and Fruit
One-Year Discipleship Course
The Pastor's Authority and the Church Member's Responsibility
The Pentecostal-Charismatic Movements
A Plea to Southern Gospel Music Fans
A Portrait of Christ: Tabernacle, Priesthood, Offerings
Sowing and Reaping: A Course in Evangelism
Things Hard to Be Understood: A Handbook of Biblical Difficulties
An Unshakeable Faith: A Christian Apologetics Course
The Way of Life Encyclopedia of the Bible & Christianity
What Every Christian Should Know about Rock Music

WILLIAMS, E.S.

www.metropolitantabernacle.org/Books/Dr-E-S-Williams

E.S. Williams, a medical doctor and a member of the Metropolitan Tabernacle in London, England, has authored two important books: *The Dark Side of Christian Counselling* and

Christ or Therapy? These document the danger of the Christian psychology movement that has permeated evangelicalism and beyond to many fundamentalist churches and homes. Dr. Williams examines the lives and teaching of the secular atheistic fathers of this movement: Sigmund Freud, Alfred Adler, Abraham Maslow, Carl Rogers, and Albert Ellis, as well as examining the Christian counselors who have borrowed from this field: James Dobson, Larry Crabb, Clyde Narramore, Selwyn Hughes, Frank Minirth, Paul Meier, David Seamands, Gary Collins. Among other things, Dr. Williams refutes the psychological counseling approach to self-esteem, unconditional love, and unconditional forgiveness.

SEE ALSO THE FOLLOWING LISTS OF SUGGESTED MATERIALS ON VARIOUS TOPICS

"Helpful Music Resources"
   www.wayoflife.org/fbns/helpful.htm
"A Basic Bible Version Library"
   www.wayoflife.org/fbns/basic-biblevers-lib.html
"Bible Commentaries"
   www.wayoflife.org/database/bible_commentaries.html
"Creation Science Videos"
   www.wayoflife.org/fbns/creationscience-videos.html